HARVESTFIELDS
—*of*—
DEATH

To James From Mother 12-2002

HARVESTFIELDS
—*of*—
DEATH

*The Twentieth Indiana Volunteers
of Gettysburg*

CRAIG L. DUNN

GUILD PRESS OF INDIANA, INC.
CARMEL, INDIANA

GUILD PRESS OF INDIANA, INC.
435 Gradle Drive
Carmel, Indiana 46032
317-848-6421

ISBN 1-57860-039-1 (HARDCOVER)

ISBN 1-57860-038-3 (PAPERBACK)

Library of Congress
Catalog Card Number
99-65198

Cover design by Listenberger Design Associates
Text design by Sheila G. Samson
Maps on pages 71, 134, and 178 by Richard Day

Printed and bound in the United States of America

Contents

ACKNOWLEDGMENTS

The telling of the story of the Twentieth Indiana required the help and contributions of many fine organizations and Civil War friends. I would, first of all, like to express my appreciation to the staff of the Indiana Historical Society, the Indiana Archives, the Indiana State Library, the National Archives, the Library of Congress and the United States Army Military History Institute for maintaining a wealth of original source material and making it available to the public.

I received much specific information from libraries and historical societies throughout Indiana. My thanks to Kathleen Brown of the Kokomo Public Library, the Lafayette Public Library, the Plymouth Public Library, the Valparaiso Public Library, the LaPorte Public Library, the Logansport Public Library, the Peru Public Library, the Crown Point Public Library, and the Lake County Public Library. Also, the White County Historical Society, the Tippecanoe County Historical Society, the Cass County Historical Society and the LaPorte County Historical Society.

Many individuals came to my assistance when the call for information was sent out via newspapers, the Internet, radio, and the mail. My sincere appreciation and a debt of gratitude go to David Canright, Chesterton, Indiana; Boyd Cole, Vernon Hills, Illinois; Harold Wheeler, Crown Point, Indiana; Mark Weldon, Fort Wayne, Indiana; Larry Strayer and Richard Carlile, Dayton, Ohio; Richard Baumgartner, Huntington, West Virginia; Dr. James Brust, San Pedro, California; Brian Pohanka; *The Gettysburg Discussion Group*; Mick Kissick, Albany, Indiana; Karl Sundstrom, Riverside, Illinois; Steve Towne, Indianapolis, Indiana; Gib Young, Huntington, Indiana; David Stone, Anderson, Indiana; Ted Rupel, Fort Wayne, Indiana; Terry Laird, Valparaiso, Indiana; Merv Woods, South Bend, Indiana; Nancy Van Valkenburgh, Huntsville, Alabama; John Baum, Monticello, Indiana;

Terry Moyer, Gettysburg, Pennsylvania; Russ and Shelly Dooley, Indianapolis, Indiana; Benedict Maryniak, Buffalo, New York; Charles Erwin, La Porte, Indiana, and Larry Winkleman, Kokomo, Indiana.

John Michael Priest, noted Civil War author and a new friend, generously offered his time to review my manuscript for historical accuracy and readability. Thank you Mike.

An extra expression of appreciation goes to my editor and publisher, Nancy Niblack Baxter. Nancy nursed me through my first book, *Iron Men, Iron Will*, and taught me much about writing and research. Guild Press' wonderful *The Civil War CD-ROM* reduced my research time immensely and proved an indispensable research tool.

INTRODUCTION

But the sense of fear on this and other occasions has been subjugated by a strong sense of duty and honor, or otherwise I should have slunk to the rear.

Major Erasmus C. Gilbreath

There is a split instant with shells plowing up the dirt, bullets whizzing and popping near his head, as his captain is yelling to fix bayonets and charge into the face of the foe, when a soldier must decide, "Shall I run or shall I fight?" What makes a brave soldier willing to lay down his life for his country and the freedom of others? What motivates a citizen to leave the safety of home and hearth and the warmth of family to answer the call to service? These questions about personal behavior, and many more, have led me to the study of history.

The talented modern historian Stephen Ambrose refers to the writing of the history of Americans in their great conflicts as triumphalism. He believes that we live in the greatest country in the world and that we need to study those who have sacrificed to make it great. I concur.

Today's youth suffer from misplaced hero worship that adulates malcontents, miscreants, and others who have prospered from the fruits of our nation's freedom but have offered little in return. We are a nation in desperate need of heroes. When a society fails to recognize its true heroes: teachers, scientists, doctors, policemen, honest government officials and other noble men and women, it becomes a ship without a compass, fated to go off course.

It does not have to be so. Heroes are everywhere if we simply look for them. A good place to discover them is in the pages of this history. The Twentieth Indiana Volunteers, an odd assortment of farm boys, coopers, clerks, laborers, blacksmiths, clergy, doctors, lawyers and businessmen, came together for a brief time in our nation's history, rallied by the call to duty and love of country. While none could imagine the horrors and deprivations he would see and suffer, each man freely swore his oath of allegiance and volunteered in the service of his country. It was a time when simple character counted and ordinary men became heroes.

Many of these brave men never returned to their homes and families; those who did return bore the physical scars of warfare and suffered for the rest of their lives, and all were profoundly affected by the experience. In fact, for the fifty years immediately following the Civil War, our national fabric was directly woven by incredibly strong men and women who suffered through the great conflict and were touched by it in one way or another. I write about the Twentieth Indiana Volunteers, not to tell others about who they were, but rather to tell us all about who we can be.

When I was sixteen years old,
I traded the golden harvestfields of grain
for the red harvestfields of death.

Private James C. Stephens
Twentieth Indiana Volunteers

CHAPTER ONE

THEY MAKE LITTLE FUSS OVER US

William Lyon Brown looked on with pride as the ragtag gaggle of farm boys, clerks, and laborers stumbled into order on the parade grounds at Camp Tippecanoe. Located a few miles from the Indian War battleground of the same name, Camp Tippecanoe had become a mustering point for yet another war. Brown had witnessed a similar scene years before as the flower of Hoosier youth hurried to answer the call to arms during the Mexican War: he had joined General Winfield Scott's forces fighting to free Texas from the yoke of Santa Anna's tyranny—and in the process to grab millions of acres of land for the United States. Brown, an attorney, had seen this first Hoosier effort at soldiering come to disaster at Buena Vista, where the ill-clad, ill-armed, and ill-led boys from Indiana ran like jackrabbits from the advancing Mexican army. But that was then; now hope sprang afresh as this new crop of cannon fodder prepared to swear their oaths and be mustered into the service of their country.

Shortly after the bombardment of Fort Sumter, President Abraham Lincoln had issued a call for seventy-five thousand volunteers to help put down the rebellion. Oliver P. Morton, governor of Indiana, responded and easily delivered more than his fair share of eager young Hoosier men, filling the quota almost at once. The surplus enlistees were ordered back home, but there were some in the Hoosier State who would not accept the verdict that they could not go. William Lyon Brown went directly to Washington, D.C., in June of 1861 and pressed his case directly to the President and the War Department, with the assistance of Senator Henry Lane. Lincoln listened to the Mexican War veteran plead his case that his avid patriotic urges should not be foreclosed on and agreed, authorizing Brown to raise an infantry regiment.[1] Brown immediately set to the task by contacting friends and associates throughout north central and northern Indiana in an attempt to organize a recruiting campaign that would raise the thousand men necessary to form an infantry regiment. If successful, Brown would be the colonel of the regiment.

On June 17, in an effort to stimulate the enlistment response, Brown sent the following letter to several men who he believed could muster the one hundred men necessary to form an infantry company:

> *Dear Sir: Hasten and fill up your company. Each one must have 101 men. Send roll as soon as you can and bring the company as soon as you have the proper number; a less number will not do, and it will be but safe to have a few extra ones. Each company is entitled to two musicians. Every man will, if possible, bring with him a blanket or comfort, his ordinary woolen clothing, no fancy, all plain and substantial. Each volunteer honorably discharged will receive in addition to his pay and clothing one hundred dollars in gold, and no doubt, 160 acres of land, besides.*
>
> *W. L. Brown, Colonel*[2]

James M. Lytle, while visiting his father in Logansport, fell under the persuasive charm of Colonel Brown and committed himself to helping raise a company of men for the regiment. Lytle had been the engineer responsible for building the railroad between Logansport and Valparaiso. With valuable experience in leading men, he was an ideal choice for the task of raising what would become Company I of the new regiment. Lytle traveled to Valparaiso by train and as luck would have it, immediately bumped into Erasmus C. Gilbreath, a former subordinate of his on the railroad construction project. Lytle, full of excitement, cried out to Gilbreath, "You are just the one I wanted to see, for you are going to war with me."[3] Gilbreath at first demurred, but fell victim to Lytle's enthusiasm and on June 5, 1861, began the task of raising a rifle company. He rode through Valparaiso and LaPorte, towns in Porter County, calling men to arms like a modern day Paul Revere.[4]

Thomas, James, and Asbury Stephens rode together to Monticello, Indiana, where they hoped to join the new company being organized by Alfred Reed. Thomas Stephens was raised a farmboy, but he had higher ambitions. He was attending school at Asbury College, now DePauw University, when the news of war came. Caught in the mood of the day, the fledgling medical student would drop his studies and go off to war with his two younger brothers in tow.[5] Alfred Reed was a Monticello attorney and had assembled an infantry company as early as May of 1861. Since the initial enlistment requirements of seventy-five hundred recruits had been filled by then, the muster of the Monticello Rifles, as Reed called his band of men, could not be accepted and many disappointed men returned to White County. They would return again to form Company K.

George Uhl was like many of the enlisted men of the Western troops who served in the Union army. Born in Austria in 1842, he had emigrated with his mother and two brothers to America in 1854. Eva Uhl had lost her husband and couldn't bear the thought of losing any of her three sons to the army. The Revolution of 1848 had prompted besieged autocratic governments to require compulsory military service. The strong-willed mother moved to rural Pulaski County, Indiana, and immediately set about the task of transforming swamp land into a fertile farm. Her desire to keep her boys from the army was thwarted when young George heard the siren call of war and ran off to Monticello to become one of Alfred Reed's soldiers.[6] At least it was his own choice.

John Wheeler of Crown Point (in Lake County) was a powerful man and an ally of Governor Morton. As publisher of the *Crown Point Register*, Wheeler had done his best to further the Republican cause of both Lincoln and Morton; now he used his paper to whip the boys of Lake County into an enlisting frenzy. In the process he fell victim to his own appeal, and on June 16 Wheeler signed the company muster rolls as a mere private in what would become Company B.[7]

Although Wheeler mustered in as a private, his leadership abilities were soon recognized, and he was elected captain of the new Company B. In time, many companies of soldiers throughout the Union would deeply regret having elected the men they chose to lead them. In Wheeler's case the election proved wise: the man was brave and a capable leader. Shortly after muster Wheeler led his Lake County charges to Lafayette, Indiana, and Camp Tippecanoe. They arrived at the camp on June 25 and found it empty; nobody else had arrived yet.[8] In a matter of days the camp would be overflowing with men, tents, horses, cannon, and wagons.

While John Wheeler may have been a political ally of Governor Morton, John B. Van Valkenburg of Peru, Indiana, definitely was not. Van Valkenburg was a strong Jacksonian Democrat. He had grown up in Cleveland and had run off to join the United States army, possibly to avoid imprisonment for theft. He spent five years serving in the artillery fighting Indians in the upper Midwest. When his service ended, he gratefully accepted the four hundred acres which the government tendered to all those who had served honorably and relocated to Indiana. In Peru, Van Valkenburg found prosperity dealing in agricultural implements and seed. He was a community leader. When war clouds gathered, he raised a company of men to put down the Rebellion, not because he approved of President Lincoln or desired an abolition of slavery, but because he loved his country.[9] He would lead the men of Company A.

On June 15 James Lytle arrived for the rendezvous of the Porter County men who were destined to fill the ranks of Company I. Nearly every able-bodied man, woman, and child in Porter County came to Valparaiso for the great mustering rally. The war enthusiasm was so great, as was undoubtedly the salesmanship of Lytle and Erasmus Gilbreath, that one hudnred and fifty men were enrolled, fifty more than were needed. Lytle and Gilbreath knew so little about military affairs that they assumed all of the men could stay with the company.[10] After the 150 men were enrolled, a vote was taken, and to no one's surprise, Lytle was elected captain and Gilbreath first lieutenant.[11]

The men comprising Company I were a sturdy lot. Every occupation and social status was represented in the company. Almost to a man they were born and raised in Porter County. One exception was an Irishman named Patrick Maloney. As he stepped up to the mustering officer he was asked his name, age, occupation, height, and his place of nativity, to which Maloney replied, "I was born in Ireland sir, but I think Indiana is me native state."[12]

Colonel Brown wisely chose July 4 for the departure of the various companies to Camp Tippecanoe. The Fourth of July was a grand occasion in Valparaiso. Once again, virtually the entire county population turned out to see the boys off. The full musical talents of the town were called upon to stir up the martial spirits of the crowd—one fife and a drum, the former played by the sheriff and the latter by the town blacksmith. This talented duo tweeted and thumped all day and finally led the departing company to the railroad station, where a train awaited to take the men to Lafayette.[13]

The path to Camp Tippecanoe and service in the Twentieth Indiana Volunteers varied greatly from man to man. Although they all shared the common bond of being Western men, their individual backgrounds were as variable as Indiana's weather. Among those destined to play a significant role in the life of the regiment were a number of interesting first-time soldiers.

Twenty-five-year-old William C. L. Taylor was city attorney for Lafayette. A graduate of Indiana University, he was influential in Tippecanoe County. He enlisted as a private in Company G.[14]

John Luther was a vice-president of the First National Bank of Crown Point and a wealthy landowner.[15] He joined the ranks of Company B with his brother, Albert.

Another unique character in Company B was William S. Babbitt. Babbitt was born in Vermont in 1825, making him, at age thirty-five, relatively old at the time of his enlistment. Babbitt had grown up fast: he had gone to sea as a cabin boy at age eleven, and before he was fifteen he had sailed around Cape Horn five times.[16] Babbitt brought experience, a fearless demeanor, and a salty tongue to a hard-boiled group of men.

John C. Brown was a shoemaker when called to service. He had plied his trade lucratively in the Baltimore, Maryland, area for most of his life. Forty-two years old at the time of his enlistment, Brown had seen the profitability of his shoemaking business steadily decline. John Brown was a husband and father, raising a large family in rural White County. At dinner one evening, Brown looked up at his wife across the huge oak dinner table and said, "Wife, I'll just have to enlist. I know I shall die if I don't."[17] Brown reported to Alfred Reed the next day and enlisted in Company K.

Thomas Hamilton Logan was born in 1840 and hailed from Logansport, Indiana. Logan's grandfather had been chaplain of the army at the Battle of Tippecanoe. After the victory over Tecumseh and the Prophet, General John Tipton had been given twenty-six hundred acres of land along the Wabash River. He named this land Logansport in honor of Logan's grandfather. Logan had long had an interest in military affairs and had been a member of the local militia.[18] The rebellion presented him with an opportunity to fulfill his youthful ambition by joining Company F.

The spiritual needs of the rapidly assembling force were tended to by Reverend William C. Porter. Born on the Isle of Jersey in 1834 and educated at Knox College and Wabash College, Porter, a resident of Plymouth, Indiana, had been licensed to preach in 1859.[19] If ministering to the sick and wounded and converting sinners was his life's ambition, Porter now had the opportunity of a lifetime.

Private William Archer represented what may have been the typical Indiana farm boy turned soldier. From Forest Township in Clinton County, Archer was vulgar, uneducated, and as rowdy a young man as you would find in Mr. Lincoln's army. Consequently, he reflected the sentiments of many when he wrote home, "I won't come home until the war is over for I want to see this damn thing over. I won't come home until I get to kill some of the god damn devils for they are the ones that got me into this fight."[20]

The mushrooming numbers of new soldiers found accommodations rather spartan at Camp Tippecanoe. The boys were assigned to large, three-sided sheds floored with nothing but straw.[21] There were to be no big, fluffy feather beds like those many of the boys had shared with a brother or two back home. They would sleep on the ground with nothing but those few strands of straw for comfort. Blankets were not to be had either, and the evening chill portended misery in days to come.[22] New uniforms were as rare as the blankets; the men were forced to make do with the clothes on their backs.[23]

With his regiment almost full, Colonel Brown began the arduous and not altogether successful process of training his new charges. Each company was drilled religiously in movements by the captains and lieutenants. This came off well enough, but when Colonel Brown tried to put the entire regiment through its paces, the men collided in a confused tangle of humanity.[24]

Discipline was lax at Camp Tippecanoe and that situation resulted in any number of breakdowns of conduct, both serious and good-natured. Mr. J. Finley wrote Governor Morton to report that Captain Nathaniel Herron of Company G was intoxicated and had no business being an officer.[25] Strong-willed farm boys also tested their new superiors at every turn. First Sergeant Harvey Miller caught one of his men from Company F sneaking into camp with a big stone in his pocket, swearing that he was going to knock down one of his comrades. Miller ordered him to give up the stone but the soldier refused. Miller told the man that he was on a course for the guardhouse, but the insolent private told him that he couldn't be taken. Miller called for reinforcements and the offender was callaboosed off to jail.[26]

There was a wealth of horseplay in the ranks at this early date. The favorite prank was to challenge a camp sentry to give up a musket for inspection and then run off with the gun. One hundred of the men staged a mass, short-term desertion and left the boundaries of the camp for a lazy stroll about the hills of Tippecanoe County and the town of Lafayette. They returned shortly thereafter and were not punished. In fact, no act of insubordination or flouting of orders seemed to draw the ire of Colonel Brown.[27] After all, here were over one thousand new soldiers, untrained, unequipped, lacking uniforms, devoid of significant military training, sleeping on the ground and being led by inexperienced officers. How could one expect them to act?

One day while at Camp Tippecanoe, Colonel Brown was visited by two plain country women, one of them the mother of a new recruit. Two of her other sons had joined the army and she wanted her third back, having the impression that you could muster out with the same ease that you had mustered in. Colonel Brown told the woman that her boys were brave and were just what the country needed. The grief-stricken mother stood there, tears streaming down her face, and said, "Well, if John really wants to go, and his services are needed, I reckon I must let him go." The boy quickly informed his mother and the colonel that he wanted to go to war and the saddened mother left the camp weeping.[28]

Another parent was not quite as cooperative. J. L. West came to Lafayette determined to get his boy James released from Company F. Mr. West had been absent from Logansport when the mustering officers enlisted his son. When he returned to find his Johnny had gone for a soldier, he determined he did not want the eighteen-year-old serving in the army. The elder West could not understand why his somewhat sickly son would want to enlist anyway. Young James informed his father about the riches his military service would earn him: eleven dollars a month, one hundred dollars bounty, and 160 acres of land. The boy told his astonished father that Colonel Brown had promised all of these things to him if he enlisted. The furious Mr. West, intent on taking his son with him, was taunted by several of the officers and enlisted men, and when he became unruly he was escorted to the camp boundary by a guard and sent back to Logansport.[29]

On July 22, 1861, the regiment was declared full. Shortly after breakfast the men were drawn up on the parade ground by companies and the process of official enrollment into the service of the United States commenced. The process was simple and straightforward. Major Thomas J. Wood, First United States Cavalry, a dignified old soldier who had served in the army since 1845, began by announcing to the assembled regiment that if any of them were too cowardly to be a soldier and face actual and dangerous battle, now was the time for such cowards to show it by immediately leaving the ranks and camp. A few took him up on his offer and slunk off amid the jeers and hisses of the regiment.[30] Then Wood slowly walked along the line of each company, examining each man for physical flaws and questioning each as to his general physical condition. Asbury Stephens was rejected in this manner and was forced to leave his two brothers behind as he departed the ranks.[31]

As Major Wood passed along the line of Company I, he spied John Smith standing tall in the second file in the rear rank. Wood noticed that Smith had lost his index finger. Sensing that a missing trigger finger could prove a serious detriment to a soldier in a rifle company, Wood exclaimed, "You can't shoot a gun with that hand!" Smith responded that he most assuredly could. The doubtful major asked, "Do you think you could hit a man at four hundred yards?" The quick-thinking and cocksure Smith boldly replied, "I wish you would step out and let me try."[32] Smith's response evidently pleased the old major and he proceeded on to a small boy who, he discovered, had placed wooden blocks under the heels of his boots to appear taller and older. Wood had the blocks removed and the young private, named Boulson, ran off crying like the child he was. Thus rejected, Boulson would hang around camp as a servant to the men until he grew old enough to pass muster.[33]

It seems almost comical, in light of subsequent problems the Union army had in recruiting or drafting a sufficient number of soldiers to sustain the war effort, that any willing man would have been turned away. The folly of it all would be exposed by later disasters. The picky pre-enrollment physical inspections would fade into memory, along with ninety-day enlistments, one-hundred-dollar bounties, promises of land, and assurances of quick, decisive victories.

After the inspections were completed, a magistrate was brought before the men. They raised their right hands and swore their oaths of allegiance and obedience.[34] With this process completed the assembled companies could proudly claim to be members of the newly formed Twentieth Indiana Volunteer Infantry. One man, Jack Forgus, reported to camp, took the physical exam and stood in line ready for enlistment. However, when it came time to swear the oath of allegiance to the United States Constitution, he refused. He then had the audacity to ask Colonel Brown for money to make the trip home. Brown had his men line up forming a gauntlet and ran Forgus between the men, with his soldiers pushing, kicking, and screaming derisions at the man.[35] With this nasty bit of business out of the way, elections were conducted and officers were elected by their companies.

The new regimental officers were as follows:

Colonel William L. Brown, Logansport
Lieutenant Colonel Charles D. Murray, Kokomo
Major Benjamin H. Smith, Logansport
Adjutant Israel N. Stiles, Lafayette
Quartermaster Isaac W. Hart, Attica
Chaplain William C. Porter, Plymouth
Surgeon Orpheus Everts, LaPorte
Assistant Surgeon Anson Hurd, Oxford

Company A
    Captain John Van Valkenburg, Peru
    First Lieutenant William B. Reyburn, Peru
    Second Lieutenant Jonas Hoover, Peru

Company B
    Captain John Wheeler, Crown Point
    First Lieutenant Charles A. Bell, Corydon
    Second Lieutenant Michael Sheehan, Crown Point

Company C
    Captain Oliver H. P. Bailey, Plymouth
    First Lieutenant William C. Casselman, Plymouth
    Second Lieutenant Joseph Lynch, Plymouth

Company D
    Captain George F. Dick, Attica
    First Lieutenant Charles Reese, Attica
    Second Lieutenant James A. Wilson, Attica
Company E
    Captain James H. Shannon, LaPorte
    First Lieutenant John W. Andrew, LaPorte
    Second Lieutenant John E. Sweet, LaPorte

Company F
    Captain John Kistler, Danville
    First Lieutenant Thomas H. Logan, Logansport
    Second Lieutenant Ed C. Sutherland, Logansport

Company G
    Captain Nathaniel Herron, Delphi
    First Lieutenant William C. L. Taylor, Lafayette
    Second Lieutenant William B. Brittingham, Lafayette

Company H
    Captain George W. Geisendorff, Indianapolis
    First Lieutenant George W. Meikel, Indianapolis
    Second Lieutenant William O. Sherwood, Indianapolis

Company I
    Captain James M. Lytle, Valparaiso
    First Lieutenant Erasmus C. Gilbreath, Valparaiso
    Second Lieutenant William T. Carr, Valparaiso

Company K
    Captain Alfred Reed, Monticello
    First Lieutenant John T. Richardson, Monticello
    Second Lieutenant Daniel D. Dale, Monticello [36]

Serving under these officers were more than one thousand enlisted men and noncommissioned officers. Each man came into service of his country for his own special reason. Most joined out of an intense feeling of patriotism and a sense of duty to the country they loved. Many joined for adventure and to find "fame and glory." Some enlisted for financial reasons, and a small minority signed the muster roll to help eradicate slavery. Whatever their personal reasons, they were now united by a common bond. From this date forward, their personal histories would be the history of the Twentieth Indiana, written in blood on a hundred fields of battle.

Immediately after taking their oaths, the regiment marched to the train station and boarded rickety old freight cars bound for Indianapolis and Camp Morton. At Indianapolis, the men were to continue to drill and to draw all necessary equipment before their departure for Washington, D.C. Camp Morton, just outside the city limits of Indianapolis, was "a beautiful place," just the kind of place to drill and complete the process of becoming soldiers.[37] Each of the men excitedly looked forward to the coming days. They couldn't wait to get their hands on the new Springfield rifled musket that was surely waiting for them. The recruiting officers had promised the men who enlisted that they would be a rifle regiment, not one of those outfits firing ancient muskets that had been converted from flintlock to percussion during the Mexican War.[38] This fact made the men proud and made the marching and close-order drill in scalding hot weather less tedious.

Captain Oliver H. P. Bailey was one of the few men who found his enthusiasm dampened during the stay in Indianapolis. On July 31, Bailey received the terrible news that his infant son had died.[39] Bailey's company was completing its drill and these hard times left little opportunity for mourning. He would stay with his men and fulfill his new responsibilities.

The five days at Camp Morton passed swiftly and on August 1, the men of the Twentieth were told they would draw their gear and then depart for Washington. The boys could barely contain their excitement. They were rip-roaring and ready to go teach the Rebs a lesson or two. Dr. Orpheus Everts, the finest-looking man in the regiment and loaded with enough medicines to kill a horse, arrived in camp just as the troops prepared to depart.[40]

At the appointed hour, the regiment lined up by companies and marched into Indianapolis, down a side street to the rear door of a large warehouse where accoutrements were stored. The new soldiers stripped off vestiges of civilian life and packaged them for shipment home. They then entered the warehouse through an alley door and were herded through various stations where they were issued everything they would need as soldiers.[41] First they picked up their uniforms which consisted of a pair of shoes, cotton socks, flannel underwear, pants, and a short coat of a very heavy gray cloth.[42] Next, each soldier picked up a belt, cartridge box, haversack, canteen, and finally a gun. After passing through the building the regiment again formed on the main street outside.[43]

However, the boys of Company K had other business to attend to before they could leave town. As they passed through the warehouse, the last company in their regiment to do so, they discovered that all of the available uniforms had been distributed. There they stood in long johns, their civilian clothes on the way home. Before they could return to camp they marched through the streets of Indianapolis, in their long underwear, to a local tailor who quickly fitted them for new gray uniforms, the standard issue for militia and state troops. The greatly embarrassed men were heartened by the thunderous applause and resounding cheers with which they were greeted by the townsfolk of Indianapolis.[44]

This should have been a triumphant moment for the regiment, but events just short of a riot broke out. The gun that was distributed to each was not a rifle as promised, but a Mexican War-issue smoothbore musket.[45]

Smoothbores had been manufactured for the United States government since 1795 at Springfield, Massachusetts, and fired by means of a flint and firing pan. They shot a round ball, kicked like a Wabash mule, and were not accurate beyond a hundred yards. In 1842 the government had paid an armory at Harper's Ferry to convert the muskets from flintlock to percussion cap. Most of these altered muskets were used in the fight against Santa Anna, and after the triumph in Mexico, the guns found their way into armories of the various states. Now, faced with a shortage of new Springfield rifles, Governor Morton was forced to send his men off to a modern war with relatively ancient weapons, regardless of what the recruiting officers may have promised as an inducement to enlist.

But if Morton thought the recruits were only a bunch of compliant farmers and clerks, he was wrong. The grumbling started immediately and rose steadily as each company emerged from the warehouse. Recruiting officers, regimental officers, and the governor himself were cursed loudly and long. Soon the men broke ranks and unceremoniously began to throw down the muskets in a heap on the street. Morton was summoned, and upon his arrival, demanded that officers be arrested for failing to control their men. After a great deal of persuasion, the officers of the Twentieth convinced their charges to pick up the guns and return to camp.[46]

If Morton and his officers thought the matter was settled, they were mistaken. The following morning as the officers emerged from their tents, they were confronted with the sight of all of the muskets belonging to the regiment stacked in a huge pile outside the boundaries of the camp. The governor again hurried to the site of the insurrection and tried to speak to the men about the shortage of rifled muskets. Morton's oratorical skills were legendary, but they failed him on this morning in August. The men simply refused to listen to the frustrated and increasingly angry governor. They jeered and hissed Morton at every word. Finally, frustrated by all other approaches, Morton reached an agreement with Colonel Brown to immediately equip Company A and Company B with rifles and then supply the remainder of the regiment at the earliest possible date. This final compromise mollified the men and the tense situation abated.[47] Governor Morton was a proud and powerful man, one who didn't take kindly to negotiating with privates or colonels. He could sense a problem regiment when he saw and heard it. He ordered Colonel Brown to take his men and get out of town on the first train east. The men were happy to comply.

Because of this sudden and unexpected departure, triggered by their defiance of the governor and obstinate behavior in general, the friends and loved ones from back home were not afforded the opportunity to come to Indianapolis to properly send the boys off to war. In fact, the regiment literally raced through town, ordered by Colonel Brown to run to the train depot. Men fell along the way from the ninety-degree heat. Private Henry Gamble, Company H, collapsed from heat exhaustion and was carried to the awaiting train. He would suffer for several days as the train proceeded eastward before becoming the first man to die in the regiment, killed at the hands of his own officers.[48]

The thoroughly fatigued regiment boarded the empty cars with nary a band, a tear or a speech in their behalf. One of the regimental officers turned to Colonel Brown and in reference to the unappreciative townsfolk of Indianapolis remarked, "They make little fuss over us."

"Yes," Brown replied, "but they shall when we return."[49]

Colonel William Lyon Brown, first colonel of the Twentieth Indiana. A veteran of the Mexican War, Brown was killed during the regiment's attack at Second Manassas. (Dunn collection)

Major George F. Dick (*left*) was promoted in 1862 to lieutenant colonel of the Eighty-sixth Indiana Volunteers. (Dunn collection) Captured aboard the *Fanny*, Quartermaster Isaac W. Hart (*right*) was later transferred to the Union army's quartermaster department, and promoted to major. (Dunn collection)

Captain John Wheeler, Company B, led the Crown Point men until his promotion to major in 1862. (Cole collection)

Charles D. Murray was the first lieutenant colonel of the regiment. His conflict with Colonel Brown resulted in his resignation, but later he was appointed colonel of the Eighty-ninth Indiana Volunteers. (Morrow's *History of Howard County*)

Second Lieutenant Charles R. Pew, Company A. (Dunn collection)

Chaplain William C. Porter (Carlile collection)

Private George W. Hughes, Company G. (Young collection)

Israel N. Stiles served as adjutant until 1863, when he was promoted to major of the Sixty-third Indiana Volunteers. (Meserve collection, New York State Library)

Private Edwin Chesley, Company D, played the fife in the regimental band. Later in the war he traded his fife for a rifle. (Dunn collection)

Private Will Emery Brown transferred to the Twenty-eighth U.S.Colored Troops as second lieutenant. He was the Twentieth Indiana's regimental association secretary. (Dunn collection)

Private Phillip Wolf, Company G. (Young collection)

CHAPTER TWO

STRANGERS IN A STRANGE LAND

After what seemed an interminable wait in the hot and dusty station, the train finally lurched forward like a giant serpent heading east into the approaching dusk. The telegraph operators let stations on down the line know that the Twentieth Indiana was on its way. In each little town along the route, the train was hailed with shouts and cheers, and at stations where the train stopped to take on water, the men were offered ice water by the grateful Hoosier townsfolk. At 7:00 A.M. the train made its final stop in Indiana on the state line. Private Robert Stoddard received a cup of "good coffee from a nice lady and a bouquet of flowers from the woman's daughter" as humble parting gestures.[1]

The train carrying the Hoosiers proceeded eastward across Ohio, meeting with enthusiastic greetings at every stop. It was still early in the war and everything seemed heroic. At Crestline the regiment changed trains and the townsfolk of that small burg treated the boys to every imaginable delicacy that orchards and ovens could provide. After arriving at Pittsburgh at 1:00 A.M. on Sunday and changing trains, the regiment proceeded to Harrisburg.

The day-long trip through the beautiful hills and hollows of Pennsylvania greatly impressed the Hoosiers, who were accustomed to prairies. Many of the boys in the regiment had never been east of the Wabash River, let alone east of the Alleghenies, and the trip gave them a sense of the immensity of the nation that they were preparing to defend.[2]

Instead of stopping at Harrisburg as the soldiers had hoped, the train turned to the south and moved on. Ten miles south of the Pennsylvania line the train groaned to a halt and discharged one of the companies from the Twentieth along the rail line to serve as guards for the bridges in the area. Colonel Brown had received orders from General John A. Dix as the train passed through the Harrisburg station: the regiment was to be temporarily spread along the line between Harrisburg and Baltimore. Two more companies were dropped off as the train moved south to a point near Cockeysville, Maryland, where the bulk of the regiment went into camp. Company A, under the command of Captain Van Valkenburg, proceeded on to Baltimore, where it was to assist in guarding the Federal arsenal.[3]

Colonel Brown was no doubt less than pleased that his regiment was dispersed before it had time to get a feeling of organization, but his disappointment was ameliorated by the excellent condition of the site selected for the camp of the Twentieth. The camp was nestled among the rolling pastoral hills of Maryland, where neat, well-cultivated farms with whitewashed houses rested next to strong stands of oak, chestnut, pine and cedar trees. Abundant springs of fresh cool water flowed, making Cockeysville an Eden among Civil War camps.[4]

Brown did not have to be told by General Dix of the importance of guarding the rail line and bridges along the Baltimore, Harrisburg and Williamsport Railroad. The rail line was now the lifeline to Washington and Baltimore. The Baltimore and Ohio Railroad line had been rendered unusable by the burning of the great wooden rail trestle. The line guarded by the Twentieth Indiana provided troops, materials of war, and food to a capital already panic-stricken as a result of the Union disaster at Bull Run. Brown intended to keep a tight rein on his men, hold them close to camp and enforce discipline and drill. He planned to be ready when the time came for his regiment to be truly tested.

Two days later secessionist guerrillas moved on the "Gunpowder Bridge." Whether they intended to set fire to the bridge or merely harass its defenders is unclear. Company G fired a few rounds from their Enfield muskets and drove the pestering intruders away.[5] In the grand scheme of the war this was a small-potatoes affair, but to a new regiment itching to make a name for itself, this initial "combat" seemed to be Austerlitz and Waterloo rolled into one.

This little affair at the Gunpowder Bridge was the only action that the regiment would see for several weeks, and the men were quickly forced to adapt to the drudgery of camp life. Brown put the time to good use and drilled the men several times a day in infantry march and tactics. The idle time gave the men an opportunity to reflect on their situation. Private Harvey Bassett of Company H penned a letter home on August 16:

The daily routine of camp is finished; the pale moonlight sleeps on grassy banks or struggles faintly through the dense foliage overhead on our snow-white tents; the sentinels are pacing the lonely watches in silence; the smouldering fires are fast dying out; the shrill cry of the katy-did mingles with the voices of men, as gathered in groups around in tents or on the grass, they make the clear night resonant with their Methodist song singing, now their only solace after the long tedious drills and previous to the last roll call at nine o'clock and the tap for all lights out.

Today I heard a quail and a meadowlark in a stubble field near us. You cannot imagine how such things affect one under peculiar circumstances. The whistle of Bob White, the first heard since I left home, made me home-sick, tired of my situation and long to be again at home in the West.[6]

The camp monotony was broken with trips to Baltimore and Washington, dinners with some of the local farmers and merchants, visits by dignitaries, and the occasional brush with Rebel troops or sympathizers. Surgeon Orpheus Everts and Adjutant Israel Stiles visited Baltimore on August 8 and found "the city of monuments and plug-uglies" to be quiet.[7] Quiet in Baltimore was welcome; four months earlier, on April 19, a regiment of Massachusetts volunteers was attacked by a mob of Confederate sympathizers, and several of the Union men were killed. Stiles was reassured to see the "Star Spangled Banner" waving over the imposing fortress of Fort McHenry and happier still when his visit to the fort revealed as many guns pointed at Baltimore as out to sea. Stiles commented to Everts that if there was to be blood spilled on Pratt Street in the future, it would be the blood of traitors.[8]

Private Robert Stoddard, Company I, and a comrade received permission for a leave of absence; they immediately headed to the nation's capital. They were struck with awe as they viewed the yet-to-be-finished dome of the Capitol Building, climbed the spiraling stairs of the dome and stared out at a vast array of encampments and soldiers for as far as the eye could see. The beauty of the city impressed them and increased their disgust for those who would tear the Union asunder. They next visited the Patent Office, the forerunner of the Smithsonian Institution, and made the same pronouncement many make today upon taking a similar excursion: "You just can't see it in a day."[9]

Captain Lytle took time away from his company to visit the huge Warren Cotton Factory. Mr. Thomson, the plant superintendent, showed Lytle around and explained that prior to the war the plant had employed over a hundred and fifty workers who manufactured thirty-three hundred yards of fabric each day. The plant was now idle from the obvious difficulty of acquiring the critical raw material. Thomson didn't complain. He was a Union man from New Jersey, and he did not let the fact that he had a Southern wife keep him from inviting Lytle to his home for dinner.[10]

Other men from the regiment experienced similar kindness from the locals around Cockeysville, but one of the Indiana boys found Southern hospitality lacking. This particular Hoosier had relatives in the area and went in search of them. Upon inquiring at one farmhouse he was directed to another, where he was assured that he could get good information and directions. At the next farmhouse he was met, not by a helpful local, but by forty rebels who immediately took him prisoner. After some time in captivity, he asked his captors for water. They directed him to the pantry. No guard accompanied him and while in the pantry he noticed a door leading to the woodshed. He seized the opportunity to escape, but not before absconding with a pound of cheese and a fresh-baked blackberry pie that was cooling in the pantry window. With arms full the Hoosier made good his escape to his relief and gastronomic delight.[11]

Colonel Brown traveled to Washington on August 17 to meet with Governor Morton. The Indiana governor was in town visiting President Lincoln and to urge his fellow Westerner to send Indiana troops to the forefront in any movement against the Confederacy. Morton was concerned about the current role of Hoosier troops in the Eastern theater serving as "water boys and bridge guards."[12] Brown took the train from Washington on the evening of August 21, with the governor in tow. It was to be a brief stop for Morton. After an introduction that consisted of "Governor Morton, boys," Morton made a short speech about the safety of Indiana being in good hands. The train whistle sounded and the good governor set off for Indianapolis with the men of the Twentieth still left guarding the bridges.[13]

Captain George Geisendorff, Company H, was also bound for Indianapolis. The regiment had departed Indianapolis without their appropriate regimental colors. Geisendorff's father, who owned a successful dry-goods store, had ordered colors, to be paid for by appreciative ladies of Indianapolis who had donated one hundred and seventy-five dollars for the purchase. On September 17 a large crowd of women gathered on the porch of Geisendorff and Co. and presented the two new flags to the lieutenant. The regimental flag was deep blue, fringed in gold with thirteen stars and the national coat of arms. The American flag was the traditional stars and stripes, but with the added name of the regiment in gold letters on one of the stripes.[14] Even though the men were clad in gray uniforms, they would at least have flags to distinguish them from their enemy.

Despite the untold suffering that the Twentieth would experience from foul weather, poor victuals, and exhaustion in the future, the time at Camp Belger around Cockeysville would always be remembered as a time of feast and plenty. The fact was that the boys worked less and ate better than they had back home. Captain Lytle wrote home that his "starvation" rations consisted of chicken, roast beef, sweet potatoes, cabbage, corn, beans, tomatoes, bread, shortcake, apple pie, fresh butter, tea and coffee.[15] Albert Luther, who had gained four pounds since leaving Indianapolis, told his father that he would give up his bounty money if his parents could be in Maryland to eat some of the blackberries growing wild along the roads. Luther boasted that, "They are as big as walnuts and as thick as hail."[16] Sergeant Moses B. Mattingly reported that Corporal John Turner had gained twenty-five pounds. Mattingly told the *Marshall County Republican*, "You know he was a big fellow, imagine what he is now. 'Laugh and grow fat' is an old adage and John seems to have proven its truth."[17]

Still, experiencing the fat of the land was not experiencing war. The Hoosiers had volunteered to fight. They were "tired of guarding bridges and shooting at cows and white rocks for want of a sight of a live secessionist bent upon mischief."[18] They also grumbled about inconsistencies in governmental bureaucracy. The government could not provide them with regulation uniforms, they still wore gray jeans and jackets trimmed with black velvet, yet could provide them with a brass band bedecked in spanking new Federal blue uniforms.[19] With autumn having arrived and winter fast approaching, the men had not received a single overcoat or blanket, yet Captain Geisendorff arrived back in camp bearing two new silk regimental flags that cost the citizens of Indianapolis one hundred and seventy-five dollars.[20] The men guarded the bridges with smoothbore muskets that "kicked as hard as they shot" and watched as trainload after trainload of volunteers from down East passed by armed with Springfield rifles.[21]

The men's rising frustration and anger was alleviated temporarily by the first visit of the army paymaster since they had been in the army. The pay was in gold and silver at the princely rate of eleven dollars per month. Little did they know that this would be the first and last time that they would be paid in gold. From that day forward, greenbacks would be the compensation.[22]

Internal conflicts within the ranks began to fester as a bored regiment of men turned to liquor and horseplay to keep occupied. Colonel Brown was intolerant of drinking and lax discipline, so he tightened his rein on the regiment. Brown apparently confused discipline with tyranny and began a gradual process of losing the respect of many of his subordinate officers and men. He blasted offenders verbally, over-punished for simple offenses and earned a reputation for unfairness. Private David Pealer wrote his brother:

"The only thing preventing us from being a good regiment is dissatisfaction among our officers with our colonel who is not liked by any man in our regiment."[23] The tension level in the camp rose to dangerous levels but was abated by big news.

On September 22 the regiment was given orders to recall all of its stray companies out on guard duties and reassemble, ready for movement into Dixie. At evening dress parade, Adjutant Israel Stiles read the following order:

> *The regiment is now under orders to march immediately. The good name already acquired by this regiment will be to each one, officer and man, a stimulus, until we excel in all that is glorious in arms—until this accursed rebellion is wiped away, and our beloved country again smiles in the happiness, the prosperity and blessings of peace.*[24]

The regiment exploded with wild cheering and excitement. Officers and enlisted men alike joked and slapped each other on the back. The neat rows of tents came down and surplus items were auctioned by humorous self-proclaimed auctioneers. Few slept that night. By 9:00 A.M. the small military town was packed up and ready to move. In thirty-five rail cars a regiment of men "who believe in the justice of the ballot and are prepared to enforce it with the bullet" were on their way to the heart of the rebellion.[25]

To the surprise of the Indiana boys, the regiment, following its spiffy band down the narrow street, was loudly cheered by many of the citizens of Baltimore. These Southern sympathizers viewed with admiration the big, raw-boned men from out of the West. Fuss-and-feathers Yankees from New England had not impressed them: New Englanders were viewed as having caused the war. These Hoosiers may have been poorly dressed and dirty farm boys, but they were honest. There were some scowling faces snarling at the boys from the windows above, but the overall reception was a pleasant one.[26]

The regiment passed down St. Paul Street and on to Baltimore Street then down to the wharves, where they took a steamer. The boys landed at Fortress Monroe early on the morning of September 24, marched to the mainland and went into bivouac at Camp Hamilton under the command of Brigadier General Joseph K. Mansfield. For the next two days the Twentieth was drilled incessantly.[27] Major General John E. Wool, commanding the Department of the East, had a job for the Hoosiers, and Mansfield wanted to be sure the boys had the pluck and training to carry it out.

From the beginning of the rebellion, the Confederacy had realized the necessity of securing and defending the sounds of North Carolina and guarding their approaches against Federal gunboats. The series of channels connecting with the Chowan, Neuse, and Roanoke rivers were natural routes for military goods to be smuggled into the Southern states. Brevet Lieutenant General Winfield Scott's Anaconda Plan called for isolating the Confederacy by imposing a naval blockade of the Atlantic and Gulf coasts to protect the coast from the smuggling of weapons. The main entrance to the sounds of North Carolina was through Hatteras Inlet, and the Rebels had thrown up heavy earthworks to protect this vital smuggling route.[28] The Twentieth and other Northern units were to aid in taking these forts.

On August 27 a large Federal naval squadron anchored in a shallow bay off Hatteras Island, not far from Forts Hatteras and Clark, which were separated from the main island by a shallow bay. At 8:45 on the morning of August 28, the naval forces commenced their bombardment of the two Rebel forts. Twenty-four hours later the Rebels surrendered and the forts were occupied by Union forces.[29] With the capture of Hatteras Inlet, the entrance to Albemarle and Pamlico sounds was effectively closed.

The Twentieth Indiana was to move to Chicamacomico at the extreme northern end of Hatteras Island to deter Rebel troops from landing and moving on Fort Hatteras. The Twentieth Indiana, less three companies, marched on September 25 from Fortress Monroe under the command of Lieutenant Colonel Murray, to the steamer SS *Spaulding* and shipped to Chicamacomico.[30]

The sophisticated Yankee soldier from down East would have found nothing exciting about boarding a plain troop transport bound for some isolated, godforsaken strip of barren sand, but the landlocked Hoosiers found the experience exhilarating. The ocean was as foreign to most of them as Timbuktu.

As the *Spaulding* moved away from the wharf and into the widening sea, Private E. M. B. Hooker, Company H, observed "schools of little fishes circling about the surface of the water, porpoises plunging to and fro, flying fish darting around," while during this nautical entertainment the big guns at Fortress Monroe boomed away during gunnery practice.[31] Hooker later wrote home that "some of you quiet fellows living cozily on farms, ought to go around with us and see what a great country you have and how well worthy it is to be kept together."[32]

The trip to Hatteras began uneventfully enough. But with the men bedded down throughout the ship, the light breeze of early evening became at dawn a full-forced gale. Captain John Kistler described it as a "perfect hurricane." Kistler, the Methodist minister, went on to explain in a letter home:

Most of the boys was awful sick and lay around on the decks throwing

Hatteras Island

Uncle Sam's grub overboard in a shameful manner. I have been one of the lucky ones, nary sick. I could not help laughing although the poor fellows was nearly dead, but I knew it was not a fatal disease. I stood on the bow to gratify my curiosity of a storm at sea, looking at the white capped billows roll. One moment so high that it looked dicey, the next a wave sweeping the deck so that I had to hold to the rigging. Then to look up at the masts and see them at an angle of forty-five degrees forward and then the same back. Pitching and puffing through the waves apparently but a speck upon the mighty waters.[33]

Sergeant Thomas M. Bartlett reported that the men had "vomited so hard as to throw up the pegs in the soles of their shoes."[34] It may well be that the seasick Hoosiers were too ill to appreciate the danger that the *Spaulding* was in. Hatteras had served as a graveyard for many a previous ship, and the basic navigational hazards had not improved over time. Numerous sandbars made sailing into Hatteras Inlet a dangerous undertaking in good weather. In weather such as this the possibility was great that the boys from Indiana might find sand a little sooner than expected. Through luck or the fervent prayers of Chaplain Porter, the ocean, in one mighty upheaval, lifted the *Spaulding* over the bar and deposited it between Forts Clark and Hatteras at 11:00 A.M.[35]

The seas were too rough to allow the men to leave the ship so they were forced to spend the entire day and night on board, looking toward land. Private Seymour Montgomery pronounced Hatteras "the most dismal place on earth."[36] Private Hooker opined that the bleak spot "blows great guns most of the time and when it doesn't, the sun roasts you. The chief productions are sand crabs, wrecks and dilapidated men."[37]

While rolling about at anchor, the regiment learned that they would be transferred to three steamers and three barges to go forty-five miles north to Loggerhead Inlet and the small village of Chicamacomico. With a few tents and two days' rations, the regiment departed Hatteras bound northward. All day the regimental band played patriotic songs and the men sang as the small flotilla made its way. At sunset the ships cast anchor about three miles from the shoreline and Colonel Brown, Major Smith, and Adjutant Stiles took a small boat to reconnoiter the landing spot.[38]

The landing party was greeted by the rough-looking women of the island, but as time wore on and the intentions of the officers became clear, the men of the island slowly made their appearance.[39] On Sunday, September 29, seven companies of the regiment, less a few men from each company who were accompanying the baggage of the regiment on a different steamer, set foot on Chicamacomico. Terra firma it was not. The water was so shallow that the landing boats could only approach to within one hundred feet of the shoreline. This forced the men to carry heavy loads of baggage and equipage through chest-high water to the shore.[40] The men immediately christened the new quarters of the Twentieth Regiment "Camp Live Oak."[41]

Two days later the steamer *Fanny* arrived at Chicamacomico bearing a large amount of ammunition, supplies, tents, uniforms and a Sawyer gun for the Twentieth Indiana. She had on board Quartermaster Isaac W. Hart and a group of men from the Twentieth and the Ninth New York. The *Fanny* had already earned a place in history as the first aircraft carrier, when on August 3 she launched a hot-air balloon from her decks to observe Confederate artillery positions at Sewell's Point, Virginia.[42] The U.S. naval steamer *Putnam* met the *Fanny* within five miles of her destination and convoyed her to a point three miles from shore where she lodged on a sandbar. The *Putnam* transferred a rifled cannon and ammunition to the Hoosiers and then returned to Hatteras, even though it had earlier seen a menacing Rebel vessel in the vicinity. The reason given for the *Putnam's* departure was that she was short of coal. At 2:30 P.M., a large, flat barge from the shore came alongside the *Fanny* and took on board a load of supplies consisting of tents and bread.[43]

Captain Oliver Bailey's barge had no sooner reached the shore when three Rebel steamers rapidly bore down on the stranded *Fanny*. Before the Rebels could fire a shot, the ship's civilian captain decided he had seen all that he wanted to see and abandoned the ship, fleeing in a small rowboat with his son and two band members from the Twentieth as his crew. Shortly thereafter the Rebel steamers opened up on the helpless ship with their guns. The *Fanny*, now under the command of Captain Hart, an infantry officer, responded with cannon fire of her own. In all, the Rebels fired fifteen shots, none of them hitting their target while the *Fanny* fired twelve shots, one of which struck one of the Rebel vessels.[44]

The fight was over in thirty-five minutes, and Captain Hart was forced to hoist the white flag. The Rebels captured twenty-three men, two artillery pieces, ammunition, coats, uniforms, and knapsacks for an entire regiment, all of it without the spilling of one drop of Rebel or Union blood.[45] Although Colonel Ambrose R. Wright, commanding the Third Georgia Infantry, which confronted the *Fanny*, considered that Captain Hart put up a "gallant resistance," others weren't quite sure.[46] Some of the men in the Twentieth thought that an officer with Hart's much-vaunted military experience and skills should have put up a better fight.[47] Brigadier General Mansfield was chagrined that Hart would ignore the suggestions of the first mate and engineer of the *Fanny* to dump both artillery pieces overboard and scuttle the ship.[48]

The camp at Fortress Monroe

Lieutenant Thomas Logan, watching the unfolding disaster from the shore, sized up the potential disaster and grabbed a small fishing boat and rowed out to the *Fanny* with the intent of setting her on fire. Without support of the crew or Captain Hart, Logan was forced to watch the painful capture.[49] The capture of the *Fanny* was a disaster for the Twentieth Indiana. The regiment now found itself on a cold, desolate island without ammunition, uniforms, knapsacks or food. This just wasn't the kind of glory that the boys had dreamed about on the train ride east.

Colonel Brown, expecting a Rebel landing at any time, called the regiment into battle line. There, hungry and tired, the men shivered throughout the night in the cold sand, awaiting their fate like sand crabs about to be scooped up by seagulls.[50]

Thursday, October 2, was a miserable day for the boys of the Twentieth. With their food supply captured and no relief anticipated, the Hoosiers were faced with a situation of "root hog or die" and root they did. The boys rolled up their pants legs, waded out into Pamlico Sound and proceeded to dig for oysters. With haversacks slung over their shoulders, the boys toiled throughout the day in the blistering sun, searching desperately for the elusive bivalves. Some of the fellows were sickened by the thought of eating the oysters, but hunger worked its magic and soon all were willing participants.[51]

A few of the men soon liberated hoe cakes and sweet potatoes from the near-destitute islanders.[52] But this meager supply of "Hoosier food" was soon consumed and it was back to oysters for the Indiana soldiers.

The next morning, as the first few rays of sunlight beamed over their shoulders, the weary Hoosiers cheered as they faintly made out a few specks on the horizon. Anticipation grew as the size of the specks grew, soon giving way to apprehension. The small flotilla of seven vessels veered off to the north of the camp of the Twentieth before the boys could tell exactly what flag the ships were flying. Pickets from Captain John Kistler's Company F ran into camp breathlessly informing Colonel Brown that Rebel transports had landed approximately fifteen hundred men a mere three miles above the Hoosiers' camp.[53]

Brown quickly dispatched a courier to Colonel Rush Hawkins, Ninth New York Volunteers, the commander of the Hatteras expedition, informing him of the dire situation, asking for reinforcements, and stating his intent to retreat to the lighthouse on the cape where he hoped to meet said reinforcements.[54] Brown then had the regimental drummers sound the "long roll" and called his regiment, totaling approximately five hundred men, down to the beach to receive the Rebels' anticipated landing. After dropping off their men, the Rebel flotilla moved to a position in front of the camp of the Twentieth and commenced a steady bombardment of the Hoosiers. One of the early shells shattered the only windmill serving the camp, cutting off the sole source of fresh water for the men. The Rebels were indiscriminate with their shelling, as shot flew over the heads of the battle line and smashed into the camp, destroying all of the regimental tents and splintering the camp hospital, killing its incapacitated inhabitants.[55] Shells overshot the narrow island completely and splashed harmlessly into the Atlantic Ocean.[56]

It became obvious to Colonel Brown that while the heavily armed Rebel ships kept the Twentieth Indiana pinned down, the troop transports were moving south of the regiment's position in an attempt to land forces between the Hoosiers and Fort Hatteras. Brown was forced to take a quick inventory of the predicament and make a decision in the midst of a desperate situation. He had 550 men with him on the beach armed with inadequate smoothbore muskets without any fortifications to protect them and without any artillery support. One full company of his regiment was six miles to the south on picket and three companies were still at Fortress Monroe. He was low on ammunition, he had no food, and his only source of fresh water had been destroyed. The futility of the situation left him no choice. Brown ordered his men to retreat as fast as possible to the south with the hope of being able to either cut their way through the blocking force or to slip by them. Word also arrived that Colonel Hawkins was aware of the plight of the regiment and he intended to march north from Fort Hatteras with six hundred men to meet the Twentieth near the Hatteras lighthouse.[57]

Brown ordered the regiment across the thin narrow band of sand to the Atlantic Ocean beachside where they might find some shelter from inquiring Rebel eyes and guns. Somewhat out of sight, the Hoosiers started the long, agonizing march toward survival. Lieutenant Thomas Logan, Company F, was given the tough task of leading the procession and Captain Alfred Reed, Company K, had the dangerous job of rear guard.[58] The sun scorched the men as they trudged through the soft, deep sand. Each step sapped what little energy that remained from the disheartened boys, who discarded shoes, jackets, and pants in an attempt to quicken their progress and find some relief from the oppressive heat. Throats became parched and tongues swollen from thirst. Desperate men dug into the sand and drank the vile water. Some men waded into the surf to drink the salt water and then fell victim to its effects.[59]

Somewhat as an afterthought, after struggling through the sand for six miles, Colonel Brown sent a party of volunteers, led by Sergeant Charles H. Comly, back to the camp at Chicomacomico to start the cooks in retreat, destroy the little remaining ammunition and to burn anything of value to the Rebels including the regimental paperwork. With this task accomplished, Comly started back towards the main body of troops, but he had gone only a mile when he saw a body of men from the Third Georgia Infantry blocking his path. Colonel Ambrose R. Wright called out to Comly to surrender; Comly responded by taking a shot at the colonel. The bullet missed Wright but hit the colonel's horse, bringing both horse and man down in a heap. The furious Georgians stormed in around Comly, and when he saw he was totally surrounded, he surrendered.[60]

Privates Lucias Bennett, Charles White, and Abram Hays, Company H, tarried too long around camp while destroying military stores and found themselves cut off by a detachment from the Seventh Georgia. Bennett was killed trying to escape and White and Hays were captured. The two unfortunate privates were tied together and held by Captain Wilson, Seventh Georgia. Toward sundown the Georgians stopped to build a fire and cook some ducks that they had looted from the residents of the island. The smell of the food nearly drove Hays and White crazy. Hays begged the Georgians for a bite and one of the Rebels looked up and called Hays "a dammed black republican son of a bitch" and told him, "We don't eat with niggers!"—their ultimate insult.

The next morning, after working all night to free his hands, Hays untied himself and White. Hays had secreted a gun under his shirt before his capture and he now removed it and shot Captain Wilson. The two Yankee privates ran as fast as they could amidst a hailstorm of bullets, hotly pursued by their former captors. After putting some distance between themselves and the Georgians, they buried themselves in the sand up to their heads in an effort to hide. Several times the Georgians nearly stepped on them as they frantically searched for the Hoosiers who had shot their captain, but to no avail, and when darkness came Hays and White made good their escape.[61]

The straggling of the column increased as men fell by the wayside stricken with hunger, fatigue and thirst. Captain Reed drove the stragglers before him like cattle on a cattle drive, but occasionally a near-dead soldier was left behind to his fate.[62] Hotly pursued by the Rebel party from the north, the Twentieth Indiana was being driven into a bag in the south. The Hoosiers had plodded twenty miles by 8:00 P.M., when they discovered a Georgian landing party disembarking on the beach in rolling seas. The Georgians were clearly illuminated against the last light of dusk, while the Hoosiers were concealed by the blackness of night coming on from the east. Perhaps the Georgians had not anticipated the Hoosiers making such good time or perhaps they were merely absorbed in their labors. Whatever the reason, by stealth, Colonel Brown was able to slip his thinning regiment past the Rebels and move them three miles further south before the complacent Confederates learned of their missed opportunity to net the Indiana boys.[63]

At 9:00 P.M. Colonel Brown ordered the men to halt at a point some seven miles from the Hatteras lighthouse. His charges collapsed in the sand and fell instantly asleep with the exception of those who were tormented by hunger. At midnight, Captain Alfred Reed of Company K arrived with the remainder of the straggling regiment pushed before him. Colonel Brown heartily greeted Reed and expressed his profound thanks for the valuable service the captain had rendered the regiment.[64]

Before dawn, the first men of Colonel Rush Hawkins' Ninth New York Zouaves met with the worn and weary Twentieth Indiana. Hawkins had double-quicked six companies of men to the relief of the Hoosiers immediately upon learning of their predicament. He also requested that two Federal gunboats move from Fort Hatteras in support of the regiment. At dawn Brown resumed his retreat accompanied by the New York soldiers. Confederate gunboats sailed parallel to the island and bombarded the men as they moved to the south, closely pursued by the angry Georgians of the Third Infantry. Shortly thereafter, the Federal gunboats *Monticello* and *Susquehanna* arrived on the scene and commenced a bombardment of both the Rebel flotilla and of the Rebel units on shore. For over two hours the Federal guns wreaked havoc on the Confederates, who now found the tables turned. The Rebel fleet was forced to withdraw as were the infantry forces, allowing the Hoosiers and New Yorkers an unmolested return to the relative security of Fort Hatteras.[65]

While the main body of the Twentieth marched back to Hatteras, those unfortunate few soldiers who had been cut off in their retreat or who had straggled badly, now saw the arrival of the Union gunboats as an opportunity for salvation. Seeing the *Monticello* near the shore, Privates Hays and White ran from their cover behind some sand dunes down to the beach and yelled for help to be sent. The Federal ship dispatched a boat to their rescue, but the two terrified privates did not wait for its arrival. They started to swim out to the advancing launch. While Hays was being dragged over the side of the boat, the utterly exhausted White could fight no longer, and to the horror of both Hays and his naval rescuers, Charles White slipped beneath the waves and drowned.[66]

Extricated from their disaster, with time to reflect on their near destruction, the men wrote home describing the perilous events. Most were concerned about how their retreat would be viewed by the folks back home. Private Wesley Kemper wrote:

> *It was not our fault. There were six times as many of them, and we were in a tight place. I never was in so tight a place in all my life. But I can tell you one thing, I have the first man to see who is a coward in our regiment. We were ordered to retreat and we obeyed orders.*[67]

Another soldier inquired, "What do Indiana people say about the affair? Is the impression out that we acted cowardly?"[68] Captain John Wheeler certainly viewed the affair as cowardly and placed the blame for the retreat squarely on Colonel Brown. He confided to his diary that, "The colonel and staff officers were a little cowardly, I really think they could have held out if they had been cool and determined."[69] The affair made big news not only in Indiana but in other newspapers in major cities. What was a relatively trivial event, when measured against the scope of the entire Civil War, took on greater significance during the relatively quiet days of October of 1861. The retreat by the Twentieth Indiana and the bombardment of the pursuing Rebels was viewed in much of the North as a victory of sorts. Private Seymour T. Montgomery, the former newspaper reporter for the *Indianapolis Daily Journal*, summed the situation up best:

> *We left the place reluctantly and if we had had a few pieces of artillery we would have died before leaving. Now to sum the whole matter up—we had only about five hundred men armed with muskets and the enemy numbered about three thousand and had plenty of cannon, we got away with a very small loss—probably none killed; so you see they gained no victory to boast of. Why we were placed at that point without a proper means of defense God only knows, and I hope the Department will not again tie our hands in this way. Give the Twentieth a chance and they will do good work, but no regiment fixed as ours was could do more than we did on this last expedition. The only wonder is that any escaped, but thank God we yet survive to work for the good of our beloved country.*[70]

It certainly took the work of an optimist to snatch victory from the jaws of this defeat. The Twentieth Indiana now found itself at Fort Hatteras in a miserable condition. The regiment had no tents, no coats, few shoes and pants (most were discarded on the retreat) and a force diminished by the prisoners taken on the *Fanny* and the seventeen men captured by the Rebels on the retreat. In addition, ninety men were confined to the hospital at Fort Hatteras suffering from exposure or exhaustion. Brigadier General Joseph K. Mansfield, placing the blame for the affair on Colonel Rush Hawkins, gave his verdict on the performance of Colonel Brown in a report to Lieutenant General Winfield Scott where he declared, "Under the circumstances, Colonel Brown probably did well."[71]

Upon the return of the regiment to Fort Hatteras and Fort Clark, the famished men of the Twentieth found an ample supply of food awaiting them. However, there were critical shortages of everything else a soldier requires. As Lieutenant John W. Andrew wrote his sister, "Our boys here are in a very bad situation, no blankets, no overcoats, many without shoes, the clothing furnished them worn out, seven companies having no change of shirts or clothing of any kind."[72] Many of the boys in the Ninth New York Zouaves felt sorry for the weary Hoosiers and gave up their tents and beds for them and slept in the sand. This greatly appreciated gesture won the permanent friendship of the Indiana boys for the strangely dressed New Yorkers.[73] Despite the temporary generosity of the Zouaves, a more permanent arrangement had to be found for the Hoosiers' accommodations, and they were shortly assigned to the barracks at Fort Clark, the former Rebel stronghold.

Rebel troops who had previously occupied the barracks had been forced to quickly evacuate their barracks and fort during the previous Union bombardment. In their haste to abandon the island, they had left behind valuable supplies and camp articles, but the one comrade they gratefully abandoned to its Federal fate was the louse. The bunks and barracks were crawling with the little beasts.[74] Soon, each of the Hoosier inhabitants of the barracks had his own set of "lodgers"—the infestation was maddening. Tempers were at the boiling point when every officer in the regiment fired off an angry petition to Governor Morton demanding that the Twentieth be returned to Indiana and sent to Kentucky to fight where they would get better treatment. The petition complained, "This regiment has been in service nearly four months and yet have never received a single article of clothing or a single blanket. Send us to fight for the good cause anywhere, but give us protection from the inclement weather, comfort for our sick and blankets for our men."[75] They wanted new uniforms so the old gray ones could be burned and along with them their ever-multiplying inhabitants.[76] The men continued to burn over the hard work which Colonel Brown had driven them to under their harried condition in camp. Captain Wheeler felt that Brown was "rather vindictive and puts the oppressor's screw down at least one turn too much."[77]

In a letter to Major General John E. Wool, Brigadier General Joseph K. Mansfield stated:

I have only time to say to you that the troops—say the Twentieth Indiana Regiment—are suffering for want of clothing, blankets, shoes, tents, &c. There should be a large supply of lumber for huts, consisting of four by four joists, two by four joists and boards and shingles. Shingle nails are much wanted and all the articles on the requisitions. We should have some dozen hand carts for the men to move their provisions by hand over this sandy beach to their camps. The weather has been intolerable and the exposures have been great. There are ninety sick of the Twentieth Regiment and one hundred thirty six sick in all. . . .[78]

The officers and men of the Twentieth Indiana were distracted from their grumbling by orders that kept them busy constructing breastworks and fortifications. After the fortifications were completed, Brigadier General Thomas Williams, the new commander of the Hatteras expedition replacing Colonel Rush Hawkins, ordered that a thirty-foot-wide and twelve-foot-deep moat be constructed around the entire defense perimeter. While the Hoosiers labored at their task, they were somewhat chagrined to find the Ninth New York lolling around, doing nothing but light drill. And, when the alarm was sounded announcing that a Rebel force had landed at the Hatteras lighthouse, the Zouaves immediately moved into the safety of the defenses.[79] The Rebels proved to be no threat to the Federal forces, so life soon returned to drill, work and more drill.

The regiment arose daily at 4:00 A.M. and drilled by companies until 5:00 A.M., at which time they had breakfast. After breakfast the men drilled, strengthened fortifications and drilled some more. This routine continued more or less unabated until 8:00 P.M. and bed.[80] The boys did steal away occasionally to explore the island, meet its inhabitants and taste its delicacies. Private Charles Reese and Captain John Kistler went on a foraging expedition and found oysters which had washed up on the beach. They picked up the oysters, cracked them open and ate them raw. They later were able to purchase fish from the local fishermen for three cents a pound.[81] Firewood was difficult to procure, however, and required the men to walk two miles to find the small pieces of wood which were the remains of shipwrecks washed ashore.[82]

The days of October turned cloudy and cold, but only promises of warm clothing arrived. The steamer *Spaulding* called on Hatteras twice a week bringing letters and newspapers. The news was mixed, the Pacific Telegraph was completed; the battle of Leesburg fought and lost by Lincoln's men; the battle of Wildcat fought and won by the North. By day, the men gathered round smoky fires of green wood and at night they huddled close together on the bare wood floors of their barracks for warmth. Wherever two men gathered, there was grumbling.[83]

At last, on October 31, the *Spaulding* brought more than just broken promises and unfulfilled dreams; it brought the long-awaited clothing. A cheer arose from the ragged Hoosiers as they ran to the shore, shouting for joy at the prospect of clean, warm uniforms. A detail of seventy men was ordered to unload the steamer and place everything on the sandy shore for distribution in the morning. It was midnight before all of the noise of merriment subsided and the men dropped off to a sound sleep with visions of blankets and shoes and pants dancing in their heads, not a man noticing the almost imperceptible change in the wind.[84]

At 4:00 A.M., the shocked soldiers awakened to shouts that the barracks was floating away. Private Joshua Lewis sprang from his bunk and landed in two feet of frothy sea water.[85] Lieutenant Gilbreath heard, "Ed, you better get up, your trunks are gone."[86] As the men staggered and waded out of the barracks, they could hear a terrific gale and the crashing of gigantic waves on what had earlier passed for a shore, as monstrous mountains of water cascaded across the island. In this time before early hurricane warnings, this was as much warning as was ever received. Major Benjamin Smith, whose only maritime experience before the war had consisted of paddling a canoe on the Wabash River, was in an absolute state of panic. He struggled through the surf screaming, "Boys we are lost, we are lost!" Water was up to the shoulders of his horse, as the depths of the angry sea ranged from three feet to twenty feet deep around what had been the camp of the Twentieth Indiana.[87] Many of the Hoosiers who had been taking the storm as a lark or a joke turned solemn as buildings began to wash into the sea. Captain James Shannon, Company E, trying to make his way to high ground, found himself nearly swept away by the onrushing tide.[88]

Private Harvey Bassett described the situation to his father back home in Lafayette:

> *While the soldiers were sleeping the wind rose, water gurgled through the floors of the shanties and aroused the men. In a few minutes everything was submerged and the tide poured in waves. Our danger was extreme. It was too dark to see and the water everywhere was three feet deep. A deep channel was cut across the island between us and the fort, where dry sand had been the day before. The breastworks we had constructed were swept off like so much cobwebs. There we stood, cold and wet, shivering until daylight.*[89]

The boys were cut off from both Fort Hatteras and Fort Clark by the deep channel; there was nothing to do but try to find the highest ground possible, even though it too was under water.

In their quest for survival the men almost forgot the newly arrived boxes of clothes and provisions that had been left on the beach. Now, after wading in chest deep water to a point that offered safety, they had time to realize the magnitude of the natural disaster. Along with the breastworks, guardhouse, watchtower and barracks, the entire supply of coats and clothing were washed away.[90] And all of the embankments that a thousand men had spent their time constructing were swept away in a single hour.[91]

This retreat to the high ground had left the Twentieth Indiana even more destitute than before. As the storm abated around noon, it was a cold and shivering, disheartened and demoralized group of Hoosiers who stood as the Federal presence in North Carolina. They passed the day and evening without food, fire or shelter.[92]

As soon as the flood waters receded and communication with Fort Hatteras could be established, Major Benjamin Smith braved the channel, several times finding himself submerged along with his horse, to ask for orders.[93] General Williams ordered the Twentieth to secure what had been Fort Clark with a limited number of men and to send the bulk of the regiment three miles further down the island. Lieutenant Colonel Charles Murray, himself demoralized even though he had missed the debacle at Chicamacomico, led seven companies of grumbling, worn-out Hoosiers to their new camp south of Fort Clark.[94] Colonel Brown remained behind with a small detachment of men.

On November 7 all of the camp was astir over reports that they would soon be evacuated to Fortress Monroe. Private Seymour Montgomery approved of the possibility, writing his friend, T. C. Phillips, publisher of the *Howard Tribune*, "I tell you that no regiment can make a successful campaign in these parts where the enemy are very scarce and the waters of the Atlantic and Pamlico so very flush. If this proves true (leaving Hatteras), you may set it down on your fourth page that our Indiana Regiment is out of purgatory."[95] Confirmation of the relocation came on November 8 when the steamer *Spaulding* arrived with orders to embark the men of the Twentieth and transport them to Fort Monroe. Never did a happier group of men board a ship. Oceans of Indiana wheat was what these boys wanted to see, but they were content with the prospect of feeling firm soil under their feet.

After a daylong voyage, as the *Spaulding* passed the point in front of Fortress Monroe, the regiment was greeted with the playing of "Root Hog or Die" by the regimental band. Captain James Lytle acknowledged that they had done "root hog" duty and had thankfully avoided the dying part.[96] Despite the future hardships that the regiment would endure, many a man would look back on their month at Hatteras as the worst month of the war.

The regiment spent their first evening at Fortress Monroe aboard ship. The next morning, Sunday, November 10, the boys disembarked the *Spaulding* and went into camp sans tents. Some in the regiment may have thought the treatment of the soldiers was not to be any better here and possibly worse, due to the marked decline in temperature. However, the doubting Thomases were relieved the next day when the much-hoped-for supplies arrived in camp.[97]

In a scene that must have reminded the destitute Hoosiers of Christmas past, the regiment now received every last item they had so longed for at Hatteras. Captain Lytle described the scene:

> *In the short span of six hours we have been provided with new tents, uniforms, coats, blankets, cooking utensils and, in short, everything even to a nice little "sibilator" for each tent and we now feel that we are once more to be numbered among the civilized soldiery of the country.*[98]

The "sibilator" that Lytle referred to was a stove that both heated the Sibley tent and served as a cook-stove. The men of the Twentieth felt as if they had found "tall cotton," and much of their misery and suffering of the past few weeks quickly passed into memory.

The service of the Twentieth Indiana on Hatteras, however inconclusive and frustrating as it may have seemed to the men of the regiment, did not go unnoticed by those in higher command. Brigadier General Thomas Williams wrote Brigadier General Joseph K. Mansfield telling him that, "the Indiana men can undergo more fatigue, wade deeper water, go bare footed, ragged and hungry longer and finally eat more, build more breastworks, sing louder while at it and complain less than any class of men that I ever met."[99]

It had now been two months since the Twentieth Indiana had resembled anything similar to a cohesive, well-drilled infantry unit. While in Maryland the regiment had been scattered out along the railroad line. When the regiment departed for Hatteras, it had left three companies behind at Fortress Monroe under Lieutenant Colonel Murray. Now, the Twentieth finally had all of its companies together in one camp. It was time to restore order and discipline to the ragtag regiment. Colonel Brown knew that he had let his horses run free for too long and there were only a few short winter months to break them in again. It would be a long winter.

CHAPTER THREE

IRON SHIPS AND LEAD BULLETS

To combat the inevitable loss of morale and respect for military order caused by the events of the last two months, Colonel Brown reinstituted the process of perfecting drill at Fortress Monroe, with particular emphasis on skirmish and battalion drill.[1] Brown drove the men hard and became increasingly agitated and unforgiving of his regiment's mistakes on and off the drill field. The colonel had demonstrated his bad temper and strict discipline as early as August, a fact noted in the *Indianapolis Daily Journal.* Captain James Lytle, a close friend of the colonel, however, observed that the strict discipline was justified in light of Brown's earlier liberal treatment of the men.[2]

Colonel Brown's brother, the Reverend Dr. Fred T. Brown, sent a note to the *Cleveland Herald* (and later reprinted in the *Valporaiso Reporter*):

> *The Colonel is a rigid disciplinarian and something of a martinet in drilling. As soon as he got to the field he began drilling and disciplining his men. The men were not allowed to pitch their evils anywhere but must use the "sink." He required them to wash their faces and comb their hair before sitting down to breakfast, as also to keep their clothes clean and their shoes blacked. He also strictly forbids profanity and excluded intoxicating drinks.*[3]

Colonel Brown's method of dealing with the wayward soldiers who imbibed demon rum was to tie the offenders to the nearest tree and have them "paddled."[4] This corporal punishment garnered the respect of a limited few and the ire of many, including most in the officer ranks, who viewed the colonel's conduct as outrageous. The colonel apparently could sense the lack of respect from his fellow officers; his way of dealing with it was to step up his criticism of any and all who did not support him fully. A discharged private told a reporter for the *Marshall County Republican* that Colonel Brown was insulting to his officers and nasty and tyrannical to the enlisted men and that he once saw Brown strike a private with the edge of his sword, cutting through his coat, because the private did not place his feet exactly right on parade.[5]

Battle lines were drawn in camp. On one side were the boys from Logansport and the few supporters of the colonel, including Captain James Lytle and Lieutenant Erasmus Gilbreath. On the other side were the vast majority of the regiment, including the ringleaders of the discontented Lieutenant Colonel Charles Murray and Captain George Dick. Captain John Wheeler was impressed with neither Brown nor Murray. He viewed Lieutenant Colonel Murray as "a poor thing, drunk, cross and doesn't know his duties as well as half the privates."[6] Wheeler had witnessed Brown accepting three hundred and fifty dollars from residents on Hatteras Island in exchange for a favor which he could bestow. He was particularly incensed that Brown had pilfered the contents of a relief package which had been mailed from Indiana for the welfare of the common soldiers. Brown took his pick of shirts and socks and delicacies and then passed the package to other officers for their select pilfering.[7] Enough was enough. Wheeler intended to file charges against both men in an effort to clean up the regiment.[8] A tempest was brewing and finally broke when Murray suffered his final insult and resigned on November 24.[9]

While Murray was awaiting word on whether his resignation would be accepted, he dashed off a scathing letter to Governor Morton blasting Colonel Brown. He blistered Brown by stating, "The simple truth is the regiment is demoralized. I am authorized by the company officers to say that they have lost all confidence in Colonel Brown due to his failure to control his temper and his tongue."[10] Captain Dick joined the fray by getting a leave of absence under the pretense of returning home to help avoid a "serious loss of personal property." Instead of returning home, Dick hightailed it for the governor's office and a face-to-face with Indiana's highest official. Dick further sullied Colonel Brown and demanded his removal from command of the Twentieth Indiana. When Morton notified Brown of the attacks, Brown conveniently dismantled Dick's accusations by reminding the governor that Dick was "one of the musket troublemakers in Indianapolis."[11] Morton recalled the regiment's embarrassing refusal to accept smoothbore muskets and then he sustained Brown by accepting Murray's resignation. The mutiny ended and Brown was free to continue his ruthless insistence on precision drill and military order. Although harsh medicine, it was probably necessary to restore organizational and disciplinary health to the regiment.

As the raging controversy over Brown subsided, the regiment turned its focus to the returning prisoners of war who had begun trickling back into camp as they were exchanged for Confederate prisoners of war. These men of the Twentieth Indiana brought back widely divergent tales of captivity upon their return. Sergeant Charles H. Comly believed that he was treated well by his captors. He wrote his girlfriend, Muggie, "I cannot complain of either my quarters or treatment. I have plenty to eat and a comfortable cot: am very well supplied with reading matter and manage to while away my idle hours very pleasantly. The prisoners here are considering their confinement very healthy. The Confederate surgeons pay our sick every attention and do all in their power to alleviate their conditions."[12]

Comly and Quartermaster Isaac Hart were lucky to escape the deprivations of Chicamacomico and Hatteras Island for relatively decent treatment in the converted tobacco warehouses of Richmond, Virginia, where they spent their time in captivity. Private Charles W. Demotte had not been as fortunate. Demotte and three other soldiers had been surrounded and captured on Hatteras Island by elements of the Third Georgia Infantry. After briefly being threatened with execution, the men were marched back to their camp at Chicamacomico and embarked on an old steamer for Norfolk, Virginia. The men spent ten days in jail in Norfolk before being transported to Richmond on October 19. While at Richmond, Demotte also was confined in an old tobacco warehouse. There, Demotte witnessed several murders of prisoners by their guards, as some of the Rebels delighted in taking pot shots through the windows of the warehouse at any head that might show itself.[13]

Basically, the levels of food and comfort of Richmond prisoners seemed to be similar to that of the boys in the regiment back on Hatteras—not good. Prison camp food intake was limited to thirteen ounces of beef bones, nine ounces of pilot bread, one pint soup and a small quantity of rice. Most of the prisoners were ill-clad and for lack of blankets were forced to sleep on the bare floor of their prison. When donated clothing did arrive for the Twentieth prisoners from the sympathetic folks back home, the Confederate captors charged outrageously high express bills before the men could claim their goods. Only after a generous gift of seventy-eight dollars from Hoosier Representative Schuyler Colfax could the captured boys of the Twentieth afford to pay the express bill.[14]

Demotte's sagging spirits were lifted by the revelation that there was a loyal Unionist living in proximity to the prison. A woman who declared herself loyal to the Union sent a welcome note by a young slave-girl to the imprisoned Hoosiers, stating her support for them and wishing them well. This unexpected event heartened the men and thus began an exchange of notes and newspapers carried by the daring young slave between soldiers and Unionist. This process kept the men informed of war developments, strengthened their loyalty and bolstered their flagging morale.[15]

Quartermaster Isaac W. Hart finally returned to the Twentieth Indiana amidst pomp and fanfare suitable for an arriving king. At this point of the war, prison-camp survival was viewed as a heroic deed. Little concern was given to the somewhat ignoble manner in which Hart and comrades were captured aboard the *Fanny*. He was now treated as a hero and every soldier in camp strained to hear his every word. Hart loved the adulation, and took to the stump like a natural and regaled the men with tales of Rebel captivity and cruelty. He was immediately given leave to return to Indiana, and the reception he received in Lafayette and in his native Attica far surpassed his welcomed return to the camp of the Twentieth. At Attica Hart addressed a huge crowd of fawning admirers who had gathered to hear of his exploits in captivity and of the conduct of his gallant comrades in Virginia.[16]

Hart would return to the Twentieth by train after three weeks of making speeches on behalf of the war cause. Others would make the tortuous journey to and from Indiana in different ways. The wife of Daniel Biser, Company E, was so lonesome for her man that she made the long journey from LaPorte, Indiana, to Virginia on foot, experiencing far more prolonged hardship than her husband had experienced on Hatteras Island.[17] This was proof positive that a Hoosier woman was just as tough as a Missouri mule when she set her mind to it. Mrs. Biser was the talk of the camp for her loyal and heroic journey.

Not all of the men captured on the *Fanny* or on Hatteras Island returned to the regiment. Sergeant Theodore Bartlett contracted "the fever" and died in a lonely prison in Columbia, South Carolina, far from the adoring crowds who had warmly received Quartermaster Hart on his triumphant return to Indiana.[18] The men of the Twentieth Indiana gradually forgot their ordeal on Hatteras and the bitter command disputes and settled into winter quarters Ample supplies and shelter made the long period of winter inaction almost tolerable.

The Hoosiers found the Virginia environs surrounding Camp Hamilton to their liking and spent their limited leisure time exploring the countryside and the nearby towns. A Union line of fortifications, anchored on one end by the massive Fort Monroe, ran for nine miles to Newport News. The fort, bristling with huge cannon, was an impressive and comforting sight. Moving west from Fort Monroe, the men could see a constant line of military camps and artillery batteries running through Hampton, Virginia, to Newport News Point and Camp Butler. From Newport News, Virginia, it was only four short miles to a large Rebel encampment. Across Hampton Roads, the confluence of the Chesapeake Bay, James, Mansemond, and Elizabeth rivers, the Hoosiers could see their Rebel counterparts staring back at them from Sewall's Point.

Men straying too far inland from the shores of Hampton Roads might encounter Rebel pickets or patrols, so vigilance was in order. An officer touring the town of Hampton found the great mansions of the city ransacked by Union soldiers for lumber and brick which were used in construction of winter quarters. A piano stood on a street, propped up on sticks, to be played by any passing soldier. Trees everywhere were indiscriminately cut down for firewood. Even the fine old mansion of President John Tyler, reviled by Unionists as a traitor, was filled from top to bottom with contraband Negroes who had taken up residence in a kind of limbo created by a confused Federal policy governing escaped or abandoned slaves.[19] Captain John Wheeler visited Tyler's home and came away with a piece of the piano which had been unceremoniously dumped in the yard and a sprig from a tree near the front door of the home as souvenirs of his visit.[20]

As winter weather reached the Union army camped on the shore of Hampton Roads, Colonel Brown was called upon to fold his regiment of unruly Hoosiers into a brigade then consisting of soldiers from New York, Pennsylvania, and Michigan. The duties of drilling the brigade fell to Colonel Max Weber. Weber, a German, with military experience gained from the Prussian Revolution, was another martinet, but his firmness of tone and expectations accelerated the "education" of the Hoosier farmboys. This brigade was put together for drill purposes only and it would be several months before the Twentieth would move and fight within a real brigade.

Captain Lytle wished that "our friends back home could see the five Regiments of infantry in full dress with their bright bayonets sparkling in the bright sun, and the twelve hundred mounted horsemen making a grand charge while the horse artillery is dashing over the field at furious speed, it halts, bang, bang, bang and is off in retreat, . . . the scene is very grand."[21]

If the boys of the Twentieth marched a little prouder and held their heads higher during brigade drill, it may have been as a result of the arrival in camp of their long-awaited new rifled muskets. On December 5 the new Enfields arrived and the boys felt less like forgotten orphans and more like soldiers.[22]

They had new uniforms, coats, tents, and rifles. They had even received two months' pay and could afford the luxuries provided by the omnipresent camp sutlers.

Added to the routine of drill was the important role of picket duty. Squads of men were detached from the regiment and spread outside of camp for the purpose of providing an early warning of Rebel armed intrusion and for the additional purpose of turning back homesick boys planning to high-tail-it for home. Picket duty was a dull and boring, but significant responsibility. There were always temptations to distract a picket: pretty Rebel belles, blackberries, or a shady spot under an oak tree for a well-deserved rest. Vigilance was the word, however. Passwords and countersigns were given out daily, and failing to use them invited trouble this far into Southern territory.

Poor old General Mansfield learned his lesson the hard way. To test the effectiveness of his pickets, Mansfield donned civilian clothes and attempted to slip through the Union lines. He was promptly stopped by one of the Hoosier pickets and asked, "Who goes there?" He responded, "General Mansfield." The doubtful Hoosier demanded the countersign, but Mansfield would give none. The stubborn soldier cocked his rifle and informed the elderly general, "The devil himself can't pass these lines without the countersign!" Mansfield wisely withdrew and moved to another point along the line where he was passed on through.[23]

Men on picket were posted two hundred yards apart and required to stand guard for two hours at a time. It was dangerous duty with Rebel cavalry active in the area. General John Wool had observed from a distance a farmhouse where Rebels came and went frequently. While the Twentieth was on picket, Wool ordered that a sharpshooter be sent up a tree with instructions to shoot anyone coming or going from the house. Private A. C. French climbed to the top of the tree lugging his heavy rifle with him. French spent the best part of a day straddling a branch with his rifle poised for a shot, but as luck would have it, the house was quiet the entire day.[24]

Another night on picket the Hoosiers stopped a spruced-up young lad making his way through the lines with the obvious intention of courting a young lady at a nearby home. While he vigorously protested his detention, his intended lass watched the activity and decided to make her way to him. She too was stopped short. The two stood twelve feet apart for several hours, separated by the picket guard, carrying on their courtship and certainly hoping that the war might move elsewhere.[25]

A lieutenant making his rounds as officer of the day came upon a picket and just as he was challenged with "who goes there?" stubbed his toe and fell into a ditch. The thoroughly irritated lieutenant cursed, "Jesus Christ!" to which the quick-thinking and diplomatic picket called out in a loud voice, "Turn out the twelve Apostles, Jesus is coming!"[26]

There were good times around the campfire on picket duty. The war, slavery, women, and booze were always ripe topics of discussion among the men. Private Richard Rusling liked to clean his rifle during these fireside chats and one night accidentally discharged the gun and shot off two fingers, scaring the men out of their wits and rendering himself useless as a rifleman.[27]

A much more serious situation developed when Lieutenant Colonel Charles Murray, Captain James Lytle, and Private Seymour Montgomery were making the rounds along the line of pickets extending five or six miles around the camp. The three men came upon three pickets, each sleeping soundly. The three were promptly awakened and arrested. They were turned over to the provost guard and duly reported.[28] The three boys, all from Delaware, were court-martialed and ordered to be shot. The civility of 1861 was turning into the harsh reality of war for 1862.

Men were dying now, of bullets and bacteria. Private J. D. Rauland, Company I, died of the fever, and his death spurred many of the Hoosiers to the conclusion that there would be hard times for all in the coming months. They also concluded reluctantly that three men shot now might save the lives of many more in the future.[29]

The Twentieth Indiana may have avoided the stain of dishonor that came with having men shot for dereliction of duty, but they could not avoid the hailstorm of controversy that hit them full force from Secretary of War Simon Cameron himself. The controversy started in September when the Twentieth Indiana departed its camp near Cockeysville, Maryland. At that time a young mulatto slave girl attached herself to the regiment and departed with it for Fortress Monroe and Hatteras Island. Her owner, a Mr. Jessup, was furious and wanted her returned to him. The departure of the regiment by ship for Hatteras made pursuit by Mr. Jessup an impossibility, but with the return of the regiment to Fortress Monroe, he was bound and determined to reclaim the young girl.

When confronted with the situation, Colonel Brown was shocked. The girl had dressed herself like a boy and was working for another free camp servant in his employ. Brown refused to turn the girl over to Jessup and forced Jessup to turn to higher authorities for help in the matter. His appeal to the secretary of war, alleging theft for the purpose of prostitution, resulted in an order from Cameron for her release to Jessup. Brown refused, risking the ire of his superiors, on the grounds that he had investigated the matter and found that she was not induced to follow the regiment by any soldier, that she was not a prostitute nor freely granting sexual favors, and that he had no reason or authority to hand her over. General John Wool sustained his colonel, and the matter was finally settled when Representative J. P. Shanks, Eleventh District, Indiana, introduced legislation barring the girl from being returned.[30] As time would show, many Hoosiers of the Twentieth were definitely anti-slavery and to a certain percentage in the regiment, this war was already a war for emancipation. They were certainly in the minority at this point in the war.

It definitely was not a war for emancipation for Private William Stone of Company K. Upon hearing a rumor that seven hundred black men wearing Confederate uniforms had wounded four Federal soldiers, Private Stone loosed this invective to a friend back home, "I am going to kill every Negro that I can find outside the guardline or any when I want because I have a good gun and I am going to try it when I am on the line and then mister Negro had better watch his manners."[31] Of course, the rumor was unfounded, but it belied a deep fear among many of the Midwestern soldiers.

As in all armies since the beginning of warfare, a surplus of time, inaction and bad weather brought the inevitable backbiting and second-guessing of the higher command. General George B. McClellan, in command of the Army of the Potomac, was a cautious fellow; his slow mustering of men and material for an advance on Richmond was viewed in many quarters, most notably the Republican media, as incompetence, cowardice, or treason. Many in the ranks of the Twentieth were eager to advance on the Rebels, camped just a few miles away, and end this war immediately. The temperature had dropped, snow and rain had fallen regularly, and thick gooey mud made any movement almost impossible.[32]

Private E. M. B. Hooker wrote a scathingly sarcastic letter to the *Indianapolis Daily Journal* taunting the high command for its inaction:

> *It is decided here that no forward movement will be made. The Army of the Potomac is quiet and no forward movement will be made. The army here is quiet also and no forward movement will be made. It is inconvenient to make a forward movement. Besides, it involves danger and it might make the rebels mad and a reconstruction of the glorious Union will be impossible, therefore no forward movement will be made. . . . The army will positively go into Winter quarters. From the piled up orders and so forth, we will never emerge.*[33]

Private Harvey Basset wrote his father: "Yes, the War will be over at last in sixty days, with the great tree of liberty left lying on the ground, uprooted and branchless."[34]

Of course, not everyone was discontented. Men involved themselves in a variety of enterprises and activities. Private A. P. Ireland worked on perfecting a remedy for chapped face and hands. He determined that an equal quantity of mutton fat and camphor gum melted over a moderate fire, when blended, would do the trick.[35]

Sergeant Lorenzo Corey was dispatched by the men of his company to Baltimore for the purpose of finding a suitable gift for their esteemed Captain Lytle. He returned with a new Sharp's breech-loading carbine and a "spendid set of epaulettes." Sergeant Corey was also given the task of making a formal presentation of the gifts and a speech to the company. Corey, a man known more for his deeds than his words, unafraid of bullets but terrified of public speaking, ambled into the captain's tent, handed him the gun and epaulettes and said, "Here is a gun and a pair of epaulettes for you—take them." Lytle, surprised but pleased, responded, "Well, that's a devil of a way to present such valuable gifts." To which Corey retorted, "Well, if I gave a speech you know what I'd say."[36]

On Friday, January 3, excitement shot through the camp as the Twentieth formed up for a reconnaissance in force toward the Rebel camps and fortifications in the direction of Yorktown. They found the Rebel stronghold of Big Bethel deserted. The environs on the road to Yorktown had been laid waste, contrasting sharply with the pleasant Virginia countryside around Camp Hamilton. Near nightfall, the regiment encountered Rebel pickets and, not wishing to press the matter, returned to camp.[37]

Six days after what was apparently a diversionary reconnaissance in force, the men of the Twentieth witnessed what to them seemed a modern-day version of the Spanish Armada. Major General Ambrose Burnside, in command of a thirty-thousand-man expeditionary force, was assembling his forces and his flotilla in the relative safety of Hampton Roads. Ship after ship of every type and description arrived for the purpose of ferrying Burnside's men to the coast of North Carolina, to accomplish with a sufficient force what the slim forces had not been able to achieve on Hatteras Island in October. The Hoosiers were disappointed that they would miss this show and an opportunity to pay back their Rebel tormentors. The appearance of the powerful flotilla and forces in Hampton Roads threatened Confederate Major General John B. Magruder on the narrow Virginia peninsula. Not knowing that Burnside's ultimate destination was North Carolina, Magruder drew back his forces from the Norfolk area toward the more defensible line of Yorktown. Although Private Hooker was upset that he would continue in winter quarters, he did take heart from his belief that "the gun boats that banged us and shelled us out of our camp at Chicamacomico, will be hunted to their holes like so many rats."[38]

The boys of the Twentieth did get an opportunity to hunt their own "rats" when on January 20 they ran thirteen Rebels to ground at a house near the Union lines. The Hoosiers marched their captives off to Colonel Brown, who had them conveyed up the line. The Rebels had protested their capture, claiming that they were civilians, even though several were in

Confederate uniforms. The Indiana men were shocked when to their dismay, the prisoners were released upon signing an oath of allegiance to the Union.[39] The parole policy of both governments appeared to the Hoosiers to be utter insanity. The North could choose to lightly dismiss its enemies, yet shoot some poor, tired Delaware farmboys who happened to fall asleep on duty.

With the upcoming change of seasons, there were also changes in the command structure of the Twentieth Indiana Volunteers. Colonel William Brown was still firmly in control, but he had a new subaltern with the promotion of Major Benjamin H. Smith to lieutenant colonel. Smith, however, was in such bad health that he was forced to resign his position. This provided the opportunity for two fine officers and men to ascend to higher rank. John Van Valkenburg of Peru was promoted to lieutenant colonel, and John Wheeler of Crown Point was elevated to major. Both advancements were well received by the regiment. Of course, several captaincies needed to be filled also. Van Valkenburg was replaced in Company A by William Reyburn. Company B was now commanded by Charles Bell, who replaced John Wheeler. Oliver Bailey had resigned on December 31, to return home to his grieving wife, and he was replaced by William Babbington. Company G's Nathaniel Herron was replaced by William C. L. Taylor, when he was transferred to the Seventy-second Indiana Volunteers. Captain George Geisendorff, in Company H, resigned and was replaced by the able George W. Meikel.[40] The time between the return to Fort Monroe and the end of February had been a time of organizational bloodletting and renewal. This was certainly not a situation unique to the Twentieth Indiana. The office-seekers, the weak, the discontented and the cowards had to be weeded out before the deadly game of killing in earnest could begin.

The Twentieth Indiana had a strange addition to the regiment at this time. Dennis Tuttle, from Hudson, Wisconsin, mustered into the regiment in Virginia. Tuttle was enlisted as a quartermaster sergeant and assigned to Company E. How Tuttle came to join the Hoosiers in a position unknown at the time in the U.S. army is not clear. He may have been visiting the camp of the Fourth Wisconsin Infantry, which was encamped nearby, and contained a company of men from Hudson. Fearing the war might pass him by, he may have sought a nearby regiment with a vacancy he could fill. It may have been because he was an acquaintance of Dr. Orpheus Everts, surgeon of the Twentieth Indiana. What is known for certain is that regimental Quartermaster Isaac Hart felt he needed an assistant, and Tuttle filled the bill. Hart was forced to pay Tuttle out of his own pocket, an arrangement that pleased neither Hart nor Tuttle. What was most interesting about Tuttle, who was an 1850 graduate of Yale University, was the fact that he had given up his position as state's attorney for St. Croix County, Wisconsin, to serve in an Indiana regiment as a sergeant. Whatever his reasons, his 175 letters written to his wife Anna during the war would excellently detail the daily life of the Twentieth Indiana.[41]

On February 26, 1862, the Twentieth Indiana, in good health and spirits, was ordered to fall into line of march moving to a new camp near Newport News, Virginia. The men made an uneventful, nine-mile march and commenced laying out their camp on a "very fine location on the banks of the James River about thirty feet above the water."[42] Major Wheeler was so impressed that a full year later he described it "as nice a camp as I had ever seen."[43] Little did the Hoosiers know that by some luck of the draw, this march to new quarters would make them both witnesses and active participants in one of the most significant events in military history.

When Union forces abandoned the Norfolk navy yard at the beginning of the war, Union naval officers put the torch to the facility, hoping to deny use of any of the boats, ships or materials of war from falling into the hands of the Confederate navy. As soon as Federal forces departed, a detachment of Virginia volunteers rushed into the navy yard and tried to douse the flames engulfing the facility. A Federal navy steamer, the *Merrimac*, had been burned down to the water line, but her hull and boilers were still intact. Lieutenant John M. Brooke, formerly an experienced Federal navy officer and newly commissioned in the Confederate navy, at once recognized the potential of converting the *Merrimac* to an iron-covered ram.[44]

After much hard work the *Merrimac* had been altered into a 170-foot-long, powerful, ironclad ram boasting ten heavy guns. The ship was renamed the *Virginia**** and was given over to the skillful command of Flag Officer Franklin Buchanan, with the intent of having it prowl the coastal waters of the Northern states and wreak havoc against commercial and military shipping. A short trial run had been authorized, but now Commodore Buchanan saw an opportunity to strike a mortal blow against the Union navy. A large flotilla of heavily armed Federal ships was anchored at Hampton Roads between Fortress Monroe and Newport News. Buchanan determined to steam down the Elizabeth River, past Sewall's Point, and engage the Federal fleet in battle.

Morning dawned in all its beauty on March 8. The previous day had been stormy, but this eventful morning was bright and sunny with the water of Hampton Roads as smooth as glass. The Federal ships swung lazily at their anchors, with small boats banging at their sides, laundry hung on lines to dry. No one in the Federal navy had the slightest inkling that naval history was rushing headlong at them from the Norfolk navy yard.

---

* To avoid confusion, the ship is referred to as the *Merrimac* throughout this book.

Near 1:00 P.M., the signal station at Newport News and officers on the *Congress* and *Cumberland* signaled that vessels were coming out from Norfolk. The long roll was sounded and men from the Twentieth stacked arms in the middle of the camp streets and headed for high ground from which to watch the unfolding drama.[45]

Lieutenant Erasmus C. Gilbreath, Company I, described the scene:

Off toward Norfolk we observed dense clouds of smoke and soon were able to distinguish a large vessel and two smaller ones drawing out toward Sewall's Point. Reaching a position off that place, they followed their leader; turned west and steamed for the James River. It seemed a long time but was only a few minutes till we could plainly see the Merrimac. *She was black and moved slowly. When three-quarters of a mile away she opened the battle by firing at the* Congress *with a bow gun. She was answered at once by a broadside from the* Congress *and the battle was on. Our batteries on shore joined in—the gun boats with the* Merrimac *fired as rapidly as they could. The roar of the guns, the smoke and the whole scene cannot be described.*[46]

Adjutant Israel N. Stiles described the hulking black Confederate monster as looking, "very like a house submerged to the eaves, borne onward by a flood" as she bypassed the nearby *Congress* and steamed directly for the *Cumberland*.[47] As the *Merrimac* passed within two hundred yards of the *Congress* she received terrific multiple broadsides from the Federal ship but "all to no use as the shot glanced off like hail from a roof."[48]

The *Merrimac* struck the *Cumberland* in the hull with such force that her ramming prow was broken off. She backed away from the *Cumberland*, revealing an enormous hole in that ship which was sucking in seawater. Her gunners moved from gun to gun, firing at the black monster in a final futile gesture. Then with a roar she quickly sank, with only seven feet of her main mast visible above the surface of the water.

Next the *Merrimac* turned her attention toward the *Congress*. While the *Merrimac* had been engaged with the *Cumberland*, the *Congress* had run aground trying to get into position to level another broadside at the Rebel ironclad. When the *Merrimac* turned toward her, the *Congress* stood motionless on a sand bar immediately adjacent to the camp of the Twentieth Indiana, no more than three hundred yards from shore. The *Merrimac* stood off from the *Congress* and fired shot after shot into the helpless frigate, killing its commander and compelling the surviving officers to haul down the colors.[49]

Commodore Buchanan dispatched a small boat to heave to the *Congress* and bring off prisoners. A Confederate officer boarded her and, seizing the Union flag, started to carry it back to his tug.

General Mansfield, witnessing the naval disaster, galloped up on his horse into the midst of the Hoosier infantrymen standing gape-jawed on the shore and asked Private Joshua Lewis if he could not hit the Rebel officer holding the flag. Lewis responded by shooting the officer, dropping him between the *Congress* and the little Rebel boat.[50]

Emboldened by this success and by the prospect of denying the Confederates their prize, General Mansfield ordered that two companies of men be sent down to the shore line for the purpose of driving off the Rebels. Colonel Brown ordered Company K and Company A under Captains Reed and Reyburn to take their positions and commence firing. Commence firing they did and in less than five minutes, the Rebels were compelled to leave the deck of the *Congress*, cut loose, and push off. The two Hoosier companies poured volley after volley into the Confederates. Colonel Brown rode his fine horse calmly up and down the beach, encouraging his men to load and fire as rapidly as possible.[51]

Now into this fray charged Captain Alfred Reed. Captain Reed, an attorney by profession, started to argue with General Mansfield about the legality of firing on the Rebels. He argued a point of military law as to whether it was legal to prevent the capture of the *Congress* since she had surrendered to the Confederates. This legal discussion was brought to an appropriate conclusion when "Judge" Mansfield unceremoniously informed Reed that "I know the damned ship has surrendered, but we haven't!" The legal discussion ended and the two companies continued their withering fire at both the small Rebel boats and the *Merrimac* herself.[52]

It was a first-class melee at the water's edge. Commodore Buchanan sent another boat of nine men toward the *Congress*. The Hoosiers turned their fire on this boat almost immediately, killing seven of its crew.[53] Buchanan now turned his guns to the infantry on shore and sent upwards of two hundred rounds of shot toward the two companies at water's edge and over the protective sand dunes into the ranks and camp of the remaining eight companies of the Twentieth, now prone behind the dunes. The shells made terrible noises and kicked up immense clouds of sand as they landed and exploded; however, not one Hoosier was injured. One shell passed directly over Colonel Brown's head, but his horse instinctively kneeled and the shot landed at the foot of Captain Lytle, who claimed its fragments as a table decoration. Lytle's Negro cook had seen enough of the bombardment and ran as fast as he could to the safety of Fortress Monroe.[54] The wives of Adjutant Stiles and Lieutenant Colonel Van Valkenburg were visiting the camp at this time and one huge shell landed near them, frightening and completely covering them with mud.[55]

The shells thrown at the Hoosiers by the *Merrimac* were so large that the men could see them coming and dodge them. The boys later agreed that they learned to dodge the shells quicker than they had learned the mandatory McClellan bayonet drill.[56]

Corporal David Kitchell, Company I, realizing that the water was shallow between shore and the *Congress*, led a party of taller men through the surf and out to the ship, where Kitchell manned an abandoned bow gun and poured shot after shot into the side of the *Merrimac*, a deed of valor which would earn him sergeant's stripes and a fine presentation sword.[57]

Five times Rebel boats attempted to bring off prisoners from the *Congress* and capture their prize, but each time the blistering fire of the Hoosiers drove them off. Angry and frustrated, the gunboats and the *Merrimac* gave up and decided to blast the *Congress* into the fires of Hades. Shot after heated shot ripped into the *Congress* as the ship sat helplessly awaiting her fate. With darkness approaching, the *Merrimac* chose to withdraw into the friendly confines of Norfolk and leave the broken Federal fleet behind for a return bout on the morrow.[58]

The toll for the day had been high. Federal losses had been 181 killed and wounded on the *Cumberland*, 126 killed and wounded on the *Congress* and 19 killed and wounded on the *Minnesota*. Confederate losses were 26 killed and wounded; among the injured were Commodore Buchanan and Lieutenant Miner, both severely wounded by infantry fire.[59]

The surgeon of the *Congress* in a description of the fight stated, "To the skill and gallantry of the sharpshooters of the Twentieth Indiana alone do officers and crew of the *Congress* owe their deliverance."[60] This may have been true for the survivors, but there were many dead seamen who owed their sad fate to the infantry fire of the Twentieth. Without infantry fire they might have been imprisoned instead of killed and maimed.

All in all, the boys of the Twentieth, under the cool leadership of Colonel Brown, had acquitted themselves quite well. Joining Companies A and K at the beach were another one hundred men of various companies who couldn't resist the temptation to get into the fight. Each of these men expended almost his entire issue of forty bullets, and all could be quite proud of their work.[61]

The evening of March 8, however, was filled with gloom and despair. The men of the Twentieth worked with the navy to evacuate the horribly maimed and mutilated survivors from the *Congress* and assist survivors from the *Cumberland* who managed to swim ashore. The carnage was terrifying and sickening. Bodies and body parts, both large and small, washed ashore throughout the evening. The rescuers' work was illuminated by fires still raging on the *Congress*. Among the shouted orders and crackling of the fire, the Hoosiers could hear the tortured moans and cries of the wounded sailors.

Private Alpheus French wrote his cousins: "Well I must tell you what is the hardest thing in war. Some may dislike to hear the whistle of a shell that weighs one hundred eighty pounds and still worse when it bursts overhead and scatters its death dealing pieces in every direction but there is one thing that touches me in a more tender spot. I mean the handling and taking care of the wounded, mangled groaning and dying soldiers. Oh, you don't have any idea of such things till you see them yourself."[62]

As the fire spread on the *Congress*, "loaded fire arms were discharged, then the cannon were discharged and when the fire got to the tarred rope, it lit up the whole country around. At about midnight an awful explosion occurred that brought the sleeping soldiers to their feet as the magazine exploded."[63] This sent "cinders far heavenward amidst clouds of sparks and flakes of rope; then the mass sank beneath the waves carrying down the burned and charred bodies of many a gallant tar."[64]

Fear gripped the Hoosiers, and for that matter, all who had witnessed the events of the day. The men feared that the black monster would return the next day and complete its work, the destruction of the *Minnesota*, the shore batteries, the land forces and Fortress Monroe. In short, most men felt the days of the Union were numbered at the hands of the *Merrimac*. Exhausted and thoroughly shocked Hoosiers drifted off to sleep, each pondering what the morrow might bring.

While Northern citizens slept soundly in warm beds, comforted by their ignorance, and exhausted sailors and soldiers collapsed under the strain of the day, Confederate patriots celebrated. The word of the overwhelming Confederate naval victory spread like wildfire as fast as the telegraph could carry it. All hopes and dreams of the Southern people seemed possible now. The *Merrimac* would venture forth again the next day and destroy the remainder of the Federal fleet. Next, it would steam up to Washington, compelling the evacuation of the capital. Finally it would cruise up the Eastern seaboard, forcing harbors to pay tribute and allowing England and France to officially recognize the Confederacy. It all seemed so easy to the cheering and dancing Confederates celebrating in the streets. There was just one problem unbeknownst to them: a small, almost insignificant, sardine can of a Northern ship that nobody knew about.

For months Captain John Ericsson had been diligently at work in New York City constructing an unusual-looking ironclad floating battery. After experiencing many problems with construction, it was not quite finished when its commander, Lieutenant John L. Worden, was given orders to proceed to Hampton Roads. His little ironclad, christened the *Monitor*, steamed out of New York Harbor and made fast for Virginia. She arrived around 2:00 A.M. and took a position alongside the *Minnesota*.[65]

The morning of March 9 dawned clear and bright, with the water of Hampton Roads once again smooth and calm. As the men of the Twentieth Indiana stirred from their short slumber, they were taken by surprise by what they saw steaming toward them. At four hundred yards distance they saw what one man immediately described as "a cheese box on a raft."[66] Not a man cheered and all shared the same opinion: they saw little to inspire confidence. As if going to a Sunday ice cream social, every man for miles around streamed to Newport News to see what events would unfold. Thousands lined the shores for a firsthand look at this odd response to the mighty *Merrimac*.[67]

The *Monitor* plowed through the water down to where the *Cumberland* rested, its American flag still visible above the surface. Then the *Monitor* turned and cruised back to where the burnt-out hull of the *Congress* lay smoldering—and thence to the side of the *Minnesota*. The *Monitor* carried two eleven-inch guns to contest the six big guns on the *Merrimac*.

Near 7:00 A.M., the *Merrimac*, accompanied by her escorts the *Yorktown* and the *Patrick Henry*, emerged at Sewall's Point. It was 8:10 A.M. before the *Merrimac* decided on a course of action and opened fire on the *Minnesota*. The Monitor now swung around the bow of the *Minnesota* and steamed directly for the *Merrimac*. The ships traded shots in a mad battle that lasted nearly four hours. The powerful *Merrimac* plodded along like a bull in a bullfight, trying to gore the *Monitor*. The *Monitor*, smaller but much quicker, sidestepped the bull and poured shot after shot into the side of the behemoth. Shots bounced off each ship, doing no apparent damage to either.[68] The blasts from the guns of the two ironclads were so loud that birds flying in the area fell dead from the force of the concussion.[69]

After noon a shell exploded near a slit in the pilot house from which Lieutenant Worden was peering out. The powder from the explosion temporarily blinded Worden and without his direction, the *Monitor* moved away from the battle in an aimless fashion. The *Merrimac*, believing the *Monitor* to be disabled and content that she had acquitted herself honorably, chose to withdraw past Sewall's Point and return to Norfolk. However, the *Monitor* was only temporarily leaderless, and when Executive Officer Lieutenant Samuel Green assumed command, the *Monitor* returned to the side of the *Minnesota*.[70] Thus, ended one of the most significant naval battles in history. An observer from the Twentieth Indiana, Dennis Tuttle, best summed the situation up when he wryly remarked, "A little insignificant tub spoiled the Rebel plans."[71]

The "insignificant tub" was accorded a high degree of respect by most of the thousands of men who witnessed the great events of the day. They assigned a much more descriptive name to Captain Ericsson's floating battery. Forever after, the men of the Twentieth Indiana referred to the *Monitor* as "our savior."[72] In countless fireside chats, the Hoosiers would recount their salvation through the grace of God and that "insignificant tub."

CHAPTER FOUR

I CAN DIE WITH A CLEAR CONSCIENCE

The Twentieth Indiana quickly settled back into the routine and drudgery of camp life after its introduction to modern naval warfare. The mighty *Merrimac* might emerge once again and wreak its vengeance on the Hoosiers, but other than occasionally cruising down the Elizabeth River to Sewall's Point, the *Merrimac* had no intention of tangling with the *Monitor* anytime soon. The men had no way of knowing that the damages to the *Merrimac* were so severe that she took on large amounts of water as she cruised and was unarmed for much of the time after her battle with the *Monitor*. Every time the Hoosiers would see the *Monitor* patrolling up and down Hampton Roads, one of the boys would yell, "Here comes our savior" and the regiment would run to the nearest vantage point to see the ironclad.

The health and morale of the men were excellent. In fact, in the nine months since the Hoosiers left Lafayette, the regiment had lost only seven men to death, and Colonel Brown reported back home: "We have scarce a sick man in the regiment. Were you to take a stroll through the camp, you would find with all an air of comfort, the men a healthful, cheerful regiment."[1] This was a rather unique circumstance given this time of epidemics, deprivations, limited medical knowledge and inclement weather. In fact, another Indiana regiment serving in Virginia, the Nineteenth Indiana Volunteers, had lost over sixty men to typhoid fever by the end of November 1861.[2]

Throughout March and early April the men busied themselves with eight hours of drill per day and policed their camp with the usual soldiers' tomfoolery. Private Seymour Montgomery gathered up one of the thirty-two-pound shells that the Merrimac had thrown at the Hoosiers, boxed it up and shipped it back to Valparaiso for family and friends to inspect.[3] There were dress parades and visits by dignitaries. Vice President Hannibal Hamlin and Representative Albert G. Porter, the Indianapolis boys' congressman, visited the Indiana camp on April 1 and lifted spirits even higher.[4]

Spring arrived and with it came the Army of the Potomac, under the command of Major General George B. McClellan. McClellan had graduated in 1846 from West Point, ranking second in a class of fifty-nine. He had served ably and bravely in the Mexican War on the staff of Major General Winfield Scott. Prior to the Civil War, McClellan had both a distinguished military career and a business career which had culminated with his appointment as president of the Ohio and Mississippi Railroad. When war broke out, he was immediately made a major general of Volunteers. He possessed charisma, organizational abilities and elan that led to swift victories in West Virginia and appointment as a major general in the regular army. In August of 1861 he was given command of the Army of the Potomac, and on November 1 was made General-in-Chief of the Union army. By the end of 1861 his Army of the Potomac had grown to a force approaching 150,000 men.[5]

President Abraham Lincoln placed his faith in the new general and called on his young subordinate to rally the Union forces to victory. His faith was not well placed. While McClellan did possess tremendous organizational skill and was very popular with his men, he lacked essential traits necessary for any good commanding general. He failed to adequately communicate with his superiors and to respect civilian authority over the military. He tended to blame any setbacks or failures on others. He was an incurable pessimist who continually took counsel of his fears. He delegated virtually all tactical authority to his subordinates. Finally, and most importantly, he lacked the will to fight. These flaws were, of course, not known to Lincoln in the war's first year, but they became painfully clear as time went on and disaster piled upon disaster.

In early December of 1861, McClellan conceived a plan of action which he dubbed the Urbana Plan. The plan involved the movement of the Army of the Potomac by water down the Chesapeake Bay to the Rappahannock River town of Urbana, forty-five miles from Richmond. From Urbana the Union army would advance on Richmond over land. The plan would interpose the Army of the Potomac between Richmond and the Confederate forces at Manassas and Centreville, thereby forcing the Rebels to rapidly fall back toward the Southern capital. But in early March the Confederate forces fell back from Centreville on their own volition, and their withdrawal made Urbana an unsuitable landing site for the army. McClellan then changed his plan to one of moving his troops by sea to Fortress Monroe and thence up the peninsula to attack Richmond.[6]

President Lincoln, while essentially approving the McClellan plan, made one critical, and to the general, fatal change: he insisted that fifty thousand men be left behind to protect Washington. Feeling shortchanged and hobbled by unreasonable civilian interference, McClellan departed for the Peninsula in a pessimistic bad temper.[7]

The grand Army of the Potomac began arriving at Fortress Monroe in the middle of March and at once assembled and advanced toward the elaborate line of Confederate defenses laid out across the narrow neck of the Peninsula near Yorktown. The Twentieth Indiana excitedly anticipated the arrival of the army, supposedly armed and ready for conflict. The Hoosiers had been hard at work building forts, redoubts and a wide variety of rifle pits and earthworks and were ready to fight. But the army passed them by and left them to their manual labor; "a madder set of fellows you never saw."[8]

On April 5 the Army of the Potomac laid siege to the Confederate stronghold at Yorktown, and while the men could hear the constant boom of cannons, they were forced to continue the very dirty, tiring and boring life of a backwater regiment.[9] Captain James Lytle described the joint arrival of spring and the Army of the Potomac:

Along this road is some of the most beautiful farms in America, all deserted, fences down or destroyed, large orchards of the most choice fruit exposed to the destruction which a large army naturally leaves behind; the peach and plum trees were in full bloom and shaded as they were by the rich grown pines in the background gave the scene a most magnificent appearance, but upon reflection, left the heart melancholy and sad.

At every step was to be seen nothing but devastation and soldiers-soldiers of every corps and brigade, on foot and mounted in eager search of their brigade. For miles we met them hurrying forward to join their command. We passed batteries after batteries, infantry and cavalry, the gay dragoons and Regulars, the vulgarly dressed Zouaves, with their long turbans, the swift dash of some General and his staff, the slow heavy drag of the long supply trains, a balky mule team blocks up the road and the driver swears, the rapid gallop of an orderly with orders to some division, the din and clatter of camp kettles, mess pans and tin plates, the savory odor of the steaming pot of chowder. Every breeze that stirred bore towards us the softened strain of military music.[10]

Private Montgomery saw the same sights and heard the same sounds, including the increasing intensity of the dueling cannons at Yorktown, and predicted that the Twentieth Indiana would miss the surrender of the Confederate army on the exact same ground where Lord Cornwallis had surrendered to General Washington at the conclusion of the Revolutionary War.[11] Tired and angry, the Hoosiers were forced to feel that history was again slipping away from them as they camped on the banks along Hampton Roads.

While McClellan was away at Yorktown, engaged in a torpid stalemate with the Confederates, President Lincoln had an excellent strategic idea. Lincoln knew that Norfolk had been denuded of troops to provide reinforcements for Major General John B. Magruder's Rebel forces at Yorktown. With Norfolk lightly defended, Lincoln felt that this was a good excellent time to mount a military operation aimed at securing this strategic Confederate port and naval yard. Without consulting McClellan, Lincoln had orders issued through the War Department to commence an advance on the Rebel city. Accordingly, late on Friday evening, May 9, the Twentieth Indiana Volunteers received orders to be prepared to march at daylight.[12]

At 5:30 A.M., the Hoosiers, "wild with joy," arose and in less than thirty minutes were in line ready to march.[13] Owing to an unfortunately typical delay caused by lack of transportation, the regiment did not commence its march until 8:00 P.M. after a short patriotic speech by Colonel Brown.[14] The Hoosiers excitedly set out on the march, almost on the double quick, winding their way through fields and groves for the ten miles to Fortress Monroe. They arrived at Fortress Monroe in under three hours and at midnight started the process of boarding the little steamer *Nelly Baker*.[15] As the Indiana men marched past the hotel at the fort, they were given a hearty salutation from an unexpected observer. Standing on the porch, President Lincoln, who had come down to supervise his military inspiration, yelled out, "What regiment is that?" The Hoosiers answered with an identifying answer and a cheer, and Lincoln responded, "Bully for the Indiana Twentieth!"[16]

A slight glitch in the plans now confronted the regiment. After eight companies had been loaded onto the steamer, it became obvious that two companies would be forced to remain behind as a result of lack of room on the vessel. The regiment had been split up before to no good effect, and Brown was troubled by the situation. Companies E and H were detained at Fortress Monroe as the *Nelly Baker* steamed for Willoughby's Point across Hampton Roads.[17]

In attempting to get close enough to shore to land the regiment, the boat ran aground; the Hoosiers were forced to remain on board throughout the night, while the surf pounded and rolled them about until the change of tide at daylight. Then, three small canal boats came alongside and were lashed together to form a passable wharf for the purpose of disembarking the troops. By 7:00 A.M., the Indiana boys were once again on terra firma in the midst of a beautiful pine forest.

The eight companies started on their march toward Norfolk, trudging through deep mud and withstanding the unseasonably warm weather. An occasional deserted Rebel encampment or broken-down cabin were all that served to remind the men that this land had ever been lived in by upright, walking inhabitants. After covering eight miles of the swampy ground, the regiment emerged into a good pike which wound its way past some respectable farms, even by Hoosier standards. The farm land was unplanted, the men obviously absent serving the Confederate army.[18] The focal point of the march was easy to discern from the billowing clouds of black smoke rising from the Gosport Naval Yard, where withdrawing Confederates had put the match to ships and boats of all descriptions, including the vaunted *Merrimac*, which was burned down to the water line.

After a twelve-mile march on the pike, the Twentieth Indiana halted along the road as the Twentieth New York, marching in the advance of the column, came in sight of the Rebel breastworks protecting Norfolk and deployed in preparation for an attack. What few defenders remained in the breastworks caught sight of the Federal troops and hightailed it to the South. Immediately, the New Yorkers and the Hoosiers moved into and through the Rebel defense line and proceeded on their advance to Norfolk, a scant two miles distant.[19]

The advance of the column was met at the city limits by city fathers carrying a flag of truce. Major General Wool and Secretary of the Treasury Salmon P. Chase, obviously looking for a little political capital, were escorted by a guard of cavalry to the Custom House, where the Mayor formally surrendered the city to the Federals. And learning that Norfolk had been virtually abandoned by the Rebel army, the transport steamer carrying Companies E and H was rerouted directly to the Norfolk wharves and discharged the first troops to arrive in the town, their flag flying proudly upon the arrival of the Federal dignitaries.[20]

In the early afternoon on Sunday, May 11, with colors flying and led by their regimental band playing "Yankee Doodle" and "Dixie," the Twentieth Indiana Volunteers themselves proudly marched into Norfolk.[21] The only "Secesh" the Hoosiers saw were "women, children, Negroes and a few men who said they were neutral."[22] One old black man cried out, "Bless de Lord, de Yankees is come and we is free."[23] General Wool decided to ring the city with encampments, lest the residents get any ideas about misbehaving. Accordingly, the Twentieth Indiana was ordered to camp on the grounds of the naval hospital, "one of the finest buildings on the continent, surrounded by the most beautiful grounds imaginable."[24]

The boys were feeling quite chipper about the change of scenery and their march into Rebeldom. They took pride in the fact that while the regiments ahead of them marching on Norfolk had quickly shed their excess coats and knapsacks, which littered the route of the march, the parsimonious Hoosiers had held onto their equipment. The long, hot march had been made more bearable by the often disparaged leadership of Colonel Brown. Brown dismounted, walked the entire length of the march and led his men by example, sharing their hardships with them.[25] The men were impressed with the colonel and became even more impressed with his wisdom in not allowing them to discard their heavy overcoats along the march when, later, transports failed to deliver tents and blankets for several days, leaving the overcoats as the only item to use for shelter or comfort.[26]

Five days after arriving in Norfolk, the Twentieth Indiana's encampment was moved across the Elizabeth River to Portsmouth. The boys took a liking to this camp for more reasons than one. It was a pleasant camp with ample shade and water, and it was also the former camp of the Third Georgia Infantry, the same Rebel regiment that proved to be their nemesis on Hatteras Island. The Hoosiers took particular delight in hastening the departure of the Georgians. Adding to the enjoyment of the Indiana boys was the fact that they were able to reclaim much of the camp equipment the Georgians had captured on Hatteras, including blankets and tents. The best find of all was the little camp writing table and desk that belonged to Quartermaster Isaac Hart, who had been captured on the *Fanny*. The boys presented the desk to Hart and reunited the two former Rebel prisoners.[27]

The atmosphere of the place was decidedly cooler than the weather. At Hampton and Newport News the Rebel inhabitants had long found themselves under the big guns of Fortress Monroe and modified their behavior to reflect the realities of military occupation. The citizens at Norfolk, on the other hand, had lived in a sovereign nation, at least they thought so, for a full year. They had tasted their brand of freedom and they deeply resented these "blue bellies" in their midst.

From the outset the Hoosiers were subjected to a variety of petty insults at the hands of their new wards. There was grudging acceptance from the merchants and commodities brokers who could see dollar signs, the greenback variety, from so many newly arrived residents with insatiable appetites for a wide variety of goods and services. The deepest insults, though, came not from able-bodied men; they were away serving in the Confederate army.

They didn't come from the Norfolk politicos, who could see who held all the cards. The insults came from the hoop-skirted, crinolined Rebels, the Southern belles.

The women invariably turned up their noses and shook their skirts whenever a Union soldier passed them on the streets. Many wore little Rebel flags on their bosoms while taking dinner in the finer hotels of the city.[28] Private Harvey Bassett heard himself referred to as one of "Lincoln's plug-uglies."[29] Captain George Meikel met a pretty eight-year-old girl playing in front of her home. He stopped and talked to her and patted her on the head. Her mother observed this from a window, rushed to the doorway of the home and yelled out, "Come right straight in the house, Susanna, and I will wash your head!"[30]

Private Montgomery was walking through Portsmouth on a fine Sunday afternoon when he heard a loud laugh coming from a half dozen adult Rebel women sitting on the verandah of a very stylish house. When Montgomery looked up he could see the object of their laughter, a little girl tauntingly shaking a Rebel flag at him. When Montgomery went to confiscate the flag the little girl hightailed it, whereupon the Hoosier informed the hoop-skirted Rebels that he had never seen a Rebel that wouldn't run at the first sight of a Union soldier. Montgomery enjoyed his little victory but plainly meant it when he declared in a letter back home that the Southern women were "the meanest rebels I ever saw."[31]

Of course, not all of the Rebel women avoided the Union boys and the money that came with them to the Norfolk area. Private David Archer wrote a friend back in West Middlefork: "There is some pretty girls in town. Most of them are whores. I will send you one of the pictures that one of the whores gave me when I was in town the other day. I don't want you to show this picture to any of the girls that is around there or let anybody see this, for if the general would find out that I sent this picture, he would Court Martial me."[32]

An occasional contrary adult male Confederate would get his back up and display his loyalty or plain stupidity. One day, a farmer brought a wagon-load of potatoes, an eagerly sought-after delicacy for the Indiana troops. He had no objections to selling his wares to the Hoosiers, but he refused to accept the Northern bank notes they offered in payment. He demanded Southern script instead, an incredible act of patriotic foolishness on his part, considering that he would have to travel many miles to find anyone else who would accept it.[33]

Major John Wheeler had an idea for dealing with the inhabitants of Norfolk. He wrote his wife that, "If I had command of this department three hours I would imprison the Mayor, Common Council, a few men and at least three hundred women and order them fed on bread and water until they would take the oath of allegiance or leave the country.[34] He apparently missed the irony that leaving the country was what the war was all about.

The officers of the various regiments encamped around Norfolk made their men take the obligatory trip to the graveyard where more than forty doctors and nurses from Northern states were buried after the great yellow fever epidemic of 1855. These brave Northerners came to Norfolk to treat the suffering of the Southern people while their cowardly medical professionals left town to avoid contracting the disease themselves.[35] At least, that's what the men were told. Whether it was exactly true or not wasn't the point of the visit. The intent was to show Northerners as enlightened deliverers.

In addition to drill, the Hoosiers were marched about the countryside in search of Rebels or contraband articles of war. One such search mission to a small village named Deep Creek turned up forty muskets, several swords and about one hundred cartridge boxes left behind in haste at the homes of civilian Rebels.[36] This was a reminder to the men that, in time, they might have more than hoop-skirted women and Rebel children to contend with.

Of immediate concern to the Hoosiers was their new brigadier general, John C. Robinson, "the hairiest general . . . in a much-bearded army."[37] Robinson began his army career at the United States Military Academy in 1835. He was dismissed during his second year for disciplinary reasons and returned to civilian pursuits. In 1839 he was commissioned directly into the army as a second lieutenant in the infantry. He served with distinction during the Mexican War and spent the years between that war and the Civil War at outposts in Florida and Utah. At the outbreak of the Civil War he was in command of fabled Fort McHenry in Baltimore Harbor. He was able to hold the fort for the Union cause when it was threatened by Confederate sympathizers. After his service ended at Fort McHenry, he went to Ohio and Michigan for the purpose of recruiting volunteers. He was appointed colonel of the First Michigan Infantry in September 1861 and served in that capacity until his appointment to brigadier general.[38]

The Indiana boys were understandably reluctant to lose their beloved General Mansfield. Still, they were willing to give the crusty Robinson a chance. Besides, the Twentieth needed to understand and participate in the organizational structure at brigade level. The Hoosiers had done light drill with other regiments but had not quite grasped the concept of fighting as a brigade. Interestingly, whereas many other Civil War regiments, both in North and South, would derive greater fame and identity from their brigade affiliation than for their individual regimental exploits, the Twentieth Indiana never quite felt an affinity for brigade identification.

Camp inspection day was customarily "looked forward to with as much interest by the soldier as is the Fourth of July by our dirty faced young Hoosiers."[39] The April inspection conducted by their new Brigadier General Robinson was a grand affair. For two days prior to the inspection the boys were busy decorating the parade grounds and their quarters with flowers and evergreens. The Hoosiers transplanted bushes and trees bearing berries and blooms to spruce up the camp streets. Tents were decorated around the doorways with magnolias and colorful flowers, many tents having their own flower beds with tulips, roses and honeysuckle. In the square in front of Company I was a complete representation of the *Monitor* complete with painted guns in the turret.[40]

Each man paid as much attention to his own personal appearance as he did to beautifying the camp. Shoes, buttons and bayonets all gleamed from the careful shining given by diligent soldiers. Knapsacks were clean, neat and well organized. These Hoosiers were spit and polish, not at all the dirty and ragged ruffians many Easterners expected. The Twentieth certainly defied the stereotype and went the Massachusetts and New York soldiers one better.

Just when it looked as if the Twentieth would spend the war as florists and landscapers, the order came to report to Major General George B. McClellan's Army of the Potomac. It had rained incessantly for three days and nights, but the boys didn't seem to mind the mud and inconvenience as they broke camp and boarded a steamer bound for the front. In fact the men were "as cheerful and happy as though about to start on a picnic excursion on a lovely day."[41] The regiment departed on June 6 and spent that evening lying at anchor in a driving gale off of Fortress Monroe. The following day they continued on their journey.

The regiment sailed up the York River to West Point, where the transport entered the Pamunkey River, a crooked, "meet yourself coming round" body of water. The Hoosiers passed "at least a thousand boats" loaded with stores for the army between West Point and their final destination of White House. The transport arrived at White House, the nondescript little farmhouse where George Washington was reputed to have met Martha Washington, in the early afternoon, and the men pitched tents and prepared rations for the twenty-two-mile march they would make to the Army of the Potomac.[42]

The Twentieth Indiana Infantry began marching to rendezvous with McClellan's forces early the next morning. For many days it had rained constantly and the roads leading to the Army of the Potomac were muddy and virtually impassable, save for the brave or the foolhardy. Colonel Brown decided that it would be easier for his men to proceed along the railroad line, stepping from tie to tie, than to wade it out in the mud. This odd way of marching required stepping and stretching in a manner unfamiliar to the men and they quickly tired and became sore.[43] As the Hoosiers slowly trudged past the camps of the various brigades and divisions, many of their new comrades in arms called out to inquire what brigade they were. The Twentieth had arrived at White House with nine hundred and ninety-nine men and were mistaken for a full brigade on the march.[44] Many of the Army of the Potomac regiments had seen their ranks greatly reduced by illness and combat and were mere shadows of themselves, so it was a rare occasion for them to see a full-strength regiment. It was a weary, but clean and dry bunch of Hoosiers who arrived in camp that evening. Most of the men of the regiment hurriedly erected their tents and fell into a deep sleep.

The next morning, the regiment slowly awakened to discover they were now camped on the battleground of Seven Pines, also known as Fair Oaks, a vicious little battle which had occurred on May 31 and June 1. There was an overpowering smell of rotting and decaying flesh which hung thick over the battleground. The heaviest fighting occurred four hundred yards to the south of the Indiana camp; the ground was still littered with unburied Confederates.

Sergeant Ezra B. Robbins described the scene in a letter home:

It is worth any man's while to look over the battlefield of Sunday, which took place in the woods, the trees are filled full of bullets from the ground up as high as a man's head, showing that the firing was very accurate, and many a poor Rebel found it to be so. Walking over the battlefield the eye soon discovers many secesh, some half-buried and some with one foot and some with one hand above the ground and yet others with no covering at all, but are being devoured by vermin. The sight is sickening to behold and one readily turns away, being glad to leave the sight to some other beholders.[45]

They also got to see Rebel prisoners up close. Private David Archer declared them, "the darndest set of humans that I ever saw in my life, not fit to be with Union folks and looking worse than sheep killing dogs."[46]

Although the battle of Seven Pines had been a narrow Union victory, they possessed the battlefield at least. The Confederates lost more than six thousand men killed, wounded, and missing. Federal losses were five thousand. The Confederate loss seemed catastrophic, but it had one positive outcome: Lieutenant General Joseph E. Johnston, commanding the Confederate army, was severely wounded and was replaced by Lieutenant General Robert E. Lee. Lee immediately pulled his troops back and commenced planning the first of his many brilliant victories.[47]

In their new camp the men of the Twentieth Indiana learned that they were now brigaded with the Eighty-seventh New York and the Fifty-seventh, Sixty-third, and One Hundred and Fifth Pennsylvania, under the command of Brigadier General John Robinson.[48] Their brigade was in Brigadier General Philip Kearny's division.

Philip Kearny was one of those unique military men who transcend the ages. He was born into the wealthiest of New York families, graduated from Columbia University, then studied law and traveled extensively. At twenty-one he inherited more than a million dollars from his grandfather and used that instant financial security to pursue the love of his life, a career in the military. He was commissioned a second lieutenant in his uncle's First Dragoons regiment in 1837, attended the French Cavalry School and fought with the *Chasseurs d'Affrique* in Algiers in 1840. He served as an aide to General Winfield Scott in the Mexican War and at Churubusco had his arm shattered by a musket ball, necessitating amputation. He returned to Europe in 1859 to serve in Napoleon III's Imperial Guard during the Italian War, where he participated in every cavalry charge by holding the reins clenched in his teeth while holding a sword in his hand. Phil Kearny was a born fighter, and the Hoosiers joining the division would fit his mold just fine.[49]

While Robert E. Lee plotted his strategy, the Army of the Potomac planned for the worst, constructing trenches, breastworks and redoubts, even sending full regiments out on picket duty. It was muddy, hot and tiring work. For many long weeks, the weather on the Peninsula had been ugly, with torrential downpours interspersed with heat and humidity. The camps and roads were quagmires, making any movement tortuous and labored.

Working at digging trenches in water which often reached to his knees, Private Wesley of the Twentieth showed he had long since lost his romantic vision of warfare. He wrote his mother:

> *I belong to Uncle Sam and I am just like a slave. When I am ordered to do anything I know it's no use talking, for I have to toe the mark. You must excuse all of my mistakes for it is nearly forty-eight hours since I had any sleep. It will soon be one year since I left home to defend my country and in that time I have slept in a bed but one night. I hope the war will be over before many days; then I want father to kill the fatted calf.* [50]

The men toiled in malarial conditions that rapidly eroded the strength of the body and depressed the mind. Mud choked the roads and prohibited the free flow of supplies. Warm food was nonexistent: The average meal consisted of three hardtack crackers, a cup of coffee, and salt beef. On rare occasions there might be bean or rice soup, but for stretches of several days the men were often forced to subsist only on crackers and water. The hard work, mud, disease, heat, and poor nutrition killed many men in the Army of the Potomac and left many more with afflictions from which they would never recover.[51]

Lieutenant John Andrew summed up the environs and his personal frustration with a soldier's life when he wrote his sister:

Mosquitoes are plenty, ticks are plenty, chiggers are plenty, the water we drink is warm, sutler is out of matches, the boys are out of blacking, the paymaster has not come, our cook, a contraband, wants to get to a free state, can't get fresh meat but once a week, food won't keep, mud shoe deep and my shoe string is broke and I can't get another. Those are just a few of my troubles.[52]

Andrew and the rest of the men in the Twentieth had the continuing problem of Colonel Brown to contend with. Andrew thought, "he needs a good thrashing, which no one can give him and stay in the service."[53] William Brown was apparently still confusing the power to control with the freedom to abuse subordinates.

Horses and mules attached to the army suffered too. Six horses or mules would be tied to a supply wagon and might only be able to pull one or two barrels through the deep mud. After mules became stuck in the mud and fell down, heartless teamsters would beat and drag them about trying to get them to move and often end up killing them. Private William Reeder summed it up when he wrote home, "They have no mercy on the poor dumb brutes and damn little for us."[54]

The strategic situation in June 1862 found the Army of the Potomac in a quandary. The massive Federal army was at the end of a perilous, mud-bogged supply line running all the way back to White House. Two Union army corps were on the opposite shore of the rain-swollen Pamunkey River, detached from the main body of the Federal forces. Virtually impenetrable thickets and swamps forced communications and supplies to funnel down the few passable roads. It was difficult for McClellan to get a proper strategic perspective of exactly where his army was and where the Confederate forces were concentrating. The situation might have been unnerving to an aggressive, offensive-minded commander, but McClellan had siege warfare on his mind. He could cautiously push out his forces and bring up heavy siege guns to pound the Rebels into submission. It might take months, but the Union army could slowly inch toward Richmond and might eventually capture the Confederate capital.

Robert E. Lee had a distinctly different situation and perspective. He did not have the luxury of building defensive works and waiting for the Federals to move. He knew that he could not withstand a siege and that he must strike a blow against the Union forces. However, his intent was not to merely bloody McClellan's nose. His intent was to plan an operation which would destroy the entire Federal army on the Peninsula. He would plan for nothing less. He did find himself in the same confusing swamps as the Union army, but he was fighting with a more dependable supply line and had the incentive of fighting for the survival of the Confederacy.

Not all of his army was present, however. Major General Thomas Jackson was on duty baffling and defeating Yankees in the Shenandoah Valley. Under orders to prevent Major General Irwin McDowell's forces from linking up with McClellan outside of Richmond, Jackson first defeated part of Major General John C. Frémont's forces near Staunton, Virginia, then returned to the Valley and struck Major General Nathaniel Banks a hard blow at Port Republic. Jackson had struck the right nerve in Washington, D.C., and McDowell's troops were withheld from McClellan.

Lee's master plan called for a swift return of Jackson's command to the Richmond area. Its unanticipated arrival should surprise and destroy the unsuspecting Federal flank. Jackson arrived, and the attack could begin, Lee keeping the Army of the Potomac pinned down by shelling them with constant artillery fire and aggressively probing the Federal lines for weaknesses.

It was into this intense environment that the Twentieth Indiana had come. The Hoosiers were rotated alternatively between picket duty and building defenses. Even when not on picket, according to Private William Reeder, they were "close enough to hear the Rebel shells whistle very plainly and some of them did not fall very far from our camp."[55] The pickets kept up a lively fire with hardly a minute passing when a soldier couldn't hear the crack of a rifle or the boom of the cannon. Each morning Rebel units would test the Union pickets with an isolated attack here or there, raising the alarm and putting the Hoosiers on edge.[56]

Private David Archer could sense the nearness of battle as he wrote his friends in Indiana, "I think I can tell more hard yarns than I could when I left home. I think that the old devil is in me and I don't think that I will ever get it out until I get to kill a god damn Rebel and then I can die with a clear conscience."[57]

General Kearny ordered that each man be ready to move and fight. Private Reeder reported that his haversack contained three days' rations. He noted, "My haversack hangs right by my side with twenty-seven crackers and a hunk of salt horse, some coffee and sugar and twenty rounds of cartridges as we have sixty rounds to carry and our cartridge boxes only hold forty rounds."[58]

The Twentieth Indiana nervously went out on picket on June 18. The incessant rain, the oppressive heat hanging over the misty veil of the swamps and bogs haunted the Hoosiers. They were now settled in beside the Charles City Road, too near the Confederates for comfort, and they were tired to the bone. Days of exhausting labor building breastworks stretched into three consecutive sleepless nights building breastworks. And now, the boys were to face forty-eight hours more of sleepless vigilance on the picket line.[59]

Captain Charles A. Bell's Company B was given the task of anchoring the line of pickets on the left end of the line, with his men taking their place on the Charles City Road while the remainder of the regimental pickets spread out between the road and White Oak Swamp. Picket duty was uneventful, save for the random, sporadic rifle and cannon fire which reverberated in the mugginess of the humid June air. Dusk and the blackness of night came on slowly, as sleepy pickets maintained their vigils. At 2:00 A.M. on June 19, exhausted soldiers were relieved by fresh pickets, who settled in for the nerve-wracking task of serving as human early-warning systems for the Army of the Potomac.

At 4:30 A.M., with the fuzzy grayness of dawn, a rifle volley announced an advance by three hundred screaming Rebels.[60] Captain Bell had himself been responsible for bringing on the fight. Shortly before that first Rebel volley, Bell and three subordinates ventured out from the picket line to investigate suspicious noises. When they got to the point of the earlier noise, they discovered a Rebel "torpedo," an early version of the land mine. While examining it, they heard voices and accosted a small Rebel scouting party. When ordered to surrender, the Rebels refused, and Bell gave his small party an order to fire on them. Simultaneously, the bushes and brambles erupted with the volley of three hundred rifles and Bell and his men fell back to the regimental line where the captain quickly rallied the company.[61]

Colonel Brown, hearing the musketry, came riding up the Charles City Road and quickly called upon Companies D and E, under Captain George F. Dick and Lieutenant John Andrew to come to Bell's assistance on the left. For good measure, Brown also dispatched fifty sharpshooters to the scene. With Bell holding the road stubbornly against the superior numbers of the advancing Rebels, Lieutenant Andrew's Company, supported by Captain Dick's, passed through the Union pickets and charged straight into the graybacks.[62]

Surprised by the quick response, the Rebels quickly pulled back. As the last Rebel left the Charles City Road, he stopped, turned and aimed a hasty shot at the charging Indiana boys. Private James Grant from Logansport, one of the select sharpshooters, had his hip shattered by the musket ball, and blood sprayed on those near him. He tumbled to the ground in agony.

The Rebels plowed down along the line toward the right flank of the Twentieth and directly into the advance picket post commanded by Second Lieutenant William T. Carr, Company I. Carr's small group of men and almost a full Rebel company opened up on each other. Carr was wounded severely in his hand and Private John Smith was hit in the right arm, rendering it useless. Carr's sword undoubtedly saved his life when, for after the excitement of battle he discovered that three separate bullets had struck the sheathed weapon.[63] For Smith it was just another bad break. He was the soldier who had passed his physical examination by offering to shoot the examining officer when questioned about his lack of a trigger finger.

With both the left flank and the right flank refused, the Confederates had only two choices, attack the center of the line or retreat. The Rebel forces now were funneled into the waiting arms and rifles of Companies A and F, under Captain William Reyburn and Lieutenant Thomas Logan. A brutal blast from the volley of these two companies convinced the attackers that this was not the time or place for further heroics. The Rebels retreated through the underbrush, dragging their dead and wounded as they went.[64] The Fourth Michigan, relieving the Twentieth Indiana on picket, counted fifteen dead Confederates in the thickets in front of the Hoosiers. Blood trails indicated the severe condition of other wounded soldiers dragged away.[65]

Corporal Archer wrote his friend Zack Scott:

My Dear Friend,

I take my pen in hand to inform you that I received your kind letter this evening and it found me well and I hope when these few lines come to hand that they may find you the same. Zack, this is the first letter that I have written to anyone but to you and to mother since we left Norfolk nor I haven't received one from anyone else. . . . I am with the sharpshooters. We have got a company of sharpshooters and they are the best shots in the regiment. There are sixty in the company and I am a corporal. . . . The Rebels tried to surround a company of our men that were on the outpost and they drove them back about two hundred yards until we could get to their assistance. We tried to surround them and we couldn't for they didn't like the sharpshooters. They ran like the devil and then we deployed as skirmishers and followed them. One of the boys in the company was looking at one of the Rebels and drawing his gun up to shoot him when he was shot by another Rebel behind a tree. They then ran like ran like damn cowards and our boys did not get a shot at either one of them. We went on and saw two Rebels standing

behind a bush and we shot at them and one of the jumped up in the air
about four or five feet and then he let down. The other one ran like the
devil. . . .[66]

Given time and the absence of further fighting, the Hoosiers might
have been able to stretch this small skirmish into one of great magnitude, a
story worthy of being told to one's grandchildren by a stone fireplace in
Logansport or Crown Point. The truth of the matter was that three men
were wounded, one mortally. The regiment had not bolted for the safety of
the rear. Colonel Brown and his subordinate officers had been brave and
quick-thinking. Now, in the magnified glory of the campfire, the Hoosiers
proudly dozed off into a deep sleep, content with a job well done, yet knowing
that a Rebel army stood between them and their return to Indiana.

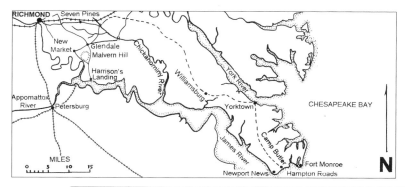

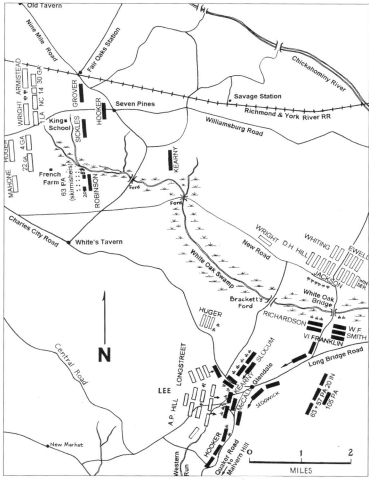

The Peninsular Campaign: (*Top*) The route from Camp Butler to the Battle of Seven Pines and the Battle of Glendale. (*Below*) The Battle of Seven Pines (Fair Oaks), May 31, 1862, and the Battle of Glendale (Frayser's Farm), June 30, 1862.

CHAPTER FIVE

SEVEN DAYS OF HELL

Union General George McClellan and Confederate General Robert E. Lee faced entirely different strategic challenges in June of 1862. McClellan's challenge was one of inches and yards, as he slowly and cautiously moved his huge army toward Richmond, while at severe risk of having his army divided by the Chickahominy River, until his giant siege guns could smash the Rebel capital and the Confederacy into submission. One Hoosier after the war compared McClellan's condition to that of "a timid Alpine traveler, who is described as becoming transfixed with trepidation at the unfortunate moment when he has set one foot over a chasm of little breadth but of fathomless depth. He desired to be across the river, but he was afraid to move."[1] Lee's challenge was no less than the total destruction of the Union army. Only the removal of the Federal forces from the Peninsula could save the Confederacy.

McClellan's next move was simple and transparently obvious to his Confederate counterparts. His goal was the seizure of the small town of Old Tavern, which occupied high ground on the Nine Mile Road, a mile and a half in advance of the Union lines as they then stood. From the high ground at Old Tavern, McClellan's big siege guns could breach the main Confederate defense line and open up Richmond to direct assault. Before an effective attack could be made on Old Tavern by Major General William B. Franklin's Sixth Corps and Major General Edwin V. Sumner's Second Corps, McClellan determined that he wanted to launch a flank attack on the town which would require seizing the woodland called Oak Grove to the south of Old Tavern in an area between the Williamsburg Road and the York River

Railroad. Major General Daniel Harvey Hill had launched his attack on Seven Pines on May 31 from this spot and it was the point of contention for opposing pickets ever since.[2] The responsibility for the Oak Grove operation slated for June 25 would be given to the Third Corps of Samuel P. Heintzelman.

While McClellan carefully calculated and planned his move on Oak Grove and Old Tavern, Lee planned his own strategy. Taking advantage of the predicament of the Union army, with its forces divided by the frequently rain-swollen Chickahominy, Lee determined to smash the Union Fifth Corps which was isolated on the north side of the river and then cut McClellan off from his supply base at White House. Lee, a calculating gambler, decided to leave a relatively small force of twenty-five thousand men under Major General John B. Magruder to hold the bulk of the Federal forces in check while the majority of his forces, including the just-arrived Stonewall Jackson's foot cavalry from the Shenandoah Valley, would crash down in a surprise attack on Union General Fitz John Porter's Fifth Corps. If all went according to plan, part of the Union army would be destroyed and the remainder cut off from food and ammunition. Lee selected June 26 for his attack.

After their brief brush with the enemy on the Charles City Road, the boys from the Twentieth returned to the laborious task of constructing redoubts and breastworks. Sweltering heat and humidity continued to make the work doubly tough and when coupled with the malarial conditions, quickly thinned the ranks. Many who reported sick were diseased and broken down, but many more were "playing off." Corporal William Reeder complained of the Pew boys in his company who were very "cute" about shirking work duty. Reeder wrote home to Peru, Indiana: "When we are out of camp they can run about and feel fine, but as soon as we come in they go right and lay down and put on a long face. To tell the truth they eat more than any two of us for they are in the cook house most of the time when out of their tents. I hate such skulkers. It shows a mean principle."[3]

Private E. M. B. Hooker wrote a letter to the editor of the *Indianapolis Daily Journal* offering his idea for dealing with the irksome and fatiguing task of digging earthworks and trenches:

And now there is something I would speak of which will have to be done before this war will be brought to a successful issue, and that is the employment of a regiment of Negroes in every brigade to do the fatigue duty. Fighting and marching does not wear the soldier out half so fast as ditching and fatigue duty, and the prevalent opinion in the army is in favor of Negroes doing that kind of work, while white soldiers do the fighting. It injures and degrades the soldier to impose so much heavy labor upon him, and he loses that martial spirit and vim so necessary to success. Our boys came here to fight, not to dig; not to be mere hewers of wood and drawers of water; not to be dragged to death in swamps and trodden under foot by upstart regulars, who never work, and hardly do anything else, except wear white gloves and put on style. The musket and bayonet are the weapons we volunteered to use, and are ready to use all the time. But spirits give way, muscles wear out, and the clammy sweat of death gathers around the handle of the spade in the swamps and under the burning sun of the South. Truly this has been an army of grave diggers, for they have dug the graves of thousands of comrades in the trenches. These Negroes could be useful in many ways. They could drive teams, cut wood, throw up breastworks and our soldiers would all the time be fresh. The Rebels use them for such purposes, why shouldn't we.[4]

In time, the President would come to reflect these same views as to the efficacy of using black soldiers in the war effort, and the Union army would be stronger and more productive as a result. But that was long after the thousands of graves in the trenches had been filled and covered over. Of particular interest was the work on an advanced redoubt, Redoubt Number Three, a spot from where McClellan intended to launch his attack toward Oak Grove.[5]

Lieutenant Andrew wrote his sister, Weck, on June 15, with his thoughts about going into battle, a possibility much closer than he knew:

Now Weck, you must not be uneasy about us. You know we believe that a kind providence watches over us and that no one falls unless it is His will. The only fear of death we have is the pain of dying and the separation from our friends here below, but to die in battle would take the sting away from both. It seems that the thought that one was doing his duty would over balance all other considerations. I don't expect to be killed so I'll not bore you with the possibilities.[6]

The picket fire around Redoubt Three was intensive at times. On Sunday, June 22, the diggers and trenchers from the Twentieth Indiana were bombarded, but the Rebels never got the range correct and continually fired over the Indiana boys' heads. On Monday, the Hoosiers advanced to a Confederate redoubt from which the artillery fire had come and found it deserted.[7] After Brigadier General Silas Casey's disaster at Seven Pines, caused by surprise attack and their own brief experience with being attacked unaware, the Hoosiers were on edge and ready to fight. And they now knew the sound of rifle fire in the distance might be an early warning of a surprise Confederate attack.

Although the boys could never be quite sure of how many men fell due to picket firing, Corporal William Reeder speculated: "There is a good many killed and wounded, picked off every day from both sides. They are mighty bold chaps around here and when they come out to fight they are generally in liquor."[8] He must have meant the Rebel pickets, because Colonel Brown and his senior officers seemed to be unanimous in their insistence on temperance and enforced a strict sobriety policy throughout the ranks.

Between June 19 and 24 the Twentieth Indiana was shelled, shot at, worked half to death, and called from short periods of sleep to full battle readiness, only to be dismissed after sweating fruitlessly in line of battle. There was precious little time for rest and hardly any time to think and ponder one's fate. Many who pondered that fate did not feel secure about the future. On the evening of June 24, as the men lay down to rest for the night, Sergeant Nelson Sweet paced nervously back and forth in his tent. He refused to sleep because, as he told his tent mates, he knew he would be killed the next day. His comrades laughed at his plight and made light of his concern, there being no battle anticipated, but all decided that to get any sleep, Sweet needed consoling and sympathy.[9] With Sweet mollified or just exhausted, the regiment bedded down for the night, with anticipation of more digging and chopping on the morrow.

While the common soldier slept, the generals planned their fate. The next day, Third Corps would advance Major General Joseph Hooker's division down both sides of the Williamsburg Road toward Oak Grove, and three regiments from Robinson's brigade would support that attack by covering the left flank of the advance. If all went well, a general attack on Old Tavern could follow the next day by the combined forces of Second, Third, and Sixth Corps.

The Hoosiers awakened at dawn and prepared breakfast, not quite suspecting what the day would bring. Their meal was scarcely done when the long roll was beat, calling the regiment to fall in, then to march out toward the enemy.[10] Brigadier General John Robinson ordered four companies of the Sixty-third Pennsylvania out front as skirmishers, with six companies held in reserve. The Twentieth Indiana then followed in line of battle with the Eighty-seventh New York in reserve at the edge of the thick forest from where the attack would begin.[11] As drums beat and hearts pounded, the Hoosiers marched off to an uncertain but surely important destination.[12]

Moving south of the Williamsburg Road, the skirmishers of the Sixty-third Pennsylvania soon met the enemy's pickets and steadily advanced on them, driving them back on their supports. With reinforcements to bolster them, Confederate resolve stiffened and the Pennsylvania skirmishers gradually fell back on the main brigade line. The entire line continued its advance through the thick woods and dense undergrowth.[13] The going was slow and dangerous as the brigade picked its way through the brush and brambles of the swampy terrain: the Rebels concealed themselves behind trees and took potshots at the Hoosiers as they advanced. The only time the Rebels could be seen was when they would dart from tree to tree falling back.[14] The forward movement continued until the brigade line reached King's School, its left flank resting in a peach orchard. Finding that his men had outpaced Hooker's skirmishers, Robinson ordered a halt in order to let the entire Union line time to solidify.[15]

While the brigade rested, General Robinson reconnoitered the ground ahead. The terrain opened up into a wheat field, from which the enemy instantly commenced an ineffective heavy artillery fire of shell and canister. Near the artillery position was a two-story frame farmhouse, providing shelter to Rebel sharpshooters who were finding much better range and accuracy than the artillerymen.[16] As Company H emerged from the dense woods, they congregated a little too closely together and their raucous noise drew the attention of the Confederate marksmen. A quick, blazing volley rang out from the French family's farmhouse and five men were wounded, one, Orderly Sergeant Ed Abbey mortally, with a bullet in the spine.[17] The Hoosiers quickly ducked back into the edge of the woods to their rear and lay down in the bushes to rest and take cover. In almost two hours the brigade had covered only a few hundred yards.[18] With the farmhouse full of marksmen and a section of Colonel Bryan Grimes' Confederate battery staring at him across an open expanse of 850 yards, General Robinson sent word to General Kearny that he could use artillery support himself.[19]

Quickly, two ten-pounder Parrott guns of Battery B, First New Jersey Artillery, arrived on the scene and fired four percussion shells through the French farmhouse, rendering it untenable and forcing the removal of one of Grimes' field pieces. With this threat removed, Robinson sent Battery B packing and waited for orders or Hooker's men to catch up to his brigade.[20]

In a somewhat odd style of field command, General McClellan attempted to conduct command from three miles in the rear of the main battle line, communicating by telegraph and courier. The scattered reports which came to him were interpreted as an indication that the advance was not going well with Hooker and that the plan might be in peril. Fearing the worst, McClellan ordered his forces to stop in their tracks and withdraw, a fateful error. Hooker had found the going slow, owing to the swampy wooded terrain and steady fire of from the Confederate brigades of Brigadier General Ambrose R. Wright and Brigadier General Lewis Armistead.[21] While progress was slow, there was progress; the attack, if pressed vigorously, might have succeeded. Now, with Hooker's division and Robinson's brigade stopped in their tracks, Confederate Major General Benjamin Huger could bring up reinforcements to his division and prepare for act two of this tragedy.

Facing Robinson's brigade across the wheat field were the Sixth, Twelfth, and Forty-ninth Virginia regiments, the Fourth and Twenty-second Georgia, the First Louisiana, and the newly arrived Forty-eighth North Carolina Infantry. The Fourth Georgia hid from view by lying down in the wheat, north of the French house, which blocked them from Robinson's sight. During the lull in action, Robinson ordered the Eighty-seventh New York to the front as skirmishers and the Twentieth Indiana to form the first battle line, supported on its right flank by the Sixteenth Massachusetts of Grover's brigade. The Sixty-third Pennsylvania and the One Hundred and Fifth Pennsylvania would serve as a reserve for the brigade.[22]

General McClellan finally arrived on the field of battle at 1:00 P.M. and, realizing that the situation was not as bleak as he had assumed, ordered a renewal of the attack by Hooker's division on Oak Grove.[23] Birney's and Sickles' brigades moved back out over the same ground which had been so dearly paid for in blood during the morning attack. Stepping over their dead and dying comrades, amidst constant and intense fire, Hooker's men finally were able to drive the Rebel forces back across the six-hundred-yard expanse of field to the edge of a thick woods. At around 5:00 P.M., Hooker's division stopped and formed a consolidated battle line, dispatching skirmishers.[24]

Early that same morning, when the affairs of battle seemed bleak for Confederate General Huger, he had sent an urgent request for reinforcement back to Richmond. Several new and untested North Carolina regiments had just arrived in Richmond by railroad and were immediately dispatched the seven miles down the Williamsburg Road to the scene of the fighting. The first regiment to find its way to Huger, the Forty-eighth North Carolina Infantry, commanded by Colonel Robert C. Hill, was sent directly into battle as it arrived, near 5:30 P.M. As Huger ordered the North Carolina rookies to attack the left flank of Robinson's line at King's School, he also ordered the Forty-ninth and Forty-first Virginia regiments to be prepared to launch a flanking motion if the opportunity presented itself.[25]

The enthusiastic charge of the Forty-eighth North Carolina hit the Eighty-seventh New York hard and drove them back on the supporting Hoosiers. General Robinson ordered the Hoosiers to support the left flank and the Indiana men raced to the support of the New Yorkers.[26] At this moment, by chance or by choice, Colonel William Lyon Brown ordered the nearly six hundred men of the Twentieth Indiana to charge the North

Carolinians. It is difficult to sort out fact from fiction in this matter and to assess responsibility for the order. By some accounts, General Robinson ordered the Hoosiers to cheer and the command was misunderstood as an order to charge.[27] However, Robinson's battle report fails to mention this and he takes no credit for ordering a charge. He did indicate approval for the daring move in the report.[28] The most likely scenario is that old Mexican War veteran Brown, who had witnessed the power of the bayonet charge during that conflict, simply did what made military sense and gave the order to fix bayonets and charge.

When the order to "fix bayonets" was given by Colonel Brown, it was received by some with blanched cheeks and by others with joy and excitement. The company officers passed along the line, encouraging the men and begging them to do honor to Indiana, challenging them to wipe out the stain of insult given the state by Jefferson Davis during the Mexican War. Shortly after the Hoosiers formed their battle line the men of the Twentieth charged pell-mell through the woods "not an enemy in sight."[29]

The Twentieth was divided into two wings for the attack, the left being commanded by Captain George B. Dick, acting as major for the ill John Wheeler, and the right wing commanded by Lieutenant Colonel John B. Van Valkenburg. With Colonel Brown leading the way, the two subalterns exhorted their men to increase their pace. The force of the charge was powerful as they plowed through the woods and out into the open ground in front of the Forty-eighth North Carolina. The Hoosiers stopped and fired a volley which riddled the ranks of the raw Rebel regiment, causing heavy casualties. They then resumed the charge, whooping, and cheering with all their might, as they drove the North Carolinians through the clearing and back toward the French house and the woods in its rear.[30]

The Eighty-seventh New York had followed on the left of the Twentieth Indiana as they made their headlong charge into the face of the Confederate line. However, as the Twentieth charged through the French farmyard, past the wheat field concealing the Fourth Georgia, and past the wood line on their left which concealed the Forty-ninth and Forty-first Virginia, a soldier in the New York regiment cried out that there was a Rebel artillery battery coming to bear on their left flank. This frightened, erroneous warning panicked the New Yorkers and sent them in headlong flight, despite the best efforts of their Lieutenant Colonel Richard Bachia, for the safety of the rear. The desertion of the field by the New Yorkers and the failure of the Sixteenth Massachusetts to keep up on the right flank left the Twentieth Indiana alone, under fire on three sides.[31]

It was into this crucible that the Twentieth rushed, unsupported and unaware of what awaited them. As the Forty-eighth North Carolina reached the edge of the woods, they regrouped and turned to fire a volley at the pursuing Hoosiers. Instantly, almost as if it was choreographed and coordinated, the concealed Virginians and Georgians opened up a murderous fire on the unsuspecting but gallant Twentieth.

Lieutenant Colonel Van Valkenburg had his horse shot from under him, mounted again only to have the horse shot down again and finally went down himself with a severe wound to his right leg, below the knee.[32] Captain James Lytle ran at the head of his company, waving his sword until he was shot in the hand and then immediately wounded severely through both hips.[33] Private Edward Farnsworth fell gut-shot to the ground and Private Harvey Bassett tumbled as he charged with a mortal wound.[34] Private George Warren of Company B stopped to assist Captain Lytle and was horribly wounded in the thigh. Private Adam Young, Company C, received four wounds in less than five minutes.[35]

The bravery of the young and inexperienced Hoosiers was admirable. Not a man blinked in the face of this murderous fire as they either raced toward the Confederates in their front or stopped and fired on the Rebels who were peppering them from the flanks. Private Arthur Richardson, Company E, grabbed a Rebel flag from the color bearer of the Forty-eighth North Carolina and had it shot out of his hand, which spurted blood like a fountain. Leander Burditt, Company G, raced ahead of everyone in his company and was downed with a critical wound. Private George Templin had been "fearless" in battle and stood alone in the open, firing calmly at his enemies until shot down. Private John Hann fought "like a tiger," but was almost disemboweled by a musket ball. Private Louis Grant and Corporal George Uhl showed their "dash and daring," blazing away at the concealed Rebels until both fell wounded.[36]

Private Thomas W. Stephens was shot in the right hip and witnessed his brother Jimmie's hip being shattered by a musket ball.[37] Lieutenant William Vatchett had a bullet rip into his shoulder, spinning him round and knocking him to the ground. Private Nicholas Dumphrey nearly had his arm severed by a Rebel shot, and William Reeder received the same wound as his lieutenant colonel.[38]

Young Private William Reed from Monticello, frightened but brave, boldly stood by his father, Captain Alfred Reed, and fired round after round into the Rebels. Private Francis Osborn, Company I, steadfastly made his own personal stand. After Colonel Brown gave the command to retreat, Osborn found himself standing alone in the face of four Rebel regiments. He coolly fired and killed two of his enemies and wounded five others before his luck ran out and a ball shattered his left arm, forcing him to run, his lifeless arm dangling.[39]

Sergeant Nelson Sweet, fulfilling the battlefield eve prophecy he had made to his tentmates, dropped to the ground with a mortal wound.[40]

The precariousness of their unsupported situation had not been apparent to the Indiana men as they furiously loaded and fired at the Virginians and Georgians, but when they started their retreat, it became all too clear that this had been for the Confederates the Civil War equivalent of shooting fish in a barrel. The retreat became a race for life. As the boys retraced their steps they could see the bloodied bodies of the dead and the wounded, who lay begging for help which could not be given—any delay meant certain wounding or death.[41]

As the desperate men ran through the cacophony of whizzing bullets and shouts and moans of dying comrades, they were greeted by a strong volley from the One Hundred and First New York Infantry, which had been sent by General Kearny from Brigadier David Birney's brigade in support. The friendly fire wounded several men and further terrorized the retreating Indiana men.[42]

When the fleeing Hoosiers reached the brigade line, they were met by Brigadier General Robinson, who bravely rallied the men and formed them into some semblance of ordered resistance. He had not been as lucky with the retreating rabble of the Eighty-seventh New York, who left the field of battle and did not return. The Twentieth Indiana rallied around its colors, and Colonel Brown and General Robinson were able to get the regiment to turn and move forward again, accompanied by the One Hundred and First New York, on loan from General Birney. The stiffened resistance of the Union line forced the pursuing Confederates to withdraw. Birney's unit was removed from support and was replaced by the One Hundred and Fifth Pennsylvania. Thus, nightfall came and the deadly game was halted for the evening.[43]

From the time the charge began until it ended with the return of the Twentieth to its lines, no more than ten to twelve minutes had elapsed.[44] In this brief span of time the Twentieth Indiana suffered eleven killed outright, eighty-two wounded, many mortally, and thirty-two missing, for an aggregate loss of 125 men.[45] To be sure, the Hoosiers had given as well as they had received. The Forty-eighth North Carolina lost over 135 men, most killed or wounded by the fire of the Twentieth Indiana.[46] Parts of five other Confederate regiments suffered casualties at the hands of the Hoosiers.

For the thoroughly exhausted and badly shaken Indiana men, the dream of glory in war died at 5:30 P.M. on June 25, passing into the hell that became the Seven Days Battles. To Major General Philip Kearny, the crusty veteran of wars around the world, it was merely a "genteel fight."[47] To the farmboys and clerks of the Twentieth it was all seven rings of the Inferno. The reports of Robinson, Kearny, and Heintzelman greatly lauded the bravery and skill of the Twentieth Indiana and Colonel Brown, but the plaudits were of small comfort to men lying on the ground near King's School and French's farm.

Four hundred yards from the battlefield, the Twentieth passed the night listening to the "mournful wail of the wounded."[48] Any attempt to relieve the suffering of the fallen men was met with volleys of rifle fire from the Confederate pickets. Several brave men from Company I crawled cautiously through the lines onto the bloody field to the area where they believed the beloved Captain James Lytle had fallen. After a long, grisly time rolling over bodies, they found their captain, bloodied from his wounds, but conscious and alert.[49] They returned him to the Union lines and Surgeon Orpheus Everts, who won high praise from the men for his dutiful care of the wounded.[50]

The One Hundred and First New York, which had already fired one blistering mistaken volley into the Twentieth Indiana, became spooked by noises between the lines during the night and again opened up on an imaginary foe. This time the volley soared over the heads of the Hoosiers, but it certainly did nothing to change the low esteem in which the Twentieth held New York soldiers.[51]

The next morning as the first light of day appeared, Colonel Brown sent a flag of truce across the battlefield to Brigadier General Ambrose R. Wright, requesting permission to retrieve his wounded and bury his dead. Declining to recognize the authority of Brown to ask for the truce, Wright refused.[52] He had already sent a detail out to recover the wounded, (though many of the party had ransacked the pockets of the Union dead and wounded for valuables); William Reeder, however, reported that he had been treated well by his captors.[53]

June 26 was a warm and windless day for Robinson's brigade as they worked to throw up breastworks in front of their new defensive line. The work was of no avail when later in the morning General Heintzelman sent orders for the brigade to withdraw one mile back to the line from where the attack of the previous day had been launched.[54] The only movement, for the lion's share of this day, for the Army of the Potomac, was this retrograde movement. Once again, McClellan, the alpine traveler, was stuck straddling the chasm. While he was frozen with inaction, the Confederate army was in headlong motion. Thus, the full circle of futile effort was completed, and there was no one who could explain to the widows and orphans back home exactly why it had to happen.

Adding to McClellan's inaction were the disturbing and confusing reports that he had been receiving from the contraband slaves streaming into the Union lines. Fantastic tales of two hundred thousand Rebel soldiers moving from Richmond, the arrival of General P. G. T. Beauregard's army from the West, Stonewall Jackson's troops arriving, and a host of conflicting reports drove McClellan to despair. Undoubtedly, there were some threads of truth among the stories, but which ones? Maybe all. Who could tell? McClellan panicked and rode to his extreme right flank to begin preparations for defense and retreat. He ordered that supplies be sent up the James River in anticipation of a retreat of the entire army toward the James. Worried dispatches were sent by the general to Washington, predicting doom and casting blame.[55] It was well and good that the common soldiers did not know of their commander's disposition, for it was only an abiding faith in McClellan's skills as a leader that kept their morale high in the dismal swamps.

Military movements, however carefully calibrated, do not often fall out like moves on a chessboard. Although General Robert E. Lee's strategic plan for the destruction of the Union army was brilliant, it did require a difficult set of tactical maneuvers that had to fall in place like so many dominoes. The most important of all the tactical movements was the one by Stonewall Jackson's troops. It was absolutely vital for Jackson to arrive early in the morning of the twenty-sixth, squarely on the flank of Major General Fitz John Porter's Fifth Corps. A coordinated attack by Jackson, in conjunction with Major General A. P. Hill's division, would smash Porter's Fifth Corps and threaten the entire Union army.

Jackson, although fully cognizant of his orders for the that date, did not seem to be fully willing or able to keep the timetable set by General Lee. For a variety of reasons, some explained and others not, Jackson failed to move with his usual alacrity and was nowhere near the Union flank on the designated morning. At 4:30 P.M., with no sign of Jackson's men, A. P. Hill became impatient and, sensing the evaporation of a golden opportunity, decided without orders to launch his own attack. Lee soon arrived on the scene, obviously piqued by the brash young Hill, and was forced to make a quick decision. The decision had to be made to either stop the attack and surrender the initiative to Porter's forces or continue the attack and hope that the dilatory Jackson would finally arrive. Lee opted for the latter option and ordered Hill to press the attack.[56]

The Hoosiers had taken turns sleeping during the day and gradually began to recover from the ordeal of the previous day. Sparse rations were consumed and stories were swapped of the little piece of battle each man had seen. Little of note occurred until late in the afternoon when the silence and stillness of the day was broken by a rising crescendo of musketry coming from north of the Chickahominy River. The boys were too tired to be much disturbed by the sound.

Instead of the 56,000-man assault on the Union flank which General

Lee had envisioned, he got a weak attack made by eleven thousand men on Porter's entrenched Fifth Corps. Lee's battle plan had become as befuddled as General Joseph Johnston's had been at Seven Pines—and with the same disappointing result. By the time the firing had died down, after 9:00 P.M., 1,475 men had fallen from A. P. Hill's ranks. Porter had lost merely 361 and his defensive line was unfazed by the desperate Rebel assault.[57] The Battle of Mechanicsville, as this fight would be called, had been a stinging defeat, partly as a result of the very complicated movements designed by Lee, but more directly the result of the Stonewall Jackson's failure to show up when expected.

McClellan's spirits were temporarily lifted by the victory at Mechanicsville. He euphorically announced his triumph to Washington, but then within a span of five hours, resigned himself to a full retreat of his army down to the James River. The cause of this swift turn of affairs was the information that Stonewall Jackson's men had not been involved in the assault on Fifth Corps. McClellan knew that Jackson was lurking out there somewhere, and with his usual pessimism assumed Jackson's arrival would be devastating to the Army of the Potomac. Accordingly, McClellan put in motion plans to retreat to the James. His ego would not allow it to be called a retreat, a change of base of operations sounded much nicer, but in reality it was nothing but a pure unadulterated skedaddle.

Major General Fitz John Porter was ordered to withdraw his forces from their present defensive lines and move to another defensive position closer the Chickahominy, near a gristmill owned by Dr. William G. Gaines. The position was not nearly as well prepared as the Beaver Dam Creek location, but still offered an excellent field of fire for the Federal forces.

General Lee had two problems as he planned his next move during the early morning hours of June 27. First, he grossly misjudged his opponent. Although he correctly divined that McClellan would remain on the defensive, he failed to realize the full extent of the man's timidity. Lee estimated that McClellan would defend his supply line running back to White House, and so he planned accordingly. He could not envision an opponent giving up the ghost after winning a substantial victory. His second problem was the continuing question of Stonewall Jackson's location. Lee had a vague idea by now as to Jackson's whereabouts, but had not been able to communicate with him about the more important question of where he was going next. Lee would have to contend with an ever-evolving strategic and tactical situation as the day progressed if he was to bag Fitz John Porter's Fifth Corps.

Firing began from one end of Porter's line to the other as the sun rose on June 27. When Major General George McCall's division withdrew from its position at the Mechanicsville Bridge, Major General James Longstreet, accompanied by General Lee, crossed the bridge with his forces and took up a position at noon across from Porter's left and center. The battle commenced in earnest near 2:30 P.M., when A. P. Hill's division attacked the Federal line on its left flank. The fight had the appearance of the battle of the previous day as Hill's twelve thousand men attacked over a quarter mile of open space against the prepared lines of Fifth Corps. Attack after attack was made and the results appeared headed in the same direction as the fight of the previous day. Stonewall Jackson was still wandering around, looking for the Confederate army and trying to get some kind of a tactical feel for where the right flank of the Fifth Corps rested. While Confederate losses piled up, both General Lee and Fitz John Porter fretted and worried. Porter frantically called upon McClellan to send up reinforcements. Lee spent the day wondering when his dynamic general from the Shenandoah Valley might grace the day with his appearance.[58]

Finally, in late afternoon, Stonewall Jackson's men arrived on the field of battle and took a position on the left flank of the Confederate battle line at the end of the exposed Fifth Corps flank. Lee and Jackson met on the Telegraph Road and privately discussed the strategic and tactical situation. History does not record what was said between the two, but when their discussion had ended, Jackson returned to the left of the Confederate line and rejoined his troops, who were by now heavily engaged with the Union forces.

Near 7:00 P.M., with the sun turning sunset red, General Lee ordered an assault along the entire line. The attack should have been launched simultaneously, but instead it was a series of herky-jerky lurches forward, fierce and bloody in every quarter. Porter's men bravely held their own, stretched to their limits by the unrelenting pressure exerted by the attacks of Major General Daniel Harvey Hill's division. At last, with the final fleeting light of day passing into twilight, the Union line broke in several locations at once. Rebel soldiers poured into the gaps in the lines and focused their efforts on capturing the Union artillery. The day was lost for Porter and his absent commander, McClellan. Their only task now was to rescue as much of the corps and the army as was possible.[59]

Only darkness saved Fifth Corps from total destruction. As the exhausted and bloody Union troops retreated to the few bridges spanning the Chickahominy River, there was an air of desperation. The massive supply organization of the Army of the Potomac blended in confusion with the retreating soldiers being funneled towards safety. Artillery caissons, supply wagons, horses, mules, and thousands of head of cattle competed with thirty thousand soldiers for the quickest route over the Chickahominy. Whether McClellan's plan for a change of base of operations to the James River was prescient or a self-fulfilling prophecy is a matter of conjecture. What was known was that it was imperative for McClellan to buy time for his army to retreat, regroup and form a defensive perimeter under the safety of the protective guns of the Union navy on the James River.

Although McClellan had definitely made up his mind to move to the James, he failed to share his plans with his corps commanders. He held a session late that night with all but Erasmus Keyes, who had already been ordered to retreat, and informed them of the plight of the army. As he perceived it, there was an insurmountable barrier of Rebel troops between the Federal forces and Richmond, making an advance on the Confederate capital difficult. There were unknown thousands of Rebels flowing into the Federal flank and rear, making a retreat to the James probable. The general informed his corps commanders that he was considering a cataclysmic fight, a veritable dice-roll for the Union to prevent that, but quickly backed off when questioned by his subordinates about specifics. Instead of the fight to end it all, he ordered Generals Heintzelman and Sumner to hold their lines as Porter's and Keyes' corps moved southward and until a final decision was made as to the next movement of the army. What McClellan didn't tell his generals was that he had already decided to race pell-mell for the James River.[60]

McClellan put into motion his army's *en echelon* retreat to the James. Keyes' corps, the closest Federal corps to the James, had already retreated. Porter's corps would follow them along the narrow roads and bridges to the south. Upon the passage of Porter's men, the Sixth Corps of Major General William B. Franklin would pull out of line and retreat, with Sumner's Second Corps and finally Heintzelman's Third Corps completing the total removal of the Army of the Potomac to the James River. It was an extremely hazardous task to disengage from the enemy and always carried the risk of a calculated retreat turning into a rout. The movement would require stealth, elan, luck and rainless weather to be successful. In addition, for the unfortunate rear guard of each corps, it would also require immense courage.

By dawn of June 28, Federal engineers were hurriedly reconstructing bridges across White Oak Swamp, the same bridges that they had earlier destroyed when this region was the anchor of the left flank of the army. Soon, Keyes' men passed over the bridges, and before noon Porter's Fifth Corps passed through the same narrow corridor of escape. To the men left holding a fraying battle line, the fact that the army was in headlong retreat, passing behind them, was unnerving and demoralizing. The men of the Twentieth Indiana had heard the stiff fighting on the evening of the twenty-sixth and again in the late afternoon of the twenty-seventh. The firing grew more intense and nearer to them as the days wore on. Now, as they rested behind their entrenchments, still stinging from their ordeal of the June 25, they were forced to listen to the rattle and clanging of the huge Army of the Potomac, lumbering away. Rumors that the army was surrounded or cut off circulated down the Federal line, which added to the already tense mood of the Hoosiers.

The Confederate army did not press their attack on the rear of the Fifth Corps because they had guessed wrong as to the probable route of retreat for Porter's men. Assuming the most logical path of withdrawal was back toward White House, Jackson's men moved in that direction until they reached the burning Federal supply dump, which told them that the Union army had retreated southward.

Now, they were forced to retrace their steps and hunt down the fleeing Fifth Corps.[61]

At midnight on June 28, General Phil Kearny received orders from Heintzelman to be prepared to retire from Fair Oaks at dawn.[62] Heintzelman had received no specific orders from McClellan, and in that vacuum decided on his own to withdraw to the rear, uncovering the Second Corps' flank.[63] During the early morning hours, Kearny informed his brigade commanders that they were "the rear guard of all God's creation."[64] At 6:00 A.M., Colonel Brown ordered his men out of their trenches and gave the order to fall back with the remainder of Robinson's brigade to entrenchments the Hoosiers had occupied only a few days earlier. After determining that the Rebels had no intention of attacking them during this move, the brigade fell back further to a strong line of fortifications behind Savage's Station. By this time, the Confederates were wise to the movements of Kearny's division and pressed the retreating troops, seeking to take advantage of any opportunity for attack that might be offered. The Rebels followed fast on the heels of the Hoosiers and took possession of previous Federal positions and the shucked-off excess baggage a retreating army leaves in its wake, as fast as the positions were abandoned.[65]

Upon reaching their breastworks behind Savage's Station, Robinson's brigade was ordered to halt and remain in defensive position. From here they listened to the sharp fighting of Second Corps, standing alone against the advancing Rebels and then, for several hours, the Hoosiers were witness to an incredible display of waste and destruction, conducted at the hands of the Union army. A huge supply dump had been created at Savage's Station and McClellan had given orders for its destruction before it fell into the hands of a supply-short Confederate army. Every imaginable type of item necessary for maintaining an army in the field was set to the torch and the entire supply dump went up in smoke and flames, a vast billowing cloud rising high into the sky.[66] The destruction of the depot further served to depress the spirits of the retreating soldiers, adding to the feeling of impending doom.

Private William P. Russell, Company H, fidgeted and worried behind the log-and-earthen entrenchment. From his perspective, all was lost. Overwhelming numbers of Rebels were closing in on the rear of the Union army and, as he saw it, the Hoosiers would be gobbled up by the Confederate behemoth. He was depressed beyond consolation and he emptied his pockets of money and other valuables and gave them to a friend to be sent to his wife in Indianapolis when he was killed.[67]

Was Private Russell being maudlin and irrational? His fear seemed justified at 4:00 P.M., when General Kearny gave orders for his division, with the exception of the "Twentieth Indiana marksmen" and Battery G, Second U.S. Artillery, to retire across White Oak Swamp. The unfortunate Hoosiers, their laurels for bravery won at Oak Grove, were rewarded with the unenviable task of being the only infantry unit between the Confederate army and the fleeing columns of the Army of the Potomac.[68] Here at Savage's Station, supported only by a small artillery battery, the boys from Indiana were forced to wait for an open-ended eternity, which it seemed would only end with the arrival of pursuing Rebels. The orders issued by Colonel Brown were simple: hold the position until the graybacks showed themselves in force and then get out of harm's way as quickly as possible.[69]

In order to make the expected getaway easier, the boys were ordered to remove all excess baggage and equipment and throw it away. Clothes, socks, tents, blankets, food, haversacks, and coats were all pitched into piles, later to be picked up by eager Rebels. This was one order that was obeyed without hesitation. When it came time to hightail it for safety, these Hoosiers were going to travel light and fast.[70]

The Twentieth waited anxiously behind their works, straining their eyes to gain a glimpse of the first Rebel. They didn't wait for long. As dusk approached Confederate picket fire started peppering the line of the Twentieth. The Indiana boys kept their heads down and weathered the fire with little worry. Then, Rebel forces boldly emerged from the wood line opposite the Union works and advanced. The Hoosiers and Battery G opened up with a rifle volley and case shell into the face of the attackers. The Rebels withdrew and regrouped. Again, they came gamely on, only to be thrown back a second time by the concentrated fire of the Hoosiers and their artillery support.[71] It was going to take more than a furtive infantry attack to drive these abandoned defenders away.

The Hoosiers shivered with excitement and apprehension as they heard the unmistakable shouts, thundering hooves, and orders from a Confederate artillery unit emerging from the trees and going into battery. Colonel Brown had done his duty. The Twentieth Indiana and Battery G had bought time for the retreating army and now, in the face of this ominous threat, it was high time to go. Brown shouted, "About face! Double quick!" as the first Rebel shells flew over their heads. The Hoosiers jumped to their feet and turned to run when the next artillery barrage of canister and grape shot hit them full force. The first exploding canister tore through the ranks, shattering the head of Private Russell and striking down several others. The shots fell quickly and murderously into the fleeing Hoosiers. Ten men fell killed and wounded in the span of seconds as a panicky flight ensued.[72]

It was now every man for himself, a stampede of desperately frightened men, shells exploding and plowing up dirt around them as they ran. The regiment, by no apparent design, divided into two groups. The majority of the regiment followed Colonel Brown down the road toward White Oak Bridge, but two or three hundred men followed Captain George Dick, in charge of the regimental colors, into the dense thick underbrush of White Oak Swamp, where they immediately became lost. Confederate skirmishers rushed headlong after the Hoosiers, intent on ensnaring the regiment, but the Indiana boys, motivated by fear, were far quicker this evening. They blindly rushed through the bushes and brambles, dodging enemy patrols which they discovered front, flank, and rear. Fortunately for the Hoosiers, they kept to a course that was roughly parallel to the road traversed by Colonel Brown and at 9:00 P.M. crossed White Oak Swamp at the bridge. Upon making inquiries of the Union forces there, Captain Dick's remnant force was directed to the point at which Colonel Brown had assembled his men. There was much cheering and elation when Captain Dick reported with the regimental colors. The Twentieth Indiana was reunited.[73]

The regiment was in surprisingly good condition, considering its ordeal. It had been offered up by General Kearny as a sacrificial lamb to save the army, but the lamb bit back. Although relatively intact in number, the Twentieth was thoroughly exhausted and hungry. Now with an absolute deluge of rain pouring down on them, the men ate the meager hardtack crackers that had been stuffed in their pockets and collapsed into a deep sleep.[74]

While the men of the Twentieth Indiana enjoyed a few fitful hours of sleep in the oozing mud, General Lee plotted to crush the Army of the Potomac. Lee planned for the divisions of Stonewall Jackson and Benjamin Huger to smash into the rear guard of the Union army, and if the opportunity presented itself, to cut it in half. His plan once again required prompt movement on the part of his generals, a continuing problem in light of the difficult communications problem and now torrential rainstorm. The focus of the Confederate attack would be the small crossroads of Glendale, where the Charles City, Quaker, New Market, and Long Bridge roads intersected. The capture of that hamlet would render an escape of the Union army to the James River impossible.

On the morning of June 30, the Union army was in an extremely precarious position. General McClellan had left his army behind to move to his new headquarters at Harrison's Landing on the James River. Before he left, he failed to delegate authority to any of his corps commanders; the result was leaderless confusion in the rear of his army. When the resultant Battle of Glendale began, parts of four Union army corps would find themselves intermingled and spread out along three roads from the White Oak Bridge to the Willis Church on the Quaker Road, with each corps commander making his own strategic and tactical decisions.[75]

General Heintzelman, commanding Third Corps, sent troops to destroy the bridge at Brackett's Ford and ordered Kearny's and Brigadier Henry Slocum's divisions up the Charles City Road to fell trees across the road and impede any Rebel advance. Heintzelman instructed Slocum to anchor his division's left flank on the Charles City Road and Kearny to connect his right flank there with his left flank extended to the New Market Road. From the New Market Road to the right flank of Hooker's division was a wide gap into which the Fifth Corps division of Brigadier General George McCall inserted themselves. Behind this defensive line ran the Quaker Road, down which the Army of the Potomac's huge wagon and artillery train proceeded.[76]

After a miserable, soaking night, the hungry and worn-out Hoosiers of the Twentieth staggered to their weary feet and fell into column of march, bound for Glendale. The misery of the rainstorm was now replaced by the torment of a sweltering summer sun. Woolen uniforms, heavy from rain and mud, clung to bodies as the brutal sun beat down. Bellies growled from hunger. Sergeant Dennis Tuttle wrote his wife that he had eaten only a cracker as big as two fingers in the last twenty-four hours, "This may seem rather rough, but I suppose it is nothing where a man gets used to it. Something like an eel getting used to being skinned."[77]

The Twentieth marched with their brigade at a very quick pace for three hours from the edge of White Oak Swamp to their new position between the Charles City Road and New Market Road. The Indiana boys were greeted at their new location by General Kearny, who had taken a distinct liking to his Western men and their tough, capable colonel. Kearny, looking every inch the splendid fighter he was, told Brown, "Here are some logs and a fence that your men can throw together for breastworks. I promise not to move you during the fight which will be a hard one." Although many of the Hoosiers had heard Kearny as they milled around him, Colonel Brown repeated the command to his men. Battle-tested men did not have to be told twice about the benefits of fighting behind breastworks and went to the task in earnest. Forgetting their fatigue and hunger, within an hour they had constructed a good defensive position staring across a two-hundred-yard field to the wood line behind it.[78]

Brigadier General Robinson, commanding the brigade, ordered two companies of the Twentieth into the woods in front of the battle line as skirmishers. Robinson's brigade was deployed with the Sixty-third Pennsylvania on its left flank, the Fifty-seventh Pennsylvania in the center, and the Twentieth Indiana on the right flank. Behind this brigade line was the One Hundred and Fifth Pennsylvania in reserve. Between the left flank of the Sixty-third Pennsylvania and the right flank of Brigadier General George Meade's brigade of McCall's division was Thompson's Artillery Battery. The right flank of the Twentieth Indiana adjoined the left flank of Brigadier General David Birney's brigade.

Adding to the confusion over this battle in later years has been the fact that two names were ascribed to it. It is called in various histories the Battle of Glendale or Frayser's Farm. The truth of the matter is that the majority of the fighting occurred on and near the Nelson farm, formerly owned by the Frayser family. Thus, the Confederates from the area referred to it as the Battle of Frayser's Farm and the boys from the Twentieth Indiana would hereafter refer to it as the Battle of Glendale.

General Jackson spent most of the day wondering when Stonewall Jackson and Benjamin Huger would launch their attacks on the Union rear. He held the divisions of Longstreet and A. P. Hill on tight leashes as they strained, ready to pounce on the Union line at Glendale. Lee wanted a concentrated attack and not a piecemeal battle such as had occurred over the last several days. As the long summer day began to melt away, he sensed that his best opportunity for a smashing victory was fading with it.

Finally, in the distance, from the direction of the White Oak Bridge, came the deep-throated booming of artillery, indicating that Jackson had begun his attack. At 2:00 P.M. Huger's division was reported to be advancing down the Charles City Road. Soon after A. P. Hill's Rebel division launched a vicious attack on McCall's division. In less than an hour, McCall's battle-weary division gave way and evaporated into the surrounding countryside. Brigadier General Joseph Hooker's division moved to their right and along with Brigadier General John Sedgwick's division of Sumner's Second Corps plugged the gap in bitter fighting that degenerated into a hand-to-hand, life-or-death struggle. With Huger's advance stymied on the Charles City Road by Slocum's division as Hill's attack ground to a halt, the fighting naturally evolved to the left of Kearny's line.[79]

It was now nearly four o'clock, with only four more hours of daylight remaining, and Lee had no choice but to commit his forces to the attack. Major General James Longstreet sent an order to Brigadier General Roger Pryor, instructing him to advance his brigade to the attack on Robinson's brigade. The woods in front of Pryor were dense and difficult to cross. Pryor was forced to send his brigade through one regiment at a time. With a whooping scream that sent chills down the spines of the skirmishers from the Twentieth waiting blindly in the woods, the Fourteenth Alabama crashed down on the two Hoosier companies and drove them, in a hailstorm of bullets, back towards their brigade line. When the Alabama boys emerged from the woods into the open field separating them from Robinson's line, they were instantly met by a devastating fire from the Federal infantry and Thompson's battery. It was murderous annihilation for the Alabamans.[80]

Captain Alfred Reed, leading the two companies of skirmishers, was forced to lie prone between the two blazing lines of rifle and artillery fire to avoid being hit by either friend or foe. Lying beside the captain was his sixteen-year-old son, William, severely wounded. Privates Martin Dobbins and Horatio Brunnel were killed instantly by the torrent of bullets. The firing was so intense that many of the men in the skirmish companies never had the opportunity to hop to their feet and make a run for their lines.

Following the Alabamans into the slaughter in the field were the Fourteenth Louisiana, Second Florida, Third Virginia, and the First Louisiana Battalion. Wave after wave of screaming gray-clad demons ran toward the Union line, only to be mowed down like hay before the sickle. The Twentieth Indiana, protected by their hastily thrown up breastworks, in the words of Colonel Brown, "behaved with the greatest coolness, jesting, cracking jokes, loading and firing deliberately as if at a target."[81]

The Confederate officers tried as best as they could to rally their shaken men. General Pryor called on the brigade of Brigadier General Winfield S. Featherston to come to his assistance. Featherston responded and formed his men in line of battle and marched them through the woods to a fence line on the edge of the open field. Featherston's men stayed in place behind the split-rail fence and opened fire on Robinson's brigade. His Mississippi regiments poured a heavy fire into the breastworks, but with little effect. The Hoosiers directed a brutal fire toward the Mississipians, piling the Rebels up like cordwood at the foot of the rail fence. Featherston himself was wounded in the shoulder and was carried from the field.[82]

During this time A. P. Hill launched the first of three successive attacks on the left of Robinson's brigade, focusing on Thompson's battery. Thompson's guns were loaded with double canister, and their fire tore huge holes in the advancing gray lines.[83] General Kearny, witnessing the battle from this point, called upon the Sixty-third Pennsylvania to leave their protective breastworks and charge Hill's men. Kearny grabbed the regimental flag in his lone arm and, placing the reins of his horse in his teeth, led the regiment in a headlong charge into the Rebels.[84] The effect of the charge was overwhelming. The brigade of Brigadier General Charles W. Field was shocked by the brutality of the charge and was decimated by the horrific fire.

It was now Brigadier Maxcy Gregg's turn to enter the crucible of Glendale. Ordered by A. P. Hill to support the brigades of Longstreet's division, Gregg moved his men to the left of Hill's division. Gregg's South Carolina boys were a tough outfit itching to get into the fight. The Fourteenth South Carolina led the brigade to the field, passing through the dense undergrowth. Captain West led his company forward as skirmishers in advance of the brigade by about three hundred yards. This movement through the woods flushed some of the Hoosier skirmishers out of their lairs and sent them running like jack rabbits in all directions. The South Carolinians paused at the fence line, as had Featherston's men, and opened a hot fire into Robinson's line. The men of the Fourteenth expended over seventy bullets per man in their attempt to drive Robinson out of his works. The Twentieth Indiana and Fifty-seventh Pennsylvania poured a "very hot and fatal fire" in return, killing and wounding a large number of the South Carolinians.[85] The remainder of Gregg's brigade arrived on the field near 6:30 P.M., loaded rifles, fixed bayonets and formed in column of companies preparing for an assault. At 7:30, with the merciless sun beginning to set, the First, Twelfth, and Thirteenth South Carolina, and the First South Carolina Rifles set off across the open field in a hard driving attack on Robinson's brigade. By now the Hoosiers had been joined behind their breastworks by the Second Michigan, who found it a much safer place to make a stand than the slightly elevated ground behind the Hoosiers. Together, the Hoosiers and Wolverines loaded and fired as swiftly as possible and created many a widow and orphan in the Palmetto State. [86] The attack of Gregg's brigade was repelled as swiftly as it had started, with fearful slaughter.

It was during this attack by Gregg's brigade that the Twentieth Indiana experienced the only casualties of the men fighting behind breastworks. During this final violent thrust by the South Carolinians, Lieutenant John M. Andrew fell, shot in the head while exhorting his men to load and fire quicker. One other private was wounded here, but the remainder of the wounded of the Twentieth lay between the lines and in the woods and thicket across the field of battle. Twenty-seven men were wounded, many mortally, and another twenty-two missing in action.[87]

With Gregg's brigade repelled, the battle in front of the Hoosiers evolved into a shooting match across the two-hundred-yard expanse of field. Intense rifle and artillery fire tore into the massed ranks of the lightly protected Rebels of three Confederate brigades who were stacked up along the wood line behind the rail fence. Casualties mounted. Thompson's battery finally ran out of ammunition and with his murderous work completed, he limbered up his guns and left the field.[88] Darkness fell and, as if on cue, both sides of this bloody struggle ceased firing.

It had been exhausting, bloody, and dirty work for the Hoosiers. Each man had fired his ration of a hundred and fifty rounds of ammunition. The faces of the Indiana men were blackened from the powder of their guns, and sweat streaked down tired faces. They simply collapsed where they were and slept.[89]

As soon as the firing ceased, Confederate rescue parties scoured the intervening field for their friends and comrades. The torch-lit details came to within forty paces of the Union line, but Robinson's men let the Southerners do their humane work unmolested. By the sheer numbers of torch lights bobbing up and down in the blackness of night, the Indiana men knew they had inflicted a fearful loss on the Confederate attackers.[90] The moans and pleas of the wounded chilled the Hoosiers' hearts. One poor, suffering soul cried out through the entire night, calling for water and aid from his company. He kept yelling, "Company B, Fortieth Virginia, both of my legs are shot off. Company B, Fortieth Virginia. . . ."[91]

Regimental Adjutant Israel N. Stiles, completely exhausted from the past several days' ordeal, was dispatched by Colonel Brown through a gap in the Union line for the purpose of determining the identity of a large body of men amassed to the right front of the Twentieth Indiana.[92] Adjutant Skiles foolishly rode his horse directly into the midst of the Fourteenth South Carolina and demanded to know to what unit they belonged. One Rebel turned the question back at him and when he answered that he was from the Twentieth Indiana, Colonel Samuel McGowan informed Stiles that he was now a guest of the Confederacy. Stiles was herded to the rear under armed escort, along with Captain Reed and several other prisoners from the Twentieth.[93]

When analyzing battles with perfect hindsight, it is easy to ascribe to the Battle of Glendale a high level of importance. If the Union line had been broken and Glendale had been captured, much of the Army of the Potomac would have been lost to the Confederate pursuers. Who can tell what July 1 would have meant, if the army had not reached Malvern Hill relatively intact? Brigadier General Philip Kearny characterized the battle as the most desperate of the war to that date, and as the one most fatal, had it been lost. He was effusive in his praise for Brigadier General John Robinson, crediting the success of the day to Robinson's brigade above all others.[94] For his part,

General Robinson gave high marks to Colonel Hays of the Sixty-third Pennsylvania and to Colonel Brown of the Twentieth Indiana.[95] The fighting performance praised by Robinson was something in which the Hoosiers could take great pride.

At 2:00 A.M. on July 1, a messenger from Kearny rode up to Colonel Brown, informing him that he was to pull quietly out of line and withdraw his regiment down the Quaker Road to Malvern Hill. Pulling out of line in the face of an enemy was tricky business at any time, but was made all the more difficult here at Glendale because Confederate rescue parties were operating almost to the very edge of the breastworks. With catlike stealth, the Twentieth Indiana slowly slipped out from behind the breastworks and tiptoed through the adjoining woods to the Quaker Road where they proceeded on to Malvern Hill. The Twentieth Indiana was the last regiment to leave the Glendale battlefield.[96]

General McClellan had decided that he would concentrate his army at Malvern Hill and make a fight of it. By noon July 1, the whole army was collected on Malvern Hill, one of the highest of the slight eminences which border the James River. From the broad top, buried in vines and trees, it slopes down gently towards the east and north and falls off abruptly to the northwest into a ravine, which extends to the river. To the rear ran the river and on every other side spread fields of grain, bounded by woods and crossed by broad, smooth roads. The green corn was in tassel, the wheat either awaiting the sickle or already cut and bound in sheaves. The harvesters had fled, leaving the fruits of their labor to be trodden upon and soaked in blood. The men of the Twentieth Indiana viewed this location as a paradise, particularly when compared with the tangled thickets and swamps of the Chickahominy.[97]

On the James River lay five gunboats, prepared to bombard any advancing Rebels with their huge naval guns. On the top of the hill were nearly three hundred cannon. The infantry was massed below the artillery in shallow rifle pits which had been hastily dug during the night. Up until this time, the Army of the Potomac had been sent to battle in a piecemeal approach. McClellan had rarely been seen at the scene of battle, choosing instead to direct affairs from a remote headquarters, with only the telegraph serving as his eyes and ears. Here, at Malvern Hill, the entire Army of the Potomac, bloodied and exhausted, were defiantly ready to make their stand.[98]

At 6:00 A.M. the Twentieth Indiana arrived on Malvern Hill, along with their division, and were placed in reserve on the right flank of the army in a golden wheat field. As the sun rose in the sky, the Indiana boys, scorched by its blazing heat, could find no shelter or relief. Having borne the brunt of the fighting on the thirtieth, the Hoosiers were placed out of harm's way, on the opposite slope from where the Confederates were anticipated to attack.[99] Quartermaster Sergeant Dennis Tuttle described the scene as the battle was about to begin, "I saw a sight, over fifty thousand troops at one view drawn up in line of battle, standing in soft mud nearly to their knees. It was a grand but sad picture."[100]

This was also the first opportunity that General Robert E. Lee had achieved for massing his army. For the first time, every division and brigade was on the battlefield and ready to fight. Six days of frustrating opportunities, near victories, and dashed hopes had made the Confederate army dangerous. They had tasted blood; only when McClellan's forces had been driven into the James River would their hatred and desire for revenge be assuaged.

The Rebel assault was opened by a heavy fire of artillery on Kearny's left flank and upon Brigadier General Darius Couch's division, and it was quickly followed up by a brisk advance of infantry over the open ground. This attack was repulsed, but the Rebels came on again, screaming their bone-chilling yell, determined to carry the attack over Porter's Fifth Corps. Brigade after brigade came on a run across the open field, storming through canister and shell into the awaiting rifles of the infantry. Gunboats rained down their destructive fire on the advancing hordes, which added greatly to the slaughter. Time and time again Lee drove his men against the unbreakable Union line only to see them crushed and cut down.[101]

The Indiana men, presumably out of harm's way, found themselves standing wide open in their field of wheat, exposed to a heavy artillery barrage. Unable to bring their rifles to bear on the attacking Rebel infantry, they were nonetheless sitting ducks for any shell which happened to fly a bit too high for the first line of rifle pits. No man was killed by this artillery fire, but thirteen men went down with wounds from flying shrapnel. In some ways, waiting for the next artillery shell to pass overhead or explode in the midst of the regiment was more terrifying than fighting the battle of the previous day.[102] Joshua Lewis was sitting down in the wheat when stray rifle bullets came whizzing by him, striking near enough that he was sure he was hit. He moved farther back and lay prone to present as little of a target as possible.[103]

The intense fighting at Malvern Hill continued until dark before the roaring guns fell silent. The Hoosiers were withdrawn at dark to a bivouac area in the rear. At midnight they were aroused from their slumber and marched down off the hill across a muddy stream to their new camp in the mud flats near Harrison's Landing.[104] There in this hot, slimy, mosquito-infested haven, the men of the Twentieth Indiana had their first opportunity to reflect on what they had done. Dennis Tuttle summed up the attitude of the Hoosiers in a letter to his wife, "I have experienced more in the last ten days than all I have experienced before since I have been in the army. I have seen more suffering than you ever dreamed of but it was only a necessary consequence of war."[105] Sergeant E. M. B. Hooker, in the days after the Seven Days battles, when some Northern papers called the Peninsula battles a great triumph, wrote, "They may be all glorious battles and glorious victories, but we don't see it. If you do, why it is all right."[106]

Each battle of the Seven Days had its nuances and ramifications, and debates went on and go on to the present day about whether battles prior to July 1 were "won" or "lost." However, there could be no debate on Malvern Hill. It was a smashing Federal victory. McClellan's frantic withdrawal to the James River could have gone down in the annals of warfare as a strategic masterpiece if the little general had had the nerve to exploit the victory at Malvern Hill. A concentrated Union counterattack, as proposed by General Fitz John Porter, might have won the war before the end of the summer. McClellan would not hear of an attack; he intended to withdraw from Malvern Hill to the safety of his new base at Harrison's Landing, head in the sand, countless opportunities ignored.

Phil Kearny, ever the fighter, was furious with McClellan's decision to evacuate Malvern Hill. Within earshot of common soldiers and directly to his subordinate brigadier generals, he heatedly proclaimed, "I, Phil Kearny, who am an old soldier and a member of the Legion of Honor of France, do say, and I am personally responsible for what I say, that George B. McClellan is either a traitor or a coward!"[107]

McClellan's conduct on the Peninsula would be debated in the White House, the War Department, around campfires, in front of fireplaces in the North, and in the newspapers. Everyone would have his say it seems, except the dead and dying, on the fields of Oak Grove, Mechanicsville, Gaines' Mill, Savage's Station, Glendale, and Malvern Hill. Their silent voices spoke much about the Federal disaster that has become known simply as the Seven Days.

An exhausted and hungry Private John H. Hendricks, Company E, wrote his mother from Harrison's Landing:

July 6, 1862

Dear Mother,

As the mail leaves for Old Point Comfort in fifteen minutes, I can't say much but by this you will see that I am alive and well after forced marches of three days and four days of hard fighting, we have arrived here. We have lost over four hundred braves out of our regiment and over one half of our company is killed and wounded. Lieutenant Andrew of our company was killed while making a desperate charge at the head of his company. In that charge we drove the Fourth Georgia and the

Fortieth Virginia before us. He was shot through the head. We have lost nearly all of our officers. We have lost one lieutenant, two sergeants and two corporals out of our company. Our orderly was killed early in the first battle. I have had no ball hit my clothes yet. Excuse the shortness of this letter. I will write as soon as I can.

Yours truly,
John [108]

The Twentieth Indiana Volunteer Infantry had started the Seven Days Battles with more than eight hundred men. At Harrison's Landing, the roll call could account for only three hundred and fifty. The rest were killed, wounded, captured, or lay rotting in the tangled underbrush of the White Oak Swamp.

CHAPTER SIX

WE HAVE ROUSED THE REAL CRITTER

After a brief two-day respite at Harrison's Landing, the Twentieth Indiana was sent by General Robinson out on picket on July 4. On the day which commemorated the signing of the Declaration of Independence, there were no parades, bands or the usual Independence Day celebrations, just the omnipresent Confederate pickets and cavalry lurking in the hot, muggy underbrush. On the Confederate side Brigadier General Jeb Stuart had pushed his cavalrymen up against the Union lines, looking for any weakness or tactical opportunity. He thought he had found one when his men discovered a rise in the ground near Harrison's Landing from which artillery might be brought to bear on the assembled Union masses. Stuart impetuously moved men to the hill without consulting General Lee, thereby tipping the Confederate hand prematurely. Colonel Brown, realizing the importance of the position, ordered his pickets forward to help drive Stuart away. The firing was brief and sharp, but Stuart's cavalrymen knew better than to tangle with infantry and deserted the hill. The Twentieth had four men wounded in the action and returned to their camp in the mud flats the next day.[1]

Back in camp, Private E. M. B. Hooker had time to reflect on the army's status in a letter to the *Indianapolis Daily Journal*:

> *If there had been less digging, less parading and less fussing generally, and a good deal more fighting, things might have been different. In fact we are now like the man that went out after a grizzly bear. He had been taunted by his comrades till he got desperate and one morning*

started out in search of one. He came upon him sooner than he expected, dropped his gun, turned tail and put for cap, with the grizzly in full chase. As he broke into view, he exclaimed, "Here we both come, God darn us!" And that's the way it is with us, we have roused the real critter and we are both here.[2]

The critter of war itself was horrible beyond what happened on the battlefield. Private Ed Farnsworth was severely wounded on June 25 and was carried back into his lines late that evening, placed on a wooden plank and loaded into an overcrowded ambulance which made the bumpy twelve-mile trip back to White House Landing, where he was transferred to a hospital transport. The transport ship made a slow voyage to New York Harbor, a voyage slow enough to have allowed his mother in LaPorte, Indiana, to be informed of his wounding and to arrive by train in New York three hours before her son. He received rudimentary medical treatment in New York; Mrs. Farnsworth made daily trips out to the hospital ship and spent the days attending to her son. Three days after his arrival in New York Harbor, Ed Farnsworth died of his wounds. His mother returned to LaPorte with her son's remains.[3]

The wounded men and boys of the Twentieth Indiana were sent to hospitals in varied locations, for no apparent rhyme or reason. Twenty-three men were sent to New York and a large number to Fortress Monroe, Baltimore, Philadelphia, and Washington, D.C. Many men were treated, or died, on the hospital transports which lay at anchor in the James River or in Pamlico Sound.[4]

Such huge influxes of wounded from the Seven Days battles stretched the medical service to its breaking point. Overworked doctors and hospital stewards showed less and less compassion for the wounded, and thoughtful medical practice in many cases evolved into sheer butchery. Once the amputation of a leg or an arm was accomplished, the victim of this enlightened medical treatment of the day would be consigned to a cot, stretcher, or bed, and left to the fate of God's good grace. Less severely wounded men were pressed into service as nurses for the more seriously wounded. Corporal William Reeder, wounded on June 25, was driven to exhaustion by the necessity of keeping constant vigil on the bleeding stub of a comrade's amputated leg. After several close calls with death, the life of his hospital mate was saved when Reeder carefully tied off the bleeding artery which had been tied haphazardly during surgery.[5]

Despite the horrible hospital conditions and the omnipresent suffering and dying around them, the spirits of most of the wounded were surprisingly good. Private Francis Osborn, who had been a jeweler before enlisting, had staggered back to the Union line on June 25 holding his near-lifeless left arm in his right hand. The field surgeons found the arm ripped from its socket and hanging by its sinews. There was no choice but to amputate the arm all the way into the socket area, leaving a ghastly indentation. Still, Osborn greeted the comrades who visited him with a serene and peaceful attitude. When his friends saw his mangled body and thought about the questionable future that would face Osborn, their eyes moistened with tears. Osborn, trying to lift their spirits, simply assured them, "It is a small sacrifice for me to make for my country."[6] His visitors nodded solemnly, for they knew Osborn would not repair another watch in the years left to him.

Captain James Lytle, who so bravely led the charge at Oak Grove, was feeling pretty chipper for a man who had been wounded three times. He wrote the following letter home to an inquiring friend in Valparaiso:

My Dear Mrs. Larned:
This morning, for the first time, I am able to write you a short note. I was shot in the left side and the left thigh, and the right wrist (slightly the latter). Three shots pierced my coat, so you see I was very fortunate to get off at all. There are no bones broken, and I am improving rapidly. My folks at Baltimore come over to see me, and I will go home with them as soon as I am able to ride. I think it will be from four to six weeks before I could think of venturing West, but will go as soon as possible. Of my own brave boys, fifteen are gone and five are here wounded. They did their duty to a man. God bless them; but we all did so.

Lytle [7]

Lytle's thoughts of returning home in four to six weeks would prove prophetic. Infection invaded his wounds and in four weeks, Lytle began his journey home in a pine coffin, accompanied by his parents. One of the regiment's best officers had been lost to unsanitary medical practices.

The officers of the Twentieth who were wounded and able were allowed to return to Indiana to recuperate and also empowered to act as recruiting officers. These were the lucky ones; they found their recovery and rehabilitation came much quicker under the attentive (and clean) hands of family and friends. Lieutenant Colonel Van Valkenburg knew how decimated the regiment had become and would work diligently, along with his brother officers, to recruit good men to join the ranks of the Twentieth.[8]

If being wounded in battle wasn't a big enough challenge, falling into Confederate hands while being wounded certainly was. Overcrowded in wagons or forced to drag themselves to Richmond, many died along the way or arrived debilitated, unable to face the rigors of prison life. So while many men were killed instantly in battle, several wounded men from the Twentieth would slowly wither away in the tobacco warehouse prisons of Richmond.

Orderly Sergeant Ed Abbey, Private Nathan Bunnel, and Private William Reed were a few of the wounded of the Twentieth who made their way to a Richmond prison hospital only to die there. Captain Alfred Reed, unfortunate enough to be taken captive, was fortunate enough to spend his son's final hours with him, comforting the boy before death took him.

There were a number of Hoosiers with interesting tales of captivity to tell, perhaps none more interesting than Adjutant Israel N. Stiles, who was captured late in the evening of June 30 and embarked on a remarkable sojourn. Upon capture, Stiles looked around as he was transferred to the Rebel rear and decided that during the night he would slip off into the blackness and escape. Stiles' escort halted their march for a rest, and he decided that this would be the best time to escape. He closed his eyes to pretend he was asleep and very quickly fell into the reality of deep sleep from which a Rebel sergeant aroused him at daylight. With his escape option closed, Stiles resigned himself to captivity.[9]

The sergeant took his prisoner to the colonel of the Sixteenth Georgia Infantry and offered to place Stiles in their charge. The colonel carried a very heavy cavalry saber and politely offered to exchange it with Stiles for his much lighter infantry officer's sword. The exchange was made and the colonel buckled on his new sword.

On the afternoon of July 1, while the Battle of Malvern Hill was blazing, Stiles trudged toward Richmond under the benign supervision of the Rebel sergeant. As they neared Richmond, the two encountered two mounted civilians making their way toward the sound of battle. The riders stopped in front of Stiles and one of the men shook his fist under Stiles' nose and declared, "You are on the road to Richmond, are you, God damn you! On the road to Richmond, well I reckon you'll get there a good while before your damn Yankee army."[10]

Apprehension grew for Stiles as he drew nearer the Rebel capital. After the initial greeting from the angry civilians, he wasn't quite sure how he would be received. The next civilians Stiles passed flew by quickly in a buggy. The sergeant and Stiles instantly recognized one of the passengers as the Confederate president, Jefferson Davis. A short while after, Stiles passed through the fortifications of Richmond.[11]

During his long march to captivity, Stiles and the Rebel sergeant struck up a conversation. The sergeant had been a printer in civilian life. As Stiles walked and the sergeant rode the adjutant's horse, they discussed a variety of issues such as secession, slavery and state's rights. They formed a respectful bond and after a short distance the Rebel allowed Stiles to tie his personal possessions to the pommel of the saddle. A while later, Stiles was invited to ride as the sergeant walked and before they reached Richmond, the riding time was divided equally. Upon passing through the Rebel defenses, Stiles found a horse-drawn street car waiting at the end of its line. The sergeant, wanting to pay a visit on some friends of his in town, invited Stiles to ride the street car with the instructions to meet him on a street corner up town. Stiles stepped off the street car and patiently awaited the sergeant on the corner. Before long a good-sized crowd had gathered around this lone Yankee officer, still carrying his sword. A Confederate lieutenant appeared on the scene and approached Stiles, demanding to know where the intruding invader had come from. Stiles told his story to the greatly disturbed lieutenant who promised severe punishment for the friendly Rebel sergeant. The lieutenant escorted Stiles to the Guy Street Prison and along the way offered a handsome sum for the adjutant's boots. Stiles refused to sell, which confused the Rebel lieutenant. He had been raised with the belief that a Yankee would sell his mother to make a profit. When Stiles informed the lieutenant that he was a Hoosier, the enlightened Rebel responded, "You are an Indianan and they are more like us." At the gates of the prison, Stiles presented the grateful, but embarrassed, lieutenant with his new canteen and entered his life of imprisonment.[12]

Adjutant Stiles entered a prison that was grossly overcrowded, filthy, and disease-ridden. The food was scant and of poor quality: regular rations consisted of boiled beef and bread and a broth in which the beef had been boiled. There was no salt available to add flavor to the bland beef. Whiskey could not be found at any price, but there was an abundance of chewing tobacco. Class distinctions were obvious: there was a distinct rift between the regular army officers who were imprisoned and the incarcerated volunteer officer. Among the Regulars who held themselves aloof from the group were Brigadier General John F. Reynolds and Brigadier General George McCall. In addition to this spat was the one between the religious officers and those more inclined to curse and gamble to pass the tedious days. Neither side was sympathetic to the other and there was a continuously rancorous verbal battle between those fearing God and those fearing "snake eyes." Eventually a compromise was worked out and quiet was observed during religious services, with protests kept to a minimum regarding the rampant gambling. Thus a miniature and less bloody civil war was avoided in the cramped prison.[13]

The boredom of captivity was alleviated one day for Stiles when he was given a pass to go outside the prison walls into the city. Donning a gray jacket and Rebel hat, Stiles entered the city and wandered around for several hours, taking in the sights. He struck up a conversation with a slave in the town and was told that his life might be in jeopardy if he was discovered. The slave also informed him, erroneously, that McClellan had crossed over to the south side of the James River and was advancing on Richmond. Stiles hurried back to prison and informed his fellow captives who rejoiced at the news.[14] Many of the prisoners detained at the Guy Street Prison were eventually transferred to the notorious Libby Prison. There Stiles found even greater overcrowding and deprivation. At Libby Prison, slow starvation and rampant disease ate its way through the resistance of even the healthiest men. The lucky prisoner made it to the infirmary where the food was ample— a brief relief from a certain slow death. There was the hope of release after Seven Days, however. In 1862 the cartel regulating prisoner of war exchanges still freed prisoners from the worst of the Rebel prisons. In later months of the war, when prisoner exchanges had been slowed or halted altogether, the death toll would mount in the hell hole of Libby Prison.[15]

In the first week of August, virtually all of the men taken prisoner from the Twentieth Indiana were returned to their regiment via prisoner exchange. They were grateful to have survived their ordeal of starvation and suffering at the hands of the less-than-hospitable Confederate government. They could now sprawl in the comfort of the new camp at Harrison's Landing.[16]

By the time the prisoners returned to their regiment, the Hoosiers had long since moved their camp from the mud flats of the James to a more suitable location. In fact, as Dennis Tuttle noted, the Twentieth was now encamped in "a rather pleasant location within a few rods of a good sized stream of water and only about thirty rods from a dam and a large pond which sets back a mile and a half."[17] This mill pond afforded the Hoosiers a wonderful opportunity to escape the oppressive heat of the summer by taking a daily swim or a refreshing shower under the cooling sheet of water spilling over the dam.[18]

The health of the men improved, as did the bill of fare. The regiment erected ten bake ovens and Private Hooker could declare, "We have eschewed hard crackers and chewed fresh bread."[19] The sutlers gradually returned to the army and brought with them their high-priced delicacies, but there were a few items that could not be had at any price. Quartermaster Sergeant Dennis Tuttle wrote his wife requesting that she send him a box filled with "Will Tuttle's best brandy, chewing tobacco and lemons or something tart."[20]

The health and sustenance of the regiment may have improved but morale was low, further damaged by the raging debate over George McClellan's performance. When a division commander such as Kearny accused McClellan of cowardice or treason, then no better treatment could be expected from the likes of Horace Greeley. Although Kearny's comments were overheard by only a limited number of men, Greeley's thunderous condemnation rang throughout the entire North, carried by numerous Republican newspapers. The knife thrust into McClellan's back by the skillful Greeley was made even sharper by the Lincoln administration's silence. Adding to the natural Republican mistrust and dislike of Democrat McClellan was the opportunistic anti-war shrill of Copperhead Democratic newspapers. Papers such as the *Plymouth Democrat*, published by the virulent Daniel E. Van Valkenburg, were attacking the war effort to reinforce their own anti-abolitionist and pro-Confederacy positions.

The men of the Twentieth suffered to see their hero disparaged. They had been fooled by McClellan, but instead of accepting that he had ignominiously retreated, they endowed him with superhuman attributes and placed the blame on hidden enemies in the War Department and in the press. Dennis Tuttle reflected this when he told his wife, "If some men who are so wise in military matters, who never saw a battlefield and never will except in times of profound peace, should show themselves here, they would stand a good chance to get roughly handled. Nothing will quicker rouse the ire of this army than insults against its gallant and noble commander. Say what they will, McClellan will stand among the first if not the first general of the ages."[21]

Private Hooker had a somewhat different attitude, blaming neither McClellan, the administration nor the press when he penned a letter to the *Indianapolis Daily Journal*, "Truth compels me to say that the army is not in the best of spirits. In fact we feel as if we were pretty well tired out and want rest. We want to see more troops here and that soon. If the North would go into the fight with half the earnestness of purpose that the South does, it would soon be settled, but it doesn't. It is very easy to talk patriotism, but we want men, not promises. If there were about fifty regiments of Western troops here, it would not long be quiet on the James River."[22]

The tolerance of seditionist Copperheads, both at home and in the press, didn't sit well with any of the Hoosiers in the camp of the Twentieth Indiana. Sergeant Seymour Montgomery summed up the general attitude of the men in a letter home: "Why don't you shoot them at first sight? Either do this, or for God's sake, call your brothers from the field. It looks to us like folly for the Administration to keep this army here in the burning sun and sickly climate to put Rebels out of the way, whilst in the North, the Union men are protecting from just punishment, Rebels of a deeper dye than these poor deluded victims of Jeff Davis. You have within the lines of your county men who are doing the cause more damage than could be done here by a whole division of Rebels."[23]

The debate on the conduct of the war would continue to rage for months to come, with McClellan as the focal point. However strongly the Northern press might condemn him, his men loved him and had the confidence that with adequate forces and nonmilitary obstructions removed, McClellan would whip Robert E. Lee.

Before they could assist in the whipping of the Rebels, the Twentieth Indiana would be compelled to reorganize, recruit and refit. The losses of the Seven Days battles would have to be replaced and officers appointed to fill casualty-created vacancies in the regiment. Most companies in the regiment had fewer than fifty effective men. Lieutenant Colonel John Van Valkenburg, Lieutenants William Babbitt, William Carr, Henry Quigley, William Vatchett, William Babbington, and John Davis were detailed as recruiting officers in Indiana, their work to be done as they recovered from their battle ordeals.[24] Major John Wheeler was appointed as acting lieutenant colonel while Van Valkenburg was away from the regiment and Captain George Dick was appointed acting major.[25] Lieutenant Erasmus C. Gilbreath was promoted to captain to fill the vacancy created by James Lytle's death.[26]

One officer was under close scrutiny, and disapproval of him was obvious. Second Lieutenant Frederick Geisendorff had flat-out run from the battle on June 30, dropping his sword and all of his possessions at the first sign of trouble. The lieutenant had actually reached Harrison's Landing two days before his regiment had. Brown filed charges and asked that Geisendorff be dismissed for cowardice.[27] The lieutenant wisely resigned before official action could be taken and was spared the humiliation that dismissal would bring back home.

Major John Wheeler, enjoying his new status as acting lieutenant colonel, secretly began working for appointment to colonel in one of the new regiments being organized in Indiana. He wrote Speaker of the House of Representatives Schuyler Colfax, soliciting his support in influencing Governor Morton. Writing his wife he said, "I may as well be a colonel as a major if I can get it." He noted that he knew as much about soldiering as some of the brigadier generals.[28]

Illness accomplished what Rebel bullets and shells could not, as several of the men in the Twentieth either died or were forced to resign because of the ravages inflicted on them by mosquitoes, brackish water and sweltering heat. Private Edwin Sprague died of typhoid fever, and Wheeler had Sprague's body embalmed and shipped back to Crown Point.[29] Private James Conner from Pulaski County, Indiana, died of the same fever. His fifty-year-old father, who had walked with James to Monticello to enlist, was forced to bid farewell to his son and send his remains home to a mother who now had lost a son and feared losing her husband.[30] Private William Clark surveyed the broken, sick and battered bodies of the regiment, noted the sorrow they were causing, and proclaimed in a note to his sisters, "Here is one child that would give all he ever expected to have if he could get an honorable discharge."[31]

The renewed boredom of camp life was lessened somewhat by reinstituted drills, reviews and inspections. The regiment was drilled twice each day, once by company and the other time by either brigade or division. On July 23 McClellan conducted a grand review of Heintzelman's corps, which required the Twentieth Indiana to stand in an oppressive sun from 7:00 A.M. until 1:00 P.M. The men looked at it stoically and resolved themselves to its inevitability. The highlight of the review for the Hoosiers was their being singled out by General Kearny as the best marching regiment in the entire corps.[32]

Philip Kearny's admiration and respect for the Hoosiers was not feigned. A tough fighting general naturally loved a tough fighting regiment, and the Twentieth was tough. Kearny singled the Hoosiers out for merit to General McClellan and came to rely on the Western men to do the dirty work of his division when it came to fighting. Brigadier General Robinson felt the same about his fighting regiment. One afternoon, Robinson ordered Colonel Brown to conduct battalion drill instead of brigade drill because he did not want the Twentieth to become demoralized by the poor drill and attitudes of his New York and Pennsylvania regiments.[33] The admiration was reciprocated by the Hoosiers. They had the highest regards for Robinson, Kearny and, at last for their own Colonel Brown, who had demanded discipline and "conducted himself as cool, collected and brave as a Spartan in battle."[34]

While the common soldier on both sides was sweating under the burning Peninsular sun, generals and high elected officials plotted and planned the next moves in the bloody chess game. When McClellan's Army of the Potomac departed for the Peninsula, President Lincoln had taken the precaution of retaining a large Federal force in northern Virginia to protect Washington from any Rebel advance. This fifty-thousand-man force was divided into three widely dispersed corps and placed under the overall command of Major General John Pope. Pope, ever striving to advance his personal career, urged President Lincoln and General-in-Chief Henry W. Halleck to return the Army of the Potomac to northern Virginia and allow him to lead it in an advance on Richmond.

John Pope had parlayed several small successes achieved in the Western theater of the war into a position of high trust and responsibility. Pope blustered self-confidence to an extreme that disgusted most of his subordinates who frankly saw him as a windbag. He also issued a series of cruel orders: his men would live off their enemy's citizens, foraging at will with no regard to private property, guerrillas would be summarily executed and citizens sheltering them would be deprived of property, and disloyal citizens would be exiled outside the Union lines. This order, which dismayed the professional officers in the Union army and infuriated the Confederacy, was tantamount to a license to loot and pillage at will.

Robert E. Lee felt so strongly about it that he was disposed to write President Jefferson Davis recommending that Pope be suppressed. Lee's army, recovering from the loss of twenty thousand men in their recent battles, was not in the best of positions to suppress anyone. Firmly interposed between two large Union forces and the Rebel capital, Lee's troops were hard pressed to defend Richmond, let alone take offensive measures. However, Lee, the gambler and psychoanalyst, had faith that McClellan's offensive days were over, and on July 13 he dispatched Stonewall Jackson and two divisions sixty miles to the northwest of Richmond.

George McClellan was ordered to remove his army from the Peninsula and return them to northern Virginia. McClellan was certain that this movement was a preface to his removal from command and he dragged his feet, greatly delaying the process. While Pope made plans to concentrate his far-flung corps near Culpeper Court House, the proposed jumping-off location for his advance, Jackson's troops strained at the leash for their chance to get at the bragging general. The two Confederate divisions, protected by a cavalry screen, began moving up the Orange and Alexandria Railroad toward the Rapidan River near where Pope was concentrating his forces.

After much delay, McClellan surrendered to the inevitability of his orders and started his army in motion for their return. His grandiose strategic plan for the capture of Richmond was in ruins, as was, it appeared, his grandiose career. His subordinates regarded him highly and it was a demoralized group of generals who now made their way to join John Pope, whom they personally detested. They were in no hurry to join him or come to his assistance in any way, but, of course, duty called.

On August 10 the Army of the Potomac, then resting at Harrison's Landing, received their marching orders. The sick were removed to transports, knapsacks sent off, artillery mysteriously spirited away, and on August 15 the rear guard of the army, Heintzelman's corps, broke camp at daylight and proceeded down the Charles City Road on a very hazardous march through the heart of enemy territory. The army marched in two parallel lines, the main body, baggage and artillery taking the road running along the banks of the James River, with the right flank protected by gunboats and the left flank protected by the divisions of Hooker and Kearny. Heintzelman's corps was accompanied by its artillery and sufficient provisions for six days.[35]

The Twentieth Indiana filed through the Union army entrenchments at

10:00 A.M., following a brigade and its wagon train. The Virginia countryside rolled up to greet them in graceful slopes sharply contrasted against the clear blue sky and ripening fields of grain which bordered them. The column marched ten miles through beautiful country to Charles City Court House, where it halted for a brief rest before the march was resumed for the Chickahominy River.[36] After another hike of nine miles, the regiment encamped for the night within two miles of the Chickahominy, to the sound of engineers noisily and hastily building a bridge across the river.[37]

The next morning the regiment was up at 4:00 and marched without fanfare for two miles to the vicinity of Christian's Mill, where they halted and cooked breakfast. At this point, Colonel Brown energetically went to work having his men fell trees, dig rifle pits, and prepare breastworks for defense.[38] The men not engaged in this endeavor spent their time, according to Seymour Montgomery, "looking out for number one by causing hogs to stop squealing, hens to stop squawking and corn to stop ripening."[39]

General Robinson, expecting an incursion by Rebel cavalry against the rear guard of the army, prepared an ambuscade for them. Artillery was hidden in the bushes and overlapping fields of fire were laid out in preparation for the gray-clad horsemen. All of the men in the brigade were awake and on alert throughout the entire night but to no purpose, as the Confederate cavalry failed to make an appearance. At 3:00 A.M., with the main body of the army moving on, the Twentieth Indiana withdrew from their defensive position and marched for Burnt Ordinary, a point twelve miles from Williamsburg.[40] When the long march concluded at 5:00 P.M., the Hoosiers were greatly relieved to find excellent drinking water, the first they had experienced on the Peninsula. The thirsty soldiers gulped the cool, clean water until their stomachs ached.[41]

Colonel Brown roused the men at 4:30 A.M. on August 18 and started them on the road to Williamsburg. The marching column passed through James City and Orrinsville before finally arriving at Williamsburg at 1:00 P.M. The camp was established and the Hoosiers played tourist as they visited the historical buildings of the venerable capital of Virginia. With no pressure from pursuing cavalry, the brief stay at Williamsburg proved enjoyable and restful. However, the next morning found the Indiana boys up and marching at dawn, down through the tangled scrub and woods of this particular parcel of the Old Dominion, sloping down toward Yorktown and the York River. Passing through land so poor that "white beans would starve to death upon its soil," the men pushed on for miles with nothing to drink. They arrived at Yorktown at 4:00 P.M., but were too worn out from their trek to appreciate the historical significance of the ground where Cornwallis had surrendered to Washington.[42]

The men did appreciate the view of the York River which greeted them. Transports lined the river and assured the men that their hard marching was done for at least a little while. The hot, dusty, and thirsty Hoosiers rushed down the steep banks of the York River and dove into the salty river. Like schoolchildren on a lazy summer day, the men splashed and played with reckless abandon, forgetting for a time that they were at war. To the great surprise of the men, cascading from the side of a hill at the water's edge was a cool, crisp waterfall. After jigging in its refreshing spray for quite some time they dressed and pitched tents for the night.[43]

At noon the next day, the Twentieth Indiana marched down to the York River and boarded the transport *New York*. The work of loading baggage took many hours—it was 3:00 A.M. before the transport steamed down the river to the Chesapeake Bay. They sailed on up the Chesapeake until moving into the Potomac and advancing to Alexandria, Virginia. In the early morning light, the Hoosiers passed Mount Vernon, the home of George Washington, and then in the distance could see—"rising up like a pillar of salt"—the unfinished dome of the Capitol Building. The steamer continued to chug along and at sunset the men disembarked at the wharves in Alexandria.[44] The Hoosiers marched three miles out of town and lay down without tents or blankets on the wet ground and got what sleep they could. By morning they were thoroughly soaked and more then ready to move on.[45]

The regiment moved out on the morning of August 22 down the line of the Orange and Alexandria Railroad. There was much excitement as the men approached Catlett's Station, where it was discovered that Rebel guerrillas had made a raid on the place and burned wagons and supplies. They continued their march to within six miles of Warrenton, where the regiment made their camp in a large woods and were immediately detailed on picket duty.[46] There was a disturbing trend developing as to the use of the Twentieth Indiana. It reflected the high regard for the regiment that both Robinson and Kearny held the Hoosiers, but it did not bode well for the Indiana men. The Hoosiers were regularly being relied upon to serve as pickets for Heintzelman's corps, a corps generally being placed in the forefront of the action—first among the first to meet the danger. It became obvious that Kearny wanted the Hoosiers out front if and when he bumped up against the Confederate army.

The Indiana boys embraced Pope's "live off the land" strategy with vigor, quickly stripping the surrounding farms. Pigs, chickens, turkeys, geese, corn, and honey were bagged and eaten.[47]

The Twentieth Indiana continued its march, along with the rest of Heintzelman's corps, down the line of the Orange and Alexandria until they reached the Rappahannock River where, once again, they were sent to picket duty at water's edge and around the railroad bridge crossing the river. With the arrival of Union troops at this point, the army now controlled the line of the Rappahannock from its mouth to the Blue Ridge mountains.[48] Neither Stonewall Jackson nor any other Rebel general would be able to advance across the Rappahannock and successfully attack the Union army head on. But while the Hoosiers basked in the relative security of the Rappahannock River defenses, the Confederate army was on the move.

General Robert E. Lee had no intention of pitching into the Union army head on. On August 24 Lee ordered Stonewall Jackson to move west along the Rappahannock River, cross over the Bull Run Mountains and using the mountains and Jeb Stuart's cavalry as a screen, pass through Thoroughfare Gap and strike the Union army in its rear. James Longstreet's forces would take Jackson's place in the Confederate line and pin the Union army along the Rappahannock.

Jackson moved with much more speed than he had demonstrated during the Seven Days battles and drove his men mercilessly, covering fifty-four miles in forty hours. He had successfully passed by the Union army and now firmly straddled the Federal supply line on the Orange and Alexandria Railroad at Manassas Junction. Jackson's twenty-four-thousand-man corps created formidable damage at the Union supply station. Huge mountains of supplies of every description fell victim to the starved Rebel army. What couldn't be carried off was consumed by flames. The Union surprise was total, leaving nothing for General Pope to do but order his army to fall back to Manassas.[49]

The first indication for the Hoosiers that something was amiss came when they were disturbed from their slumber on August 26 by the sound of cannon fire coming from the direction of Washington. Any doubts about the source of the artillery fire vanished as the Hoosiers saw the dull orange glow of the Union supply dump burning in the black evening sky. As word of Jackson's coup ran like electricity down the Union line, officers hurried their men to their feet and ordered them in line for the forced march to Manassas.[50] The column pushed on without rest for twenty miles and finally arrived near Manassas where they went into camp at midnight.[51]

At noon on August 28 Heintzelman's corps slowly advanced in three columns on Manassas, expecting to bump into Jackson's Confederates at any moment. But to their surprise and the relief of many, Jackson was nowhere to be found. The Twentieth filed past the terrible destruction of military supplies and pressed on for Centreville, where they finally got to take a few pot shots at the rearguard of Jackson's forces. With no Rebels in sight, the regiment made camp and boiled coffee.[52] It would be a long, frightful night without sleep or knowledge of the whereabouts of a very potent enemy.

At twilight on August 28, Stonewall Jackson had finally found a location to make a defensive stand. Running roughly from southwest to northeast was an excavated, but not completed, railroad cut. Within this entrenchment-like position Jackson would make his stand while waiting for the arrival of General James Longstreet. Jackson struck the marching column of Brigadier General John Gibbon's troops—which would soon be dubbed the Iron Brigade—who were moving wearily along the Warrenton Turnpike, at 6:00 P.M. In a brief fight that lasted a little over an hour, he piled up the dead in heaps and decimated the Union brigade and large parts of two of his own divisions. This brief, sharp fight served as merely a prelude to the next day's events and Jackson was determined to make a fight here at Brawner's Farm at first light of day.

The early light of August 29 revealed no Union forces at the Brawner Farm. The Federal troops had decided to withdraw to Manassas in compliance with their earlier marching orders. Jackson did discover the Union corps of Major General Franz Sigel forming for battle to the north of him, on the exact grounds of the first Battle of Bull Run. This time the opposing battle lines would be flip-flopped from the positions they had held in the battle in 1861. Whether it was irony or the poetry of war, Jackson determined to repeat his earlier triumph.

At first light the Twentieth Indiana struggled to their feet and reluctantly fell in line for the move to the front. They were to have moved before this time, but Major General Phil Kearny had not moved with his traditional alacrity.[53] Consequently, by the time Kearny's division reached the field of battle, Sigel's attack on Jackson's Confederates was in full force, with Sigel sending brigade after brigade into the Rebel ranks. The Twentieth advanced over broken terrain for about three miles until they found themselves on an open hillside. To the Hoosiers' right and front, the Rebel lines extended along the ridge of a hill; to the left was a thick woods. A furious artillery duel was conducted between Sigel's batteries and those of the Confederates on the opposite ridge, with the Hoosiers in the middle.[54]

The results of this brutal fighting were inconclusive, although losses were great for both armies. Major General John Pope still hoped for a breakthrough with a frontal assault or, in lieu of that, a gradual decimation of Jackson so that Fitz John Porter's Fifth Corps could successfully crash down on the Rebel's right flank when he arrived on the field. Joseph Hooker saw the futility of an advance across open ground into the face of the menacing Confederate artillery. He persuaded Pope to allow an attack through a dense stand of cedar which might dislodge the Rebel batteries. He would need flank support from Kearny's division, but with any luck a great victory might be achieved. Hooker selected Brigadier General Cuvier Grover's brigade to make the attack and Phil Kearny chose his stalwart, Robinson's brigade, as the flank support.[55]

General Grover was startled when a staff officer rode up, pointed westward through the thick stands of cedar scrub and ordered him to attack. Grover asked if he would be supported and was curtly told that support would be coming. Grover followed orders and immediately launched a bayonet charge with his fifteen hundred men into the teeth of Jackson's forces. Grover's charge hit Brigadier General E. L. Thomas' brigade of Georgians flush on the chin and sent the Confederates reeling towards the rear. As Grover's men rushed out of the woods and up over the unfinished railroad cut, they could now see, if they had looked around, that their support was nonexistent. But there was no time to look around. Grover's brave men continued their headlong rush in pursuit of their quarry.[56]

Robinson ordered his men forward through the cedar woods in his front, with the Sixty-third and One Hundred and Fifth Pennsylvania in line of battle on the Leesburg road and the Twentieth Indiana and a stray Ohio battalion in reserve. The men could hear a terrible crashing of musketry on their left and front, signaling that Grover's attack was going on in full force. Kearny ordered that the men push their advance further and look for the opportunity to turn and wheel into the retreating Confederate flanks. That strategy might have worked had the movement been coordinated, but Grover was significantly forward of Robinson's brigade and the current brigade position was of no tactical use at this time.[57]

The headlong rush of Grover's unsupported brigade was now ripe for the picking by Jackson's men. Brigadier Generals Dorsey Pender's and Maxcy Gregg's brigades, without any immediate threat in their front, were in perfect position to stage a smashing counterattack on Grover, and this they did with a roaring vengeance. Grover's brigade was taken totally by surprise by the furious attack, and with his men worn out by the exertions of their running advance, they were in no condition to make a stand. Grover's men now were pursued across the same ground they had just won with casualties mounting. Without any attempt at rallying, the thoroughly beaten Federals rushed for the rear with Pender's and Gregg's Rebels in pursuit.[58]

The Twentieth Indiana admired the natural strength of the defensive position behind the railroad cut and its chin-high protective rim. From this position the regiment could repel any attack coming from its front, but Grover's retreat had eliminated this cut as a possibility. The dense column of screaming, gray-clad men passed within three hundred yards of the waiting Hoosiers, who were somewhat sheltered from view by the cedar trees. The head of the counterattack was six hundred yards east of the Twentieth; it appeared as if they might to be surrounded. Then one of those little accidents of war occurred which turned the tide.[59]

Stray bullets were flying all along the Union line; one of them, a .54-caliber minié ball, had pounded into the knapsack of Peter Schwartz, Company I. Schwartz was shaken by this near-death experience and mad as hell. He rose to his knees in the firing position and, while shouting curses in German, began firing at the passing Rebel forces. The entire regiment, "on the anxious bench" from their nervous predicament, also rose and joined Schwartz in firing volley after volley into the Confederates. Unsure as to who and what was on their flank, Pender's men made a quick about face and returned to their original lines, firing at the Hoosiers as they went.[60] This fire, much of it above the Hoosiers' heads, poured into the flank of the remainder of Robinson's brigade. Phil Kearny, sensing that the moment was right to strike, ordered his men forward across the high banks of the railroad cut and wheeled them as to advance down the cut.[61]

Kearny stood on top of the ridge of the unfinished railroad cut, waving his sword and hurrying his men forward. Colonel Brown ordered the Twentieth by right of companies to the rear and then had them cross the railroad cut in a grand wheeling motion, which the regiment executed as if on parade.[62] The Twentieth came under a fierce volley of musketry from the Thirteenth South Carolina, wounding several men in the regiment.[63] Colonel Brown shouted commands to advance and spurred his horse forward in the lead when a bullet struck him in the temple, killing him instantly and sending his horse galloping wildly to the rear. Captain George Dick, surviving bullets which three times struck near him, lifted the colonel's lifeless body onto his own horse and removed him from the battlefield.[64]

Robinson's brigade slowly drove the Thirteenth South Carolina backwards and then, behind it discovered the First South Carolina coming to their sister regiment's support. The First South Carolina crashed into the Twentieth with its full fury, blasting volley after volley into the Hoosiers.[65] Major Wheeler, now commanding the regiment, sat tall in his saddle and exhorted his men to hold their ground. A bullet ripped into Wheeler's instep and another struck his horse, causing both beast and major to fall in an awkward and painful heap. For Wheeler, who had yet to fully recover from the illness he'd contracted during the Seven Days, this was more than his weak body could handle. He turned the command over to Captain Dick, who had returned to the battlefield.[66]

The regiment, aligned roughly perpendicular to the railroad cut, took whatever cover they could find and returned the fire of the South Carolinians. Here Privates Edgar Ferguson and Daniel Heinmiller fell, killed by the intense rifle fire.[67] As Private Asher Chapman rose from behind his protective cover to fire at the South Carolinians, a bullet ripped into the end of his nose, leaving him with a lifelong reminder of Second Manassas.[68] The Hoosiers, recovering from the shock of seeing their colonel and major struck down, increased their fire and, with the Sixty-third and One Hundred and Fifth Pennsylvania, drove the First South Carolina back some three hundred yards.[69] It was tough work for Quartermaster Isaac Hart and his assistant struggling to run ammunition to the Twentieth, dodging both friendly and enemy bullets as they went. With ammunition running low, they were all that stood between the Twentieth and annihilation.[70]

General Kearny now sent three regiments of Brigadier General David Birney's brigade into the fray. The Fourth Maine, the Fortieth and the One Hundred and First New York advanced against the first line of the enemy. Assault after assault was made, depleting the strength of Stonewall Jackson's line and exhausting supplies of Rebel ammunition.[71] The Confederate line teetered on the brink of destruction, but Maxcy Gregg's battered regiments and Brigadier General Lawrence Branch's withered brigade bravely stood their ground. When it appeared that Kearny had successfully broken Jackson's line, the Union forces were blindsided by the arrival of Brigadier General Jubal Early's large brigade. Twenty-five hundred howling Rebels ran pell-mell into the breach and drove the battle-weary Federals backward. Adding to the fury of Early's attack was the enfilading artillery bombardment by Crenshaw's and Braxton's batteries posted on Stony Ridge.[72]

The hunters became the hunted. The Twentieth Indiana watched as hundreds of battle-shredded men fled by them, running for the rear. As artillery shells pounded all around them and bullets whizzed by, the Hoosiers hugged the ground and fired supporting volleys when they could. Captain Dick, supported by the "brave coolness" of Captains George Meikel, Charles Bell, William Taylor, and James Shannon, ordered a fighting withdrawal and the men of the Twentieth slowly moved back to a spot under the protection of an elevated Union battery. From there, Kearny's division was rallied by the heroic one-armed general and beat back the repeated charges of Early's brigade. Early's men rushed forward with hideous yells, confident of the destruction of Robinson's brigade. They emerged from the woods behind the railroad cut and, catching sight of the battery, formed and charged, only to be driven back. Again they charged and the bullets and shells from the Union position drove them back. A third time they appeared in larger force, with a fresh regiment and charged to within four hundred yards of the battery when a "perfect storm of shell and grape" from several batteries opened upon them and sent them reeling back into the woods. Kearny launched a counterattack, driving the Rebels back through the woods and over the railroad cut.[73] When the blackness of night overcame the battlefield, the Hoosiers found themselves in roughly the same position as they were when they first advanced to the railroad cut.

The Twentieth Indiana was thoroughly depleted due to little sleep, hunger, the exertions of battle, and the worry about the immediate future. What would come next? Once again, the regiment rested on their arms, unable to sleep peacefully, expecting a Rebel attack at any moment. A burial detail brought in their dead comrades and hastily buried them in shallow graves. The casualties in the regiment had fallen heavily on new recruits who had just arrived. Of the seventeen new men, only two were left standing in the ranks; the remainder were casualties of the brutal fighting.[74]

At daylight on Saturday, August 30, Kearny's weary division was pulled out of the battle line and was moved to the extreme right of the Union line, in a supporting position. It was replaced by Rickett's division of Irwin McDowell's corps. Kearny directed the Twentieth Indiana to guard one of the fords of the Bull Run from the heights of a considerably elevated hill. From this location, the Hoosiers were within easy artillery range of Rebel batteries at Sudley Springs. In addition, this elevated position offered the Indiana men a panoramic view of the entire Union line.[75] From their cedar thicket blind of the previous day, it had been difficult for the Hoosiers to appreciate exactly what was going on around them. From this elevated view, they could readily understand their hotly contested fight for the railroad cut.

The battles of the two previous days had not given Major General John Pope any reason to panic. Gibbon had fought two Confederate divisions to a standstill at Brawner's Farm on the August 28, and the battle of Groveton, as the fight on August 29 has come to be called, was a stalemate as well. True, the Union brigades were fed into the fight piecemeal with little tactical cooperation, but Pope was really only fighting a holding action while he awaited the arrival of Major General Fitz John Porter's Fifth Corps. What Pope failed to account for was the dilatory march of Porter's corps to the field of battle and for the surprising, timely arrival of Major General James Longstreet's Confederates. Misunderstanding these events would destroy his army and his career.

Porter's Fifth Corps sauntered too slowly down the Sudley Springs road on August 29 to be of any use in that day's fighting. Had these ten thousand men been thrown on Jackson's right flank, the Second Battle of Manassas might have been the final battle of the Civil War. John Pope still hoped to take advantage of this formidable force and intended to use them as the spearhead of an attack on Jackson's right flank on August 30. Even though Brigadier General John Reynolds had informed Pope of a large presence of the enemy on the Federal left flank, the Union commander chose to ignore the ominous warning and launched the attack. The Federal attack had no more started when it ground to a halt, shattered by a tremendous artillery bombardment from a line of cannon in the direction of the Brawner Farm. As the attack faltered, McDowell, in nominal command of the Union left flank, ordered eight thousand additional troops northward from Chinn Ridge, leaving only one thousand men to guard the left flank. The fateful moment had come for the Union army. James Longstreet ordered his twenty-five thousand men to attack down the Warrenton Road, squarely into the lightly defended Union left flank.

Longstreet's soldiers rushed with abandon down the Warrenton Road, brushing the token Federal resistance aside. The surprise of the attack was complete and overwhelming. There was no time to organize an effective defense; as Longstreet's divisions poured into the Union rear, Pope's hope for a decisive victory went up in smoke. It was now a case of simple survival as the Union army fell back in a rout in the direction of Washington.

The Hoosiers of the Twentieth Indiana had witnessed the grand spectacle before them as Porter's corps advanced against the Confederate lines. The had seen the great puffs of smoke from the hundreds of artillery pieces and heard the deep-throated booming of the cannon. The pageantry of the Federal army moving forward, turning and rushing away as a leaderless mob was displayed before their eyes in panoramic form. To Erasmus Gilbreath it was "an awe inspiring picture of disaster."[76]

Near 5:00 P.M., as the fighting died down and the battle evolved into a footrace between the pursued and the pursuer, the Twentieth Indiana was drawn back from their position for a mile to the Brown House. The Hoosiers took their new position in a small woods adjacent to the farmhouse and hastily stacked a hurried breastwork for defense. While staunchly waiting for the victoriously pursuing Confederates to arrive, thousands of battle-weary, demoralized soldiers either trudged by in despair or ran by like scared rabbits. An unknown, gallant man of the cloth came running into the midst of the retreating mob and exhorted the men to rally and halt the advancing Rebels. He appealed to them for the sake of their homes and their parents to defend the ground at all costs.[77] His appeals, as one would imagine his sermons, fell on deaf ears; the only response was the derisive laughter of the soldiers who had learned the ancient axiom that "he who fights and runs away, lives to fight another day."

At this time an advance Rebel battery got the range of the Hoosiers' positions and opened a destructive fire on and around the Brown House. Several men were wounded, including Gilbreath's loyal Negro servant Zeke, who was killed by the flying shrapnel. This artillery fire startled the loyal chaplain, who now forgot about God and country and sprinted for safety as quickly as any soldier that he had tried to rally. It was in this exposed position that the Twentieth Indiana and the remainder of Robinson's brigade were ordered to wait while the rest of the army melted from sight.[78]

Darkness came and caused the relentless Rebel pursuit to stop. Robinson's brigade was now virtually surrounded by Confederates. Phil Kearny had taken charge of the rearguard, and his placement of Robinson's men left them out on the line to dry. At 8:00, Robinson received word that he could withdraw his men as best he could and passed orders along for the Twentieth Indiana to hold their position until the rest of the brigade had marched off. Slowly and quietly, listening to the shouted orders and boisterous yelling of Rebels in the darkness, the Hoosiers slipped away from their position and marched almost in parade order to Centreville. They arrived a little after midnight and immediately prepared a defensive position for the attack they knew would follow the next morning.[79]

The skies were overcast and a steady rain drizzled down on the Hoosiers on August 31, as they prepared for the worst. Another sleepless night and hunger-crazed day passed as the weary Indiana boys waited for an attack to be made. The rearguard action of Saturday evening had stalled the Confederate pursuit just enough to allow a formidable defensive line to be erected at Centreville. Robert E. Lee wanted to avoid a head-on attack with his dead-tired soldiers and resolved to maneuver the Union forces out of their position at Centreville or, if lucky, stage another Second Manassas. To that end, Lee sent Jackson's men on a swooping seven-mile end run with the eventual goal of interposing them between the Union forces at Centreville and Washington, D.C. To support this action, Longstreet would follow Jackson and attempt another of his smashing flank attacks. Jackson's men were just too weary to move and did not reach Ox Hill until late on the afternoon of September 1, by which time two Union divisions awaited their arrival.

In a driving rainstorm, punctuated by bolts of lightning and claps of thunder, Brigadier General Isaac Stevens drove into Jackson with two divisions of Federal troops. Stevens himself was killed leading the charge. Phil Kearny's division rushed to the support of Stevens, and Brigadier General David Birney's brigade became locked in furious combat with Major General A. P. Hill's Confederates in a cornfield on the estate known as Chantilly. As the wounded men of Stevens' force fell back toward Kearny, the characteristically brave and reckless general rode his horse into the cornfield to rally them. In the premature darkness of late afternoon, Kearny confused a group of Georgians for Federal troops. Discovering his error, he spurred his horse and wheeled around to make his getaway. The Georgians fired a quick volley at the hard-riding general and their bullets found their mark, killing Kearny instantly. The firing quickly sputtered out and brought the brief vicious fight to a close with each side losing about five hundred men.[80]

Robinson's brigade, bringing up the rear of Kearny's division, arrived on the field too late to engage, but once again was given the onerous task of serving as rearguard. The evening proved uneventful and the brigade marched back to Centreville and from there to Arlington Heights, Robert E. Lee's home (and the present-day location of Arlington National Cemetery). At Arlington Heights, Robinson's brigade and its Hoosiers went into camp and began the long process of healing, both physically and organizationally.

The deaths of Colonel William Lyon Brown and Major General Philip Kearny were terrible emotional blows to the Hoosiers of the Twentieth Indiana. Colonel Brown had been a stern disciplinarian whom the men had come to respect at last for his dedication and attention to detail. He had proven his bravery on several occasions and, although he may not have been loved by his men, his leadership certainly was going to be missed. Sergeant Marquis Winch still thought otherwise and wrote: "He was disliked by both officers and men and there were not many tears shed over his death."[81]

Kearny's loss was another matter altogether. His renown had grown to almost mythic proportions for the men in his division. He was a general of unquestioned personal valor and reckless fighting qualities. A lesser man might have relaxed with his million-dollar fortune and let poorer men fight the war, but Phil Kearny loved to fight and loved his country too much to sit by. The Hoosiers loved the one-armed devil and it was reciprocated. The Twentieth Indiana was, perhaps, Kearny's favorite regiment. He treated it as he did himself, always putting it in the way of danger. Instead of feeling mistreated, the Hoosiers took great pride in this proof of Kearny's high regard. There would be many fields of battle in the future for the Twentieth Indiana and many commanders, but they would never be as ably led as they were by Philip Kearny.

CHAPTER SEVEN

THE LEAST POSSIBLE GOOD

While his comrades in the Twentieth Indiana spent August marching and fighting, Lieutenant Colonel John Van Valkenburg had spent his time recovering from his leg wound and recruiting fresh men for his regiment. The late summer days passed in the company of his family were pleasant, but his life changed abruptly when Van Valkenburg received the telegram informing him of the death of Colonel Brown and his promotion to colonel of the Twentieth Indiana.

Van Valkenburg gathered up his recruits and proceeded to Indianapolis to depart by train for the seat of war. It had been quite some time since he had been paid, owing to his absence from the regiment, and Van Valkenburg found his personal finances in distress. When he arrived in Indianapolis, he went to an acquaintance of his in town and asked to borrow fifty dollars. The friend, Mr. Reynolds, hesitated to loan the colonel money with the blunt pronouncement, "I don't like the idea of loaning money to a man that is fighting under this damned nigger administration." Van Valkenburg promised to send the money as soon as he arrived at his regiment and Reynolds relented and gave him forty dollars.[1] With his financial burden eased, Van Valkenburg returned to his regiment in Virginia with his eighty-five new recruits and assumed his command.

What had caused Mr. Reynolds' venomous response to Van Valkenburg's request? The answer was simple: emancipation. For more than a year, the Northern states had put aside their disparate regional interests and differences in social philosophy to fight the Confederacy on the one basis on which they agreed, the preservation of the Union. To be sure, from the outset of the war, there were those who had other agendas and advocated war for financial or personal gain. Simmering just below the surface of the Northern people was a large and growing group, the abolitionists, who felt war was the only answer to the burning question of slavery. In the first year of the Civil War, the abolitionists were a distinct minority of the populace, a group merely to be used and tolerated by the government. However, as the war ground on and Union forces occupied Southern territory, giving the common man and the inquiring media a close-up view of the ugly institution of slavery, the ranks and shrill outcry of the abolitionists grew.

The typical Northern soldier, particularly those from the Western states, looked down on the Negro as inferior. As for slavery, the attitudes of the men could be broken down into one of three views on the institution. The first group believed that the United States government had no right to interfere with the Southern states on the issue of slavery, but believed that the necessity of preserving the Union overrode their beliefs on slavery. These men did not view the Negro as an equal in any respect and harbored deep-seated prejudices. The second group had a benign attitude about slavery. They felt that the institution of slavery was wrong, but certainly not worth a civil war to end it. The general attitude, one originally shared by Abraham Lincoln, was that the institution would eventually die out on its own accord. The final, and smallest, but most vocal group, were the abolitionists. This growing element of the population, for reasons either of religious or personal conviction, believed in the absolute equality of man. To the abolitionist, the Civil War was a holy war and, as they viewed it, there could be no just conclusion to the war without the total destruction of slavery.

Added to the red hot debate over abolition and slavery was intensely partisan politics. Political differences had been set aside for the first year of the war as the Union rallied upon itself. Now, after bitter defeats on the Peninsula and in northern Virginia, veteran politicians of both parties— both in Washington and in the state capitals of the North—jockeyed to benefit from the chaos. The stakes were high and there were no Marquis of Queensberry rules of fair play. Quarter was neither asked nor given.

Abraham Lincoln was prepared to add the final ingredient to this national stew of open rebellion, military disasters and social upheaval. That ingredient was emancipation of the slave. The President had long contemplated a decree that would free the Negro from the yoke of slavery. He had debated it with his cabinet openly during the summer, but these careful men suggested that to issue such a proclamation on the heels of a defeat would appear to be the last act of a dying government. Lincoln pocketed his proposal, but told his cabinet that he would revisit the issue at the appropriate time. That time quickly arrived with the Union victory at the Battle of Antietam on September 17, 1862.

From the great despair following the disastrous Federal defeat at Second Manassas, Union fortunes took a decided turn for the better with the discovery, by two Hoosier soldiers from the Twenty-seventh Indiana, of Special Order 191, the top-secret order detailing the distribution of Rebel forces then invading Maryland. Armed with this intelligence, George B. McClellan, once again in command of the Army of the Potomac after Pope's terrible performance at Manassas, ordered the concentration of his army with the intent of destroying Lee's Army of Northern Virginia in piecemeal fashion. After fighting the bloodiest one-day battle in the history of the United States, Lee's severely outnumbered army was compelled to retreat across the Potomac River into Virginia. Although the Battle of Antietam was a tactical fiasco for McClellan, once again showing his ineptitude as a battlefield commander, the Confederates did leave the field of combat in the hands of the Union army, the standard method of determining who was the victor of the day.

This victory provided the opportunity for which Lincoln had sought to issue his Emancipation Proclamation and, accordingly, he did so on September 22, 1862. This single act became the defining moment of the Civil War and forever changed the face of the war and the history of this country. No longer would this be just a war to preserve the Union. It became a war to address the one issue which had eaten away at the national fiber since the birth of the United States. The Civil War officially became a war between the preservation of the Southern way of life, (including the almost indefinable concept of state's rights) and the preservation of the Union (including the reaffirmation of "We hold these truths to be self-evident . . .").

With the Emancipation Proclamation, the nation entered into possibly the most controversial and tumultuous six months in our history. Wars of words and deeds were fought within the greater Civil War which came closer to toppling the government than any of the fighting had done. The vicious, take-no-prisoners, philosophical war touched everyone, including the Hoosiers of the Twentieth Indiana, who were now drawn up on Arlington Heights, defending Washington and licking their wounds from their ordeal at Second Manassas.[2]

After the disaster at Second Manassas, the average soldier clamored for the return of George B. McClellan to the command of the Army of the Potomac. Sergeant Harvey Miller wrote his grandmother, expressing his disdain for those he blamed for the Union disasters: "Little Mac is the man. Let abolitionists howl and politicians do their best and the generals all combined do their worst, for he has one hundred thousand brave men on his side."[3]

Captain Charles Reese revealed the typical attitude toward the Negro, which he shared with many of his comrades, in a letter to his brother:

How is Joseph Fisher and his nigger regiment? Has he got it full yet? He ought to command a lot of niggers, let him get up a nigger regiment and arm them with shovels and picks, make them ditch. That's the way to use niggers, they will never fight.[4]

Sergeant Seymour Montgomery reflected the views of the majority of the men in the regiment when he wrote to the *Howard Tribune* for the purpose of publicly expressing his views:

I am not opposed to the spirit of the Proclamation, but thought then, and do now, that it was brought forward at an improper time. By saying that I am not opposed to the spirit, it must not be inferred that I am an Abolitionist, on the contrary, I am as much opposed to that principle, as advocated by a faction at the North, as any man can be; but the South, in bringing about and waging this unholy rebellion have thrown the institution of slavery into the scales, and if the blotting out of the whole thing will bring about a peace, I say Amen to it. The South have thrown down the gauntlet, and if it is taken up, they alone are to blame. Opposed as I have always been to meddling with that peculiar institution in the states where it already existed, I can now go for wiping the entire system out, without the least compromise of principle.[5]

Lieutenant Colonel Wheeler had a more pragmatic attitude about emancipation when he wrote in his diary:

Well the Proclamation is at last out and I suppose the North is satisfied. But I can't for my life see any benefit to be gained from it. Are slaves free as they will be in ninety days in Virginia, the Carolinas and all the other states unless we conquer them? I am confident that the Rebels have got to be whipped, conquered and subdued before that Proclamation can reach a single slave. But any way to quiet and settle the divisions constantly getting up among our people and all by those who know no more of war, of battles, of the enemy, their strength, determination and all connected with the War. A little more attention to honest sober and candid conclusions would be a benefit to the Nation. Slavery is the cause and must be rooted out, but why this clamor for such a

Proclamation. I can't see as a thing is gained by it, except to pacify a clamorous division of the people. It will do no harm or good, unless I am much mistaken.[6]

It was into this environment of hatred, bigotry, and hope that the Twentieth Indiana now passed. The single unifying issue which provided the only glue binding the Union army together was the preservation of the Union. Other issues would divide and demoralize as time went on, but men with names of Oliver Hazard Perry Johnson, Benjamin Franklin Cook, George Washington Foster, and William Harrison Dawson would put issues of emancipation aside and fight on to preserve a unified nation.

Before the Twentieth Indiana could be a formidable fighting force again, they needed to replenish the ranks and restructure their command. Serving as Colonel John Van Valkenburg's immediate subordinate would be newly appointed Lieutenant Colonel John Wheeler. Captain George Dick, in reward for his brave conduct in battle, was promoted to major. Israel N. Stiles received the good news that he was promoted to major of the Sixty-third Indiana Infantry, thereby creating a vacancy which was filled by John F. Thomas. William S. Babbitt, Charles Reese, John E. Sweet, Thomas H. Logan, Erasmus C. Gilbreath, and John C. Brown were all promoted to captain, filling vacancies caused by casualties or promotions.[7]

The men of the Twentieth had just caught their breath on Arlington Heights when they were dispatched on picket duty. Early in the morning on September 16, the Hoosiers, accompanied by the One Hundred and Forty-first Pennsylvania, passed through the Union line and made their way over hills and through valleys in the direction of Bull Run.

The regiments in the brigade had been charged with returning to the Manassas battlefield and burying the dead. They found the dead in "every condition of decay and rottenness." Dead horses and scattered pieces of clothing and equipment of all description lay thick on the field of battle.[8] It was stomach-retching work, and the men were happy to leave the battlefield and take up picket. Rebels had been reported in the area and the regiment spent a worried twenty-four hours in a driving rainstorm, peering out into the deluge, looking for an enemy that did not come. A few Rebel stragglers were discovered and apprehended, and it gave great pride to the Hoosiers to escort these ragtag vagabond remnants of the great Confederate army back to their camp at Arlington Heights.

These few prisoners were not exactly the flower of the Confederacy. General Lee had taken the best the Confederacy had to offer and headed north into Maryland. After Antietam, Lee was forced to withdraw into Virginia, while Major General George B. McClellan plotted his pursuit of the wounded foe. The beautiful early days of autumn passed without the exchange of hostile rifle fire and the regiment spent its time drilling, policing its camp and doing the obligatory picket duty. General McClellan seemed in no hurry to tangle with the Army of Northern Virginia any time soon. Many of the men in the Army of the Potomac viewed this inaction favorably, a sign of McClellan's military brilliance. President Lincoln, his cabinet, Congress, the Northern newspapers, and a few anxious military men viewed the inaction as a continued indication that McClellan just didn't have the heart to prosecute the war with the dedication necessary to bring the Confederacy to its knees.

The Hoosiers didn't give it much thought. In the past twelve months they had experienced hunger, thirst, exposure to the elements, hard marching, and even harder fighting. This period of inactivity in the relative safety of their current camp seemed to satisfy most of the men. Grand reviews occupied the time and energy of both officers and men. On October 1 General Heintzelman held a review of his corps at Bailey's Crossroads, a grand affair, but one conducted in a sweltering heat. As a result of the four-mile march to the review ground, the exhausting all-day wait in the sun, and the return march to camp, the Hoosiers were thoroughly tired. The review had taken its toll on the men, but on none more than Private William Mutchler, Company B. Mutchler was standing guard the next day when he fell flat on his face and died, the apparent victim either of a heart attack or of a general's excesses.[9]

The common soldier and the parasite-like sutlers who plied their wares existed in a love-hate relationship in these Army of the Potomac camps. The sutler business was the epitome of supply and demand, with soldiers demanding the goods and comforts which were not provided by their government. Sutlers continually drove up prices to the maximum possible, and when the soldiers' cash ran out they were more than happy to extend credit. On October 1 tempers flared. Whether it was a disagreement with sutler John Watson, from Peru, Indiana, or just the reaction of a tired and angry group of soldiers returning from the review who came upon the sutler and remembered past issues, the result was a full-fledged assault on the sutler's wagon. The men looted every last item from the distraught sutler and even dismantled the wagon for their campfires.[10] Thus, learning what many Confederate soldiers already knew—you didn't tangle with the Twentieth Indiana—sutler Watson returned to Peru and less dangerous, albeit less lucrative, pursuits.

Celebrity political visits provided temporary relief from boredom. The Hoosiers received a welcome visit from Governor Oliver P. Morton on October 7, during the tour he was making of Indiana regiments serving in the east.[11] Gone were any feelings of animosity that the men may have felt about the governor who sent them off to war with smoothbore muskets. Instead, Morton was warmly received and vigorously cheered at the conclusion of his congratulatory remarks to the men. An entire lake of water had gone over the dam since the gun confrontation. The governor could tell by the bullet-tattered and battle-stained regimental flags that these Indiana boys had not only seen, but had been trampled by the elephant in the past several months. He proudly announced to the regiment that the state of Indiana would present the Twentieth Indiana with a new stand of colors to replace the current sad remnant. He asked the men to return their flags to Indiana where they could be displayed to the public, attesting to the bravery of the men who defended them. The Hoosiers gave a most hearty three cheers for the governor.[12]

With the exception of Morton's visit, the month of October proved uneventful for the Indiana men. As the green of summer turned to the brilliant gold, purple, and crimson of autumn, the Hoosiers passed their days in the tedium of drill, picket and the monotony of camp life. The regiment daily awaited the arrival of Colonel John Van Valkenburg, a man viewed by Assistant Quartermaster Dennis Tuttle as inferior to Colonel Brown and less desirable for the position of colonel than John Wheeler.[13] Wheeler concurred with Tuttle's opinion and shared with his wife the view that "many of the men in the regiment think Van Valkenburg is a coward."[14]

While the regiment awaited their new colonel, President Abraham Lincoln anxiously awaited some sign of movement on the part of General McClellan and the Army of the Potomac. McClellan, for his part, spent the month of October refitting and resting his army. When impatiently quizzed by the President as to why his men had not moved, McClellan responded that his horses were fatigued. The beleaguered President quickly shot back a request that he be informed of exactly what the horses had done since Antietam to become fatigued. The warning signs were undeniable to McClellan: his commander-in-chief was unhappy. The army would have to move soon or he might be back at the job of running a railroad. Accordingly, McClellan deigned to move.

In late October Robinson's brigade made a series of short marches and changes of camp which brought it to the vicinity of Poolesville, Maryland. A driving rainstorm in this area, with no tents for shelter, meant a miserable time for the Hoosiers. Sergeant Marquis Winch and a companion were forced to straddle a log, back to back, with a blanket over their heads, in an effort to get some sleep in the rain.[15] The brigade was to rejoin the main body of the Army of the Potomac which had finally started to inch its way toward Virginia. On Sunday, October 26, the Twentieth fell in line early in the morning in a driving rainstorm and marched for the Potomac River, where they assumed the customary picket duty. On Tuesday the regiment marched five miles to White's Ferry. The boys arrived expecting to cross the Potomac on a wire, chain, or pontoon bridge, but to their chagrin, they were forced to wade the waist-deep, cold river. The river was extremely wide at White's Ferry and the men quickly got over the "novelty of the thing." They went into camp, once again in "old Virginny."[16]

The "long roll" was beaten on Friday, October 31, before dawn, and the Twentieth once again formed in column with knapsacks slung and haversacks full. With flags flying and bands playing martial tunes, the army paraded through the little hamlet of Leesburg under the stares of five hundred unimpressed Confederate inhabitants, then went into camp.[17]

Late in the evening of November 1, Private John Vanderbark and Sergeant Seymour Montgomery liberated a large quantity of straw from a secessionist barn, neatly and evenly spread it on the ground, and placed a blanket over it. The two weary soldiers plunked down on the soft bed of straw underneath another blanket, quite content with this comfortable arrangement. Just as the two men were drifting into the arms of Morpheus, an orderly came running through the camp, calling the men of Companies D and I to march immediately. Jolted awake, the men quickly took their place in line with knapsacks slung and tents on their backs and within five minutes were marching down the Washington Road towards an unknown destination.[18]

The haste of the march and the necessity of using every available wagon for transporting provisions limited the Hoosiers to taking with them only what they could carry. Extra blankets, tent halves, and other items of comfort were left behind. Vanderbark and Montgomery said a sad good-bye to the straw mattress.[19]

After a quick march of nearly four miles, the men arrived at the burned-out remnant of the Goose Creek Bridge. It seems that in the haste of making camp, someone had forgotten this potential avenue of advance for the Rebel army and thought it provident to send the Hoosiers to keep an eye on the ferry. Winter was certainly on the way; the night was extremely crisp and cold. Montgomery and Vanderbark spent a miserable night peering out sleepily into the dark. Morning light revealed that the Hoosiers were in the midst of an abandoned line of Confederate fortifications. Taking turns, the Hoosiers went out in search of suitable breakfast fare and soon returned with chickens and other ingredients necessary for an enjoyable breakfast.[20]

The boys remained at Goose Creek until noon, when they marched back down the Washington Road to rejoin their regimental mates, who were already packing up and readying themselves for another move. The division of which Robinson's brigade was a part was now commanded by General

George Stoneman. Stoneman ordered the division forward at 5:00 P.M., and by sundown the men were snaking their way down the eastern slope of the Blue Ridge Mountains. At midnight the column passed through Mt. Gilead and continued on to a camp some ten miles from Leesburg, where slow, fat Rebel chickens and turkeys were found and summarily dispatched.[21] The Indiana boys also discovered the mill of a local rabid secessionist and commandeered the mill for their own use. Soon a detail of experienced millers was busy grinding up corn meal and flour for the Hoosiers to use to bake corn dodgers and pancakes. Assistant Quartermaster Tuttle confiscated the remaining grain and attended to the needs of the regimental supply horses.[22] The folks in this part of Virginia were quickly learning to keep their Confederate sentiments to themselves if they had anything of value that a hungry Yankee might need or want.

The next morning the Hoosiers commenced putting up tents and laying out the trappings of a good camp. A feast of turkey and crackers was prepared and eaten with appropriate zeal by the march-weary men. Visions of a morning nap passed from the minds of the men when a shrill bugle sounded the call to fall in. The Hoosiers passed through beautiful country of verdant pine trees, marching up hill and down through the villages of Unionville and Spring Hill until stacking arms late in the evening. As they marched they could hear the faint sound of gunfire in the distance, in the direction of Snickers Gap. The Confederate rear guard was holding a reluctant McClellan at bay.[23]

As the Hoosiers marched deeper into Rebeldom, they found their reception by the locals to be increasingly hostile. The few citizens who remained in the little hamlets along the line of march went out of their way to be rude and uncooperative. One of the privates of Company I, canteen empty and parched with thirst, made his way to the well of a farmhouse along the line of march. Finding no bucket or rope at the well, he asked the lady of the house where the well bucket was. She replied that there wasn't one, whereupon he quickly retorted that a well without a bucket was useless and should be filled in with fence rails. He started to disassemble a nearby fence and drop a rail into the well when his feisty Rebel foil came running out with the bucket.[24]

The Indiana boys spent the entire day of November 4 resting and writing letters home. The men knew better than to pitch tents only to be disappointed by a call to march again, so a blanket tossed on the ground or on a few hastily assembled cornstalks was their only comfort. The camp was full of rumors and speculation about the next move of the Army of the Potomac. While officials in Washington encouraged McClellan to bring the Army of Northern Virginia to battle on the north side of the Rappahannock, the average soldier and below-average general, McClellan, seemed content to recline or plan in camp while the Rebel army withdrew to its sturdy line of defenses south of the river.[25]

Before sunlight on November 5 the brigade was once again called to arms and set in motion. The column moved three miles to the formerly thriving village of Middleburg, where the Hoosiers found the once-proud buildings falling into decay and Rebel sick and wounded taking refuge in the beautiful church. The regiment scooped up three Rebels who were hiding in a brick house and made them prisoners.[26] It wasn't exactly stealth that enabled the Hoosiers to make the capture. They were talking to the little lad of the house when he blurted out, "You all don't wear clothes like the soldiers upstairs."[27] The Confederate stragglers were a filthy and ragged crew, and from their appearance Sergeant Seymour Montgomery concluded that the South was "pretty near out of soap."[28] The prisoners were placed in the middle of the regiment and the march resumed uphill as the column approached the table lands known as White Plains.

The column pressed on through the small hamlet of White Plains, on the Manassas Gap Railroad, and proceeded another four miles before bivouacking for the night. It had been a hard march but one that had not passed without amusing moments. Along the march, the Hoosiers had chanced upon an attractive Rebel residence. A Union sentry had been posted at the door of the dwelling to protect its contents from pilfering by the hungry horde. The Hoosiers recognized the sentry to be from a newly arrived regiment, green in the ways of the wily forager. One of the Hoosier privates impersonated a corporal and ordered the sentry relieved from his guard post. With this obstruction removed, the hungry Indiana boys cleaned out the well-stocked cellar of the absent Rebel and made off with his prized inventory of molasses.[29]

After a brief night's rest, the regiment arose in the blackness of night and headed to Salem, which was overflowing with the cavalrymen of Major General Alfred Pleasonton's cavalry corps. At Salem, the Twentieth Indiana found seven additional Rebel stragglers, bringing the total bag of prisoners in the last week to twenty-five. From Salem, Robinson's brigade moved down the Waterloo Road and at 9:00 P.M., stopped within four miles of the village, rumored to be in the hands of the Rebel army.[30]

Now came the potential dirty work of driving the Rebels out of Waterloo and, as usual, the Twentieth Indiana was called upon to do the task. The Hoosiers were allowed to rest until 2:00 A.M. and then, without any food, were started on the double quick for Waterloo. Two companies under the command of Lieutenant Colonel Wheeler led the advance, working as skirmishers as they deployed towards the river. The Hoosiers arrived hard on the heels of the retreating Rebels, who crossed an adjacent creek and burned the bridge. The Indiana boys halted their pursuit in the blackness of night and awaited the first rays of morning light to renew their advance. Morning light found the Rebels defending themselves in an old mill on the creek. A sharp and furious firefight commenced between the two forces, with neither side prepared to call off the action. Soon a solitary Union field piece was brought to the scene and four quick shots into the mill sent its occupants reeling towards the south bank of the Rappahannock. The Twentieth Indiana followed up and when evening fell, found themselves in possession of the north bank of the upper Rappahannock.[31]

While the Hoosiers were chasing their foe across the river, events of greater magnitude were occurring elsewhere. Abraham Lincoln had finally reached the end of his rope with McClellan. He knew that he must take decisive action in regard to his recalcitrant commander, and he had selected the little general's replacement. Already on two separate occasions, Lincoln had pressed Major General Ambrose E. Burnside, one of McClellan's subordinates, to take McClellan's place, but the Indiana expatriate had declined, citing inexperience in handling a large body of men. Now, faced on November 7 with the ultimatum that either he would take command or, with his refusal, allow his fellow corps commander, Joseph Hooker, whom he detested, to assume command of the Army of the Potomac, Burnside acquiesced and agreed to take the reins of the massive army.[32]

Burnside's reluctance should not have been brushed aside by Lincoln. Ambrose Burnside may have had many faults, but false modesty was not one of them. Burnside's performance as a field commander was mediocre at best and disastrous at worst. His failure to launch the attack of the Ninth Corps in a timely fashion at Antietam allowed the best chance for an early end to the Civil War to slip away. The common soldier, instinctively realizing his inadequacy, viewed him as a temporary occupant of the seat of command, a mere caretaker awaiting the return of the beloved McClellan.

Burnside's overpowering responsibilities quickly made him physically ill, but did not get in the way of his formulation of a bold plan of action and a plan of reorganization. Burnside proposed to the armchair generals in Washington that he concentrate his forces in the direction of Gordonsville as a ruse to convince General Lee that the line of movement for the Army of the Potomac would be in that direction. With the Confederates taking the bait, Burnside would quickly move on Fredericksburg, cross the Rappahannock there and then move directly on Richmond. The plan was bold and innovative. However, to be successful, it relied on speed of movement, something that McClellan's field commanders were not particularly known for. To facilitate the movement, Burnside proposed the reorganization of the Union army into three grand divisions to be commanded by Major Generals Edwin V. Sumner, William B. Franklin, and Joseph Hooker. The forces at their disposal would comprise more than one hundred thousand troops.[33]

The projected start date for the advance on Fredericksburg was November 15. This left the men of the Twentieth Indiana with little to do except wait, suffer from exposure in the freezing temperatures and chilling winds and shuffle from camp to camp. The regiment, still without extra blankets and camp goods, built enormous bonfires in the evening. Of course, this resulted in blankets and overcoats catching fire with the soldier who was on fire called upon to do a dance in an effort to put out the flames.[34]

The idle time gave the men plenty of opportunity to contemplate and evaluate the numerous organizational changes which were whirling about them. The Hoosiers bade a bittersweet farewell to Major George F. Dick, who was promoted to lieutenant colonel of the Eighty-sixth Indiana Regiment being formed back home. The boys all regarded Dick as a brave and stalwart officer, well deserving of his promotion, but they couldn't help being sad about the departure of such a gallant officer. Charles Reese, who had replaced Dick as captain of Company D, wrote home that he regarded Dick's leaving the regiment as the loss of a brother.[35] Dick's departure created a vacancy for the position of major to be filled by James H. Shannon of LaPorte, Indiana. John E. Sweet replaced Shannon as captain.[36] Captain James Kistler was dismissed from the service for being absent without leave for ten days after the fight at Bull Run. He had simply disappeared and headed for the safety of Washington, where he had convinced the paymaster that he should be paid, even without proper papers. He was replaced by Thomas Logan.[37]

Of course, the removal of McClellan was the biggest topic of conversation around the bonfires of the Twentieth Indiana. It had been stupid, they said, to remove McClellan for inaction when, since Burnside took command, the regiment had moved a total of four times, but no further than two miles from where they started.[38] They had no idea what was being planned for them or what fate might reveal in the coming weeks, but in the harsh winds of early November, they were as gray-tempered as the skies. In a letter to his sister (in which he also tells his young son Charlie that he will bring him to the regiment to make a drummer boy out of him), Charles Reese informed her, "You may expect me home in about two months or two years."[39] Ambrose Burnside, a fellow Hoosier by birth, would prove a critical factor in determining which end of the time span was most accurate.

Major General George Stoneman, now in command of the corps in which the Twentieth Indiana belonged, issued orders on the morning of November 15 for each man in his corps to be ready to march at a moment's notice.[40] The previous day, Sumner's Grand Division, followed by Franklin's, departed on their hurried way to Fredericksburg. When the order to march was finally given on November 16, leading the way for Robinson's brigade, in Birney's division, were again, the men of the Twentieth. They moved briskly along covering over twenty miles in two days to their point of destination near Hartwood, seven miles from Falmouth.[41]

When the advance elements of the Army of the Potomac arrived at Falmouth, immediately across the Rappahannock River from Fredericksburg, they found a golden opportunity awaiting. Fredericksburg was being defended by four companies of Confederate infantry, a cavalry regiment and a battery of light artillery. The nearest Rebel force of any considerable strength was Longstreet's corps, more than thirty miles away at Culpeper. Jackson's corps was still firmly ensconced in the Shenandoah Valley.[42] The brass ring was Burnside's for the taking. All the Army of the Potomac needed to do was cross the river and easily seize Fredericksburg and the protecting heights behind it, then the road to Richmond lay open before them. Charles Reese might yet be home for New Year's.

Burnside, hesitant and fearful about moving elements of his army across the Rappahannock before the full body of his fighting force could arrive, worried about the fate of any infantry which might be cut off by a rain-swollen river. Both Major General Sumner and Major General Hooker pleaded their case for a rapid movement across the Rappahannock, but Burnside was adamant in his views. Hooker even attempted a very sloppy back door effort to push his views by writing directly to the Secretary of War criticizing Burnside for his hesitancy.[43] What started out as such a promising movement, so bold in its design, had now degenerated into paralyzing hesitancy on the part of the commanding general and recriminations and insubordination on the part of his subordinates.

Fredericksburg rested in a river valley running between the elevations of Stafford's Heights on the north bank of the Rappahannock, and Marye's Heights, which sloped sharply upward from the town itself, on the southern bank. Marye's Heights commanded both the river crossings at Fredericksburg, and the road ran through it and on to Richmond. Even a soldier with limited experience could see that controlling Marye's Heights was the key to Fredericksburg and that moving against a few hundred defenders now was preferable to tangling with the entire Rebel army, soon to arrive.

When General Lee first learned of the movement of Sumner's Grand Division toward Fredericksburg, he was not sure of the intentions of the Union army. He had fully expected an advance southward from the direction of Gordonsville, and now this Fredericksburg movement puzzled him. He had loved playing poker with McClellan; he had always known what kind of hand the little general was going to play and could gamble accordingly. Burnside's movement, however, had taken him off guard and left him in a quandary. He dispatched James Longstreet and one of his divisions on a hasty march to Fredericksburg and sent another division to the south toward the North Anna River, his preferred defensive line. He left Jackson in the Shenandoah but tactfully suggested that he might move a few divisions east of the Blue Ridge Mountains, just in case.[44]

Any thoughts Burnside may have entertained for a quick advance across the Rappahannock were quickly dashed when heavy rains commenced on the afternoon of November 19 and continued for three days. The swelling rivers and thickening mud were not confidence builders for Burnside, and neither was the frustrating absence of the pontoon boats to be used in the construction of bridges. Burnside believed that he had adequately communicated his intention to cross the Rappahannock on pontoons at Fredericksburg, but General-in-Chief Henry W. Halleck was under the impression that Burnside intended to cross the river upstream from Fredericksburg and move down the south side of the river. Consequently, the pontoons were sent to where Halleck thought they should be sent and not to where they were actually needed.[45]

From their frigid, damp camp near Falmouth, the Hoosiers of the Twentieth Indiana groused about their lot in life and contemplated the calamities awaiting them. The men were forced to face the freezing nights with nothing but "a shelter tent, all but the shelter." Charles Reese made himself as comfortable as possible with his limited resources. He lined the floor of the tent, which was open on both ends, with " a little straw, then a piece of an old tent and one blanket and a piece of carpet" thrown over him. Shivering from the cold, Reese would complain to his brother that, "We don't go any faster now than we did when General McClellan was in command."[46]

Lieutenant Colonel John Wheeler was discouraged. He had been in command of the regiment until just recently when Colonel John Van Valkenburg returned, and he resented playing second fiddle to a man most of the men considered an inferior leader. Now, faced with the prospect of a dismal winter in camp, exposed to the cruel elements for no apparent good, Wheeler wrote Governor Morton on December 4, that "The Army of the Potomac is a kind of 'standing army' with no prospects of doing anything this winter." Wheeler asked the Republican governor to transfer him to a Western fighting unit.[47] Before the governor could respond, fate intervened.

While Burnside fretted over his plan of action, and the wayward pontoons slowly made their way to Falmouth, Robert E. Lee took firm action. He quickly raced the remainder of Longstreet's men and Jackson's corps to

Fredericksburg. One quick look at the place convinced him that he could not defend the town itself because of the bristling Union batteries on Stafford's Heights. Instead, he would form a defensive line along the ridge of Marye's Heights and extend the line through the protective wood line to the east. The Confederates rushed to their new defensive line and added to the natural strength of the position with their own breastworks. By December 9 the Army of Northern Virginia was in place and ready for a crack at the men across the river.

In a council of war, Burnside laid out a plan to cross the Rappahannock by pontoon at Fredericksburg. His assembled generals roundly and loudly condemned it. At the conclusion of the meeting Burnside turned to two junior officers for their opinions of the projected attack. Expecting a dutiful blessing, the general was surprised when Colonel Rush Hawkins of the Ninth New York stated flatly: "If you make the attack as contemplated, it will be the greatest slaughter of the war; there isn't infantry enough in our whole army to carry those heights if they are well defended." Burnside turned to Lieutenant Colonel Joseph H. Taylor for his views and was shocked again when Taylor told him, "The carrying out of your plan will be murder, not warfare."[48] Undaunted and unconvinced of the grim realities of the situation, Ambrose Burnside scheduled his attack for December 11.

The geography of the Fredericksburg area would leave precious little room for maneuver, as Burnside prepared his plan of action. Burnside selected William B. Franklin to assault the Confederate right flank and roll it up or, if troops were removed from the center of the Rebel line to reinforce the right, then Sumner's Grand Division would launch its attack from Fredericksburg on the heavily defended Marye's Heights. To support the attack, Chief of Union Artillery Brigadier General Henry Hunt had amassed 147 guns on Stafford's Heights.[49]

Brigadier General David Birney's division, in which Robinson's brigade resided, was one of the two divisions detached from Hooker and sent to Franklin's Grand Division. Robinson's brigade had been expanded with the addition of three new regiments, the One Hundred and Fourteenth Pennsylvania, the One Hundred and Forty-first Pennsylvania, and the Sixty-eighth Pennsylvania.[50] These additions would, once again, make Robinson's brigade a formidable fighting unit. The fighting trim of the Twentieth Indiana had been somewhat restored through the return of previously wounded men and the receipt of new recruits. In addition to nineteen officers, the regiment could boast of five hundred and eight men fit for duty.[51] With the good token of immediate action, the men of the Twentieth put aside their petty grievances and prepared to support their new commander, Burnside.

Before daylight on Thursday, December 11, 1862, Federal engineers

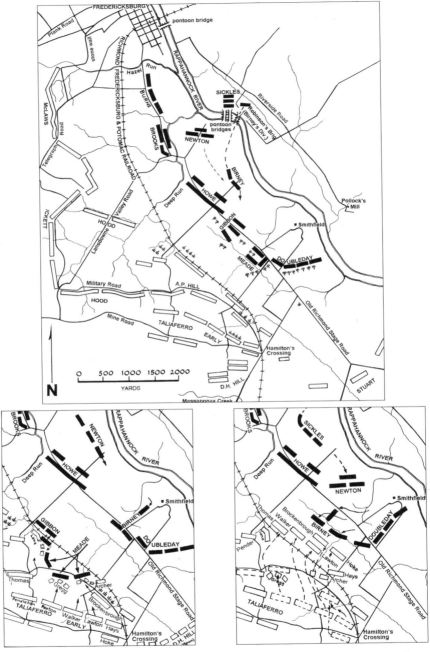

The Battle of Fredericksburg (December 13, 1862): (*Top*) In the morning, Birney's troops, including the Twentieth Indiana, move into support position. (*Lower left*) At 1 P.M. Meade and Gibbon's attack; Birney awaits orders to advance. (*Lower right*) At 2:20 P.M. Birney advances to cover Meade's retreat.

slid down the slippery slopes of Stafford's Heights lugging pontoon boats as they came. They hastily shoved off in the boats, placing them side by side, as additional engineers ran forward to nail heavy wooden planks to them. The work of the engineers was unobserved by their Confederate adversaries until the bridges were half completed, then a booming solitary cannon shot fired by the Confederate Washington Artillery on the hill aroused the Rebel defenders and instantly subjected the bridge builders to a murderous fire of small arms from the south side of the Rappahannock. The Union engineers made repeated attempts to bridge the river throughout the fog-shrouded morning with little success. Only at 1:00 P.M., when the entire line of Union artillery opened up on the town of Fredericksburg itself, driving the Rebel sharpshooters out of easy rifle distance, could the bridges be completed. Then the destruction of Fredericksburg was virtually complete, with fires raging out of control throughout the town.[52]

With the bridges secure, Sumner's Grand Division and the remaining divisions of Hooker's Grand Division filed across the Rappahannock and into Fredericksburg, their numbers unknown to the Rebel defenders on the heights above them. While this action was taking place, General Franklin's forces were able to cross the Rappahannock on two pontoon bridges where the Deep Run empties into that river. There was little opposition to Franklin's crossing, and the appearance of his large force on the plain in front of Stonewall Jackson's defenders led General Lee to assume that the main attack would occur on his right flank. The Federals, dallying as usual, used the remaining hours of December 11 and all of the next day to cross the river and prepare for their attack.[53]

Under a fog-shrouded mist, the Sixth Corps, under Major General William F. Smith, launched its attack at 8:30 A.M., on December 13. The division of Major General George Meade spearheaded the attack, supported on its right flank by Major General John Gibbon's division. Meade crossed the small ravine in his front and directed his attack at a woods angling down from the heights. The Confederate artillery on the heights at this point had been silenced by three batteries of Union artillery, so Meade's advance was swift. Meade's division crashed into the woods and drove on up the hill to the crest of the ridge, where they captured Rebel flags and hundreds of prisoners. It appeared as if Burnside's plan might work, after all. However, in the confusion of the advance through the woods, Meade's right flank became separated from Gibbon's left flank, which opened Meade's men to counterattack on both of his flanks. A desperate rush of Rebel reinforcements crashed into Meade's flanks and sent the division reeling back down the hill.[54]

Not content to merely reclaim their previous position, the Confederate brigades of Brockenbrough, Hoke, Walker, and Lawton poured over the crest of the hill and hotly pursued Meade's division in a mortal chase. Gibbon's men soon became engaged in the contest and it became apparent to Franklin that bold action must be taken immediately or his beachhead on the south bank of the Rappahannock would be in jeopardy.[55]

It was near 1:00 P.M. when Brigadier General John Robinson received the order to move his brigade across the Rappahannock to shore up the badly shaken divisions of Meade and Gibbon. No sooner had Robinson crossed the river when the immediacy of the situation became apparent to him. Brockenbrough's and Hoke's brigades had smashed the resolve of Meade's men and were moving to drive them into the Rappahannock. Moving his men into position on the double quick, Robinson hurried Company F, under the command of Lieutenant Edward Sutherland from the Twentieth Indiana, forward as skirmishers. The Hoosiers rushed into the blizzard of whining shot and shell and discovered a five-foot-deep ditch running across their front. The ditch was filled with muddy and bloody water several feet deep, but Sutherland's men didn't hesitate for a moment as they plunged into the freezing water, wet but well below the steady rain of lead being delivered overhead.[56] Robinson centered his brigade in line of battle in rear of Livingston's and Randolph's batteries, toward which the enemy was then focusing its attack. The One Hundred and Fourteenth Pennsylvania and the Sixty-third Pennsylvania, moving quickly and sharply forward, as if on parade, fired one withering volley and charged with fixed bayonets.[57]

The main body of the Twentieth Indiana, behind the first battle line, fixed bayonets and joined the fray. Brockenbrough's brigade stopped and blasted the Hoosiers with a destructive volley, immediately shooting off the shin bone of Captain Erasmus Gilbreath. Gilbreath, leading the charge, found one of his legs not willing to "do its duty" and when he looked down he saw a small hole in his pants leg. The shock then hit him and he fell headlong into the mud.[58] A Rebel artillery solid shot struck Sergeant Major George Cavanaugh in his left leg, ripping it from his body. The regimental bugler, John McCoy, was sounding the charge when he was literally cut in two by another shell.[59]

Lieutenant Albert Norris was struck down by one of the many Rebel bullets which pinged and zinged in the ranks of the Hoosiers.[60] Private Albert Cox, a lad of seventeen, had both of his legs pierced by the same lucky Rebel musket ball. He was carried to the rear by Private James Cromer, who quickly returned to the battle only to have his thumb shot off.[61]

Of course, the test of an effective fighting regiment was not merely in absorbing punishment, but in delivering it to the enemy in kind. The Hoosiers were up to the task. Colonel Van Valkenburg and Lieutenant Colonel Wheeler bravely fired their sidearms and waved their swords, exhorting the band of Indiana stalwarts to pour repeated volleys of lethal lead into the Confederate brigades in their front. A new crisis arose when Randolph's battery had shot away all of its ammunition and found itself defenseless in the face of a renewed thrust by Hoke's brigade. Colonel Van Valkenburg ordered Captain Thomas Logan's company to stop firing and go get ammunition. The Logansport boys ran to the rear and grabbed a twelve-pound shot and bag of powder each and hurried back to the nervous, unarmed artillerymen. Captain Randolph's guns began their deadly work once more, with the Hoosiers delivering the lethal loads as needed.[62]

The Pennsylvania boys from Meade's division who were assigned the task of defending Randolph's battery had seen enough action for the day. The guns had become a bullet magnet for the Rebels and the heavy concentrated fire on the guns had taken both a physical and emotional toll on the Pennsylvanians. They now abandoned the guns and started to melt away to the rear. Major General Stoneman, sensing grave danger, rode up into the midst of the steadfast Hoosiers, pointed at the artillery pieces and yelled, "My Indiana Rifles, save that brass!" The Indiana boys swiftly ran to the guns and started servicing them. Randolph's men took heart from the brave Westerners and returned to the guns and commenced a murderous repeated fire into the Confederate line. It was at this time that Lieutenant Harvey Miller was knocked out by the concussion of an exploding shell. Quickly around him fell Privates Isaac Cook, shot in the arm, and Gilbert Arnold, shot in the foot. Private Matthew Sullivan was shot twice, taking a bullet in each leg.[63]

The collective infantry and artillery fire finally took its toll on the exhausted and battered Rebel brigades. They withdrew in the storm of swarming bullets to the protection of the wood line. Brigadier General Robinson, his face showing both the haggard look of battlefield leader and the determined look of the defiant, walked among his men, accompanied by Private Ed Jennings of the Twentieth, who had been selected to carry the brigade flag. Everywhere the general went during the battle, Jennings was there by his side. The general appreciated his bravery and commended him in front of the begrimed men of the brigade.[64]

Laboring under the false impression that all was going well on the left flank of the assault and being battered by artillery fire from Marye's Heights, General Burnside ordered Sumner's and Hooker's men forward. To characterize the resultant attack as a battle would be overly generous; it was more a case of cattle being sent to the slaughter. Wave after wave of blue-coated lines moved toward Marye's Heights, only to be driven back by an irresistible fusillade. Time after time the ocean of blue crashed down and spent itself on the rock of Longstreet's corps—not battle, but murder, as Burnside's officers had predicted. Stubbornly, Burnside wasted the flower of the Union army on useless, futile attacks. Mercifully, night came on the cold, mournful, and bloody field. The Battle of Fredericksburg had proven an unmitigated Union disaster. Despite Burnside's intent to resume the attack on the following day, with himself in the lead of the charge, his generals unanimously implored him to see the futility of the situation and withdraw beyond the Rappahannock. Burnside relented and after a grueling day spent under heavy Rebel fire, the Union army quietly slipped back over the river under the cover of darkness, thus ending the ordeal.

The casualty figures revealed the one-sided nature of the battle. Union forces lost 1,284 killed, 9,600 wounded, and 1,769 missing or captured, for an aggregate total of 12,653. Confederate losses were 608 killed, 4,116 wounded, and 653 missing or captured.[65] If the action on the left flank of the Union army is discounted, with relatively balanced casualty figures, the slaughter in front of Marye's Heights is even more disastrous.

The Twentieth Indiana, engaged in the short, hot affair on the left flank, had two men killed, twenty-two wounded and three men missing.[66] The numbers do not begin to tell the grisly tale of carnage and suffering which the Hoosiers experienced. Surgeon Orpheus Everts and Assistant Surgeon Henry Grover had anticipated the heavy casualties that the battle would bring and established their field hospital on the south bank of the Rappahannock. From the first angry bullets fired on December 13 until December 15, there was a steady stream of horribly wounded soldiers—both Union and Confederate—carried to the hospital. Everts was serving as medical director for Birney's division and as such was totally responsible for the amputations and dressing of wounds of the more than five hundred casualties suffered by that division alone, along with numerous Confederates and stray wounded from Meade's and Gibbon's divisions.[67]

The first of the Hoosier wounded to arrive at the field hospital was young Albert Cox. Fortunately, the musket ball which passed through both of his legs had not shattered any bone and he was spared the horror and uncertain conclusion of amputation. While having his wounds dressed, Cox pleaded with Dr. Grover and Seymour Montgomery, who was acting as hospital steward, to be allowed to return to the firing line. A steady stream of ambulances arrived at the hospital unloading the mangled bodies, some with arms and legs hanging just by sinews. Little regard was given as to whether the wounded men wore butternut or blue uniforms—each received the same attention. The Rebel patients ranged from being defiant to overly appreciative, damning either Abe Lincoln or their own government for putting them in their present fix.[68]

Upon the completion of the fighting at Fredericksburg, squads of rescuers combed the battlefield under cover of darkness to find wounded comrades who had fallen in battle, and were unable to make their way to the field hospital. First on their list of men to seek was Captain Erasmus C. Gilbreath. He had fallen with the first Rebel fusillade and found himself lying in the mud with bullets spinning and thudding around him. The double-quick run to the battle line had brought a sweat on the captain. Now, still lying in the freezing mud and bleeding, he suffered a horrible chill. The musket ball which had removed the entire front of Gilbreath's tibia made any movement painful and crawling impossible. For seven hours from the time of his wounding, Gilbreath lay shivering, with the strength and life ebbing from his body.[69]

Sergeant John French, Company I, slowly worked his way across the battlefield, examining each body he happened upon to see whether it was that of Captain Gilbreath. He called out into the blackness of night for some sign that Gilbreath was among the dark shapes littering the field. Gilbreath, in an almost dreamlike state from the shock of his ordeal, heard the calls and, with tears streaming down his face, was able to wet his throat enough to cry out. The rescue party placed the captain on a blanket and carried him back to the field hospital, where he was put on an old mattress. Then they returned to their search for survivors.[70]

Sergeant Winch begged Colonel Van Valkenburg for permission to carry canteens out to the wounded. Reluctantly, Van Valkenburg gave his approval with the prediction that he would probably get shot. The sergeant called out to the Confederates across from him, asking permission to succor the wounded. The Rebels did not reply, but Winch proceeded out between the lines with his canteens. He gave each wounded man some water and ransacked the haversacks of the dead soldiers on the field in an effort to offer some food to the suffering wounded. The captain of one of the companies of the Fifteenth Alabama spotted Winch and came out between the lines to talk to the sergeant. The captain shook Winch's hand and apologized for their not caring for the Union wounded themselves, informing Winch that it had been all they could handle to attend to their own men. With that bit of civility taken care of, Winch returned to his lines and the killing resumed.[71]

In another paradox of battle, a skirmisher from the Twentieth Indiana gamely stood behind a wide tree and blazed away at a Rebel skirmisher behind similar protection. The men fired repeated shots at one another until they saw the humor in their inability to shoot each other. Finally, they gestured at each other, leaned their rifles on trees and walked out between the lines. With gunfire blasting all around them, they agreed that they would go find other targets and leave each other alone.[72]

For many, the horror of being wounded only commenced at the field hospital. Gilbreath was examined by one of the field surgeons in the makeshift hospital where his boot was cut off revealing the ghastly nature of his wound. The blackened foot and leg were badly swollen, and the surgeon quickly completed a little ticket and marked Gilbreath for amputation. Gilbreath desperately tried to get the attention of one of the other surgeons to protest the first doctor's conclusion, but the agonizing screams and confusion in the hospital did not allow him an opportunity for appeal. Finally, by a freak accident of war, a stray Rebel artillery shell came crashing through the ceiling of the abandoned farmhouse which passed as the hospital, sending everyone who could walk scurrying for cover. As the medical personnel returned to their bloody duty, Gilbreath gave the Masonic sign to a surgeon whom he recognized. This new surgeon re-examined the captain and promised to have him transported back across the river to the Third Corps hospital, where he might be treated by friends.[73] This lucky circumstance allowed the brave Captain Gilbreath the opportunity to save his leg and return one day to the regiment to fight again.

The recriminations over the Battle of Fredericksburg began immediately after the soldiers recrossed the Rappahannock. Most of the soldiers immediately blamed the failure on poor generalship, a logical result of the poor decision to cashier McClellan. Burnside himself, in a noble display of humility and honesty, accepted the full blame for the disaster. This raised his stock immensely among the soldiers who had quickly come to accept the rumor that officials in Washington had actually ordered the attack. Later, when Burnside confessed to his army that he had not been pressured to move, his support died quickly. Immediately after the battle, John Luther wrote his father:

> *My dear father,*
> *Since I wrote you last there has been an awful bloody battle fought, as hard a battle as ever fought, which I suppose you have heard about by this time, and we got badly whipped too, but men never fought better than they did here, but it was our generals that whipped us. We have not got a general in the field here that knows his business. The enemy killed about three to one and what an awful slaughter just piling them on top of each other. . . .*
>
> *Respectfully yours,*
John E. Luther [74]

On December 21 General-in-Chief Henry W. Halleck made the trip down to Falmouth to visit the troops and get a firsthand perspective of the calamitous situation. Halleck may have expected a welcome befitting his rank, but instead was greeted with stony silence. Assistant Quartermaster Tuttle couldn't imagine why Halleck was visiting unless it was to see "what a confounded fool he has made of himself."[75] Tuttle, a Republican and former government loyalist, had lost all patience with the armchair generals. He wrote his wife that, "We are sadly in need of strong men at the head of affairs at Washington. I am fearful that the Administration is going to turn out a total failure. I did think that we had the right man at the helm but I think 'Old Abe' of late has 'slopped over.' The President has been most fearfully bamboozled."[76]

The defeat at Fredericksburg portended the cessation of any combat until the coming spring. The soldiers of the Twentieth Indiana therefore quickly set about establishing a winter camp. The camp was situated on the top of a hill and a "very comfortable" group of log huts were constructed with large fireplaces within.[77] The scene was somewhat reminiscent of Valley Forge during the American Revolution. While some soldiers may have taken heart from the historical parallel, Dennis Tuttle did not. In a melancholy letter to his wife written on Christmas Day, Tuttle wrote: "I firmly believe the United States received its death blow when George B. McClellan was removed from the command of the Army of the Potomac. I do not believe the North will ever succeed in bringing the South into the Union. I would not make such an admission here. The thought is humiliating, but I believe it is true."[78]

Of course, Christmas is a bad time to be away from loved ones, especially in time of war. None of the Hoosiers in the Twentieth were in good spirits. To make matters worse, the Indiana boys were dispatched on picket for three days and had to spend Christmas Day alone along the banks of the Rappahannock, being taunted by Rebel pickets hooting at them from the opposite shore. The boys noticed that there was no evidence of Christmas or, as one lonely soldier put it, "Not even the death-shriek of a chicken."[79]

Private George W. Weaver, writing to a pretty young girl named Kate from a hospital on Craney Island, Virginia, worried about the prospect of the girls back home being "hard up for beaus." His suggestion to the young maiden was to turn a cold shoulder to the remaining suitors who had failed to enlist in the army. He speculated that the fellows remaining in civilian status "must feel very sheepish to call on their sweethearts."[80]

Sergeant Seymour Montgomery had different thoughts on his mind as he finished his rounds of dressing wounds and otherwise attending to the needs of his patients. He had seen the carnage of war from the massacre of the *Congress* by the *Merrimac*, the battles on the Peninsula, the slaughter of Second Manassas, and the bitter travesty of Fredericksburg. With pen in hand, Montgomery wrote the *Howard Tribune*, "When the future historian of this nation comes to make up his record for 1862, he will certainly denominate the Battle of Fredericksburg a 'great slaughter' without accomplishing the least possible good."[81]

CHAPTER EIGHT

MUD, BLOOD, AND CHEERS

Corporal John Hendricks had witnessed the worst of the fighting in 1862 and he looked forward to brighter prospects for the new year. On January 1, 1863, Hendricks took the opportunity, his first in several weeks, to write his mother. He sat down in the small, snug log hut by a rough-hewn table, warmed by the crude stone fireplace, and wrote:

Dear Mother:
It has been some time since I last wrote you but never mind, I think I am excusable and if I am not, I had ought to be at any rate. Well Ma, another New Year has found me in the army. This is two and my time is half up. I have one more New Year in the army. Well Ma, during the last year I have been in several hard fought battles. The first was before Richmond, the battles of the Orchard, Glendale, White Oak Swamp, Malvern Hill, Bull Run, Chantilly and Fredericksburg. In those seven battles we have lost over forty-five thousand men in killed and wounded. This is the very least estimation that I ever saw of the fights besides many skirmishes in which we have had more or less killed, especially those of the Oatfield, Buckhouse and Harrison's Bar. I have taken an active part in every battle or skirmish from the Orchards right down to the skirmish at Waterloo. You may think it strange that we should not be all killed but we are not. There is nineteen in camp now out of the ninety-seven that left Indiana with us. There is seven at the convalescent camp. We have discharged nineteen. This leaves fifty-two for killed and

wounded out of our company, missing six. We have received sixty-three recruits during the last three months which makes our company seventy-two strong.

I was made corporal soon after our skedaddle from before Richmond and the other day the Colonel appointed me for color guard. So you see, all I have to do is to go where the flag goes. It is an easy work in camp and a dangerous one in battle, but Ma, you know I came to war to run my chance with the rest of my friends and it is known that I will do it. I will run some risk as so many have been killed in the same place. Well Ma, the boys is sitting and talking about home and wishing they could be there tonight. I can't hardly write for wishing too, but I can wait patiently as there is only eighteen months longer for me and then if the war is over, I will enlist again.

I am well and hope this may find you all well. We expect another battle soon as we have orders to be ready to march at twelve hours notice with sixty rounds of cartridges and three days rations in our haversacks. We all know we are to march but can't tell where but suppose it is where there is rebs to be found.

Well Ma, what do you think about my New Years dinner? It was beans and fat pork made in soup or rather fat pork and spoiled water with a bean in it. But never mind, we will eat better for supper. We will have spoiled water with a coffee in it and some hardy knickknacks, such as salt horse and crackers. It is about time for dress parade and I must close. Write soon to,

John H. Hendricks [1]

Obviously supplies of good food had been scarce since the Battle of Fredericksburg, with many of the wagons of the army necessarily detailed to transporting the wounded back to Washington and making the return trip bearing ammunition and the tools of war. Fresh beef, fruits, and vegetables were as rare as Union loyalists in Fredericksburg. Until the supply trains turned to delivering sustenance, hardtack and beans would be standard fare.

In addition to the meager food ration, the common soldier in the Army of the Potomac was provided a steady diet of tripe served up by Northern newspapers intent on destroying the command structure of the army. Constant sniping which characterized the men of Burnside's army as demoralized and tantamount to rabble infuriated the Twentieth and added to their discomfiture. Seymour Montgomery felt that it was bad enough to be defeated, let alone have the stigma of demoralization attached to their record. His deepest regret was that the Hoosiers were not allowed to return to Indiana and fight the "home traitors."[2]

Ambrose Burnside was not content to while away the winter, allowing the Northern media to snipe at him. He intended to take quick action to force the removal of the Rebel army from Fredericksburg by flanking it out of the town. His plan of action was to move his army to the west of Fredericksburg and cross it over the Rappahannock at some lightly guarded crossing. With the bulk of his army safely across the river, he could either move directly on Richmond or he could take Fredericksburg from the rear. It was a simple plan and reasonable. Once again, it would require speed and full cooperation among the various elements of the army. He commenced planning the operation and ordered up the necessary tools of war to set it in motion. In the meantime, Burnside put each man on alert to be ready to move at short notice.

The men naturally looked upon any action in the winter as somewhat risky and were less than happy about going into battle with a new brigade commander. Brigadier General John Robinson had had the trust of both Phil Kearny and David Birney, trust he had earned as a strong and dedicated fighter. Now, Robinson was ascending to the command of John Gibbon's division and the Twentieth found themselves serving temporarily under the command of the colonel of the Thirty-seventh New York. A more permanent brigade commander would be named soon, but men tended to find comfort in familiarity, especially when their lives were on the line.[3]

Although there was some opportunity for the Twentieth to rest and recuperate, there was little time for Dr. Orpheus Everts and Dr. Henry Grover to relax. The job of attending to the needs of the wounded and sick rarely provided rest, but the two good physicians were up to the task, winning high marks from the Indiana men and the entire brigade. Wounds gradually healed and fevers abated and the ranks of the Twentieth Indiana began to fill again.[4]

Captain Erasmus C. Gilbreath was not quite ready to return to the regiment. He was still confined to a hospital, recovering from the painful wound to his shin bone. Gilbreath had recovered sufficiently to appreciate some of the visitors who frequented the Union hospitals. He was visited by Dorothea Dix, the wives of several members of Congress and by his own congressman, Schuyler Colfax. Mary Lincoln, the President's wife, came to visit her friend's wounded son in the room adjoining Gilbreath's. The First Lady poked her head into Gilbreath's room and presented the captain with a box of fine cigars from Havana.[5]

Not all went well at the hospital, however. Gilbreath had discovered that there was only one other officer in the same hospital, Captain George Wallace of the Fourth Ohio Infantry, and Gilbreath naturally befriended the Ohioan. Wallace had been wounded by a small ball from a shrapnel shell, the ball entering through his kneecap. At first, Captain Wallace refused an amputation, but he was informed as he grew progressively weaker that he would either lose his leg or his life. The captain relented and soon after the amputation found his health improving. A pretty young lass, Wallace's fiancee, visited him from Canton, Ohio. Captain Wallace and the young Miss Schneider decided that they would marry before she returned home. Dr. Brown, the brother of the late Colonel William Brown, happened to be in the area and was summoned to marry the two. After the ceremony, a very happy affair, the new Mrs. Wallace spent an enjoyable afternoon with her seriously injured husband, leaving late in the day.

Captain Wallace was extremely contented with his life now. He had survived the terror of amputation and its uncertainty and was now a proud husband. Life was indeed looking up for him. He ate a hearty supper and was smoking one of Mrs. Lincoln's cigars when he raised the blanket covering his stump. Horrified, he looked across the room at Gilbreath, who shouted for the surgeon. By the time the surgeon arrived, blood was soaking through the blanket. Gilbreath and the surgeon attempted to place a tourniquet on the stump, but before it could be accomplished, blood gushed out over the side of the bed and Captain Wallace cried out, "Oh, I can't breathe!" He died immediately and the newlywed Mrs. Wallace thus became the Widow Wallace.[6] Captain Gilbreath had seen enough of hospital life and he determined to regain his own health and return as quickly as possible to his Hoosier friends in the Twentieth.

Ambrose Burnside staged a series of grand reviews in early January to view the condition of the men serving under him. On January 2, and again on January 5, Burnside reviewed Stoneman's corps. Although not up to McClellan's previously grand standards, the appearance of forty thousand troops in full uniform with flags flying and bands playing made for a fine sight. It was obvious to the men of the Twentieth that some great movement was afoot—these reviews generally portended as much.[7]

The weather took a sharp turn for the worse, with fast-falling temperatures, snow and freezing rain. On days of freezing rain, the ground around the camp of the Twentieth oozed with sticky, yellow clay mud.[8] Dennis Tuttle summed up the feelings of the regiment in a letter to his wife, "Oh, such a dull, stupid place as this is. I never saw the like. Nothing to do. Nothing to see. Nothing to read. Just one stupid monotonous routine of stupidity. I wish we might move, go somewhere or do something. Give me change of any kind."[9] Mothers through all time have warned their children to be careful of what they wish for, because it might come true. Tuttle may have temporarily forgotten the admonition as he longed for something to break the boredom. In any event, change did come.

On the morning of Tuesday, January 20, the men of the Twentieth Indiana were ordered into regimental formation and an order from Major General Burnside was read to them. It said, "The movements of our troops in North Carolina and the southwest have drawn off and divided the Rebel forces on the Rappahannock, therefore the General Commanding regards this as the auspicious moment in the providence of God to strike a blow."[10] The Hoosiers had heard the bluster before from McClellan and Pope and they were somewhat less than inclined to swallow the bait in a fit of enthusiasm. They would, however, fall into column and go wherever they had to.

At 11:00 A.M. they began their march through the wintry Virginia back roads, marching twelve miles to where they were to cross the Rappahannock at Scott's Mills.[11] The march had gone well and the men lay down to rest that evening with expectations that they would make a short march down to the river in the morning and cross over on a pontoon bridge which would arrive and be constructed overnight. Then rain came and deluged the regiment. At 3:00 A.M., the Twentieth Indiana was ordered to rise and to go to the rescue of the pontoon boats, whose wagons had quickly become stuck in the mud. All day long on January 21 the Hoosiers struggled to drag wagons whose wheels were no longer useful through the unrelenting rain and deep mud down to the river landing. It was grueling and futile work. Only a few of the many wagons made it to the river's edge. One wagon, dragged by two companies of men and six mules, succeeded in moving only six hundred feet in twelve hours.[12]

The work continued throughout the night and into the next day with no better results. All the while, the rain continued. The army was dragging to a halt and there was nothing which could be done about it. Officers who found that they could not stop the rain decided to pour the whiskey, and a healthy ration of the elixir was served up to all who cared to partake. The whiskey, while welcome, did little to lighten the loads or dry up the mud. Again, all through January 22 and until noon the next day, the rain poured down. By this time the roads had become totally impassable and the provisions which the men carried in their knapsacks had been exhausted. What little sleep the men had been able to get in the past two days was accomplished in cold soggy mud. Fevers started to rise and bodies to break down. A crisis was brewing and, gratefully, the futility of the ordeal convinced Burnside that he had been licked by Mother Nature and that a return to Falmouth was in order.[13]

The return march was reminiscent of Napoleon's retreat before Moscow, except it was mud and not snow that plagued the boys. The Hoosiers waded through knee-deep slop in uniforms and overcoats which were waterlogged and heavy. Throughout the day, the regiment plodded back to Camp Pitcher.[14] Adding insult to injury, the Rebels had erected a large board near the river's edge with a life-size painting of an officer on it, with the words, "Burnside stuck in the mud" written on it. The Rebels must have gotten a hearty laugh out of it, but the Hoosiers were just too tired to appreciate the humor.[15]

Finally, just after dark, the muddy and frozen-to-the-bone Hoosiers staggered into camp and collapsed from sheer exhaustion. Those with enough energy to think did not place the blame for the disaster on Burnside. They blamed Mother Nature and General Whiskey, whom they assumed had been in charge of the late arrival of the pontoon boats at the river's edge. Instead of drifting off to sleep in Fredericksburg or on the road to Richmond, they were once again in their log huts, overlooking the defiant Rebel defenses on Marye's Heights.[16]

Ambrose Burnside had seen his fill of high command. His health and emotional stability had been shattered by the twin disasters of Fredericksburg and the Mud March, as the Northern papers were derisively calling the "abortive movement of January 20 through 23." Burnside tendered his resignation as commander of the Army of the Potomac and President Lincoln accepted it. In Burnside's place, Lincoln appointed Major General Joseph Hooker. Lincoln had many reservations about the politically astute Massachusetts general. He expressed his concerns and misgivings in the same letter in which he appointed Hooker to command. Hooker was a brave and aggressive general, but one who had served his own selfish interests over those of the army and the country. In spite of his backbiting conduct of the past several months, Hooker was now commander of the Army of the Potomac and asking his subordinates for their personal loyalty.

Instead of loyalty, Hooker received resignations. Both Major Generals Edwin V. Sumner and William Franklin resigned because Hooker was junior to them in rank and their pride would not allow them to serve the upstart commander. With himself promoted and the other two Grand Division commanders resigned, Hooker decided to scrap the current organizational structure and redesign the Army of the Potomac. Diving into the task with vigor, he laid out a new corps organizational structure which he believed offered the best means of supplying and controlling units in battle. He provided for a system of distinctive corps badges in an effort to build unit cohesiveness and the ability to recognize units on the march or on the battlefield. In short, he began to dramatically refit and reorganize the Army of the Potomac into a formidable fighting force. He was showing that McClellan had no monopoly on organizational talents.

Private John Luther wrote his father detailing his initial impression of General Hooker:

There is lots of talk here about our new commander in the army. And no two men agree or have the same opinion of the same man or the same thing. All have an idea, however that Hooker is going to find out where the Rebels are and fight. The general cry among the boys is, 'Keep your eye peeled for old Hooker,' for they think he learned a trick or two from Phil Kearny. He said in his speech to the army when he took command that we are here to hunt out and fight our enemies, instead of hunting them and taking to our heels as soon as the first shot was fired. He says that God is on our side, and though the enemy is determined, we will win in the end, and return to our homes crowned with victory. I have thought lots about this, and hope it is true. But I have often wondered if he really believes it in his heart that the rebellion will soon terminate. The roads are impassable now. Saw a mule drown in mud yesterday.

I received the paper you sent, but I am down on the man that stays at home and shouts against the War. He is as much a traitor as the man in Jeff Davis' ranks. I wish every man in the north who supports Jeff Davis was in the ranks so that we could get a clip at their noodle once in a while. They are now doing their best to prolong the War until Old Abe's time is up, and then try to defeat him, so they can elect their Blacklegs. If the men in the army can vote they will support the Government, and would like to see those who want to prolong the War sticking on the end of a bayonet.[17]

Hooker hurried the paymasters forward, and the boys in the Twentieth were given two months' pay, a princely sum, but one which was still three months shy of paying them up to date. The twenty-six dollars which the men were paid was desperately needed back home and left little, if any, for the creature requirements of the soldier in camp, such as writing paper and clean, dry socks.[18]

Colonel John Van Valkenburg, who had proven his worth on many a field of battle, was now finally commanding the brigade. Brigadier General David Birney had shown his confidence in the Hoosier and it was a promotion which was welcomed by the overwhelming majority of the men in the regiment. They now awaited the proud day when the "Miami Chief" from Peru would receive his brigadier's star.[19]

Hooker had another idea for dealing with morale and the folks back home, especially the Copperheads and the Northern newspapers. He strongly encouraged each regiment to hold a meeting of its officers and to prepare a resolution of support for the government and the war effort to be signed by each of the officers and then sent back home to be published in the papers.

This testimony to the faith and fidelity of the Union army would quell the unrest at home, rally new recruits and be looked on favorably by Secretary of War Stanton and President Lincoln. On February 19 the officers of the regiment, minus a mysteriously absent Colonel Van Valkenburg, assembled for the reading and signing of the resolution.[20]

The reading of the resolution raised little excitement or debate and the officers of the regiment had begun to sign the document when Surgeon Orpheus Everts excitedly ran into the tent and announced to the stunned officers present that Colonel John Van Valkenburg had been dismissed from the army by order of the President.[21] The charge was disloyalty to the government and conduct unbecoming an officer and a gentleman.[22] "Had a 100-pound shell exploded in the tent it could not have caused more surprise. . . ." wrote Dennis Tuttle to his wife.[23] There was much agitated speculation as to the cause of the dismissal. The officers knew Van Valkenburg to be a brave and efficient officer. There had to be some mistake or maybe it had something to do with the fact that Van Valkenburg was a well-known Democrat. Dr. Everts informed the assembled officers that the colonel and he would travel to Washington in the morning to get the misunderstanding cleared up.[24]

Colonel Van Valkenburg himself had been unaware of the summary dismissal. Apparently, a meaningless, insignificant indiscretion was to cost him his rank and cause his cashiering from the army. As has been shown, upon his first payday after returning to the Twentieth Indiana from his recuperation in Indiana, Van Valkenburg had purchased a money draft for forty dollars which he owed a sutler, a Mr. Reynolds, and mailed it to him. Reynolds, a man with strong Copperhead sentiments, had expressed his misgivings when loaning the money to Colonel Van Valkenburg because he did not like giving money to a man "fighting under this damned nigger administration."[25] When Van Valkenburg enclosed the money in an envelope, he also inserted a brief note which said, "This is the last money I expect to get from this damned nigger administration for the next four months." With this, he entrusted the delivery of the note and money to the care of the postal service for its delivery.

However, the money made its way to Indianapolis and was delivered to the *wrong* Mr. Reynolds. This Mr. Reynolds was the brother of Indiana Brigadier General Joseph Jones Reynolds, a strong supporter of Republican ideals and of the Lincoln administration. The name Van Valkenburg rang like a bell to Reynolds. Wasn't there a seditionist newspaper publisher in Plymouth with the name Van Valkenburg? Reynolds ran directly to Governor Oliver P. Morton's office in the Capitol Building and handed the note to him. Morton, obviously relishing the opportunity to get his pound of flesh from a Democrat with the hated name of Van Valkenburg, immediately sent a letter to the Secretary of War Edwin Stanton, requesting the dismissal of Colonel Van Valkenburg from service.[26]

Upon receiving his order of dismissal, Van Valkenburg quickly called upon Major General Joseph Hooker, who had witnessed the colonel's fidelity and bravery on the Peninsula. Hooker and Generals Daniel Sickles and David Birney wrote letters of endorsement for Van Valkenburg and sent the colonel on to Washington to see the President and ask for relief or a hearing. President Lincoln was surprised by the nature of the visit from Colonel Van Valkenburg. He had not seen any complaints of any type from Morton or others with the charges and he certainly had not signed the orders to dismiss him. No, the dismissal of Colonel Van Valkenburg had not come at Lincoln's hand; it was the dirty work of the Secretary of War. Edwin Stanton ran the army, and there would be no appeal and no hearing. There would not even be an official specification of charges, just the dismissal. And thus, John Van Valkenburg learned in a very unfair manner that there are casualties on the battlefield and casualties in the corridors of power. He had experienced both, but the wound delivered at the hands of his government would pain him forever.[27]

John Van Valkenburg's comrades in the Army of the Potomac offered all the support they could with numerous letters to government officials, members of Congress and military officials in the War Department. Major General Hooker wrote the President:

> *The action of the authorities in regard to Colonel Van Valkenburg is incomprehensible to his friends in camp. I can only think that there has been some mistake in this case. His loyalty has never been doubted by his brother officers, nor has his soldiership been other than the proudest soldier might envy. No injurious suspicions are attached to his name in the army.*[28]

Major General Sickles was even stronger in a letter to the Speaker of the House of Representatives, Schuyler Colfax, Van Valkenburg's own congressman, when he wrote: "I think he should not only be promptly and honorably restored to his command, but he should be promoted." [29] Brigadier General Birney wrote General Hooker, "I regard him as one of the best officers and soldiers in my division and in restoring him your army will retain one of its truest officers and loyal citizens."[30]

Lieutenant William D. Vatchett wrote Congressman Albert S. White and vouched for Van Valkenburg's loyalty, citing examples of his meritorious conduct, including stopping unauthorized medical discharges and arming seventy-five members of the regiment who had gone so long without weapons that they had forgotten how to use them. Lieutenant Colonel Wheeler, certainly viewed as a potential rival of Van Valkenburg's, wrote Schuyler Colfax pleading with the congressman to intercede and right the terrible wrong being visited on Colonel Van Valkenburg.

Petitions were sent to Governor Morton bearing the names of every officer in the brigade and division requesting reinstatement and justice. Morton, apparently misjudging the potential consequences of his actions, appealed to Adjutant Lorenzo Thomas to reinstate Van Valkenburg.[31] But there was no justice to be found. Secretary Stanton murdered a distinguished career and sent Van Valkenburg home to derision and ridicule by the people of his hometown, Peru.[32] Van Valkenburg, disgusted and depressed, wrote Lieutenant Colonel Wheeler informing him that he would travel to Mexico to fight the French.[33] Several months later, still residing in Peru, the disgraced colonel would write Wheeler, updating him on his plans to plant tobacco and to serve in the Union army as a private, if he was drafted.[34]

The agitated controversy which consumed the debates and emotions of the Twentieth Indiana for two weeks gradually died down and the reality that "life must go on" settled in.

Hooker wisely granted leaves of absence to officers on a rotating basis, which lifted their morale immensely. The opportunity to see loved ones for the first time in eighteen months was the little lift they needed to forget the terror of Fredericksburg and the fatigue of the Mud March. Organizational matters within the regiment needed urgent attention. Lieutenant Colonel John Wheeler ascended to the colonelcy vacated by Van Valkenburg. This promotion came none too soon as Wheeler, depressed and homesick, had informed his wife in February that he would resign his commission before June. The vacancy in the lieutenant colonelcy created by Wheeler's elevation caused an intense rivalry and jockeying for promotion among Major James Shannon, Captain William C. L. Taylor, and Captain George W. Meikel. Meikel was favored by Wheeler, who advocated his promotion ahead of Taylor in a letter to Governor Morton because, "Taylor will get intoxicated every time an opportunity occurs."[35] Major Shannon prevailed on the basis that he was next in line for promotion. Taylor settled for second prize over Meikel as Shannon's replacement as major.[36]

Several other positions needed to be filled in the company ranks as well as in the field command. Jonas Hoover of Peru was appointed captain of Company A. Henry Quigley of Lafayette was promoted to captain of Company G, and John C. Brown of Monticello was advanced to captain of Company K. The cream of the companies was beginning to rise to positions of leadership and would serve the regiment well in the months ahead.[37]

One shocking, yet well-deserved dismissal from the regiment occurred on March 13. Before his own dismissal, Colonel Van Valkenburg had noticed a large number of seemingly able-bodied men being discharged for disability from the regiment by Assistant Surgeon Daniel H. Prunk. Prunk had more in mind than just the health and well being of the men in the Twentieth Indiana. It appeared that discharges could be purchased at a handsome price from Dr. Prunk. The truth was bound to come out sooner or later, and when Van Valkenburg discovered the facts, Prunk was dismissed for bribery.[38]

Other men in the brigade were dismissed from service, but with less civility than Prunk received. A soldier in the Sixty-third Pennsylvania was court-martialed and found guilty of desertion during the Battle of Fredericksburg. He was sentenced to be dishonorably discharged and drummed out of the army. The entire division gathered for the proceedings and formed a hollow square. The sentence of the court was read to him, his military buttons cut from his uniform and a letter "D" was branded into his hip. Then he was marched around the inside of the square followed by the guards with bayonets at charge and the band playing the "Rogues March." Only after this pain and humiliation was he taken outside the lines and turned loose to return home to whatever reception awaited him there.[39]

There were wintertime illnesses in the regiment which needed urgent attention. Typhoid fever, chronic diarrhea and rheumatism were debilitating conditions which called for the care of Dr. Everts and his crew of hospital stewards.[40] The best cure for the men was the sunshine and warmth which returned with spring, along with an improved diet which occasionally included fruits and vegetables.

Winter hung on tenaciously. One Hoosier described March as "one hour of summer sun, two of rain, three of snow and eighteen hours of intense cold."[41] Any pretense of soldiering, with the exception of guard and picket duty, was dispensed with and the men took refuge in their small, cozy huts. New clothes and rations of the good things in life arrived daily from home, and spirits were lifted by the largess the mails brought. With no fighting to deplete the ranks, the number of officers and men in the regiment swelled to six hundred and nine men present for duty.[42]

Nonetheless, loneliness ate at the Twentieth, and the single boys turned to advertising in newspapers for pen pals. Early on in this process, a theory developed that girls tended to write men with fancy names more than they did men with boring names. As an experiment, the Hoosiers concocted a test of their theory. They ran identical advertisements requesting girls to write. On one advertisement they used the name "Reginald De Courcey" and on the other, "Edward Murphy." Their theory was correct and the mysterious and wealthy-sounding "Reginald De Courcey" received more than his fair share of mail from the Northern girls.[43] "Edward Murphy" was left out in the cold.

Adjutant John F. Thomas was in love. He had decided to ask for leave to return to Indiana to marry his sweetheart. The leave had been canceled on January 4, but Thomas determined to take the first opportunity presented to him and get the job done. In late February, Thomas got his fifteen-day leave and immediately headed for Indiana. He decided to surprise his fiancee by dropping in on her—a mistake. His intended bride had decided to leave home for a visit with friends in western Iowa; the stranded lover was left with flowers in his hand at the girl's front door. He returned to the regiment and resignedly received hoots and hollers from his unsympathetic comrades.[44]

Assistant Surgeon Henry Grover was luckier. He used his leave to return to LaPorte and, without any advance notice to his fellow Hoosiers, married Miss Jane Pratt. It was a surprised regiment of Indiana boys who greeted the return of their well-liked surgeon. He was serenaded with song by the Hoosiers and entertained by the regimental band.[45]

The Hoosiers turned their attention to other avenues of pursuit to fight boredom until the spring campaigning season arrived. Dr. Orpheus Everts and the regimental chaplain, Reverend William Porter, learned the game of chess to pass the time. What started out as a light pastime turned into a daily rivalry between the two with no quarter asked or given. The passion of these two spiritual leaders of the regiment spread to the company captains who all quickly took up the game. The sight of their officers plotting great victories over a hardtack box amused the enlisted men, who generally preferred gambling to the more intellectual game of chess.[46]

The area surrounding Camp Pitcher had been totally stripped of all but the greenest firewood, and it was necessary to move camps to a more friendly environment. The camp of the Twentieth was moved the first week of March further to the east where the boys found plenty of good oak wood to burn. Their new hastily erected log huts were warm and cozy. The new camp was near Potomac Creek, about six miles from the landing at Aquia Creek. All pronounced the camp a much better place to pass the remaining days of winter.[47]

Assistant Quartermaster Tuttle particularly liked the location for the abundance of river eels. He found the slimy creatures to be a particular delicacy and fashioned himself as an extraordinary chef. A huge supply of onions had arrived in camp and Tuttle was excited to get a crack at whipping up a culinary delight featuring the two foul ingredients.[48] Tuttle, the former attorney, also spent his time concocting ways to earn additional money to support the free spending habits of his wife. He had returned from Connecticut, where his wife was living, with sets of knives which he marked up and sold for a handsome price. To his chagrin he found that he had not brought back enough of the knives: his entire supply was sold out immediately.[49]

On March 4 the Twentieth Indiana was transferred to a new brigade under the command of Brigadier General Hobart Ward. The brigade consisted of the Third and Fourth Maine, the Thirty-eighth, Fortieth, and Fifty-fifth New York, and the Twentieth Indiana.[50] Ward was descended from a line of soldiers. His father and grandfather had both perished as a result of wounds suffered in combat. He was a tough young man and at eighteen enlisted in the United States army. He rose progressively through the ranks from private up to sergeant major during the Mexican War. After marrying a Mexican belle from Vera Cruz, he returned after that war to serve as assistant commissary general for New York. When war broke out in 1861, he was commissioned colonel of the Thirty-eighth New York. He eventually rose to command of Brigadier General David Birney's brigade, to which the Twentieth Indiana had now been transferred.[51]

The well-respected Hoosiers immediately fit into their new brigade. The reputation of the Twentieth as intrepid, hard-fighting Western soldiers was well known. Brigadier General Birney was an exceptional leader of men and tried hard to build cohesion in his division and to keep morale high. As the weather improved, he took several opportunities to stage friendly competitions between the regiments in his division. Division headquarters had been handsomely decorated and Generals Hooker and Sickles were invited, along with their large entourage, to witness the events. A large viewing stand over one hundred feet long and twenty-five feet wide was constructed for the spectators. The competitions consisted of foot races, pole climbing, greased pole climbing, sack races, wheel of fortune, horse races and mule races. Cash prizes were given, with a ten spot going to the winner in each event. There was even a mock cockfight, with two soldiers dressed up like roosters. With the day's festivities ended, the dignitaries retired to General Sickles' quarters where they enjoyed the best foods and wines that could be brought together in this part of Virginia.[52] There would be no rum or wine in the ranks of the Twentieth Indiana. Colonel John Wheeler was a teetotaler and had issued a strict order that any selling of liquor to the soldiers in the Twentieth would be punishable by banishment from camp.[53]

General Birney, in another masterstroke to boost morale, issued orders in his division that regimental commanders were to submit the names of all soldiers who had distinguished themselves on past battlefields. Each of these brave soldiers was to receive a silver cross, named the Kearny Cross, to be worn over the red patch of their division. No soldier who had been arrested or had been caught straggling could wear the red patch. The awards were an instant hit with the Hoosiers. The soldiers wore their medals of valor with great pride, and those whose breasts were bare vowed to win one on the next field of battle.[54]

By early April the weather had turned reasonably warm and the ground thawed and dried out. The time to move forward was quickly approaching. The boys had learned the distinct signs of approaching action. First, they would be visited by the governor, then the President might hold a review and finally, the paymaster would arrive. The Hoosiers were definitely more interested in seeing the paymaster than the dignitaries at this point. By the end of April, the United States government would be in arrears six months' pay to the Indiana soldiers.

True to form on March 30, the boys were just sitting down to dinner when word came down the line that Governor Oliver P. Morton was coming. The men dropped their dining utensils and marched to the parade ground where the governor, accompanied by Brigadier General Solomon Meredith and Brigadier General Ward, with their respective staffs, rode along the lines of the Twentieth Indiana and saluted them. After reviewing the men, the governor launched into a short, "soul stirring" speech. At the conclusion of the patriotic talk, the Hoosiers erupted in wild cheering for the governor. They marched past him in review one more time and returned to their now-cold dinners.[55] One wonders what kind of reception the governor would have received had the men known his role in the dismissal of Colonel Van Valkenburg.

On April 8 all the camps in the Army of the Potomac were astir at an early hour. President Lincoln was visiting the army to view the amazing transformation of the soldiers from a bedraggled, broken-down, filthy rabble to a spit-and-polish, well-equipped fighting machine. At 8:00 A.M., the Twentieth Indiana took up their line of march for the parade grounds on the plains overlooking Fredericksburg. The location had been chosen purposefully because it was in full view of the Confederate defenders on Marye's Heights. The parade of April 8 was a grand sight previously unseen on the North American continent. More than fifty thousand infantrymen with glittering bayonets and swords paraded amid the pomp and pageantry of hundreds of fluttering flags and blaring patriotic music.[56]

As President Lincoln approached the right of Sickles' corps, the bands struck up the tune of "Hail to the Chief." The President, led by a troop of lancers, rode to the front of the corps and halted in its center. Accompanied by General Sickles and many staff officers, Lincoln rode down the line of the corps, with head uncovered, smiling at the awestruck soldiers. As each brigade was passed, the general commanding it would fall into line at the rear of the procession and move on to the next brigade. After inspecting the brigades in this fashion, the assembled troops passed in front of the reviewing stand one last time.[57]

The Twentieth Indiana returned to camp at 4:00 P.M., talking along the way about how careworn the President had looked. Private Thomas Stephens thought Lincoln "very homely, but a pleasant looking man."[58] Sergeant Seymour Montgomery was impressed with how much cheerfulness and grace the President was able to muster with the weight of the entire Union on his shoulders.[59]

Two days later the Hoosiers got another look at their commander-in-chief and other military and civilian leaders, as Lincoln departed for Washington. The men were marched out to a newly constructed military road leading to the landing at Aquia Creek. The entire Army of the Potomac was lined up on both sides of the road over which the President would pass. To the west, several miles distant, the Hoosiers could hear a faint cheer and roar which grew in intensity as time went on. The soldiers were wild with excitement as Lincoln approached, his young son by his side and followed by the First Lady in a carriage. Behind the carriage rode a host of brigadier generals and their staffs, including the wives and daughters of many of the officers. It was two hours after the President had passed before the cheering to the east died out and was replaced by the booming cannon at Aquia Creek.[60]

If the intended purpose of the review was to inspire the Army of the Potomac, it succeeded. It was easy after a defeat to blame unseen politicians in Washington. This review, however, was able to put a face on the national leadership: the men liked what they saw. Abraham Lincoln liked what he saw, too, and gave Joseph Hooker the approval to take his army out again.

Major General Hooker had decided on a strategy similar to Burnside's for flanking the Confederate army which sat at Fredericksburg. His plan essentially consisted of moving one third of his army across the Rappahannock at a ford twenty miles upstream from Fredericksburg and in a move to deceive the Rebels, crossing two corps over the river below Fredericksburg. Third Corps, under Dan Sickles, and a division under John Gibbon would remain at Stafford's Heights across from the Rebel stronghold. With the bulk of the Confederate army frozen in place at Fredericksburg and a powerful Union force on their flank, Lee would have no alternative but to evacuate the town and either fall back toward Richmond or try and do battle with one of the Union wings.[61]

On April 14 the Twentieth Indiana received orders to be ready to march by 5:00 P.M. Each man was to carry three days' cooked rations in his haversack and five days' rations in his knapsack. The Twentieth would put forty rounds of ammunition in their cartridge boxes and stuff another twenty rounds in their pockets. The boys were allowed to take an extra pair of drawers, one pair of socks and an extra shirt. All other clothing was to be left behind.[62] Finally, officers would be forced to carry their own camp equipage or provide a servant to do so. No wagons would follow the army across the Rappahannock. This army would travel light and fast, no more wagons bogged down in the mud, carrying needless gear and amenities.[63]

The regiment failed to march at the appointed time. Before they could get under way the next day, it rained heavily.[64] With General Stoneman's cavalry failing to secure their river crossing in a timely fashion, and the rain washing away hope for quick movement, Hooker put the grand movement on hold for the time being. He wanted no part of another Mud March, so the Twentieth emptied their pockets of the extra ammunition and settled back down into camp life.

Colonel Wheeler took the opportunity during the delay to write Governor Morton, informing him of the good condition and morale of the regiment. He also added a politically astute notation. "Every man is ready and willing to go in and help officer a Negro regiment. This they would not do six months ago and but few of them would three months ago," he said.[65] Wheeler was not going to miss the opportunity to point out that he certainly was not a John Van Valkenburg. It might be dangerous to a man's career to give that impression.

Surgeon Orpheus Everts best summed up the state of readiness of the Twentieth Indiana in a letter to the *LaPorte Union* where he remarked, "It seems to me impossible that an army could be in a better state of discipline, health and equipment than the Army of the Potomac."[66] If only it would stop raining and dry up, this army was ready to show its stuff.

Private Thomas Stephens noted in his diary on April 25 that the ground was "drying up fast."[67] This fact was not lost on General Hooker or any soldier who understood that dry ground meant movement and movement meant battle. Hooker conducted one last grand review April 27, with Secretary William Seward serving as the visiting Washington dignitary.[68] Later that same evening, the Twentieth Indiana received their marching orders and prepared eight days' rations.[69]

Early on the morning of April 28, five hundred men of the Twentieth Indiana answered the roll call and proceeded to a wooden table, where they warmly received the Union army's paymaster and accepted their long-overdue four months' pay. Thomas Stephens and his brother, Jimmie, dutifully sent ten percent of their pay to the missionary society in Cincinnati and the majority of the balance back to Indiana.[70] It was dangerous work in battle, and no soldier wanted to carry a lot of currency or silver. If he were wounded, friend or foe could pick him as clean as a Christmas goose.

At 4:00 P.M., the regiment fell in line and began a march through tangled ravines and wild underbrush to a point approximately four miles below Fredericksburg and the next day they moved one more mile nearer the river.[71] The Union observation balloon floated lazily over Stafford's Heights, out of rifle range from the Rebels on Marye's Heights. George Washington painted on the balloon's side kept an eye on his wayward children, ready to do battle with each other again.[72]

Throughout the night of April 29 and into the morning hours of April 30, the sounds of heavy artillery fire drifted down the Rappahannock to the waiting ears of the Hoosiers. Awakening to a heavy rain, the regiment was called to formation at 9:00 A.M., where an order from General Hooker was read. Hooker congratulated his army for successfully crossing the Rappahannock, just about declared a victory and predicted that General Lee would have no choice but to flee the advancing Union army.[73] The men had heard this kind of blustering nonsense before; it smacked of John Pope, and although they were hopeful that it was true, past experience had taught them to be wary of premature pronouncements.

At 1:00 P.M., the entire Third Corps of Major General Dan Sickles moved off on a long, circuitous march along narrow back roads and the Warrenton Turnpike, heading west upriver from Fredericksburg. It was an arduous march in warm temperatures with the men each carrying forty-five pounds of provisions and a rifle. The long column finally stopped at midnight and the Twentieth fell to the ground into instantaneous sleep, too tired to even prepare a meal.[74]

At 5:30 A.M. on May 1, Ward's Second brigade was up and moving the few miles down to U.S. Ford, where they would cross the Rappahannock. At 8:00 A.M., the brigade wearily crossed the river on a pontoon bridge and halted in a field adjacent to the crossing. With the prospects of only a short rest, the Hoosiers scrounged through their haversacks and knapsacks for something quick to eat. Hardtack and raw pork seemed to fill the bill of fare for most of the men. Within thirty minutes, the regiment was back on its feet and marching for Chancellorsville.[75]

The entire Third Corps was allowed to rest at Chancellorsville while General Hooker tried his best to get a strategic handle on the battle which was unfolding. The Rebels seemed ready to fight. Hooker had every right to be confused. Only a fool would knowingly choose the area around Chancellorsville for battle: dense, almost impenetrable undergrowth surrounded the area for miles around. A few roads running through the morass and spotty fields offering small space for cultivation were all that provided any identity to this wilderness. Hooker had never intended to fight it out in this confusing maze and did not have a coherent battle plan to do so. Uncertain of exactly how many Rebels he was facing, and where they were, he was uneasy in the strategic situation. All Hooker really knew was that somewhere out in the tangled wilderness in front of his headquarters at the Chancellor House was a Rebel force of unknown size which was engaged in a heated artillery duel with Union forces.

Sickles ordered his corps to move to the right of the Chancellor House, and General Birney put his faithful Twentieth Indiana out on picket duty, far in advance of the Union line.[76] The Hoosiers were located one half mile south of the Orange Plank Road in a dense woods along the Catherine's Furnace Road. Before them was a broad field sloping down to a swamp some nine hundred yards wide. At the terminus of the swamp, the ground rose again to a high, woody hill with a stream at its base, bordered on both sides by impenetrable thickets. It was from this hilly prominence of Hazel Grove that the Rebels had been shelling the Union lines all day.[77] Pushed forward in such an exposed position, no officer had to remind his men to stay awake and keep vigil. An attack was expected at any time.

The dawn of the next day heralded a beautiful spring day, with birds chirping and wildflowers blooming everywhere. The pleasantness of the morning was only occasionally ruined by the stray shot of a Rebel sharpshooter taking a pot luck shot at an unwary Yankee. Late in the morning, the most advanced pickets could see, off to their front and left, the steady movement of wagons and Confederate troops moving to their right down the Gordonsville Road. A current of excitement electrified the Hoosiers as it appeared to them that Hooker was right and Lee must retreat before them.[78] Word was sent back immediately to Brigadier General Birney, who quickly passed the intelligence on to his corps commander, Daniel Sickles. Sickles ordered a battery of rifled field pieces to be rushed to the scene and when they arrived they immediately began shelling the Confederate column.[79] This bombardment had little effect except to hurry the Rebels on down the Gordonsville Road at double-quick speed.[80] Sensing the futility of trying to disperse the Rebel column with artillery fire from two miles away, Sickles ordered Birney's men forward in an advance down the Catherine's Furnace Road, their immediate goal being to capture the commanding elevation at Hazel Grove.[81]

When Colonel John Wheeler received the order to advance down the Catherine's Furnace Road, he knew he had to select a tough company to do the dirty work of leading the regiment as skirmishers. He selected Captain John Brown to lead Company K into the face of the Rebel defenders. Brown would lead the advance, followed closely by the remainder of the regiment and accompanied on their flank by Hiram Berdan's Second U.S. Sharpshooters.[82] The Twentieth moved out cautiously, driving back the

Confederate pickets and skirmishers of the Twenty-third Georgia Infantry, who had been ordered by Brigadier General Robert Rodes to remain behind as a rear guard for the moving Rebel column.[83] The Hoosiers pressed forward, firing steadily into the Georgians, scooping up prisoners as they advanced.

Colonel Emory Best of the Twenty-third Georgia had sent four companies of soldiers forward to act as skirmishers while he remained in a redoubt constructed from felled trees with five companies of men, supported from an elevation behind Catherine's Furnace by two pieces of artillery. From the redoubt, Best was able to delay the advance of the Hoosiers and Berdan's Sharpshooters for a while, but word soon came from his vedettes that the Hoosiers were beginning to sweep around his flank, threatening to cut off his retreat and capture the two artillery pieces. Best had no choice but to order his men to fall back several hundred yards to an unfinished railroad cut and to prepare a defense there.[84]

The Hoosier advance rushed on, snatching up prisoners by the handful, and as the onrushing tide reached the railroad cut it had parted like the Red Sea as it approached the Confederate position. Now, as it lapped around both flanks of the Twenty-third Georgia, the Twentieth Indiana came crashing in on the hapless Rebels. As the Hoosiers approached the cut, they were amazed to see a great commotion, with knapsacks, haversacks, caps, and other accoutrements of war flying in the air. Totally surprised and surrounded, the Georgians had no choice but to surrender. Only one man, Colonel Best, escaped capture, riding hard through the Hoosier throng, carrying his regimental flag. The total loss to the Twenty-third Georgia amounted to more than two hundred and fifty killed, wounded, and captured, including twenty-six officers.[85] Miraculously, the Twentieth and Berdan's Sharpshooters had made this staggering advance without the loss of a single soldier.

Still convinced that they were pursuing a beaten and retreating foe, the Twentieth Indiana pushed further forward for a quarter of a mile to the Welford House on the Catherine's Furnace Road. The Hoosiers were now close to three miles from the main body of Union forces, blissfully awaiting the rest of the army's renewed pursuit of the Rebel army in the morning. The defensive line faced south and southwest, and when it was completed the happy but weary soldiers had time to kill. The Welfords had left their home to avoid the inevitable fighting, and the Indiana boys made themselves at home. A cozy fire was built in the fireplace in preparation for cooking dinner. A fat hog and several chickens were killed and a feast was in the making, a fine reward for a fine day's work.[86] Then, as the final light of day was fading from the Wilderness, the Hoosiers could hear the unmistakable sound of heavy musketry coming from the northwest. They knew the sound signaled battle of some kind, but they were ignorant of its source or status.[87]

The source of the severe fighting was the staggering flank attack which Stonewall Jackson was launching on the unsuspecting and unprepared Eleventh Corps of Major General Oliver Otis Howard. Howard's men occupied the extreme right flank of the army and had taken up a defensive position facing south. Unmolested through the day, Howard's troops did not expect any fighting and had stacked arms and started to prepare supper. By all conventional military wisdom, a classic oxymoron, the Eleventh Corps should have been safe in their assumptions. However, Stonewall Jackson and Robert E. Lee had different ideas about what constituted military wisdom.

Joe Hooker had been right when he issued his grand proclamation that Lee would either be forced to fight at a great disadvantage or fly ignominiously. Lee chose to fight and, contrary to traditional wisdom to "never divide your army in the face of a superior foe," he split his army. All day long on May 2, Lee had funneled Stonewall Jackson's troops in a steady procession to the west on a long, circuitous march to the unsuspecting right flank of the Union army. The mass of forces which Hooker assumed to be retreating were actually shifting themselves to the exposed right flank of Eleventh Corps, dangling in thin air.

Stonewall Jackson's massive attack was overwhelming, and the Eleventh Corps disintegrated in a matter of minutes. Gray-clad demons swept the Eleventh Corps out of their way and charged forward towards Chancellorsville. Hooker rushed elements of the Third Corps and Twelfth Corps down the Orange Turnpike to meet Jackson's forces. The pause of Jackson's men to reorganize gave the Union troops an opportunity to form a defensive line, to bring up artillery and to stem the tide of defeat.

Immediately after the attack began on Howard's corps, orders were rushed to the Third Corps forces spread out to the Welford House to return to the vicinity of Hazel Grove, where the corps would make its stand. Only the Twentieth Indiana and the Sixty-third Pennsylvania would be left behind at the Welford House.[88] The Hoosiers' culinary plans were put on hold and raw pork and chicken were stuffed into haversacks as the Indiana boys marched out to build new defensive positions facing northwest.[89]

All through the evening the frightened Hoosiers and Pennsylvanians witnessed the pyrotechnic extravaganza performed by the two armies. They were, they realized, cut off. In hushed, fearful tones the men talked about how far it was to Richmond, Virginia, surely a difficult a walk for prisoners of war. At midnight, the men heard the sound of clattering hooves coming down the Catherine's Furnace Road from Hazel Grove. The men's anxiety was alleviated when they learned the rider was Captain Fassett of General Birney's staff. He informed Colonel Wheeler of the by-now-obvious fact that a terrific battle was being waged, with the fate of the entire army at risk. They were totally cut off from the remainder of Third Corps.[90]

Captain Fassett had ridden down the road past Confederate pickets and scouts, and he suggested that only by the most careful, quiet movement could the Twentieth expect to survive. Accordingly, Colonel Wheeler ordered his troops to maintain absolute silence, even to holding their tin cups so that they would not jangle, as the men moved off toward Hazel Grove. As the Hoosiers silently moved down the road, they could hear the loud voices of Rebel first sergeants calling out the rolls of their companies. Finally, the Indiana boys wearily filed in on the left flank of Third Corps along the north edge of Hazel Grove.[91] They passed the remaining few hours before daylight throwing up breastworks aimed to the north, the opposite orientation from what Third corps had faced the day before.

On the morning of May 3, General Lee had ordered his forces on the left flank to continue their attack but to move to their right as they did, joining two separated wings. Lee began the day hearing the unnerving news that Stonewall Jackson had been seriously wounded by his own troops mistakenly firing upon his mounted party. The Rebel strategy of moving by their right flank was accompanied by Hooker's withdrawing his left flank, Third Corps, to Chancellorsville. Hooker was a whipped man. Instead of following Lincoln's advice to "throw in all your troops" in the next battle, he had failed to commit either Fifth or First Corps to battle and had held back much of Second Corps. Hooker planned a defensive strategy which he hoped would allow the removal of his army to the north side of the Rappahannock.

Before dawn, Third Corps moved by its right flank to Chancellorsville, ever vigilant against an expected attack from the west. The Rebel forces coming from the west had chosen to attack down the Orange Turnpike with the right flank of their attack directed toward Hazel Grove. Fortunately for the Twentieth Indiana, they had been withdrawn before the full force of the Confederate attack could hit them. The fighting along the front lines that morning was ferocious and continued unabated for seven hours.[92] Captain Charles Bell, who had been in the thickest of the fighting on the Peninsula and at Second Manassas, noted that, "The rattle of musketry, the roar of artillery, the bursting of shells and the screaming shot mixed with the charging yells of the contending forces were beyond compare and the great battles at Charles City Cross Roads, Malvern Hills, and Bull Run were child's play in comparison."[93] Modern warfare had, indeed, come to the Civil War.

The Twentieth Indiana was held in reserve until noon and then were sent to the front to pull off a battery which had all its horses killed. With huge ropes, the Hoosiers strained to pull the guns to the rear, all the while under a blazing musketry from the attacking Rebels. Private Joseph Brown took a bullet in the face, but miraculously escaped death. Adjutant John Thomas, as unlucky in war as he was in romance, was grievously wounded by an artillery shell and left on the field for dead.[94]

With the gun safely withdrawn from the field, the regiment returned to a safer haven in the woods and took the defensive.[95] From their location, the Indiana boys could hear a great cheer rise from the direction of Chancellorsville to the east. The majority of the army was drawn up on the fields surrounding the Chancellor House, and the roar puzzled and excited the soldiers. Soon, they learned the source of the cheering was the appearance of Major General Hooker, mounted on his beautiful white horse. Hooker was well-liked by his men and his appearance was electrifying. The men rose and cheered wildly as Hooker approached.[96]

Soon after Hooker made his appearance along the front lines, the Twentieth Indiana was withdrawn to a new position to right and rear of the Chancellor House. Their sole duty at this location was to support Battery E, First Rhode Island Artillery.[97] While in support of the battery, the Twentieth Indiana came under a ferocious artillery attack from a Rebel battery which had worked itself to the north of the Chancellor House. Without any warning, shells fell fast and thick in the midst of the Twentieth. Private George Dasch, Company F, had his arm ripped off by a shot and died immediately. Several others dropped from the flying shrapnel and shells. One of the Rhode Island guns killed seven men, with one exploding shell blowing body parts for more than a hundred feet. Captain William Babbitt was slightly wounded from a piece of shrapnel, as was Private John Hendricks. Hendricks' side was struck by a glancing piece of iron which tore a gash one-and-a-half inches long.[98] Marquis Winch, struck by two pieces from a shell, was violently thrown to the ground. One piece hit him in the hip and the other pierced his left side, the shrapnel passing under his spinal column, severing the cord and immediately paralyzing him.[99] The assembled Union artillery quickly responded to the Rebel battery fire and drove the Confederates off, but not before the Twentieth Indiana had lost more than twenty men.[100]

All afternoon of May 3, the Twentieth Indiana kept their ground around the thirty Union artillery pieces drawn up at the Chancellor House. The Hoosiers, in the midst of the artillery pieces, were forced to lie flat on the ground to avoid being charred or powder-burned by the firing guns. After a shot was fired, the Hoosiers would jump to their feet and fire a volley or two at the Confederate line, then the Rhode Island gunners would call "look out" and the Indiana boys would dive to the ground. This process was repeated throughout the afternoon until darkness allowed the Twentieth some respite.[101]

Soon, however, the Twentieth was advanced one hundred yards in front of the Union line as pickets. The Hoosiers were afforded the comfort of the protection of breastworks which had been constructed earlier in the day. A lively, annoying skirmish fire was maintained throughout the night, but no direct Confederate advance threatened.[102]

The defensive position of the Twentieth Indiana was sufficiently strengthened by the further construction of breastworks and earthworks. However, the Confederates did not come, because they were concentrating their efforts against the Union Sixth Corps which was advancing on Chancellorsville from Fredericksburg on the Orange Turnpike. The Hoosiers could hear the heavy firing to the east but found the Rebels in their front to be relatively quiet.[103]

The Union army was out of immediate danger with both its right and left flanks secured by the Rappahannock River. The Union line resembled a huge V, with Third Corps occupying with the south-pointing apex. The Confederates had occupied the high ground at Hazel Grove with artillery, but found it untenable because of its exposure to Union artillery fire. Although the Confederate army had control of the field, with the Union army backed up against the river, it had been thoroughly bled and was in no shape to launch an all-out attack on the Federal line. It left only its artillery active.

The Hoosiers were inured to thundering cannons and flying shrapnel. Major Taylor, an aide to General Sickles, reported to Brigadier General Ward that he had "one of the damnedest coolest regiments in the army." He had ridden by the Twentieth Indiana during a heavy bombardment and witnessed a chuck-a-luck gambling table in full operation.[104] In fact, five men were wounded during the brisk cannonading which poured down on them for one half hour.[105]

Heavy skirmishing broke out at 10:00 P.M., and muzzle flashes glowed like fireflies in the black of night. No Hoosiers were wounded in the blind firing and they were unable to determine what effect their return fire had been able to inflict. The next morning when artillery was brought up to shell the woods in their front, it found the woods had been vacated.[106]

May 5 was warm and windy, with prospects of rainstorms. When the thunder commenced in the late afternoon, the noise was not much different from that of the artillery fire of the previous days. Cold rain however, soon soaked the men. Sergeant Thomas Stephens described the night as the most miserable of his time in the service. The pitch blackness of the evening cast a particular pall over the spirit of the men, but each soldier found whatever comfort he could in straw or brush piled up for a bed.[107] Captain Erasmus Gilbreath, freshly returned and largely healed from his wounding at Fredericksburg, was sleeping soundly on the cold ground when he felt the sting of a bullet hitting his shoulder. A stray picket shot fired into the darkness sent the captain to the hospital once more.[108]

At daylight on the morning of May 6, the regiment fell into line of march and gingerly moved back to the Rappahannock. The Indiana boys recrossed the river at 8:00 A.M. and marched through "the deepest mud this army has ever marched over" for another two miles. That was saying a lot. They soon stopped to cook breakfast. With their meal eaten, the march resumed, and the Hoosiers wearily trudged into their former camp near Falmouth at 4:00 P.M.[109] They had been gone from the camp for eight days and many of the men wondered what might have been achieved by the movement across the Rappahannock. They knew that they had taken a frightful toll on the Rebel army and had captured thousands of prisoners in the process. Their removal to the north side of the Rappahannock was orderly, a contrast to the demoralizing retreat at Fredericksburg and Second Manassas. Still, they were no closer to Richmond, and General Lee occupied the battlefield. It smelled like a defeat. They placed the blame squarely on Oliver Otis Howard's cowardly Eleventh Corps.

It had been no small miracle that the Twentieth Indiana had lost only twenty-seven men in the horrible fighting and bombardments, contrasting sharply with the brief battles on the Peninsula which had yielded so many more casualties. The losses to the Union army exceeded seventeen thousand in killed, wounded and missing. Confederate losses exceeded twelve thousand. The Union losses would be quickly filled by the regular influx of soldiers being conscripted in the North. The Confederate losses would prove more severe and harder to counteract. Southern manpower was strained to the utmost—Robert E. Lee could not afford many more of these victories. Lee's greatest loss in the battle was Stonewall Jackson, felled by a bullet shot by his own troops. Upon learning of the amputation of Jackson's left arm, Lee was quoted as declaring, "He has lost his left arm, but the army has lost its right arm."

General Joe Hooker was very interested in the mental state of the regiments returning to the north side of the Rappahannock. He set out on a grand tour, riding from camp to camp to see for himself if his men were in any mood to fight. As he rode into the camp of the Hoosiers, Hooker asked Colonel John Wheeler about the morale of the Twentieth Indiana. The colonel replied, "General, my men are happy." Hooker looked keenly at the Twentieth and nodded, "Yes, colonel, your men are happy."[110] This was one tough bunch of Westerners who could fight hammer and tong then return to camp carefree. They were itching to get at Robert E. Lee one more time.

CHAPTER NINE

A Glorious Field of Grief

The Twentieth Indiana Regiment had developed a fatalistic attitude about the war and the recent Battle of Chancellorsville. They would win some; they would lose some, and eventually they would probably win the struggle. Morale was generally high and their general, Joe Hooker, had lifted their spirits with a blustery congratulatory message read to each regiment lauding them for their bravery and heroic deeds during the seven days of fighting. Hooker proclaimed that even though the desired result of the campaign was not attained, it was only because of a factor over which the Army of the Potomac had no control: the weather.[1]

Major General Daniel Sickles wasted no time in whipping his men back into fighting fettle. On May 11 Sickles conducted a grand review of the Third Corps, personally taking a good look at each of his units.[2] Although reduced in strength from their pre-Chancellorsville numbers, the hardened veterans of Third Corps looked ready to march out and whip the Confederates, if fairly led.

At this point, in mid-May, the weather along the Rappahannock was causing far greater misery than the Rebel army. Temperatures had been warm enough to "bake a man alive" during the grand review, a heat which some of the Hoosiers noted had never been exceeded in Indiana in midsummer.[3] The companies of the Twentieth Indiana were rotated every two days on picket duty along the banks of the Rappahannock. The stifling heat made many a man on picket look longingly at the refreshing waters of the river, and it was only a matter of time before the pickets wandered down to the water's edge for a quick dip. Of course, their Confederate counterparts found the heat just as brutal and they too made their way down to the river's edge. The presence of common soldiers of both armies, separated only by the body of water, made the men appreciate the plight of all soldiers, and a truce of sorts was declared by the pickets. There was no need to take pot shots at some unknown fellow eighteen-year-old who just wanted to cool himself off or wash his socks.[4]

Conversations ensued; good-natured taunting and rumors passed freely over the Rappahannock. Then came orders which forbade any contact between pickets.[5] The orders were observed for a couple of days, but the junior-grade officers and even Colonel Wheeler didn't have the heart to enforce them, so the contacts resumed. The first day on picket, Privates Elias Reed, James Merrill, and William Johnson crossed the river and ate their evening meal with the Rebel pickets.[6] On May 20, Private George Uhl, in possession of a *New York Herald* newspaper which the Rebel pickets wanted to see, waded across the river and swapped his paper for a Confederate one.[7] The following day, two of Uhl's new friends from the Eighth Alabama Infantry waded to the north side of the Rappahannock and brought tobacco with them to trade for coffee. They found their visit a pleasant one and decided to spend the night with the Hoosier pickets. A good night's sleep in the company of their fellow Americans, boys just like themselves, convinced the Rebels that all the fighting was pointless and they informed their new friends that they weren't going to return to the Confederate army. Reluctantly, Uhl and the others forwarded the two to General David Birney for interrogation.[8] An Alabama lieutenant and sergeant crossed to the Union side of the river, ate breakfast, and played poker with the Hoosiers. The group struck an agreement that if any of them were ordered to shoot, they would be sure to shoot high.[9]

Colonel Wheeler believed the gambling had gone too far and issued orders on May 14 prohibiting gambling of any kind by his regiment.[10] Of course, this only forced the dedicated gamblers in the regiment to do a better job of concealing their vice. There was hypocrisy involved here on the part of officers: Sergeant Thomas Stephens, a strict teetotaler himself, listened to his captain, John Brown, read an order banning drinking in camp, then was subjected to his captain's drunken abuse later on.[11]

Good news filtered in at the end of May. The Twentieth heard that the Copperhead traitor, Clement Valandigham, a seditionist Congressman from Ohio, had been arrested and sent south to his Rebel brethren. It was a long-overdue punishment for the unrepentant insurrectionist, but it fell short of the hanging that most of the Hoosiers would have liked to have seen. The second bit of good news was the thrilling account of Major General U. S.

Grant's victories near Vicksburg. When Vicksburg fell, they told themselves, the Confederacy must surely fall with it.[12]

The final morale-building event of the month was the formal presentation of the Kearny Battle Crosses to deserving recipients. Dreamed up by division commander David Birney to honor the heroism of enlisted men and noncommissioned officers, the awards were named after the late, beloved General Philip Kearny. On May 27 the entire division was assembled on the parade ground and, in an elaborate and inspiring ceremony, the medals were pinned on the uniforms of the proud recipients by Major General Sickles.[13]

Private Stephen C. Wilson, Company H, had distinguished himself in the bloody fight on June 25 of the previous year. He had been wounded by a musket ball piercing clear through his ankle, but instead of going to the rear for medical assistance, he plugged the bleeding hole with mud and continued firing away with his rifle beside his comrades. After the battle, when the wounded were removed and sent to field hospitals, Wilson refused to leave his company and fought bravely during the removal of the Army of the Potomac to Malvern Hill. Since the battles on the Peninsula, Wilson had been in the thickest of the fighting at Second Manassas, Fredericksburg, and Chancellorsville. Wilson wore the Kearny Cross with sincere pride.

The presentation of the crosses was not without controversy. Colonel John Wheeler was adamantly opposed to the presentation of the medals and let everyone know it, including his superiors. He declared in writing to Brigadier General Hobart Ward that no man or officer in the regiment had done more than his duty and that he considered it the duty of every man to do all he could, even to the laying down of his own life until the Rebellion was put down. He was particularly peeved that Birney had arbitrarily limited the medals to twenty-five men in each regiment, when more than a hundred believed they deserved it.[14]

The next day a photographer who had been making the rounds of the Army of the Potomac visited the Hoosiers and took pictures of the men in companies.[15] With news of Vicksburg's fall, and the fall of the Confederacy expected at some point, the boys felt that they might not get another opportunity to have their images taken together.

The weather turned hot and windy. A blazing sun quickly dried up any semblance of moisture from the soil of the camps of the Army of the Potomac; huge clouds of dust were blown by strong gusty winds which were, at times, strong enough to knock a man down. Assistant Quartermaster Dennis Tuttle, exhausted from a busy day of supervising the transportation of supplies to the camp of the Twentieth Indiana, lay down in the open to catch a few minutes of rest. He quickly fell into a deep sleep and was startled awake, after an hour, by Lieutenant Colonel James Shannon. Shannon had awakened

Tuttle because he was almost completely buried by a huge pile of dust and sand which had drifted over his body.[16]

Dennis Tuttle was finding his military career buried as well, and he placed the blame squarely on Colonel John Wheeler. For more than a year, Tuttle had entertained visions of promotion to quartermaster. His free-spending wife was stretching his meager compensation of twenty-one dollars a month to its limits. Only the enhanced officer's pay could alleviate his financial distress. The promotion of Captain Isaac Hart would create the necessary vacancy for Tuttle's advancement. Hart had friends in all of the right places and a vacancy created by his advancement would open the way for Tuttle's promotion. Or, other options would open. Colonel Brown and then Colonel Van Valkenburg had given assurances to Tuttle that his time would come. His good friend, Surgeon Orpheus Everts, sustained him and encouraged Tuttle to be patient—he would be rewarded.

In late May Tuttle had been assured by Colonel Wheeler that he would be taken care of in the organizational changes which were soon to come. It seemed very straightforward and simple. Adjutant Thomas, on the road to recovery from his wounds, would be promoted to the captaincy of Company A, and Tuttle would be promoted to adjutant. Tuttle fretted daily to his wife in letters, worrying about whether Colonel Wheeler really intended to promote him as he had been assured. Then, on June 4, the news came to Tuttle that John Luther, of Wheeler's hometown of Crown Point, had been promoted to adjutant. Tuttle was furious with Colonel Wheeler for "playing a most dastardly and cowardly double game." Tuttle attributed his failure to be promoted to the fact that Wheeler hated his close friend and mentor, Dr. Everts. He wrote Wheeler off as a "cowardly snake in the grass."[17]

Actually, Colonel Wheeler and John Luther's father were close friends and had maintained a regular correspondence since the beginning of the war. As early as May 22, Wheeler had written John Luther's father, also named John, informing him that his son would be made adjutant. Wheeler explained to the elder Luther, who had lobbied for his son's promotion to quartermaster, that the move to adjutant was for the young man's own financial good, since quartermasters were financially responsible for every piece of equipment issued to the regiment. Wheeler predicted that "nine out of ten quartermasters will be poor men for life."[18] An adjutant had the prestige but not the financial burdens of the quartermaster.

The following day, Lieutenant Colonel James Shannon resigned his commission for "varicose veins" and returned to Indiana, seeking higher rank in the newly forming regiments. William C. L. Taylor was promoted to fill the vacancy, and his promotion touched off a potentially destructive jockeying for rank among Captains Charles Bell, George Meikel, and Erasmus

Gilbreath. Gilbreath was able to muster the support of the majority of the men in the regiment, and his supporters signed a petition to Governor Morton requesting his promotion over Bell and Meikel, who were actually senior to him in rank.[19] The issue would not be decided for another month.

The men of the Twentieth Indiana passed the first week of June looking for shade, reading old newspapers and playing baseball, a game which had spread from General Abner Doubleday's division and was the new rage in the Army of the Potomac. Sergeant Thomas Stephens had relieved a Confederate officer of a German book at Chancellorsville and was busily trying to learn the language. His studies were interrupted on June 8, when Company K was detached on picket duty. For Stephens to be sent out on picket duty—"the eyes of the army"—was ludicrous. For some time now Stephens had been suffering through episodes of blindness, probably related to dietary deficiencies, and he was in no shape to go out on picket.[20]

After his victory at Chancellorsville, Robert E. Lee found himself with a continuing dilemma. He had won a great victory and controlled the field of battle, but he had suffered losses of manpower which were difficult or impossible to replace. As a simple mathematical function, the chances of the Confederacy succeeding declined every time a Rebel soldier died or a Rebel's horse broke down. Lee realized that the South's sole chance for an enduring victory was the destruction of the Army of the Potomac. The likelihood of destroying the Union army, however, in its present location was not strong. The Federal forces were able to be supplied with troops and provender from both a direct line to Washington and by naval forces at Aquia Creek. To defeat the Union army, Lee and Confederate President Jefferson Davis came to believe that a bold movement toward Pennsylvania would be required. Such a move would have several potential benefits. First, the Confederate army could supply itself off of the rich bounty that a Pennsylvania untouched by the scars of war could offer. Secondly, a movement into Pennsylvania would draw the Union army away from its supply bases. Then too, a victory on Northern soil might be the fatal blow to Union morale, which was faltering, opening the possibility of recognition of the Confederacy by a war-weary populace. Finally, a victory might gain the international recognition of the Confederacy by Great Britain and France that Jefferson Davis so desperately desired. They would move into Pennsylvania, taking a bold risk to accomplish all these goals.

Accordingly, on June 3, with Jeb Stuart's cavalry serving as a screen to inquiring eyes, the Army of Northern Virginia became an army of invasion, as the Confederate forces withdrew from the banks of the Rappahannock, then moved into the Shenandoah Valley, heading north.

It was eight long days before Major General Joseph Hooker became aware of the intent of the Confederate army. When his own cavalry informed him that the Rebel army was heading north, he hastily rushed orders to the Army of the Potomac to be prepared to march. The pickets from Company K, who had been on duty and in continuous motion for twelve hours, had just stumbled into camp at 3:00 P.M. on June 11 when they were informed that their four-hour hike in from picket duty was all for naught. They would have five minutes to gather their gear before falling in for a march that would pass within two hundred yards of their previous picket post. Sergeant Stephens, suffering from a recurrence of blindness, had to be led along the route of the brutally grueling march. Private John Johnson, Company D, collapsed along the road from sunstroke.[21]

As they continued their march at 8:00 A.M. the following day, the men had no clue as to their final destination. The weather was somewhat cooler. Coats, spare garments, and unnecessary camp equipage were strewn along the route of the march as men choked from the stifling dust which filled the air in great clouds. Former blue uniforms were now gray from the chalk-like dust; faces dripped grimy sweat.[22] The fifteen-mile march halted a mile from Bealton Station.[23]

The Indiana boys had new company in their brigade. Earlier in the month, the Thirty-seventh and Thirty-eighth New York Infantry regiments had mustered out of the service at the expiration of their two year enlistments. Now, owing to the decimation of the Third Corps at Chancellorsville, Whipple's division was dismantled and its regiments transferred to the remaining two divisions in Sickles' corps. The new faces in the brigade belonged to the Eighty-sixth and One Hundred and Twenty-fourth New York Infantry. Brigadier General Hobart Ward could now boast a brigade approaching fifteen hundred men.[24]

As their generals debated where the Confederate army was headed, the Hoosiers were allowed to rest and recover on Saturday, June 13. There were disturbing cavalry reports filtering in that Rebels had been sighted in a variety of strategically important locales. Finally, on Sunday morning, a solitary bugle sounded assembly and the Hoosiers rose to prepare breakfast and renew the march, which, as it turned out, covered only ten miles in four hours because of straggling.[25] The biggest surprise to the Hoosiers was that the column wasn't heading south to Richmond, as expected, but was moving back toward Washington.

Ward's brigade started out at 5:00 A.M. on Monday—without breakfast—for the old battlefields near Manassas.[26] Assistant Quartermaster Tuttle wondered out loud whether the army was heading toward its annual Bull Run battle.[27] The sun was oppressively hot, and several men lay dead by the roadside from heat exhaustion.[28] The brigade halted briefly at Bristoe Station, prepared a small dinner and pressed on. The severely parched soldiers, with canteens empty, resorted to drinking green, scum-filled water from swampy pits and drainage pools. This hellish liquid soon hit the Hoosiers below their belts; the thoroughly wasted and nauseated regiment finally halted for the day two miles north of Manassas Junction.[29]

The regiment moved the next morning in a cloud of dust to a position occupying former Rebel breastworks on the Bull Run Creek. Dennis Tuttle wrote his wife for the first time in more than a week from their new position at Bull Run:

> *Union Mills, Virginia*
> *June 17, 1863*
>
> *My Dear Wife:*
> *There must be a terrible excitement in the North now and you I fear will be over anxious. Our corps is at Bull Run. I am about six miles from there this morning. It is now just after sunrise. We move on in a few minutes. Oh, the dust, the dust. I have eaten dust, breathed dust, rode in dust, and slept in dust ever since I left the old camp. I never saw it so dusty in my life. I could not see from one wagon to another when they were not over a rod apart a great part of the time. Some of the time I could not see the ground when sitting on my horse. I don't know where we are going. It may be to Maryland or to Pennsylvania and it may be we shall remain in Virginia. It is going to be hot enough today to boil owls. May God bless and protect you ever. Love to all home friends.*
> *As ever, Your Affectionate Husband* [30]

The dust and heat were finally alleviated by a heavy rainstorm in the evening of June 18. The joy of clean, fresh water pounding down was welcome. However, as was often the case in army life, nothing ever occurred in just the right amount, and the rain continued throughout the night and into the next day.[31] The march on June 20, was made in heavy mud and slop three to ten inches deep.[32] The soldiers who had only days earlier cursed the blessed dust now bemoaned the fact that they had received what they prayed for—water. Sergeant Thomas Stephens was once again debilitated with his blindness and relied on Private Ed Ferguson to lead him through the torrential rain. Their progress was painfully slow, and they ended the night three miles in the rear of their regiment. Stephens and Ferguson started early the next morning and caught up with their company in time to dine on a hearty breakfast of "hard tack, coffee and fat pork."[33]

The Twentieth Indiana was destined to spend the next few days in the vicinity of Gum Springs, Virginia. This was guerrilla territory and soldiers straying from camp or straggling along the road were fair game to be scooped up by John Singleton Mosby's Rebel brigands. Major General David Birney issued orders that no soldier would be permitted outside the lines without a pass.[34] The day after this order was issued, Birney and his escort were ambushed by fifteen Rebel partisans a short distance from the camp of the Twentieth Indiana. Birney sent a rider to summon up the Twentieth, but when the Indiana boys arrived, they found the general and his staff holding guns on the Rebels, who were now their prisoners.[35]

As if Colonel Wheeler's earlier order condemning gambling was not enough, Colonel Hiram Berdan, temporarily in command of the brigade, issued additional orders suppressing gambling. Wheeler's previous order had been roundly ignored and, much to the colonel's consternation, gambling had run rampant since the Chancellorsville battle.[36] The Christian officers in the army seemed to feel that killing one's brother was enough sin for one war. They could, at least, hold the line and prohibit gambling, drinking, and wenching.

While Hooker fiddled in northern Virginia, Pennsylvania burned. Robert E. Lee's fast-moving army had quickly pushed into Pennsylvania and spread out across the countryside from Chambersburg to Carlisle, with some Rebel units advancing to within four miles of Harrisburg, the state capital. It was not until June 25 that Hooker placed the Army of the Potomac in motion to Pennsylvania. The failure to move in the previous few days required the army to move rapidly now to the relief of Northern soil.

The regimental bugler sounded the call to strike tents at 6:00 A.M. on June 25, and after a breakfast of honey and pork the Twentieth started a northerly march. At 2:00 P.M. the regiment reached the Potomac and crossed it on pontoon bridges at Edward's Ferry. The men pressed on all afternoon and into the blackness of night, tormented by a driving rainstorm. They finally collapsed late in the evening after their thirty-mile forced march.[37]

It was a miserable night spent lying in pools of rainwater and mud, the body demanding sleep, but the rain preventing it. It was with great relief, lifting themselves out of the mud, that the Hoosiers staggered to their feet at dawn and again moved northward. The Twentieth crossed the Monocacy River at the canal and tramped eight more miles before halting on the railroad at Point of Rocks, Maryland. Tents were hastily erected and soldiers fell from exhaustion into a deep sleep.[38]

At ten o'clock the next morning the regiment moved out again, this time bringing up the rear of the corps while serving the purpose of pushing all stragglers ahead of it. In neutral Maryland, the Federal troops were on their best behavior and were kept by good manners and patriotism from plundering the beautiful farms they passed of their bountiful treasures of chickens, hogs, and sheep. Such delicacies had been fair game in Virginia, so it was with deep regret that these potential feasts were bypassed. The regiment marched through the little town of Jefferson and then went into camp on a "pretty farm" to be serenaded with a patriotic song by the farmer's "handsome young ladies." The song and the spirit of the girls brought cheers from the Indiana boys, happy to be among loyal citizens again.[39]

It was at Prospect Hall where the brief tenure of Joe Hooker as commander of the Army of the Potomac came to an inglorious end. Upon seeing the ten-thousand-man garrison holding Maryland Heights overlooking Harper's Ferry, Hooker appealed to Lincoln, Halleck, and Stanton for permission to reassign the force to his army. When the Washington triumvirate refused, Hooker dashed off a heated letter of resignation. It was a resignation that his bosses in Washington were glad to receive. They had been less than thrilled with Hooker's performance at Chancellorsville and had determined shortly after the battle to relieve him at the appropriate time. Major General George G. Meade was promoted to command of the Army of the Potomac, a post he neither sought nor wanted.[40]

The Twentieth arose early on June 28 and resumed its hard march to the rescue of the desperate Pennsylvanians, who had escaped the ravages of war to this point. The regiment passed through Middletown and at 2:00 P.M. moved into the beautiful pro-Union town of Frederick, Maryland—"a town about the size of Logansport"—and draped in patriotic bunting and the Stars and Stripes. The Hoosiers were thrilled to see Old Glory rippling in the wind from the windows of homes and buildings. The bands of the army blared their finest patriotic tunes, and the soldiers marched with a lighter gait as the townsfolk gathered along the way cheered their beloved rescuers. One bald-headed, wizened man hurrahed the flag and proudly informed the Indiana boys that he had fought under the banner in 1814. The regiment quickly moved on and finally halted at 7:30 P.M. for the evening.[41]

The men awoke at 5:00 A.M. on June 29, in the middle of another hard rain. Nonetheless, one-half hour later they were up and marching through a succession of loyal Union cities, including Walkerville and Woodborough. The Twentieth Indiana crossed Pipe Creek and tramped through Taneytown, where they were greeted by all of the inhabitants of the town and a good number from the surrounding countryside.[42] Here, the town folk lavished the finest foods available on the moving column. Cakes, pies, hams, turkey, pork, fruit, and vegetables were stacked high for the passing soldiers to grab what they could and feast on the march. It was an event that no soldier who experienced it would ever forget, and the patriotism of the citizens reminded the Twentieth of exactly why they were fighting. The dead-limbed column finally ground to a halt after covering another twenty-five difficult miles.[43]

The Twentieth rested in camp near Taneytown until 2:00 P.M., then renewed the advance to the northwest, back through the town and on toward Emmitsburg. At 5:00 P.M., another driving rainstorm struck the column and the soaked soldiers plodded on until early evening, when they rested near Emmitsburg. The Hoosiers saw their first indication of the trouble which lay ahead when a party of a dozen Rebel prisoners were escorted past them on their way to the rear.[44] Rebels were a lot like cockroaches to the Indiana men; there were never just a few. Somewhere unseen was a bunch of them that would make their appearance when and where least expected.

The Hoosiers bedded down for the night within two miles of the Pennsylvania state line. At two the following afternoon, Brigadier General Hobart Ward ordered his men to fall in line and prepare to march. The men didn't need to be told the reason—they could hear the booming of artillery coming from the north towards Gettysburg. Why they had not moved sooner was the real mystery, but each corps commander seemed to be feeling his way along, waiting for Rebels to appear in force. Panicked citizens of Gettysburg fled their homes down the Emmitsburg Road, desperate to find safety from the increasingly loud din of battle.[45] The ten-mile distance to Gettysburg was covered in quick time, with no rest, in ninety-degree temperatures and with only a fifteen-minute rest. Men fell by the roadside by the score from their exhaustion and the blazing sun. To their great relief, the Hoosiers reached the peach orchard on the Wentz farm at 8:30. From there, Ward's brigade filed off the Emmitsburg Road and moved along a small road across the Jacob Weikert farm to the high ground just south of Gettysburg. Bone-tired and longing for sleep, the men were allowed to lie down, but were ordered not to remove a single stitch of clothing or a single accoutrement. The men grumbled but obeyed.[46]

The fighting began early on July 1 at Gettysburg when the cavalry division of Brigadier General John Buford confronted Confederate infantry on the Chambersburg Pike, northwest of the town. Buford's troopers bravely stood their ground until relieved by the Federal First Corps. The fighting by First Corps along McPherson's Ridge and in the unfinished railroad cut had been desultory, with Union troops hard pressed by the massing Rebel army. The Union Eleventh Corps arrived on the scene and took up position on the right flank of First Corps. The fighting became more fierce as the day progressed and more Confederate infantry arrived on the field. Eleventh Corps had taken a severe pounding, and the arrival of a large body of Rebel infantry from the north struck a fatal blow on their flank. The Eleventh Corps, which was prone to running, used this as their catalyst and broke, falling back on Gettysburg in a rout.

Their shameful withdrawal left the First Corps isolated and flanked, forcing it to make a fighting movement back into Gettysburg. As the desperate men of First and Eleventh Corps fled through the little town toward Cemetery Hill, they were met by Major General Winfield S. Hancock, the most dashing and brave commander of Second Corps. He rallied the frightened men and formed a defensive perimeter which ran from Cemetery Hill on the left to Culp's Hill on the right. The victorious Confederate infantry, led by Lieutenant General Richard S. Ewell, pausing in the town, failed to press their advantage. This fatal delay allowed an ever-increasing number of Federal forces to file into the defensive lines, which by early evening extended southward along Cemetery Ridge. As the hot, muggy evening of July 1 faded into blackness, the Army of the Potomac was in a formation which greatly resembled a fishhook, with the eye of the hook at Little Round Top to the south and the barb of the hook to the north at Culp's Hill.

Even though the Hoosiers had grumbled about being forced to sleep on their weapons, with all clothes and accoutrements attached, they were fortunate that they were allowed some respite for the evening. Such was not the case with the Fourth Maine Infantry of the brigade. They were sent forth as pickets west of the brigade position to the Emmitsburg Road. Scattered rifle fire broke out between the Fourth Maine and its unseen enemy across the Emmitsburg Road before the morning sun could break the mist and fog which shrouded the battlefield. The firing increased in intensity, indicating a strong presence of Rebel infantry in the woods opposite their position. At 11:00 A.M., the Fourth Maine withdrew to their brigade and reported the apparent strength of opposition.[47]

Between seven and eight that morning, Birney's division was ordered to relieve Brigadier General John W. Geary's Twelfth Corps division near Little Round Top, the rocky hill which, along with its sister elevation, Big Round Top, dominated the topography of the south end of the Federal line.[48] Although taller, Big Round Top was tree-covered, providing little opportunity to crown its heights with artillery which could dominate the battlefield. Little Round Top, however, was treeless and offered artillery an excellent field of fire from which to dominate advancing Rebel forces. On the other hand, should it fall into Confederate hands, it would allow Rebel artillery an opportunity to enfilade the entire Union line on Cemetery Ridge.

The Twentieth Indiana and its brigade moved to a position about one mile east of the Emmitsburg Road at the southern slope of a rocky eminence just beyond the small stream called Plum Run, approximately one-eighth of a mile northwest of Little Round Top. There they took up a line of battle behind a stone wall.[49]

While the bulk of Ward's brigade was resting in their new position, the

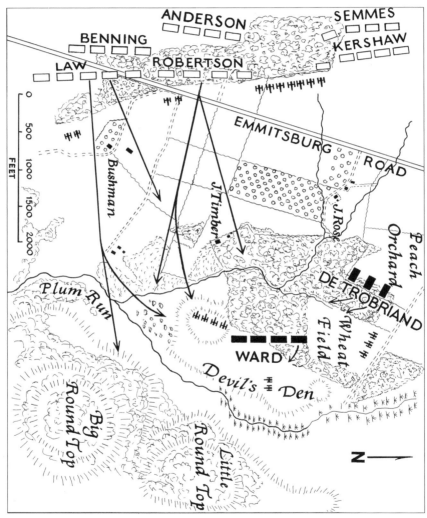

The Battle of Gettysburg, the second day (July 2, 1863): At 4 p.m., the Confederate advance into the Wheatfield drives Ward's division, including the Twentieth Indiana, into the Devil's Den.

Third Maine and two regiments of Berdan's Sharpshooters advanced across the Emmitsburg Road to feel out the Confederate right flank. A brisk fire fight broke out between the Federal sortie and Confederate General Cadmus Wilcox's Alabamans. During the sharp little skirmish, Colonel Berdan witnessed a large column of Rebel infantry moving across his front, indicating that Confederate forces were jockeying to make an attack on the Union left flank.[50]

In an action that would stir controversy to this very day, Major General Daniel Sickles moved the bulk of his Third Corps to the extreme advanced position in Wentz's peach orchard. Sickles passionately believed that this position offered the best opportunity to defend the Union line, with greatly improved fields of fire for artillery. Such a bold change of position required permission from Major General Meade, but the impulsive Sickles did not wait for the approval. Instead he moved his men forward, abandoning continuity with the rest of the Union line and exposing the left flank to a potentially disastrous Rebel turning movement.

Robert E. Lee, deeply regretful that Ewell had not pursued his advantage on July 1, was now determined to repeat the strategy which was successful at Chancellorsville and assault the Union left flank. Accordingly, he ordered Lieutenant General James Longstreet's corps to make a wide, sweeping movement which would bring them undetected in a massive attack down the Emmitsburg Road. Longstreet had favored an even wider turning movement which would bring his corps in behind Big Round Top, but Lee was insistent on the Emmitsburg Road line of approach. In the blackness of the early morning hours, Longstreet's men stealthily moved to their right, across the front of Third Corps.

Shortly after noon Colonel Hiram Berdan reported what he had seen to Major General Birney, who passed the intelligence on to Major General Sickles. Sickles then ordered Birney to change fronts to the southwest, the new anticipated line of attack by the Confederates.[51] In compliance with this order, the Twentieth Indiana moved with the brigade five hundred yards forward, crossing Wheatfield Road and proceeding into the ripened golden grain standing chest high in the Wheatfield.[52]

Ward's brigade was aligned with the Fourth Maine on the extreme left flank, the One Hundred and Twenty-fourth New York on its right, followed by the Eighty-sixth New York, the Twentieth Indiana, and the Ninety-ninth Pennsylvania on the right flank.[53] Ward's brigade anchored Birney's line on the left flank—the right of Birney's division extended for a mile to the Emmitsburg Road, perilously thin.[54]

The Hoosiers passed an uneasy half hour lounging in the Wheatfield. Faces were blanched and pulses raced quicker as each soldier contemplated what the movement across their front by the Rebels might mean. The Confederate boot was in the air, now the question was where it would come down.

Colonel John Wheeler had risen at 4:00 A.M. and had taken the opportunity afforded by the quiet predawn hours to write home, perhaps for one last time. He wrote:

> *Dear Wife and children:*
> *We arrived here last night at 9:00 P.M. The First Corps had a fight here yesterday. Major General Reynolds was killed. Our whole army is here now and we move on them this morning. I shall give this to someone who does not go into battle so that you will probably get it. It may be my last letter to you. If so believe that my last prayer for you is that God may bless you all. I believe we will whip them finely before the sun goes down. We met women, children and men all flying for safety last night and scared to death. Some had a hand box, some a valise and some were in wagons and buggies, others on horse back. All said "hurry up." We had a hard march of ten miles. We left Emmitsburg at 4:00 P.M. Once more adieu.*
>
> *Your affectionate husband, John Wheeler*[55]

While the Indiana boys speculated on the coming day's events, General Birney had moved two sections of Smith's battery (four rifled artillery pieces) to the top of a rocky eminence, called Houck's Ridge, in front of Little Round Top. The guns would require infantry support, and Ward was ordered to move his brigade to the left to handle the task. Ward's brigade, maintaining their battle line order, sidled to their left for several hundred yards until the Fourth Maine anchored the line firmly in place at Devil's Den, an outcropping of massive stones plowed up by some tormented geological action during the ice age.[56]

The Twentieth Indiana's movement to their left found the Hoosiers occupying a wooded, hilly parcel of waste scrub adjacent to the Rose Farm. The ground was littered with large rock outcroppings which provided some cover, but made quick movement hazardous. This final movement into the Rose Woods culminated a month long, two-hundred-plus mile march. The tired men of the Twentieth took the opportunity provided by their current position to rest. Perhaps it was some confusion over whether the Third Corps would be attacking or defending that led Brigadier General Ward to forego ordering the construction of breastworks. Whatever the reason, the brigade missed a golden opportunity to provide themselves with some protection other than the menacing granite boulders which littered the hill.[57]

This lazy, two-hour-long respite was shattered at 3:30 P.M. by a rain of iron blasted out by Confederate artillery posted west of the Emmitsburg Road. The object of this concentrated fire was Smith's battery, which threatened to destroy Rebel forces moving across the Emmitsburg Road. Two hundred and sixty-eight Hoosiers clung to the rocks and earth along Houck's Ridge as exploding shells splintered the treetops and showered fragments and limbs on the mass of soldiers huddled together. Colonel Wheeler bravely rode his horse along the regimental line encouraging his men to be brave, as his subordinate officers ran from rock to rock, imploring their companies to stand fast.[58] Smith's battery gamely returned the fire into the Rebel ranks, striking down officers and enlisted men indiscriminately as they massed for their attack.[59]

At 4:00 A.M. Colonel Manning had prodded his Third Arkansas Infantry into motion on a sweeping flank march. The men had eaten a hearty breakfast, were well rested, and had full canteens and cartridge boxes. Their march proceeded slowly, taking nearly four hours to move six miles. At last, a halt was called to the march and men were ordered off the road and into the adjacent fields so that artillery could pass. At noon Evander M. Law's brigade of Hood's division arrived in the area from picket duty at New Guilford. With Lafayette McLaw's brigade leading the way, the long column renewed its march on a road running parallel to Seminary Ridge, the low ridge line which concealed the Confederate movements from Union forces on Little Round Top. Soon, the Rebel column came to a bumping halt, as Law's men marched back down the road heading in the opposite direction. They had been forced to backtrack when the head of the column emerged on the Emmitsburg Road in full view of the Federal forces assembled in the Peach Orchard. This backtracking caused an even further delay to an already seriously tardy movement, forcing Longstreet's corps to cut cross country on their movement to the jumping off point. At eight in the morning Little Round Top had been deserted, now, at mid-afternoon, it bristled with artillery.[60]

When the ever-aggressive Major General John Hood saw the presence of Union troops in both the Peach Orchard and on Little Round Top, he suggested to James Longstreet that the attack needed to swing further to the south around Big Round Top. Longstreet, who had been chastised by General Lee for the delay in this attack, was in no mood to defend a battle plan with which he plainly disagreed and brusquely terminated the discussion with the order: "You will attack down the Emmitsburg Road because the commanding general has ordered it."[61]

At 3:30 P.M. fifteen thousand Rebel soldiers began crossing the Emmitsburg Road to assemble for attack. As soon as the leading file touched the road, the alert gunners of Smith's battery loosed a salvo at the Rebels, instantly ripping into the massed troops.[62] Private John Wilkerson, Third Arkansas, described the chaotic scene:

The enemy soon got range of us and it seemed they could hit our line every time. I could look down the line and see our men knocked out constantly. I was in the front ranks by the side of my captain. Soon a shell hit and killed him. I saw the orderly sergeant's head knocked off, then a corporal's leg. I don't know how long we were held there under fire, but the time seemed endless.[63]

Colonel Manning walked through the prone ranks of his Arkansans, encouraging them to be calm. Oblivious to the crashing shells around him, the brave colonel steadied his men until Brigadier General Jerome B. Robertson, commanding the brigade, rode to the front of the Arkansas regiment and shouted, "We're going in there men. There's a rail fence down there on the road. Grab it by the bottom rail and heave!"[64] Manning stepped to the front of his regiment with drawn sword, pointed to the peak of Little Round Top and commanded, "Forward, guide right, march!"[65] The huge mass of gray-clad Confederate infantry burst forth from the trees along the Emmitsburg Road, a line stretching widely left and right, red battle flags fluttering in the breeze.[66]

It was well that the Hoosiers were saved the spectacle of the massed battle line moving toward them like a *tsunami*. Through the thickets of the Rose Woods the Hoosiers could scarcely see two hundred yards in their front. Already extremely anxious, they let their ears tell them what their eyes could not reveal, that a large number of screaming Confederates were headed their way, delivering searing fire which drove the skirmishers back on the brigade line.

The men of the Third Arkansas steadily moved across the open fields leading to Houck's Ridge. They advanced under a devastating artillery bombardment skillfully fired by Smith's rifled guns, and continued over a slight ridge some six hundred yards from the awaiting Twentieth Indiana and then down into a ravine.[67] On they went toward the edge of the Rose Woods and the small stone wall which offered some protection from the hailstorm of shot and shell. On the Northern side, Brigadier General Ward had given a strict order to the regiments on the left flank of his brigade to withhold fire until the enemy had drawn to within two hundred yards.[68]

For the men of the Twentieth Indiana, Eighty-sixth New York, and Ninety-ninth Pennsylvania, Ward's order was meaningless. The trees and the smoke and dust thrown up by exploding shells greatly limited their view;

the Arkansans were nearly in their laps before they came into view. Suddenly, life-sized Rebels appeared, swarming into the Rose Woods firing a lethal volley. With pockets and cartridge boxes full, some men carrying as many as two hundred rounds, the Twentieth and its sister regiments responded with their own fierce volley. The fighting then degenerated into a melee.[69]

On horseback, Colonel John Wheeler threaded his way among the rocks and boulders, exhorting his men to aim low and make every shot count. He was shouting orders when a Rebel minié ball found its way to his throat, severing the jugular and exiting through his temple. He fell from his mount, lifeless, in a pool of blood. Adjutant John Luther placed the colonel in a blanket and tearfully carried him to the rear, where he quickly buried him.[70]

Hoosiers dropped thick and fast from the concentrated fire. Asher Chapman, already missing his nose from a close encounter with a Rebel musket ball at Second Manassas, went down with a wound to his thigh.[71] Captain Thomas Logan took a ball in his arm, breaking the ulna and rendering him useless for battle.[72] Amos Ash, Elias Briley, and David Brownlee all fell dead in this first attack.[73] George Reddick's leg was shattered by a musket ball, as were the legs of Andrew Crabb and Harrison Ambrose. All three would have their legs amputated, only to die slow, agonizing deaths in a hospital.[74]

The focal point of the attack by the Third Arkansas had been aimed more toward Smith's battery than at the Rose Woods. The Arkansans and the First Texas Infantry on their right flank listed to their right as the firing from the Twentieth Indiana and Ninety-ninth Pennsylvania intensified. This exposed their flanks and rear to a deadly enfilading fire from not only the Hoosiers and Pennsylvanians, but from the Seventeenth Maine, which had taken a position behind a stone wall bordering the Wheatfield. Lieutenant Colonel William C. L. Taylor, leading the regiment after Wheeler's death, skillfully ordered his men to turn slightly to the south, and they poured a withering fire into the flank of the left three companies of the Third Arkansas. This forced the Third Arkansas to withdraw from the ridge and regroup some three hundred yards to the rear.[75]

Bodies of bloodied and broken men from the Twentieth lay strewn across Houck's Ridge in every imaginable position of death and suffering. Smoke hung thick in the air above the wicked boulders strewn haphazardly by nature. Men cried out for mercy and relief—Union and Confederate soldiers were once again united in pain.

The brief lull in the fighting gave the Hoosiers the opportunity to give some assistance to the wounded and to take an inventory of those still able to hold a rifle. Lieutenant Colonel Taylor rode up to Captain Erasmus C. Gilbreath and suddenly slumped over the pommel of his saddle. He called

to the captain, "Gil, you will have to take charge of the line as I am wounded."
He spun the horse around and galloped off to the rear, leaving the Twentieth
Indiana in the capable hands of Gilbreath.[76]

Hobart Ward did not make the difficult duties of command any easier
on the young Captain Gilbreath. Ward's left flank had almost succumbed to
the relentless pressure exerted by the remainder of Robertson's Rebels; he
needed reinforcement quickly. He ordered the Ninety-ninth Pennsylvania
to pass from the extreme right of the brigade line to a new position in the
heart of the Devil's Den. This left the greatly diminished Twentieth Indiana
and the Eighty-sixth New York to hold the Rose Woods.[77]

Lieutenant Colonel Taylor had known that there was a dangerous gap
between his regiment and the Seventeenth Maine, who had no intentions of
abandoning the safety of their stone wall to close up on the Hoosiers' flank,
so he sent Companies B and H, under Captain Charles A. Bell, to fill the
void. Bell took his men forward of the line and to the right to create the
appearance that they were skirmishers and not the only forces in the gap.[78]

Gilbreath looked for his brother officer, Captain Charles Reese, to secure
advice but found Reese unable to provide it. Reese had received what appeared
to be a fatal wound, a bullet passing through his eye and lodging in his
brain. There was nothing to do for the captain but send him to the rear and
hope for the best.[79]

There were many lucky men in the regiment. Both of the men standing
next to Thomas Sibel were killed by bullets, yet he was unscathed.[80] Sergeant
Stephens was even luckier. He was struck in the side by Rebel bullets, but
was spared being wounded because the missiles hit his cartridge box and the
metal U.S. plate on the box.[81]

Hobart Ward felt he could shorten his brigade line somewhat and provide
additional cover for his badly exposed right flank by moving the Twentieth
Indiana and the Eighty-sixth New York 160 yards forward to a stone wall.
He pleaded with Major General Birney for reinforcements, and the general
responded by sending the Fortieth New York to Ward's support. Ward placed
the New Yorkers on his left flank in the valley between Devil's Den and
Little Round Top and awaited a renewal of the Confederate attack.[82]

The Rebels immediately renewed their furious assault on the Union left
flank. Brigadier General Jerome Robertson knew that Federal forces in the
Rose Woods and the Wheatfield had to be removed if the assault on Little
Round Top was to be successful. Robertson sent a courier back to Brigadier
General George T. Anderson, commanding a supporting brigade two hundred
yards to the rear, requesting that the general bring his men on the run and
attack the Wheatfield and the Rose Woods. Anderson wasted no time in
pushing his men forward on the double quick. His Georgians advanced in

one large mass, the Ninth and Eighth Georgia infantries on his left flank, and the Eleventh and Fifty-ninth Georgia infantries on his right. The survivors of the Third Arkansas joined the Fifty-ninth Georgia in running toward the stone wall. Together the two regiments charged through the boulder-cluttered woods toward the wall, men jumping up on rocks to fire at the Hoosiers who were loading and shooting as quickly as possible.[83]

Captain Gilbreath's moment had come to lead men in battle. He looked around for the trappings of command. He found Colonel Wheeler's horse and mounted the beast, intent on providing the Rebel riflemen the same excellent target that his predecessors Brown, Wheeler, and Taylor had done. The horse became so restive that Gilbreath could not remain mounted and he was forced to dismount and lead his men on foot, for which the horse should have won a medal for saving the captain's life.[84]

The Twentieth had expended most of its ammunition during the first assault. Gilbreath had dispatched a messenger to General Ward requesting additional bullets. Ward sent his aide, Captain Alfred M. Raphall, to Gilbreath with orders to hold his position for as long as possible, using ammunition gleaned from the bodies of the killed and wounded; when the regiment could hold no its position no longer, they were to fall back to a small cabin along the Wheatfield Road. Raphall had barely repeated his instructions when a musket ball struck him in the arm and unhorsed him.[85]

The irresistible charge of the Fifty-ninth Georgia and Third Arkansas met squarely with the immovable object of the Twentieth Indiana. One of the most fiercely fought battles of the entire war ensued. It is hard to imagine how men can stand at close range and blaze away at each other, with the sounds of crashing explosions, screaming, whistling bullets and cries for help pervading the air. Both sides rose to the moment and bravely slugged it out along the stone wall.

Lieutenant Ezra Robbins' chest was ripped open by a minié ball, and Captain Gilbreath dragged the officer off to die in peace behind a cedar tree. Private Daniel Wright had his left hip shattered by a ball, forcing his removal from the field. Sergeant Alonzo Lamb felt the piercing of his breast by a Rebel bullet and then he felt nothing more as the ball continued through his spine, paralyzing him.[86]

Adjutant John Luther, his duties requiring him to be armed with pen and paper and not with a gun, returned from burying Colonel Wheeler. He rushed into the fray wielding only his sword, then realized the futility of taking a sword to a gun battle. He sheathed the weapon, picked up the rifle of a dead member of the regiment, stuffed his pockets with ammunition, and proceeded to blast away at the advancing Georgians. He kept up the furious fire until he was struck in the belt plate by a Rebel musket ball, which knocked the air out of him and sent him tumbling to the rocky earth.[87]

The barrels of the rifles had grown so hot from repeated firing that they scorched the hands of the Hoosiers who were loading and firing as quickly as possible.[88] As Anderson's Georgians and Roberton's Arkansans crashed headlong into the Hoosiers, fighting became hand to hand and shooting was done at point-blank range. Powder flashes from rifles ignited the uniforms of contending, struggling soldiers.[89] The Rebel success was brief and deadly, as a terrific fire poured into the flanks of the attackers. The Seventeenth Maine, still anchored behind the stone wall at the Wheatfield, opened a deadly volley on the advancing Rebels which shattered the head of the attack and drove the gray-clad enemy backward, finally.[90]

The Twentieth Indiana and Eighty-sixth New York were nearly broken. The ammunition was almost exhausted and the few soldiers who weren't killed or wounded had leaden arms from the exhaustion of battle. As the Fifty-ninth Georgia and Third Arkansas regrouped, joined by elements of the Eleventh Georgia, Northern men who had the strength to move wandered along the battle line, rummaging through pockets and cartridge boxes for any precious ammunition. Precious little could be found and Captain Gilbreath knew that his brave regiment had reached the point of desperation.

Within minutes the regrouped and reinvigorated Confederates came steadily forward, the Rebel yell a little less loud and piercing. The third Confederate advance held its fire until it had come to within two hundred yards of the Twentieth line. The Indiana men opened up with what ammunition was left and tried their best to fire low and make every shot count. Captain Gilbreath had heard the cries from panicked men that they had fired their last shot and determined that the line could not be held. He ordered his survivors to slowly fall back and to stay close to the flag. The advancing Georgians, seeing the Hoosiers heading for the rear, laughed and yelled taunts at them as they came on. They concentrated their rifle fire at the regimental colors, dropping six of the eight color guards assigned to the protection of the flag. Sergeant William Horine, carrying the flag, was shot through the leg and fell hard to the ground. A young corporal rescued the flag and carried it to the rear. The Georgians got a good laugh and hooted at the corporal that they'd get the flag yet. Emboldened by the retreat of the Hoosiers, the Rebels rushed on up and over Houck's Ridge.[91]

The cockiness of the Georgians and their advance were both thwarted when the retreating men of the Twentieth were joined by the Fifth New Hampshire Infantry, rushing forward to their relief. The New Hampshire boys loosed a powerful volley which brought the Rebel advance to a standstill and sent the formerly laughing Southerners on their own withdrawal. Gilbreath reassembled his men at the rear edge of the Rose Woods and had the company rolls called, quietly and solemnly, when Captain Charles Bell returned with the remnants of his two companies. Bell ranked Gilbreath in seniority and insisted on seizing command of the tattered regiment. His first act was to grab the flag, lift it over his head, and start singing "Rally 'Round The Flag Boys." Bell was not blessed with a singing voice or charisma, and so the thoroughly uninspired men ignored him as he furiously waved the flag and ran to the rear. The regiment followed slowly and when the procession could be brought to a halt again, they were located on the ridge line to the north of Little Round Top.[92]

The Twentieth had an excellent view of the continuing pitched battle between the newly arrived Union Fifth Corps and Longstreet's Confederates. The last light of day revealed two stalemated battle lines several hundred yards apart and thousands of dead and seriously wounded soldiers on the rocky ground between them. After dark, there was little for the Twentieth to do but prepare for the renewed fighting which would surely come the next day. It had been a terribly costly day for the Twentieth Indiana. In addition to losing their respected Colonel Wheeler, the Hoosiers lost 31 killed, 109 wounded and 11 men missing.[93] Ten of the wounded would later die of their wounds or from the crude amputations hastily done in the overcrowded field hospitals at Gettysburg.[94]

The Hoosiers faced a tense, sleepless night on the rocky ridge, awaiting either a surprise attack in the blackness of night or at the first glimmer of dawn, but the attack never came. What did come was the surprise delivery of a backlog of mail. No one was able to deliver ammunition in the heat of battle, but they could get mail through as the armies poised, waiting for attack. Captain Erasmus C. Gilbreath received the welcomed news that his appointment as major had been approved by Governor Morton. He could now resume command and spare his regiment the tone-deaf choraling of Captain Charles Bell.[95]

July 3 dawned with the glaring sun which had shown at Austerlitz, and the Twentieth Indiana were left alone on their lonely outpost on Cemetery Ridge. From their elevated position, the regiment could get a good perspective of both the Union position and the disposition of much of the Confederate army. Across the wide expanse to the Rebel line along Seminary Ridge, the Indiana boys could see dust clouds as columns of massed soldiers moved behind the ridge line and batteries rushed into position. Occasionally a Rebel artillery shot would fly toward the center of the Union line as if to verify distances to the center of the Federal battle line.[96]

At 1:00 P.M. the icy tension was broken by the fire of two signal cannon on the extreme left flank of the Federal line.[97] Nerves and muscles became tightened as 150 Rebel artillery pieces belched forth their lethal lead and pummeled the center of the Union line on Cemetery Ridge. The seventy-seven guns which chief of U.S. artillery, Brigadier General Henry Hunt, positioned in the center of the Federal line, angrily replied and the largest artillery duel ever fought in the Western Hemisphere ensued.[98] For two hours the valley between Cemetery Ridge and Seminary Ridge reverberated with the thunderous rumbling of cannon fire. Sound, smoke and flames dominated the rolling Pennsylvania farmland.

The survivors of the Twentieth Indiana sat in front-row seats, one half mile from the crashing tumult of the Union center, far from their suffering comrades in the Second Corps who bravely held their ground in the face of the blistering bombardment. Veterans and recruits alike stared with utter amazement at the cataclysm unfolding before them.

Then, in an effort to save ammunition for his artillery, Brigadier General Hunt ordered his guns to cease firing.[99] Confederate Colonel E. Porter Alexander had been given the ominous and difficult task of not only directing the Rebel artillery fire, but also evaluating its success as an indicator of when to launch the infantry attack. Longstreet, commanding Alexander to decide because he could not bear to do it himself, was as unhappy as a general could be. Robert E. Lee had ordered that an infantry assault be made on the Union center after a preparatory artillery bombardment, an assault Longstreet believed would fail. The attacking force which would consist of fifteen thousand soldiers led by Major General James Pickett, would have to cross a wide-open wheat field into the teeth of the Federal line. If Union batteries and their supporting infantry could not be destroyed by the Confederate bombardment, it could mean the slaughter of Pickett's men. Alexander, his own ammunition running perilously low, judged the cessation of the Federal artillery fire as an indication that they had exhausted their ammunition, and he implored General Pickett, "For God's sake, come quick!" With an artillery colonel's innocuous order, the charge which would endure in lore forever was begun.[100]

Pickett's men emerged from the tree line on Seminary Ridge into the bright afternoon sun and, with battle flags flying, the force advanced across the open field to their front. Federal artillery resumed their fire, this time concentrating on the Confederate infantry, tearing great holes in the advancing lines. Still, never faltering, they advanced over the ripened wheat up the slight rise to the Emmitsburg Road and then down the eastern bank of the road to the Union line at the point of a small copse of trees which marked the center of the Federal line and on to the artillery.[101]

The Twentieth watched in worried silence. Then, an aide to Colonel Hiram Berdan, who commanded the brigade because Brigadier General Ward was acting division commander, rushed up and ordered the Twentieth

Indiana, the Fourth Maine, and the Ninety-ninth Pennsylvania to their feet. He then pointed at the endangered Federal artillery position and ordered this small force to the relief of the Union gunners. Huffing and puffing in the warm afternoon sun toward the Union center, they rushed on, their eyes ahead on the Rebels interspersed amongst the batteries, victoriously waving their flags, some mounting the captured field pieces in triumph. There was chaos everywhere as men yelled, cheered and feverishly slugged it out for possession of the guns.[102]

Just at their moment of potential triumph, the bloodied, battered, and exhausted men of Pickett's charge threw down their guns and surrendered in the face of superior Federal strength.[103] Their greatly thinned numbers did not allow them to hold their gains. The attack, which had looked so promising, ended in utter failure, a conclusion which Longstreet had anticipated before the attack had begun.

The newly arrived Hoosiers raised their guns and took hundreds of prisoners too tired to continue fighting. The Rebel captives were escorted to the rear of the Union lines and the Twentieth had their first opportunity to see the slaughter firsthand. Captain John Brown ventured out among the dead and dying Confederates, where his attention was captured by one horribly wounded officer who was crying out for help. The officer cried out to Brown that he was shot through the body in at least two places. Although Brown was sympathetic, there were so many wounded Rebels lying about that there was nothing that made this one unique. And then the officer asked, "Are you a Mason?" Captain Brown, who was a member of the Monticello Masonic Lodge, instantly flew into action and called for two men and a stretcher. The officer was loaded on the stretcher and quickly carried to a field hospital where he could receive medical attention. The officer, destined to die of his wounds but live in Civil War lore, was Brigadier General Lewis Armistead.[104]

Ward's brigade drew picket duty at the Cordori Farm.[105] It was an evening spent among the dead and dying on the plain in front of Cemetery Ridge. All night long the moans and groans of the wounded aroused the pity and outrage of the men. If they had not hated war before, they did that night.[106]

Independence Day dawned hot and humid with the threat of rain. At this early hour, a pervasive stench arose over the battlefield. The regiment was in a deadly and exposed forward position, trusted as always with the tough and most important work.[107] It took the Confederates in the tree line along Seminary Ridge little time to spot the soldiers huddled around the Cordori Farm. They opened up immediately, spraying a shower of lead on the Twentieth. The Indiana men fired at puffs of smoke, the only way to mark hidden potential targets. The peach trees offered scant cover; one man was killed and seven enlisted men were wounded. Lieutenants Charles Liner and Ed Sutherland fell to Rebel bullets while keeping up the Union end of the spirited skirmishing.[108]

Assistant Quartermaster Dennis Tuttle visited the regiment bringing supplies and ammunition. Deeply shocked, he wrote his wife:

July 5, 1863

My dear wife:
I have just this moment come in from the front. I went out yesterday morning with forage and shoes. I went over the battlefield or a portion of it last night. I thought I had seen some terrible sights on the battlefield before but I never saw anything to compare with this. The Battle of Gettysburg was the most bloody of the War. We were victorious but it cost us much choice blood. Everyone says the field was the most stubbornly contested of any yet fought. Our corps suffered most fearfully. Several times their whole number was thrown against them like an avalanche but they stood like a rock. There was no flinching as their ranks were rapidly thinned.

Our brigade held their ground for a long time against more than five times their number but they suffered severely. Our regiment lost over two hundred killed, wounded and missing. Among the killed was Colonel Wheeler. The proportion of killed to wounded was very small. We have taken a large number of prisoners. I should think 8,000 or 10,000. When I was out there last night one look told me I was in seven lines of battle, one behind the other. As usual, our regiment occupied the front line. I went to the front to do my business but I made my stay as short as it was practical as the bullets were circulating rather more freely than suited to my taste. I don't think I have much of a taste for bullet music anyway. Several bullets struck within three or four feet of me and many more from the sound, I think came still closer. You can have no idea of how the field looked in that locality. I think I could have walked one fourth to one half mile on dead Rebels without ever stepping on the ground. Horses and mules, the living and dead were mingled together on the field. Oh, but it was horrid and it made my heart sick to see it. I cannot tell you about it.

I have not the time now, besides it makes me heartsick to think of it. I was at the Third Corps Hospital this morning and there was another sad sight, so many brave fellows mangled so horribly. Dr. Everts is one of the operating surgeons of the corps and he has worked constantly since the fight and is tired and bloody but well. No more now. I am still

well and strong. General Lee will have his hands full to get his foot out
of this scrape.

> *With much love, I am as ever,*
> *your affectionate husband* [109]

Lee would have his hands full, but would not experience nearly the difficulty he might have. Many historians and military experts view July 4 as a day of wasted opportunity for the victorious Northerners. A concentrated Union attack on the Confederate position along Seminary Ridge might have destroyed Lee's army and the Confederacy as well. Lee expected the attack; he knew that he would have done it had the shoe been on the other foot. His men expected to be assaulted along the entire line; they were unable to defend their position for want of artillery ammunition. The Union soldiers expected to be ordered to attack and actually looked forward to the advance. Private A. W. Luther wrote his father, stating: "We are ready and anxious to give them another battle, all hoping and trusting that God and the good generals are on the side of the invincible Army of the Potomac."[110]

Major General George Meade, satisfied with the glorious victory he had won, was not going to attack. His army was mangled and bloodied, the supply and medical systems stretched to their breaking point. More importantly, Meade was himself mentally and physically exhausted. He had taken command in the face of battle, had slept little over the last several days, had seen so many of his and the other army's brave soldiers butchered over three days that he was physically and psychologically spent. Meade resolved to either fight a defensive battle in his current position or wait for Lee to move and then pursue. While Lee plotted his retreat, Meade issued General Orders Number 68, congratulating his men for their performance during the battle. His message concluded, "Our task is not yet accomplished and the commanding general looks to the army for greater efforts to drive from our soil every vestige of the presence of the invader."[111]

Meade's choice of words might have been meaningful during the War of 1812, but in this war to preserve the Union, the concept of repelling invaders was repugnant to President Lincoln, Secretary Stanton, and the radicals in Congress. The proclamation cast a shadow on the great victory and would haunt Meade in the coming weeks as Lee withdrew to Virginia.

At 4:00 P.M. on July 4 Confederate Brigadier General John Imboden departed Gettysburg, leading the long wagon train of suffering from the field of battle. He had been entrusted by General Lee with the duty of removing the wounded and most of the Confederate army supply wagons to Virginia. It was a dangerous task, hampered by the constant pressure of pursuing Federal cavalry. On July 5, the Rebel infantry slipped out of its position along Seminary Ridge and followed the wagon train to Williamsport, on the Potomac River, where Lee intended to cross over to the Old Dominion.[112]

The removal of the Confederate army from Gettysburg confirmed to the average soldier that the Union had won a great victory. Sergeant W. H. Zimmerman, Company E, now believed that the end of the Confederacy was near. He wrote to his father that, "Things look very favorable to us now. I expect to be home to help husk corn if I do not get killed."[113] The Army of the Potomac was itching to pursue Lee when Meade finally authorized the Union Sixth Corps to move out at noon on July 5. Meade himself was still at Gettysburg the following day and did not seem in any particular hurry to chase Lee down, apparently content that the invaders had been driven off.

The Army of Northern Virginia was in serious trouble. Union cavalry had previously destroyed the Confederate pontoon bridge at Williamsport, and torrential rains had swollen the Potomac River to a point where it could not be forded. When Lee arrived at Williamsport, his back was to the river and his fate in the hands of Mother Nature and George Meade. It was July 12 before the Army of the Potomac had crept far enough forward to threaten Lee's forces. Meade telegraphed Secretary Stanton that he intended to attack the next day unless something intervened.[114]

Meade prepared a plan of attack and called his corps commanders together for its presentation. Whether intentionally or not, Meade allowed the presentation to turn into a council of war; the proposed plan of attack was voted down five to two. The attack was off and so was any hope of destroying Lee's cornered army.

By the morning of July 13, Lee's quartermaster had devised a ramshackle bridge of used planks and boards torn from some warehouses. It was a rickety structure, but proved adequate for allowing his entire force to quietly slip over the Potomac and to safety, effectively ending the Gettysburg campaign.[115]

The Twentieth Indiana had mixed reactions to Lee's escape. Corporal Reeder reflected his disappointment when he told his parents, "They said we had them in a bag, but someone forgot to tie it."[116] Sergeant Seymour Montgomery cast his lot with the majority of the Union corps commanders when he opined, "To have stormed the works there (Williamsport) would have been as great a piece of folly as it would be for a column of infantry to make a similar attempt on the castle of San Juan Villoa, from the seaside. Every soldier feels grateful to General Meade for not attempting it. He has saved the Army of the Potomac from being uselessly slaughtered."[117] But the wise Assistant Quartermaster Dennis Tuttle referred to the escape of Lee as a "sad, sad mistake."[118]

President Lincoln and Secretary Stanton also viewed it as a sad, sad mistake, or something close to criminal neglect. Lincoln ached from the pain inflicted by the lost opportunity. The massive casualty figures from the three days of unrelenting carnage at Gettysburg were becoming known and the President hated the thought that the sacrifices made by the fallen had not been followed up by definitive destruction of the Confederate army. In excess of fifty thousand men had lost life or limb in a battle which, after Lee's removal to Virginia, left both armies in the same relative position they had been in two months earlier. Meade's days might have been numbered had it not been for the disturbing news coming from New York City. The first attempt to conduct the conscription of draftees into the Union army had ended in failure, and the city of New York was engulfed in flames and rioting. This was a problem in Lincoln's own back yard which had to be dealt with before serious thought could be given once more to the destruction of the Army of Northern Virginia.

Colonel John Wheeler was killed at Gettysburg. His letters to his family and friends contributed to this book. (Carlile collection)

Adjutant John E. Luther (Carlile collection)

Quartermaster Dennis Tuttle was a Yale-educated attorney. (Carlile collection)

Captain Charles Reese, Company D, was discharged in October 1863 because of the wounds he received at Gettysburg. (Carlile collection)

Private Amos Ash, Company A, was killed at Gettysburg. (Sundstrom collection)

Captain Henry O. Quigley, Company G, died of a gunshot wound at the Battle of the Wilderness. (Courtesy Shelly D. Dooley)

Corporal William C. H. Reeder, Company A, was wounded at Oak Grove. (Dunn collection)

Lieutenant Colonel James H. Shannon resigned to become colonel of the One Hundred and Thirty-eighth Indiana in June 1863. (Carlile collection)

Assistant Surgeon Henry C. Grover served the regiment from January 1862 until the end of the war. (Carlile collection)

Captain John E. Sweet, Company E (Carlile collection)

Brave and capable, Major Erasmus C. Gilbreath served in all major battles and was wounded at Fredericksburg and Chancellorsville. His manuscript contributed to this story. (Carlile collection)

Private Samuel Foxworthy, Company F. (U.S. Army Military History Institute)

Private Theodore
Day, Company D,
was killed at
Gettysburg. (Dunn
collection)

Private Elijah Roe, Company A.
(Dunn collection)

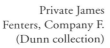

Private James
Fenters, Company F.
(Dunn collection)

Private Edward Jennings, Company F,
was the brigade color bearer at
Fredericksburg, and one of the few
men in the ranks to survive to be
mustered out. (Dunn collection)

CHAPTER TEN

BULLETS ON BROADWAY

A very simple order dramatically altered the lives of the men of the Twentieth Indiana. On July 30, 1863, General-in-Chief Henry W. Halleck telegraphed Major General Meade the following peremptory order:

> *Four regiments of infantry (not New York or Pennsylvania) will be immediately sent from the Army of the Potomac to New York Harbor, to report to General Canby. The officer in command will telegraph to the Quartermaster General the numbers for transportation. The troops to be sent east should number from 1,500 to 2,000. This detachment is all that is proposed at present to take from your army: but under no circumstances can we now give you any reinforcements. Every place has been stripped to the bare poles. Keep up a threatening attitude, but do not advance.*[1]

Meade responded the following day by telegraphing Halleck that he had selected the First and Thirty-seventh Massachusetts, Fifth Wisconsin, and the Twentieth Indiana infantries, with an aggregate strength of 1,643, for service in New York as a deterrent against any further draft rioting.

The Twentieth Indiana, tired and shaken from their ordeal at Gettysburg, had crossed over the Potomac River into Virginia and for several days made forced marches in their pursuit of the elusive Rebel army. They had heard the reports of rioting in New York City and each man had his own opinion of how best to deal with it. Dennis Tuttle reflected the common view of the men from Indiana when he wrote his wife, "I despise this cowardly Northern treason worse than I do the vilest secession of the South because we look for something better at home. I wish the authorities had some of the old troops to assist them in dealing with that mob. It would not take them long to crush it and they would do it with a will, I assure you."[2] Soon they would have an opportunity to deal with the Northern traitors personally.

After their long, bone-wearying march from the Potomac along dust-choked roads, the Army of the Potomac finally caught up with the rear guard of Lee's forces and fought a brisk battle on July 23, at Wapping Heights, near Manassas Gap. The Hoosiers and their brigade drove in the Rebel skirmishers and accelerated the withdrawal of the Confederate army deeper into Virginia. With Lee spurred onward, the Twentieth went into camp near Warrenton, Virginia and awaited further orders for a resumption of their pursuit of the Rebels.[3]

Orders arrived on July 30, but not the ones anticipated by Colonel William Taylor, newly promoted to fill the void left by John Wheeler's death. The orders detailed the Twentieth Indiana to join a detachment of troops destined for New York City. The Hoosiers had six short hours to disassemble their camp and prepare for the movement. At daylight the regiment was in line and on the march to Warrenton Junction, where they boarded freight cars bound for Washington, D.C. From there the train proceeded to Baltimore, Philadelphia, and Camden, New Jersey, where the Hoosiers left the train and boarded a steamer bound for Pier Number One in New York City.[4]

The Twentieth Indiana had started from Falmouth on June 5 during the Gettysburg campaign, leaving behind all personal belongings which could not be carried. The boys were still wearing the exact same clothes as they approached New York Harbor. Coats were stiff from the dust and perspiration accumulated over five hundred miles on the march in the last seven weeks.[5] The Twentieth may not have presented the most sartorially resplendent appearance as they stepped wide-eyed onto the pier at the Battery Park, but it may have been the look that Lincoln wanted. The President didn't want any pantalooned fuss-and-feathers soldiers sent to New York. He wanted men who looked as if they could kill, if necessary, and who had the appearance and credentials to prove it.

A surly mob of men, women and children—among them murderers, arsonists, and hooligans of every stripe—greeted the Indiana boys as they assembled in the battery. Many in this mob had been among those who had run rampant through the streets of the city on July 13, looting, burning, and murdering as they went. These were the dregs of the city who had thought nothing of murdering helpless black citizens as they innocently walked near the Colored Orphan Asylum on Fifth Avenue and then proceeded to burn the institution down. Some of the mob, it must be admitted, were legitimately concerned about the inequalities in the National Conscription Act, which allowed wealthy citizens to pay three hundred dollars for a substitute to take their place on the firing line. They resented the fact that it was a rich man's war and a poor man's fight. Many others in the mob merely looked for any opportunity to create mayhem and stuff their pockets with the rich pickings of Fifth Avenue. Still others were Rebel agents sent north to stir up whatever trouble they could.[6]

The Indiana men were welcomed with a variety of derisive calls such as, "Yez can't enforce yer draft if you bring yer whole damned Army of the Potomac up here!"[7] and "Take care of your own state and leave us be."[8] The Twentieth formed a line across the pier, fixed bayonets and marched slowly forward, driving the angry mob before them. Now and then a soldier would reach into his pocket and toss a handful of cartridges into the crowd, letting the mob know that guns were loaded and that the regiment would stand for no abuse. The men drove the mob back sufficiently to allow for a proper camp to be established for the night. The rowdies severely tested the sentinels on the outer perimeter of the camp and forced pickets to be doubled up so that there was one man for every five yards of space.[9]

The next morning, Major Erasmus C. Gilbreath left Battery Park with Companies D, E, G, and H, destined for Gramercy Park. The Hoosiers were quite a sight as they marched up Broadway, gawking at buildings they had only dreamed about before. Unshaven and filthy to a man, they proudly marched with shining bayonets and their bright red Kearny patches down the expansive boulevard, proceeded and followed by an escort of New York police. The soldiers and their police escorts were followed closely by huge crowds of curious onlookers, anxious to get a look at the veteran draft enforcers. Women and children perched in the windows along Broadway hooted insults at the Midwestern intruders, but the boys marched proudly on, loving the adventure of the moment.[10]

When the regiment arrived at Gramercy Park, they found the huge iron gates to be locked. The Hoosiers marveled at a park where people were actually locked out. Eventually, to Major Gilbreath's relief, a little old man appeared with a large key and opened the park to its soldier visitors. In a few minutes, the companies had thrown up tents and a reasonable little camp took shape. The officers fared better at this location when the proprietor of a nearby hotel came to the park and invited the officers of the four companies to partake of his hospitality. Gilbreath and his fellow officers found that the man had set aside his finest rooms for their convenience. The Indiana men were amazed and self-conscious at their appearance, when the lobby of the hotel revealed a large number of wealthy Cuban and Spanish people dressed in their finest garments. The ladies looked particularly lovely to the ragged officers of the Twentieth.[11]

The remaining companies of the Twentieth Indiana did not rest long at Battery Park before they were sent to other stations. Initially, all six companies were sent to Fort Schuyler, and Companies I and K were later moved on to Willard's Point.[12] Duty for the Hoosiers consisted largely of guarding armories and other strategic locations throughout the city. The novelty of the Western interlopers wore off, and the citizens of New York gradually came to ignore their uninvited guests.

Life had taken a distinctive turn for the better for the Indiana boys in exotic New York City. It was not, however, as good for the wounded and captured of the Battle of Gettysburg. The crude field hospital amputations, with contaminated or unsterile wound dressings applied, left the wounded susceptible to gangrene and other infections. Private Ambrose Harrison's leg was fractured by a ball on July 2. The leg was amputated and gangrene set in, slowly leeching life from the private until he died on September 8. Private John Bowman also had his leg broken by a Rebel musket ball. In his weakened condition he contracted diphtheria, and he also died on August 9.[13] For many others, the crude elixirs, ointments, and poultices used in the medical treatments of the era took time to work their wonders, and the men spent agonizing weeks recovering and longing to return either to their homes or to their regiment.

Private F. M. Head suffered at the hands of the Confederate forces, dragged along by them on the long retreat from Gettysburg. While capture may have spared his life, it certainly spared him no suffering. Head had entered the Gettysburg fight with a hungry stomach and an empty haversack. If he thought he would dine any better as a guest of the Rebel army, he was mistaken. He went without food all day on July 3 and marched many miles on July 4 before he received his sole rations for the day, a half pint of flour and a half pound of rancid meat. Head continued his wearying march as a prisoner for five more days before he was escorted over the Potomac River. At the Potomac, he had been offered a parole, a release from capture upon written promise not to take up arms until exchanged, but he refused the offer because the Federal forces no longer recognized the paroles and would immediately return him to his unit where, if captured again, he could be executed by the Confederates. This doomed Head to a further march of two hundred miles to Staunton, Virginia. During the entire ten days it had taken Head to march the one hundred miles to Winchester, Virginia, he had received only two and a half pounds each of flour and meat. He was exhausted, starving, and ready to give up all hope of survival, when unexpected rest and provisions afforded the prisoners at Winchester reinvigorated him. On July

28 the prisoner procession moved out again, marching the ninety-five miles to Staunton in five days. This march, made on half rations, quickly depleted the remaining strength of the prisoners. At Staunton the bedraggled mass of bluecoats were provided transportation by train, in jammed-tight rail cars, to Richmond and imprisonment on Belle Island, where half rations were a treat and omnipresent lice the everyday reality.[14]

Sergeant Thomas White Stephens experienced imprisonment of a different kind after his month-long recovery from his wounding at Gettysburg. He had initially limped away from the battlefield on July 2, heading for the Third Corps field hospital. He had watched as men bearing the stretcher carrying Major General Daniel Sickles, sans leg and looking beyond hope, had passed by.[15] From the Third Corps hospital, Stephens was taken to Washington, D.C., where he was admitted to a soldiers' hospital and began the process of healing amongst the other horribly wounded men who steadily flowed in from the site of the battle. On August 12 Stephens felt sufficiently well to start for New York City and his regiment. He dutifully reported to the provost marshal's office in New York on August 13, starting the next day for Governor's Island with eighteen other soldiers. When he arrived there, he was unceremoniously and surprisingly dumped into prison, without any explanation for his incarceration.[16]

Sergeant Stephens, loyal soldier to a fault, willing to march blindly and painfully along with his regiment to the Gettysburg battlefield, and seriously wounded in the thick of that battle, was now a common prisoner of his own troops. He made daily inquiries as to why he was in jail, and wrote to everyone whom he felt might come to his relief. A deeply religious man, Stephens found himself in the company of vulgar, traitorous thieves and miscreants. Only his knowledge of Job's sufferings and trials kept the young man from despair. Finally, on August 25, Stephens was called to the warden's office and remanded to the custody of Lieutenant Bartholomew from his regiment and allowed to rejoin his brother Jimmie and his beloved Company K.[17] Stephens had been arrested as a deserter because he'd failed to have a pass allowing him to proceed to New York City. The bright red diamond on his uniform jacket carried much respect in the Army of the Potomac, but to these backwater provost marshals, it meant nothing.

While his brother Thomas had been trying to survive in a Federal jail, Jimmie was soaking in all that New York had to offer in the way of sights and amusements. The draft had passed smoothly by and with it any threat of civil insurrection. This left more time for recreation for the men of the Twentieth. Strolling, playing baseball and leapfrog, young Stephens ventured off on explorations of Central Park and the pleasant environs of Fifth Avenue.[18] When he was eventually joined by his brother, the two Hoosiers from tiny Monticello visited the P. T. Barnum Museum and marveled at the many exotic sights there. The price of admittance was a princely two bits, but it was well worth it to see the eight-foot-tall boy, dancing Indians, live eels, snakes, serpents, a five-horned sheep, monstrous black sea lions, and a seal which played a trumpet.[19] It was quite a spectacle for these Hoosiers who had previously thought a trip to Logansport was "big doings."

As good as life had become for the common soldiers in the regiment in New York, it was far better for the officers. Major Gilbreath and his brethren had the run of the Hotel Gramercy and gorged themselves on four sumptuous meals each day. Liquor flowed freely for those so inclined, and painted ladies were nearby. It was with much sadness that, after three weeks in the lap of luxury, Gilbreath and crew were forced to leave it all. A momentary panic beset the Hoosiers as they scrambled to put together some money to pay the enormous bill. At the fateful moment, the proprietor of the hotel called the officers together and filled a glass of champagne for each. With raised glasses, the proprietor proudly announced that the officers' bills were canceled. The grateful group said their farewells and moved out to Fort Schuyler, where Major Gilbreath was put in temporary command.[20]

The two-and-a-half month idyll came to an end for the Twentieth on October 15, as the thoroughly reinvigorated and fattened-up men of the regiment boarded a small steamer and crossed to Jersey City.[21] For some men, the New York City experience was merely a brief interlude between killing episodes. For others, the it gave perspective to the enormity and diversity of the country they were fighting to preserve.

From Jersey City, the Hoosiers boarded the train and moved to Philadelphia and then on to Baltimore. The next day at 3:00 P.M. the boys proceeded to Washington, where they drew rations and quickly boarded their train cars for the trip across Long Bridge, which spanned the Potomac. They slowly filed off the train at Alexandria, Virginia, drew eight days' rations of hardtack and started for the front.[22]

Not all of the men from the Twentieth proceeded to Virginia and the front. Captains Charles Bell, John Brown, and Henry Quigley, in addition to Lieutenants Warren Hauk, Hiram Crawford, Ed Sutherland, and Daniel Corey, detached from the regiment bound for Indiana on recruiting duty. Captain Charles Reese, given up for dead at Gettysburg, met the detail at the train station and made his way back to Indiana with the squad. The men pitied Reese for his grossly disfiguring wound—one eye was turned up and a huge pockmark left on his face from the entry of the bullet. But he was a brave and proud man, determined to serve his regiment as a recruiter, even though his fighting days were through.[23]

Colonel Taylor sent Dennis Tuttle, his newly promoted quartermaster, to the War Department to procure blank payrolls. It was a seemingly easy task, but in Washington, capital of red tape and, as far as Tuttle was concerned, "a contemptible city of magnificent distances," nothing was easy. After hours of battling a military bureaucracy more stubborn than the Stonewall Brigade, Tuttle finally won his hard-fought battle and procured the documents. He had confirmed his low opinion of the nation's capital and condemned it in a letter to his wife: "Darn the City, darn the officials and darn everybody that won't darn them to darnnation, by thunder!"[24] This was the best tongue lashing that the Yale-educated Victorian man could give to a place that represented his ideal of Sodom and Gommorah.

When word reached Brigadier General Hobart Ward that his gallant Twentieth Indiana was approaching the brigade camp, he marched his entire brigade out on the road leading to the camp and split them into two long lines, one on each side of the road. As the Twentieth came within view, a tremendous roar rose from the brigade. The Indiana boys received a heartfelt "three cheers" from their comrades and returned them in kind. Upon arriving in camp, the regiment stood at attention in review as each of the other regiments in the brigade filed past on parade. With the formalities ended, guns were stacked, and the veterans embraced and tearfully greeted each other.[25] Jimmie Stephens was convinced that the cheers which the Indiana men heard were louder than any McClellan had received, even in his most popular days.

By the middle of October, it was clear to Major General Meade that the Confederate forces were making a strategic withdrawal to the south. Accordingly, Meade prodded his slumbering army into action and a less than "hot" pursuit. On October 19 the camp of the Twentieth was roused before dawn and started on a long march of sixteen miles down the rail line toward Bristoe Station. Before departing, the men were issued another, virtually inedible, ration of hardtack.[26] The perilously stretched Union supply lines brought the Twentieth to the unenviable decision of whether to eat the wormy hardtack and greasy spoiled pork belly rations or starve. Quartermaster Tuttle had never seen "such mean fodder in the army"[27] So it was with aching bellies that the men pushed to the south, slowly pursuing their gray-clad foes. Tuttle, never one to mince words, confided to his wife that Major General Meade had been "emphatically bamboozled and outgeneraled" in his recent movements. Tuttle feared that Meade had reached his high-water mark at Gettysburg and might never reach that level of achievement again.[28]

The Rebels had done their best to tear up the railroad as they retreated. Ties were burned and iron rails held over fires until they could be twisted into an unusable shape. Rail bridges were fired, too, making the destruction of the rail line complete. The Hoosiers followed this path of destruction for an additional twenty miles the following day, marching five miles out of the way for some reason. The tramp resumed before sunrise on the October 21 and ended at noon near Catlett's Station. Here, tents were pitched, fires started and coffee brewed.[29] It appeared that Meade wasn't overly interested in bringing the Confederate army to bay.

The next five days were passed with no aggressive action on the part of the Union army. The men lounged about as best they could, spending the majority of their time debating the relative merits of re-enlistment and the four hundred dollar inducement it would bring. Rain and cold made the conditions less than idyllic but infinitely more acceptable than the days of twenty-mile marches.[30]

The Union army found itself either unwilling or unable to engage the wily, ragtag Rebels, and orders soon came down the line to prepare to construct winter quarters. The news was well received—the average soldier preferred the comfort of a log hut to the chill and dampness of a well-worn tent. However, before construction of the new camp could begin, the regiment was advanced an additional eight miles down the line of the Orange and Alexandria Railroad and placed in line of battle.[31]

Major General Meade made the decision that his army would go into winter quarters, but that it would be on his terms. He felt that it would be to his advantage in the spring if his army started from a position south of the Rappahannock River. Much blood had been dearly shed in an effort to cross the river during past campaigns and it seemed a reasonable movement for his army to make. The problem, of course, was that the Confederates knew that the Rappahannock was worth a division or two in defense and were prepared to defend it. The Rebels had dug rifle pits and constructed defensive positions along the south bank of the river. Meade intended to use his Third Corps to force passage of the river.

There were unmistakable signs to the Twentieth that a fight was brewing. The wormy and insect-infested hardtack was replaced with the first soft bread the boys had eaten in weeks.[32] Generals still relied on a full belly to give proper impetus to soldiers flying headlong into combat. There was a more ominous indication of impending battle: Each man was issued forty rounds of ammunition for his cartridge box and another twenty rounds per man to be stored in the regimental wagons.[33]

The Twentieth didn't have much time to ponder their fate. Before dawn on November 7, the Hoosiers were up and marching for the Rappahannock River. The Union plan of attack called for the left flank, consisting of First, Second, and Third Corps, under the command of Major General William French, to force a crossing at Kelly's Ford at the same time that the right flank, consisting of Fifth and Eleventh corps, commanded by Major General

John Sedgwick, attacked Rappahannock Station.[34] Before the Twentieth could lock horns with their Southern counterparts, they would first make a wearying seventeen-mile march. Arriving at noon, the Hoosiers were impressed by what they saw. The Union-held north bank of the Rappahannock was much higher than the southern bank and afforded an expansive, unobstructed view of the Rebel entrenchments for both infantry and artillery. The Third Brigade of the First Division, commanded by Brigadier General Philippe De Trobriand, was selected to form the storming party. In an effort to strengthen the troops who would force the crossing, both the Twentieth Indiana and the Ninety-ninth Pennsylvania were temporarily transferred to the Third Brigade.[35]

At 1:30 P.M. a Federal battery on the heights opened a heavy and effective fire on the Rebel rifle pits. The fire was so destructive that the Confederate defenders scattered like ants at a picnic.[36] After a half hour of the punishing fire, De Trobriand gave the order to advance. The ford was barely wide enough for a company to pass abreast, so he executed an *en echelon* attack made in line of companies. The Twentieth Indiana was the third regiment to cross in the chest-deep river, taking scattered rifle fire which was heavy enough to wound eight of the Hoosiers. The attack was a smashing success, leading to the capture of four hundred prisoners, a large quantity of camp equipage and a supply of mail which had just arrived in the Rebel camp.[37]

Log huts which the Southern boys had painstakingly erected behind the lines bore testimony to the fact they had fully intended to pass the melancholy days of winter in this position.[38] The drenched and bone-cold Indiana men looked longingly at the huts where they hoped to find some shelter from the bitter wind and chilling drizzle. In the presence of their enemy, however, they were required to suffer on the battle line throughout the night.[39]

The joint Federal attack on Kelly's Ford and Rappahannock Station had been a success, and the morning of November 8 found the Rebels nowhere to be seen. The emboldened Union army advanced eight miles further to the south in the direction of Brandy Station. The Third Corps, leading the advance met Confederate infantry in force and fought a stiff skirmish before forcing them to retreat beyond the Rapidan.[40] Satisfied with their progress, the Union army prepared to go into winter quarters. Orders were given to erect huts which would provide refuge from the coming cold.

This locale in Virginia seemed as good a place as any to pass the winter, and the boys set to the task of constructing the log huts in earnest. The area offered an abundance of previously untapped resources catering to the culinary desires of the Hoosiers. A squad of men went out foraging and brought back a pig which they claimed had followed them. Although questioning the veracity of the story, Colonel Taylor determined the swine to be a Rebel infiltrator and ordered it executed for its impudence.[41] The story was worth a hundred laughs and demanded countless retelling. One farm in the area was definitely off limits to any marauding Union soldiers. John Minor Botts, an elderly Virginian, had sworn his allegiance to the Union and was thereby guaranteed protection by the Federal forces against its own pillaging. It was quite a battle to keep foragers from stealing the relative wealth of resources which Botts possessed, and to keep fences from being removed for firewood and livestock from being cooked over these rails.[42]

On November 15 the regimental sutler located the camp of the Twentieth Indiana and again offered his delicacies to the Hoosiers. Quartermaster Dennis Tuttle summed up the bill of fare to his wife:

> *Our sutler came up last night and I almost killed myself eating my dinner today. I must give you our bill of fare—sausages fried, beefsteak fried, sweet potatoes boiled and fried, turnips, soft bread, cheese, coffee with condensed milk, celery, canned peaches, canned pineapple and cranberry sauce. I cannot tell when my stomach has had such a surprise. Who wouldn't eat too much under such circumstances.*[43]

During this lull in the action, the Army of the Potomac formed a military commission for the purpose of examining the qualifications of all officers in order to raise the standard of performance. Through this sometimes capricious and generally subjective process, many excellent officers as well as deficient ones were removed from command. One evening, in anticipation of a visit by the commission, Brigadier General Ward asked Dr. Grover what the duties of a surgeon were in time of an engagement. Grover, a man of keen humor, replied, "A surgeon on report of the first gun should limber to the rear until he got beyond all possibility of a shot or shell reaching him, get behind a large hill, lie down behind a tree, and if any wounded man could find him, it would be his duty to dress the man's wounds."[44] Amidst the roar of laughter, his brother officers unanimously voted that he would pass muster.

In September, General Robert E. Lee had dispatched Lieutenant General James Longstreet to Georgia to help repel Major General William Rosecrans' movement towards Atlanta. With Longstreet's corps reported to be present at the pivotal Battle of Chickamauga on September 20, the Union military brain trust in the East calculated that Lee had been dangerously weakened and believed that the time was right to strike further to the south.

On November 23 the camp of the Twentieth Indiana was all abustle as preliminary orders filtered down that a move was imminent. At 11:00 P.M. orders were quickly circulated for the men to be packed and ready to march at 6:00 A.M. Pelted with a freezing rain, men suffered in their places for a half hour before an orderly came with an order countermanding the original marching orders. There was much grumbling as tents which they had just taken down had to be erected again.[45]

The uncertainty of movement was removed on November 26, when the Third Corps, including the Twentieth Indiana, finally made its anticipated movement across the Rapidan River, with eight days' rations. The army was to be concentrated about Robertson's Tavern on the Orange Plank Road which ran from Fredericksburg to Orange Court House, a distance of twenty-five miles. Robertson's Tavern was located at the beginning of the open country just to the south of the tangled morass of undergrowth and scrub pine which the locals had dubbed "The Wilderness."[46]

The Third Corps crossed the Rapidan River at Jacob's Ford, near the mouth of the Mine Run River, just before darkness fell on November 26. The column halted one half mile from the river, the men exhausted from their march and the tortuous climb up the steep, muddy south bluff of the ford. At 7:00 A.M. the following morning, the Third Corps left its bivouac and started for Robertson's Tavern. Advancing to a ridge line called Locust Grove, the corps marched directly into the flank of a marching Rebel column and a sharp fight ensued.[47]

The fighting began at 10:00 A.M. between the bulk of Confederate Major General Jubal Early's division and Major General William French's corps, and by 3:00 P.M. the unmistakable din of battle could be heard all along the Union line. The Second and Third Divisions formed in line of battle and were pouring a galling fire into the Rebel lines. At 4:00 P.M. Early formed his Rebel division en masse for a general attack on the Union line. The First Division, to which the Twentieth Indiana belonged, formed in line of battle behind the Second and Third Divisions as their support.[48]

From behind the scrubby growth of cedar and pine lining the ridge line, the Hoosiers heard the bone-chilling, infernal yell which told them that soon they would be locked in battle with Virginians, Louisianans, and Georgians. The attack crashed first into the Third Division, which fought them briefly, then fell back in disarray on the Second Division, making engaging difficult. Soon, they too fell back upon the First Division, the last line of defense.[49]

The First Division was accompanied along its line by Battery E of the First Rhode Island Light Artillery. The guns of the battery were loaded with double canister in anticipation of the onrushing hordes of Rebels. Both infantry and artillery held their fire until gray uniforms could unmistakably be seen emerging from the trees. As Rebels drew near they were greeted by a destructive fire from First Division and the artillery. Southerners by the hundreds fell in bloody piles. Some men thought the intensity of the firing rivaled that of Gettysburg. At any rate, the fire was so furious that it made any further advance an impossibility, and at sunset the Confederate survivors withdrew from the field. The Twentieth Indiana lost eleven men wounded during the powerful attack; the Hoosiers were grateful for their Rhode Island comrades and their roaring artillery pieces.[50]

The Twentieth had passed the busy previous day with nothing but hardtack and salt pork to eat. It was shortly after midnight on November 28, when regimental cooks found their way to the outfit with hot coffee. Warm food was another matter, and it was a hungry Thomas Stephens who went out at 8:00 A.M. on the ever-dangerous and lonely picket duty. Throughout the morning the Hoosier pickets could hear the not-so-distant voices of unknown Confederates shouting orders, laughing, cursing and shuttling about behind their lines. When Stephens and his fellow pickets returned to their former resting ground, they found the regiment, brigade, division and corps gone. It looked like a retreat to Stephens, but in actuality, it was just another strategic move.[51]

At first daylight on November 28, the Twentieth marched for Robertson's Tavern and, upon arrival, went into position on the right of the Second Corps, temporarily commanded by Major General Gouverneur K. Warren.[52] Meade's objective was to turn the line of the Mine Run stream defenses which did not extend all of the way to the Orange Turnpike.[53]

During the morning of the twenty-eighth, the various corps came up and were placed in position for attack, but the enemy was firmly entrenched behind their works and the corps would be advancing over unfamiliar ground. It was determined to postpone the attack for one day.[54] This temporary reprieve from battle was welcomed by the common soldier. From their position opposite the Rebels, the Hoosiers could see dirt flying from Early's Confederates' hurried digging.[55]

Assaulting the Mine Run line was no insignificant task. Although the stream was narrow and shallow, the bank on the west side was steep and abrupt in some places and a swampy morass in others. Interspersed between the escarpments and the spongy bottomland were nearly impenetrable thickets of briars and brambles. The Rebel side of Mine Run rose upward for one half mile to an altitude of nearly one hundred feet higher than the stream itself, thereby affording the Confederate army an excellent position from which to shell and enfilade the advancing Union troops.[56]

The Twentieth was given the unenviable task of assaulting the Rebel lines across a three-quarter-mile ground into the face of concentrated artillery and rifle fire. The boys were not hopeful about their chances for survival. As a sign of the fatalistic reality of their lot, each man wrote out his name on a piece of paper and attached it to his clothing, making identification easier if he died.[57]

The Twentieth Indiana was formed in three lines of skirmishers, the first line spaced at a twenty-yard interval, the second at ten yards, and the third at five. Warren's plan called for the Twentieth to be followed by the main columns of the Third Corps.[58] The Second and Third Corps were to make a demonstration in front of the Rebel lines, while the remainder of the Union forces advanced on the Confederate line. When Major General Warren felt the moment was right, the demonstration by his men and French's would become a full-fledged assault.

At 8:00 A.M. the long line of skirmishers from the Twentieth moved down and across the Mine Run, driving in Rebel pickets along the way. Confederate artillery opened on the advancing Hoosiers in earnest. Private Jimmie Stephens confided in his diary: "I never saw as many solid shot in the air as I saw today."[59]

Although French's men appeared to Warren to have made good progress toward the main Confederate line, Warren demurred. Either he lost heart or just realized the futility of the plan. He could not bring himself to call for the all-out assault on the Rebel heights and recalled the two Federal corps. A bullheaded general like Burnside might have driven his men on to utter destruction, but for whatever reason, Warren would not carry the blame for a bloody disaster.

It was a profoundly disheartened Meade who at 6:30 P.M., finally called an end to this fiasco which bore the name of the Mine Run campaign. As Civil War Union disasters went, this one was less destructive than others. The line of ambulances slowly carrying the wounded back up the Orange Turnpike was only three miles long, and a tired and relieved Army of the Potomac would live to fight again. The Twentieth Indiana was fortunate in losing only three men, bringing to fourteen the number lost in the campaign.[60] Quartermaster Tuttle summed up the campaign as a "stupendous fizzle."[61]

The Hoosiers crossed the Rappahannock River at 5:30 A.M. on December 2. The following day they returned to their old camp near Brandy Station, prepared to tough out a damp and cold winter—their third away from the Hoosier hearthsides.[62]

Meade wrestled with the decision of whether to try another run at the Confederates. The week after the Mine Run campaign was marked by furtive movements here and there and the pitching and striking of tents and camp. It was also a time for dealing with the ever-growing problem of deserters. Patience with soldiers who deserted, either cowards or just homesick men, had run its course. Now they would be dealt with in brutal fashion. On December 4 the First Division stood in formation in a three-sided square and Private Cyrus Hunter from the Third Maine was brought to the open end of the square to be executed.[63] Thomas Stephens described the event:

> *He was marched in front of all the regiments formed in two lines fronting each other. A band played the death march before him. His coffin was carried in front of him, a chaplain walked by his side. He appeared calm, yet walked with downcast eyes. The Chaplain prayed before he was executed, then a cap was drawn over his head and face. The Provost Marshal then gave the command, ready, aim, fire and the man fell over on his coffin, killed instantly. It was a hard fate, but just.*[64]

On December 18, the Hoosiers witnessed two deserters from Vermont being shot.[65] The ever thin veneer of civility and humanity had been stripped from the Army of the Potomac forever. You could fight and possibly die or run and be executed. They made it a simple choice.

The remaining weeks of 1863 were consumed by the emotional issue of veteranization. The Federal government had to offer powerful inducements to retain soldiers in an ever-thinning manpower pool. By all rights, each soldier in the Twentieth Indiana was required to serve until July, at which time he would be mustered out to return to civilian life. Summer could bring a mass exodus from the army. The solution was to offer each man an inducement to re-enlist before the expiration of his initial enlistment: veteran's stripes, a four-hundred-dollar bounty, and at least a thirty-day furlough. Of course, there were liberal appeals made to patriotism and duty in an effort to get men to re-enlist. The stated objective was the re-enlistment of three fourths of each regiment.

There was a firestorm of debate, as could rightfully be expected, as to the relative risk versus rewards of veteranization. Failure to re-enlist meant no bounty and no furlough. Re-enlistment meant a wealth of money, a visit to home and family and military service through the conclusion of the war, no matter how long. So as the Indiana boys started the process of constructing the tiny log huts in which they would pass the winter months, they debated and argued the merits and demerits of signing the enlistment rolls again.

The fate of others seemed sealed as well. The Officers Fitness Commission finally made its way to the camp of the Twentieth Indiana and took a long look at the abilities of Adjutant John E. Luther. They recommended his dismissal from the service for incompetent record-keeping. Luther, a cunning fellow, hatched a plot to resign his commission prior to dismissal, thereby saving his honor and preserving his options. Quartermaster Tuttle, who had seen his career impeded by Luther, thought the move "clever" but still characterized Luther as a "lunkhead."[66] Luther's ruse would work and he would again surface as the regiment's adjutant, none the worse for wear.

Colonel Taylor was ordered to report to General Meade's Headquarters on December 22. Taylor found himself and his regiment the subject of lavish praise, patently offered to induce Taylor to urge his men to re-enlist.[67] Taylor accommodatingly returned to the regiment and did his best to appeal to his men's patriotism and pocketbooks.

Christmas came to the camp of the Twentieth Indiana and hard liquor flowed. Quartermaster Tuttle reported to his wife that "General Drunk" was in command of the regiment.[68] Perhaps it was in this euphoric state that the first sixty-nine men signed re-enlistment papers. On January 5, 1864, this first ration of re-enlistees signed their muster papers and received their bounties, less a somewhat hefty sum for clothing accounts and lost equipment. Still, the average man received hard cash of as much as two hundred and fifty dollars, a handsome sum. This new-found wealth caused the liquor to again flow freely, and in the spirit of the moment, most of the Twentieth Indiana Volunteer Infantry re-enlisted for veteran's duty and the riches it would bring.[69]

In March the gloomy, gray Virginia days were considerably brightened by the fact that the men of the Twentieth Indiana who had volunteered to re-enlist were at long last headed for their home state and a long-awaited furlough. The returning Hoosiers left their comrades and proceeded to Washington, D.C., where each man drew a new regulation-blue uniform. The regiment enjoyed a first-rate reputation in the Army of the Potomac and with the folks back home. With their new uniforms and shiny brass buttons, they would look first class as well.

On March 8 the regiment was met at the train station in Indianapolis by Henry B. Carrington, the adjutant general for the State of Indiana. The men paraded up Meridian Street to Washington Street, escorted by a brass band, and from there to the Soldiers' Home. New uniforms and brightly polished guns belied the fact that theirs was a veteran regiment. But the torn and tattered flags hanging limp from their staffs told the real story. Colonel William Lyon Brown had noted in 1861 as the troops departed that "they make little fuss over us." Now, under Colonel Taylor, the men were welcomed with the adulation befitting their accomplishments. Before the men were dismissed to find their way home to their loved ones, the dignitaries and townsfolk of Indianapolis treated them to a dinner to rival any previous fete. At last the men were allowed to depart for home.[70]

Little is known of how the men of the Twentieth Indiana passed their time during their furlough. One can only guess about enjoyable days spent in the company of friends and family after so much time away. There would be telling and retelling of the battles and marches. Departed comrades would be lamented and lauded. Colonels Brown and Wheeler would be eulogized before countless hearths. Some of the soldiers would spend their time cajoling reluctant civilians to enlist in the cause. Others would begin the political jockeying for future consideration as elected officials, using their military experience as their prime qualification for office. Young girls would be dazzled by the new blue uniforms and swayed by the soldiers who left Indiana as boys and returned as men. On April 8 Colonel William Taylor took advantage of the brief respite to marry Lizzie McPheeters, the daughter of the surgeon of the Thirty-third Indiana Volunteers.[71]

Whatever the pursuits the men enjoyed during their furlough, there was too little time, and on April 14 the officers and men of the Twentieth Indiana were called to reassemble in Indianapolis.

The regiment was due to leave for the front on April 19, but before they departed, there were to be additional banquets and ceremonies. The most moving ceremony was the presentation of new flags to the regiment by the citizens of Lafayette and Indianapolis. After a dignitary presented Colonel Taylor with both a new battle flag and national standard, the flags and the regiment were blessed by Reverend Edson, who prayed for the safe return of all. Colonel Taylor gratefully accepted the flags, which had been sewn by the ladies of the two towns. He tendered to Governor Oliver P. Morton the two battle-scarred remnants of the regiment's once-proud flags.[72]

Governor Morton was pleased to see the regiment off. These Hoosiers had a nasty habit of making feisty demands in anticipation of shipping off, and this time was no exception. Morton had received a petition signed by each man in Company I complaining that Colonel Taylor had promised them that Captain Daniel Corey would be removed if they would re-enlist. Now, they were confronted with the fact that Captain Corey had not left and they appealed to the governor for his interdiction. The letter stated flatly that Corey was "incompetent and did not care for the welfare of his men."[73] The governor promised to look into the matter no doubt hoping that Colonel Taylor would soon take his men and rejoin the Army of the Potomac.

On April 19, 1864, the Twentieth Indiana, with new flags and recruits, departed Indianapolis bound for the Army of the Potomac. The Hoosiers would return to find a new general, Ulysses S. Grant, in command of the Union armies. Grant's reputation had preceded him. He was known for hard, headlong fighting and dogged determination. The Indiana boys knew that there would be hell to pay in the coming months. They had a job to do.

CHAPTER ELEVEN

DESCENT INTO THE INFERNO

Ulysses S. Grant had earned his "tough-as-nails" reputation. From his early victories at Forts Henry and Donelson in Kentucky, through the capture of Vicksburg and his relief of the beleaguered Federal forces bottled up at Chattanooga and the dramatic triumph at Missionary Ridge, Grant demonstrated time and again that not only was he was a fighter, but he had the determination to move forward whatever the cost.

Grant accurately explained Confederate success thus far: it lay in the impunity with which Robert E. Lee shuttled forces between himself and Generals Braxton Bragg and P. G. T. Beauregard. The new commander planned to consolidate his forces into two great armies and to apply unrelenting pressure on the Confederate forces separately, not allowing them to move men from one sphere of the war to another.

Grant's first act as commander of the Union army was to consolidate the Army of the Potomac into three infantry corps and one cavalry corps. He ordered Major General Ambrose Burnside's corps from East Tennessee to the line of the Orange and Alexandria Railroad as a guard for his supply line and as a reserve to Meade's Army of the Potomac. Further, Grant ordered Major General Benjamin Butler, along with supporting forces from Smith's and Gilmore's corps from South Carolina and Florida, to make a feint on the Peninsula and then proceed up the James River to either capture Petersburg or entrench at City Point. Major General Franz Sigel was ordered to move up the Shenandoah Valley in an effort to cut Richmond's western communications.

The Third Corps, which had been decimated in the previous year at Gettysburg, was consolidated with the Second Corps, commanded by Major General Winfield Scott Hancock. Hancock, who would earn the sobriquet "The Superb" through dynamic and outstanding generalship throughout the war, had been severely wounded at Gettysburg on the third day of the battle and was now ready to resume his brilliant career, which would one day bring him to within a few votes in the Electoral College of becoming President of the United States.

The Twentieth Indiana Volunteer Infantry remained with the First Brigade of the Third Division. Brigadier General J. H. Hobart Ward still commanded the brigade, and Major General David B. Birney commanded the division. The Twentieth Indiana found itself brigaded with the Third Maine, Fortieth New York, Eighty-sixth New York, One Hundred and Twenty-fourth New York, Ninety-ninth Pennsylvania, One Hundred and Tenth Pennsylvania, One Hundred and Forty-first Pennsylvania, and the Second United States Sharpshooters.

The Indiana boys made their triumphant return to Ward's brigade on April 24. Brigadier General Ward ordered his entire brigade out to line the route of the Twentieth Indiana as a sign of the esteem which they had earned, the only regiment to which he afforded such an honor.[1] The regiment received sincere cheers from their brigade mates, Easterners who had previously looked down their noses at the rough and crude Western soldier as unworthy of comradeship. Now, after almost three years of bitter war, the Hoosiers had earned the right to full brotherhood with the New Yorkers and Pennsylvanians.

The Twentieth reciprocated its esteem for its fellow First Brigade comrades, but they, along with most other former Third Corps troops, wanted nothing to do with the newly reconstituted Second Corps. It was obvious to all that these men were reluctant members of Hancock's corps. While conducting a division review, Major General Birney noticed that his men wore their old "Kearny Patch," Third Corps emblems on their caps and their new Second Corps trefoil on the seat of their britches.[2] This could only be an issue during a lull from action. Soon enough more pressing concerns would occupy the minds of the men.

An April 29, 1864, the Richmond paper predicted, "This is the last year of the war, whichever wins."[3] At the time, that prediction was anything but certain, especially to the troops in the field.

Quartermaster Dennis Tuttle feared a renewal of Federal disaster. He confided to his wife, "I very much fear that General Grant has been overestimated and that he will not be able to perform what is expected of him. He has never been tested in the flint mill.[4] I am looking forward to a terrible campaign. Oh! How wish I could muster a little more faith in the results. My fears are very strong. I don't think I ever had less faith in a campaign than I have in this, as important as it is, I am sorry."[5]

At midnight on Tuesday, May 3, the Army of the Potomac moved out. Lieutenant General Grant hoped to quickly move across the Rapidan River and through the Wilderness to the open ground near Spotsylvania Court House before the Confederates could bottle the army in the morass of the Wilderness. At dawn on May 4, the Cavalry Corps quickly splashed across the river at Germanna Ford and drove Rebel pickets back on their lines. This cleared the way for Warren's Fifth Corps to advance and push straight into the less-than-cordial confines of the Wilderness.

The Fifth Corps proceeded to the Old Wilderness Tavern, five miles from Chancellorsville, where they passed the night. Hancock's men made their passage at Ely's Ford and marched through thick stands of pines, huge oaks and menacing, vine-clad entanglements, halting near Chancellorsville for the night. The march covered twenty-three miles and wore out the Twentieth, who were not in marching fettle. Sergeant Thomas Stephens soaked his bleeding feet in cold water in camp, a temporary relief.[6] In addition to their normal camp gear, the Indiana men carried three days' rations and fifty rounds of ammunition.[7]

Lieutenant John Luther, back in his role as adjutant, dearly regretted his decision to leave his horse behind in Crown Point. Luther had appreciated the horse's service throughout the war and was determined that either he or the horse—and hopefully both—would survive the conflict.[8] The tender feet of the adjutant were sorely taxed by the trek.

The complexion of the regiment had changed significantly since its muster in July 1861. Sickness and battle casualties had ground the once-strong thousand-man regiment down to a remnant of itself: four hundred and fifteen men and officers.[9] The officers leading the Twentieth Indiana into the Wilderness were as follows:

Colonel William C. L. Taylor
Lieutenant Colonel George W. Meikel
Major Erasmus C. Gilbreath
Adjutant John E. Luther
Quartermaster Dennis Tuttle
Chaplain William C. Porter
Surgeon Orpheus Everts
Assistant Surgeon John Guffin

Company A
Captain John F. Thomas

First Lieutenant James De Long
Second Lieutenant Warren J. Hauk

Company B
Captain Charles A. Bell
First Lieutenant Michael Sheehan
Second Lieutenant Joseph Clark

Company C
Captain Lafayette Gordon
First Lieutenant John W. Williams
Second Lieutenant James Bennett

Company D
Captain William D. Vatchett
First Lieutenant Marquis Kinneard
Second Lieutenant Albert Norris

Company E
Captain John E. Sweet
First Lieutenant Hiram Crawford
Second Lieutenant Christopher Fraunberg

Company F
Captain Thomas Logan
First Lieutenant Edward Sutherland
Second Lieutenant Harvey Miller

Company G
Captain Henry Quigley
First Lieutenant (vacant)
Second Lieutenant Isaac Ensey

Company H
Captain Charles Liner
First Lieutenant Harry Geisendorff
Second Lieutenant William Dickason

Company I
Captain: Lorenzo D. Corey
First Lieutenant William W. Stevens
Second Lieutenant John Vanderbark

Company K
Captain John C. Brown
First Lieutenant John Price
Second Lieutenant John Bartholomew[10]

The night was passed in an eerie way with the troops sleeping among the ghosts of their fellow Twentieth Indiana and Third Corps brethren who had fallen in the previous year's battle at Chancellorsville. In the midst of the shell-shredded battlefield, still littered with the flotsam of war and human bones, the Hoosiers knew what possibly lay in store for them should their movements be resisted before they could penetrate the Wilderness and break out into the open south of Spotsylvania Court House. Still, exhaustion claimed them and they slept.

Only a thin veil of light glowed in the east when the Hoosiers were roused from their sleep and set in motion on the march. Even at this early hour, it was already uncomfortably hot and humid. The long column of Hancock's Second Corps lurched off at 5:00 A.M. and moved to the southwest along the Catharpin Road. Four hours later they had progressed two miles past Todd's Tavern when Major General Meade ordered a halt.[11] The men had not liked the looks of things when a staff officer roared past them heading north, his horse foaming at the mouth. This was their first indication that something was amiss.[12] In the distance, to the right of the Indiana men, came the unmistakable, deep-throated booming cannon fire. Warren's Fifth Corps had stumbled across the advance elements of Lee's army and were hotly engaged in combat with an unseen enemy. D. R. Jones' brigade of Edward Johnson's division, from Ewell's Confederate Corps, had been moving east along the Orange Turnpike when it crashed headlong into Griffin's division from Warren's Fifth Corps.[13]

Hancock's corps was strung out for many miles along the Catharpin Road, and Birney's division, which led the march, was afforded the opportunity to rest while the remainder of the corps caught up. Brigadier General Ward threw out a strong line of pickets and allowed the balance of his brigade to lounge along the road. At 1:00 P.M., a desperate order arrived in the hands of Winfield Scott Hancock directing his corps to proceed to the intersection of Brock Road and Orange Plank Road. Ward's brigade started for Brock Crossroads on a trot, dust billowing up from the bone-dry Catharpin Road. Every step brought an increase in the intensity of the sounds of rifle fire coming from the Crossroads.[14]

Brigadier General Alexander Hays' brigade was the first to arrive at the crossroads; he placed his men in two lines of battle astride the Orange Plank Road. Ward followed next but failed to close on Hays' men and stopped one-half mile from the crossroads. Thankfully, Brigadier General Gershom Mott arrived with his division and placed it between Hays and Ward along the Brock Road, which was a narrow path through the dense undergrowth of the Wilderness.[15] Hobart Ward apparently did not appreciate the dangerous predicament in which the Second Corps was placed. He allowed his men to lie by the road and drift off into a deep sleep while army engineers feverishly prepared entrenchments along the road.[16]

The Battle of the Wilderness was actually two distinct battles fought within earshot of each other, with little coordination of attack by either army. The first battle was fought by Warren's and Sedgwick's corps against Confederate Lieutenant General Richard Ewell's corps on the Orange Turnpike. The second battle, the one involving the Twentieth Indiana, was a corps-versus-corps affair between Winfield Hancock and A. P. Hill.

Brigadier General George Getty's divison from Sixth Corps was spread out along the Brock Road to the right of Birney's division. Mott's division was on Birney's left and the soon-to-arrive Major General John Gibbon's division would fall in on Mott's left.

Getty's division was ordered to attack down the Orange Plank Road and drive any Confederate troops away from the key Brock Crossroads. Robert E. Lee had similar designs on the strategic intersection and ordered Major General Henry Heth to move toward the Crossroads without bringing on a general engagement, a wise order but one which was impossible to carry out owing to the terrain. Therefore, Getty started down the Orange Plank Road and Heth started up the road, resulting in a collision of the two forces. Getty's division was led by Brigadier General Frank Wheaton's brigade, followed by the tough-as-nails Vermont brigade commanded by Brigadier General Lewis Grant. The Vermonters and Heth's division locked horns in a terrific fight.

The Vermont boys were shredded by the accurate fire of Heth's riflemen, who were concealed behind trees and a ridge line. The firefight raged for more than thirty minutes, when ammunition began to run low. Lewis Grant called for support in this desperate hour. Hobart Ward dispatched the Twentieth Indiana, the One Hundred and Forty-first Pennsylvania, and the Fortieth New York to the relief of the Vermont brigade. Grant had located a thinly defended spot along the Confederate battle line and proposed to smash through it. Grant first queried the officer in command of his remaining unengaged regiment, the Fifth Vermont, about whether they could punch through the Rebel line. The Vermonter responded, "I think we can." He asked the Hoosiers and New Yorkers the same question and the response was, "We will!"[17]

Ward's three regiments pushed forward in a spirited attack aimed at piercing the ridge line. Coming on a full run, accompanied by Ward himself, the men ran into heavy fire. The Hoosiers occupied the left flank of the attack and drew merciless fire from the Thirty-fourth and Thirteenth North Carolina regiments.[18] Captain Lafayette Gordon was struck by a spent bullet which thudded into his shoulder, knocking him down and convincing his onrushing men that he was mortally wounded.

Private Joseph Brown was shot in the gut and killed instantly. Privates Amos Burch and John Vinson were severely wounded in the first volley fired by the North Carolinians.[19] Bodies piled up and blood splattered everywhere as Rebel bullets ripped through flesh and obliterated arms and legs of the Union attackers. Many a man in the Twentieth counted himself lucky to have a bullet clip off a finger or rip out a chunk of thigh rather than plunge a mortal wound into his chest or stomach.

As Ward's three regiments rushed forward, they made an attractive target on the overly exposed left flank. The Fifty-fifth Virginia, of Brigadier General Henry Walker's brigade, quickly recognized this as the spot to strike a mortal blow. The Virginians tensely waited and watched as the Twentieth passed by them, waiting for just the right moment to swoop down on the rear of the attackers and destroy them. As Walker's men moved through the briars and brambles to position themselves for the attack, Hobart Ward saw the danger and ordered the Twentieth Indiana to halt the Virginians' advance and wheel to the rear in a defensive position.

The Virginians had just launched their attack, and before they could be recalled, they crashed into the awaiting Indiana men, who shocked them with the violence of their defensive fire. Now broken and beaten, having dashed into the muzzles of the guns of the Twentieth, the Virginians were easy pickings. Sergeant William Thompson, Company G, ran to the color bearer of the Fifty-fifth Virginia and snatched the "Stars and Bars" from the Rebel's hands, an act which would win him the Medal of Honor. The Indiana boys rounded up a large number of staggered and beaten Virginians and herded them to the rear.[20] All told, the Fifty-fifth Virginia lost two killed, seventeen wounded, and thirty-one captured in their abortive attack.[21]

Additional North Carolina troops rushed forward into the large gaps in the Rebel line caused by the relentless fire of the Twentieth Indiana and other units. Most movement ceased; the fighting degenerated into a turkey shoot, with soldiers of each side vying to hit the elusive head, shoulder or arm offered up as a target from behind a tree. Screams of mutilated men intermingled with the smell of powder and the hisses, pops and zings of minié balls which flew as thick as bees.

Generals U. S. Grant and George Meade grew progressively more frustrated as the day wore on. They had failed to bring about a coordinated attack or to concentrate their superior force on the Confederates. Now, as the day wound down, they hoped to see their frustrations ended by an overpowering attack down the Orange Plank Road using the collective strength of Getty's division and Hancock's corps. General Lee, too, realized the urgency of sending whatever troops he could muster into the fray. He had to give Heth's division's relief. He quickly ordered two brigades from Ewell's corps to move through the wild terrain to the Plank Road and aid their Confederate comrades.

The intense and deadly bloodbath along the Plank Road continued in unrivaled intensity as wave after wave of Union blue broke against the thinning gray lines of the Rebel position. Casualties were staggering on both sides—the Wilderness had become an appalling killing ground. In the confusion created by the fog of battle, with its roaring artillery and the constant stream of casualties passing by him to the rear, Major General Hancock did not realize how close the Union Second Corps was to breaking the Confederates. Had he known just how close to extinction the Rebel line was, he would have rushed any available man to the attack, but his fear of being taken by surprise slowed his normal alacrity, and he did not push an assault. Slowly, the last light of day slipped away, and with it went Grant's best chance for winning a smashing victory in the tangle of the Wilderness.

Gratefully, the Twentieth greeted the coming darkness, which offered greater protection from the watchful eye of Rebel marksmen. Exhausted, as the firing slowly died down to just an occasional stray shot, Indiana troops called out into the blackness of the night to locate their brothers and friends who had fallen during battle, hoping against hope that their calls would be answered. Had they survived? In the darkness of night and the confusion of distant shouted orders of officers and orderlies, there was little which could be done for the unfortunate fallen. The weary men collapsed into deep sleep. Before he drifted off to sleep, Private Jimmie Stephens, happy that he had survived the brutal fight alongside his brother, confided in his diary, "I am really proud that I belong to such a regiment."[22]

While the common soldier slept the sleep of battle exhaustion, interrupted throughout the night by the mournful wails of the wounded between the lines, the generals played their deadly game of chess. Grant and Meade labored over the best location to punch through the Confederate lines, and Lee pondered just where to position his arriving reinforcements. It appeared as if a renewed assault down the Plank Road by Hancock's Second Corps, supported by Major General James Wadsworth's division from the Fifth Corps on their right flank, was the best course of action. This movement by Wadsworth to the flank of the Second Corps would unite the two wings of the Federal army. The attack was to be a massive frontal assault by more than twenty-two thousand men of Second Corps. The decision allowed the Union Second Corps to begin its movement into battle formation before dawn. Lee's decision as to where to place reinforcements would be delayed. He was forced to anxiously await the arrival of Lieutenant General James

Longstreet's corps, which was slowly making its way up the Catharpin Road.

Brigadier General Hobart Ward called his weary brigade from sleep and started moving them toward the Rebel lines at 4:30 A.M.[23] With the men lining up south of the Plank Road, Ward dispatched the Second U.S. Sharpshooters as skirmishers across the front of his brigade. Anchored on the road was the One Hundred and Forty-first Pennsylvania. To its left were the Twentieth Indiana, Eighty-sixth New York, and the One Hundred and Twenty-fourth New York. Behind them were the remaining regiments of the brigade.[24]

Shortly after dawn Hobart Ward ordered his troops forward. Each man, armed with sixty rounds of ammunition, moved steadily forward, winding through twisted knots of trees and scrub, looking for any gray target to shoot. As the Twentieth drew nearer to the Confederate earth-and-log entrenchments, they confronted increasing numbers of startled Rebels, some sleeping. The shocked Confederates either ran, surrendered or were shot down if they resisted. Steadily, Ward's men pushed ahead toward the Rebels who manned the entrenchments.[25]

The two lines were defended by Brigadier General Alfred Scales' North Carolinians. Within sight of the Rebel lines, Ward's brigade was ordered to charge the works. Rushing forward, bayonets gleaming, the Twentieth Indiana fired and loaded as they ran. The Confederate fire was intense, with Ward's men dropping and tumbling head first on the ground. A private from the Thirty-seventh North Carolina shot Private John McBeth in the head, seriously wounding him and resulting in his capture and removal to Andersonville Prison, where he subsequently died. Privates Paris Nordyke, John Fair, and Ed Hendrickson all went down in a hailstorm of North Carolina bullets.[26]

Thomas Stephens had spent the minutes before dawn in fervent prayer that he would be delivered from the coming peril. Upon completing his prayers, he tucked his beloved Bible in the breast pocket of his frock coat and moved off on the assault with the rest of the Twentieth Indiana. As Stephens rushed toward the first Rebel line, he was jolted by a smashing pain in his chest and crumpled to the ground. Unable to move, his first thought was that he had received a mortal wound. And it would have been a mortal wound save for Divine deliverance. The bullet struck his Bible, coming to rest on First Kings, Eighth Chapter, verses fifty-nine through sixty-two.[27] The passage read:

And let these my words, wherewith I have made supplication before the Lord, be nigh unto the Lord our God day and night, that he maintain the cause of his servant, and the cause of his people Israel at all times, as the matter shall require: That all the people of the earth may know that the Lord is God, and that there is none else. Let your heart therefore be perfect with the Lord our God, to walk in his statutes, and to keep his commandments, as at this day. And the king, and all Israel with him, offered sacrifice before the Lord.[28]

Lieutenant Ed Sutherland, running and waving his sword, received a bullet in the arm, sending him to the rear.[29] The casualties were particularly heavy in the ranks of the company officers. Captain Thomas Logan was knocked unconscious by a ball to the head. Captain Henry Quigley was mortally wounded in the thigh, and Captain John Thomas was winged in the shoulder.[30]

The Twentieth crashed into the North Carolinians as they scrambled over the log ramparts of the Rebel entrenchments. The Indiana boys used cold steel and clubbed muskets as the fighting grew into a brief, but brutal, hand-to-hand melee. Scales' regiments were outmatched and fell back in headlong flight, hotly pursued by Ward's triumphant brigade. Jimmie Stephens did not pursue the North Carolina boys. He had learned of his brother's misfortune and was making his way back through the lines of the advancing Federals, when an officer accosted him and forced him to return to the front lines of the fight.[31]

It was now only 7:00 A.M. and Winfield Hancock could smell victory. The attack along the front of the Second Corps had been universally successful, and the main line of attack had advanced more than one and a half miles. Hancock sensed that this was the opportune time to call on Major General John Gibbon's division to advance and strike the exposed flank of the Confederate line a death blow. Gibbon, in command of both his and Francis Barlow's divisions on the Second Corps left flank, was hesitant to commit his division at this moment. Somewhere out in the dense wilderness were the healthy and rested soldiers of Longstreet's Confederate corps. With this peril lurking in the shadows, Gibbon only sent a single brigade into the flank of the Confederates, far too little to achieve Hancock's ambitious goal.

General Lee came riding up the Plank Road to find his forces in utter rout. He appealed to his officers and men to take heart and stand and fight, but it was to no avail. The Rebels were not whipped, they simply needed a rallying point to restore their fighting pluck. That rallying point soon arrived: the forces of Lieutenant General James Longstreet.

Longstreet's corps hurried to the battlefield up the Plank Road. Its lead elements were quickly directed by General Lee to charge into the Federal forces along the Plank Road. Lee knew that the Union troops fighting behind trees and entrenchments could stand and exchange volleys all day, so he ordered the arriving Texans and Arkansans to give the enemy "cold steel" in a headlong assault. These troops, formerly of Hood's brigade, shocked the Union troops on the north side of the Plank Road, shoving them back to the east.

While Webb's brigade recoiled from the force of Longstreet's attack on the north side of the Plank Road, Ward's brigade, including the valiant Twentieth, stood tall and fast against the determined assaults of Brigadier General Benjamin Humphreys' Mississipians and Colonel John Henagan's brigade of South Carolinians. Wave after wave of newly inspired gray-clad demons came rushing toward the Indiana boys. Each attempt to drive Ward's men backwards was repulsed—Humphreys and Henagan had nothing to show for their attempt except the piles of shredded bodies from the Confederate States of America strewn across the field of battle.[32]

The Twentieth Indiana and One Hundred and Forty-first Pennsylvania had completely exhausted their supply of ammunition, firing sixty rounds to a man in the assault on the Rebel entrenchment and then the repulse of the counterattacks south of the Plank Road. Hobart Ward ordered the two regiments to proceed to the ammunition wagons in the rear to again fill their cartridge boxes and pockets with lead, replacing the men in the front line with the Ninety-ninth and One Hundred and Tenth Pennsylvania regiments. The Tenth New York and the Twelfth New Jersey, however, failed to move into the void created by the departing Pennsylvanians, thereby exposing the right flank of the Third Maine.[33]

North of the Plank Road, Colonel William Perry, commanding Law's Alabama Brigade, had smashed into the Federal troops defending there. Colonel Pinckney Bowles' Fourth Alabama Infantry plowed into the shocked infantry of the Fourteenth Indiana Volunteers and the Eighth Ohio, driving them back on the Seventh West Virginia. The resultant retreat of these regiments revealed the dangling flank of the Third Maine of Ward's brigade. By moving into Samuel McGowan's former earthworks, the Alabamans had a perfect location from which to pour in a withering fire on the totally surprised men from Maine. With nothing to protect them, the Maine boys dropped in droves and soon the survivors were filtering to the rear.[34]

It took some time for the men of the Twentieth Indiana to wade over the dead and wounded strewn across the battlefield, make their way through the trees and scrub pines back to the wagon train carrying their precious ammunition. The march to the rear was orderly and deliberate, betraying no panic or fear. An occasional bullet would pop and zing through the trees, or a solid artillery shot would crash above their heads, serving as the only indication that their brethren in Ward's brigade were under heavy attack.

Upon arriving at the ammunition wagons, the Hoosiers hurriedly filled their cartridge boxes, knapsacks and pockets with cartridges. Colonel Taylor allowed his men to take a much-needed rest, unaware that the balance of Ward's brigade was under heavy assault. Quickly, some of the Hoosiers started fires for brewing coffee while others dropped off to sleep.

This brief respite came to a quick end when a messenger arrived from Brigadier General Ward desperately calling for the return of the Twentieth Indiana and the One Hundred and Forty-first Pennsylvanians. The Federal front had deteriorated because of the relentless Rebel attacks north and south of the Plank Road. Union forces had been forced back to the area around the first line of Confederate rifle pits which they had passed over in triumph earlier that morning.

The Ninety-ninth and One Hundred and Tenth Pennsylvania regiments had exhausted their ammunition and were anxiously awaiting the return of the Hoosiers for their relief. Brigadier General Ward had ridden out to meet the returning regiments and in their place found two Connecticut regiments of Colonel Sam Carroll lounging about. Ward ordered Carroll to move his men forward, but the colonel protested that he only had five hundred effective men and that they had just emerged from a heated battle and were fatigued. Colonel Carroll added that he did not want to move his men into an ambush. The furious Ward refused to accept Carroll's argument, and although he had no authority to do so, ordered the Connecticut men to their feet. By this time, the replenished troops of the Twentieth Indiana and One Hundred and Forty-first Pennsylvania had arrived at Carroll's brigade. Disgusted by the apparent apathy of the Connecticut men, they marched through the middle of the two regiments and moved to the front. As soon as the Hoosiers passed from view, Carroll ordered his men to go ahead and lie down.[35]

The Twentieth Indiana finally reached the front line of the Second Corps and took its place, its right flank anchored solidly on the Plank Road.[36] This was the critical point of the entire Second Corps. A breakthrough along the road would mean that thousands of Rebel forces could quickly penetrate the Union rear. The Twentieth Indiana had a well-earned reputation for standing its ground and slugging it out, and Brigadier General Ward wanted these tough-minded Westerners as the determining element in the fate of this engagement.

Lieutenant General James Longstreet planned to strike somewhere other than the fiercely defended Plank Road. The Confederate war horse intended to bring Major General William Mahone's division in on the extreme left flank of the Union line and roll up the Federal forces as Jackson had done at Chancellorsville the previous year. Mahone launched his powerful attack at approximately 11:30 A.M.; the Union left flank quickly disintegrated. Regiment after regiment fell back in disorder, in turn causing havoc in the adjacent regiments. Within minutes, most of the Federal force had been driven in headlong retreat north of the Plank Road.

A rising crescendo of rifle fire and Rebel war whoops signaled to the awaiting Twentieth that disaster was imminent. They could see to their left both the Third Maine and the Fortieth New York regiments were withering under the Confederate pressure. With the Second Corps routed, there would be no time for Hancock to organize any effective defense further to the rear. There have been well-documented cases through the years of leaders quickly sizing up a situation and taking bold measures without orders. This was one of those times. Colonel William Taylor ordered his men to charge into the attacking Confederates. The Twentieth never hesitated as they plunged forward out of the safety of their rifle pits and into the teeth of the Confederate attack, quickly followed by the Ninety-ninth Pennsylvania.[37] This bold and impetuous attack forced Mahone's men to pause and duck for cover. The delay in the Confederate attack allowed the remainder of Ward's brigade to rush east up the Plank Road to the relative safety of the previous day's first line defenses near the Brock Crossroads.[38]

Private Jacob Head, pausing to fire his rifle, was struck in the hand and the right side of his face by a Rebel musket ball. Bloody, but none the worse for wear, Head was able to make it back to the trenches and continue fighting. Private Jimmie Stephens took a spent ball in the arm which blackened the skin and numbed his arm. He was able to make it to the Federal trenches trailing his deadened arm by his side.[39] Others were not as fortunate. Corporal William Sapp and Private William Black both died blunting Mahone's attack.[40]

It was hell and chaos along the line of the Second Corps, as badly fatigued and frightened men arrived at the critical junction. It was not a demoralized force, however, and officers shouting orders and encouragement soon ushered the arriving regiments into their defensive positions. Stray shots filled the air as Rebel pickets tested the strength and resolve of the Union line. Hobart Ward spent this time of relative inaction carefully placing his regiments along the line. He anchored the right flank of his brigade to the Plank Road by once again placing the Twentieth Indiana in the critical location. Next to the Indiana boys and extending to their left were the Ninety-ninth Pennsylvania, Second U.S. Sharpshooters, One Hundred and Forty-first Pennsylvania, and One Hundred and Twenty-fourth New York regiments. The remainder of Ward's brigade occupied the second line of defense behind these regiments.[41] It was on this thin and bloodied line that the fate of the Second Corps—and possibly that of the Union army itself—rested.

At 3:00 P.M. an eerie calm fell over the area adjacent to the Brock Crossroads. Confederates scurried about in the dense woods across from the

line of Ward's brigade, reorganizing their regiments into an effective battle
order. For almost a full hour, a heavy silence hung on this section of the
battlefield, punctuated by the quick-beating hearts among the awaiting
Twentieth. Many Confederates, including Colonel James Hagood, First South
Carolina, thought this delay was inexcusable and that the hour was spent
merely "dilly-dallying."[42]

The dilly-dallying ended at 4:00 P.M. when Major General Charles Field,
replacing the wounded Confederate corps commander, Lieutenant General
James Longstreet, ordered the First and Fifth South Carolina regiments to
move forward and "feel the enemy."[43] Upon first sight of the South Carolina
troops at the edge of the woods, the line of riflemen in Hobart Ward's brigade
and the adjacent brigade of Colonel William Brewster erupted in a solid
sheet of flame running the length of their entrenchment. South Carolinians
dropped by the score from the brutal, accurate fire. The Rebels responded in
kind, but the Federal rifle pits afforded much greater protection than the
narrow trees at the Confederate line.

The veteran soldiers in the Twentieth Indiana took particular delight in
dishing out terrible punishment to the South Carolinians. Private Jimmie
Stephens was almost wild with excitement as he loaded and blazed away at
the woods, taking ample advantage of the opportunity to pay back the
graybacks for shooting him in the arm earlier in the day. A known marksman,
Stephens stopped loading his own rifle and allowed his companions to load
and pass him their own rifles so he could shoot more quickly. According to
Stephens, in the space of a half hour "I think I fired two hundred rounds.
Several in the rear loaded for me and I fired incessantly until the rebels fell
back. They overshot us but we did not overshoot them."[44]

The excruciatingly hot and intensive fire had literally driven the Rebels
to the ground, forcing the South Carolinians to hug the dirt. Leaves, tree
limbs, and bark showered down as bullets did the work of buzz saws along
the wood line. After a half hour of this humiliating and terrifying experience,
Colonel Ashbury Coward, Fifth South Carolina, jumped up, grabbed the
regimental flag, waved it, and ordered his men to their feet. If they were
going to die, they were at least going to die as brave men. Colonel Hagood
responded to Coward's action as if on cue and called the First South Carolina
to their feet. The emboldened Confederates now moved forward toward the
Union line as if they were walking into a hailstorm. Ward's men continued
to blast away at the advancing Rebels, ripping wide gaps in their lines.[45]

The advancing South Carolinians stopped at one hundred paces from
Ward's line and traded volley after volley with the Union brigade. Neither
side would give way in the heated fight, but the gods of war intervened. A
seemingly innocent muzzle flash from a rifle ignited bone-dry pine needles

and bark in the Union entrenchment. This fire quickly spread to the head logs of the rifle pits, which exploded in flame and blinding pine tar smoke. Major Erasmus Gilbreath summed the situation up succinctly when he noted, "Our breastworks took fire and we were literally roasted out of them."[46]

The scorching heat and choking smoke sent the men of Ward's brigade scurrying like rats deserting a sinking ship. The Twentieth Indiana and the Ninety-ninth Pennsylvania were driven across the Plank Road to the north. The South Carolina troops saw the looming disaster for the Union line and wasted no time in exploiting it. They charged the breastworks, intent on shattering the Union line.

Brigadier General Hobart Ward had been nervously pacing back and forth along his brigade line; now he ordered the One Hundred and Twenty-fourth New York and the One Hundred and Forty-first Pennsylvania to fall back to the second line of works. The New Yorkers and Pennsylvanians, however, were in a panic and no amount of cajoling could stop them from running. Ward himself had no intention of being captured. Within full view of Major L. B. Duff, an aide to Major General Birney, Ward raced to an artillery caisson and ordered the driver to take him as fast as possible to the east and safety. Ward thus tore down the road, leaving his men to fend for themselves.[47]

The Twentieth Indiana and the Ninety-ninth Pennsylvania resisted the excusable temptation to flee the melee and instead stood their ground and fired a lethal shower of lead across the Plank Road into the flanks of the South Carolinians and Georgians now reaching the edge of the breastworks south of the road.[48] Volunteers from the Twentieth Indiana left the infantry and temporarily became artillerymen, as a section of Rogers' battery requested assistance in muscling two field pieces over the entrenchment on the north side of the Plank Road, so they might add their fire to that of the infantry. Men from the Twentieth helped lug the big guns into position, and Rogers' men poured rifle cartridges by the bucketful down into the barrels of their guns, so that a deadly fire of shrapnel could pour into the flank of the Confederate attack.[49]

The South Carolinians and the Eighth Georgia who had joined were stopped short by the fury of the flanking fire and arrested their forward movement, though the major of the Eighth Georgia stood atop the breastwork, furiously waving the regimental flag to rally his men. Seeing the Rebel attack waver, Colonel Taylor ordered the Twentieth Indiana to charge bayonet on the dazed Confederates. The Ninety-ninth Pennsylvania joined them in a mad dash through smoke and flame to recapture the Union line of works. Sergeant Joseph Barrett blasted the flag-bearing major of the Georgia regiment at close range, killing him instantly and snatching up the prized war trophy. The initial shock of the counterattack quickly dissolved into panic, and within moments the South Carolinians and Georgians fled to the west.[50]

Rebel officers vainly tried to rally their troops, but man after man was shot down, colors fell and were captured and the day lost. The Hoosiers were wild with battle blood lust and a chance for complete victory. A boisterous chorus of "Rally Round the Flag, Boys" rang out and men ran, fired and sang as they went.[51] Union troops occupying the third and last line of defense behind the Brock Road were heartened and emboldened by this sudden change in the fortunes of war, and their officers quickly seized the opportunity to order them to the attack. Whatever chance the South Carolinians had quickly evaporated in the face of the overwhelming mass of bluecoats spilling out of the third line of trenches. All hope of victory and salvation gone, the rout of Field's division was complete.

The exhausted but exhilarated, powder-blackened Hoosiers could take great pride in their work this day. With greatly diminished numbers and the ranks of officers thinned by continual fighting, the Twentieth had faced the ultimate test of a Civil War regiment and had stood tall. Major General David Birney personally visited the Twentieth Indiana and the Ninety-ninth Pennsylvania to extend his thanks and compliments for their gallant service.[52]

The two-day bloodbath had proved costly to both sides. Confederate casualties were estimated at 7,500, and total Union casualties were pegged at 17,666 killed, wounded, or captured.[53] Union Second Corps losses totaled 5,192.[54] Birney's divison lost 2,242.[55] The Twentieth Indiana had nineteen men killed and 105 wounded.[56]

In battles and campaigns past, Union commanders would have looked at such terrible losses and retreated to regroup or reorganize, but General Grant was not your garden-variety commander. As the blackness of night fell over the smoky, surrealistic entanglement of the Wilderness, Ulysses S. Grant encountered a newspaper correspondent bound for Washington. In his characteristically succinct style, Grant told the newspaperman, "If you see the President, tell him, from me, that whatever happens, there will be no turning back."[57]

It is a generally accepted principle of warfare that it is highly unwise to make a lateral movement with an army in the presence of its enemy. The risks of such a movement usually far exceed any benefit derived. However, the great captains of war throughout the ages have been men who have taken great risks to secure great prizes, and Grant was a general willing to take the risk. Late on the night of May 6, Grant decided to move his army laterally along the Brock Road to the south while sending his wagon train back toward Fredericksburg. His immediate military objective was the small crossroads town of Spotsylvania Court House. If he could reach the crossroads before the Confederate army did, General Lee would be forced to either attack him directly or to try and keep pace with the Union army's southerly movement by traversing inferior roads. It would be a race to Spotsylvania, with the Union Fifth Corps leading the way.

The Twentieth Indiana remained in its breastworks all night and throughout the day on May 7. Enduring unseasonably warm temperatures, the men in the trenches sweated and dehydrated. Detachments were detailed to venture out on the field of battle, which had been abandoned by the routed Confederates, to pick up the thousands of rifles left behind by the wounded and dead. At 5:00 P.M., the Twentieth was called out of its trenches and put in line of march on the road back to Chancellorsville. The Hoosiers were disheartened by the apparent retrograde movement, believing the sacrifice of the previous two days fruitless. However, after marching back toward the supply trains for two and one half miles, the regiment was halted in its tracks and shortly ordered back to its breastworks along the Brock Road.[58]

General Winfield Scott Hancock called his regimental commanders together early in the evening of May 7 and informed them that the Second Corps would make its movement by the left flank during the night. It would be the duty of the Twentieth Indiana and the Fortieth New York, under Colonel Thomas Egan, to act as pickets in front of the Brock Road defenses. Major Erasmus Gilbreath was put in command of the Indiana pickets, and he and Colonel Egan were ordered to be present along the picket line at all times. The picket line ran from the Orange Plank Road for one mile to the east in the direction of Todd's Tavern.[59]

It was the task of the pickets from Indiana and New York to screen from view the true movement of the Union army. This job required extreme vigilance in aggressively driving off any curious Rebel pickets whose own task was to feel the lines of the Union army to try and determine just what Grant might have up his sleeve.

The Union army was on the move all night on the Brock Road, running behind the pickets. Rebel pickets pressed the Hoosiers the entire evening, probing for gaps in the defenses or for any telltale sign of movement. Major Gilbreath could not ride his horse over the deep entrenchment along the Brock Road, so he was required to go to the end of the line on the Plank Road, dismount and walk along the line to the left, then ride back down the Brock Road, report to Colonel Egan and then repeat the process over and over again.[60]

Confederate pickets would slowly approach the Union pickets and open fire on them. The Twentieth would lie down and return fire, the Rebels would fall back. This deadly activity continued all night long. As dawn approached, the ante was raised as Confederate cavalry dashed down the Plank Road only to be driven off by the Hoosiers. Tiring of this impertinence on the part of the Rebel cavalry, Gilbreath placed a squad of thirty men in hiding along the road, well in advance of the picket line. The next galloping graybacks were welcomed at thirty yards by a volley which shocked them and convinced them that the folly must stop until daylight.[61]

At 10:00 A.M. on May 8 the Hoosiers were called in from picket and fell in line behind the rest of the Second Corps on the march to Todd's Tavern and beyond.[62] After two days of desperate and heated battle, with little rest, it might have been expected that the march would have been weary and forlorn. However, the men were heartened by the news rippling along the lines like a current of electricity, that instead of moving back toward Fredericksburg, Grant was heading south.

The narrow Brock Road—a single-lane path running through the impenetrable mass of the Wilderness—provided scarcely enough room for a division to march, let alone an entire army, and it soon became a colossal logjam of blue-clad soldiers. It took the entire day for the Twentieth to move a handful of miles, as the heat took its toll on the marchers. The regiment stopped and camped for the night about one mile south of Todd's Tavern. In a marked change in procedure, the Hoosiers now built defensive breastworks any time they stopped.[63]

The following day, the Twentieth Indiana moved out at 3:00 P.M. with the rest of Ward's brigade in an effort to swing to the extreme right flank of the Union army, part of Grant's strategy to flank Lieutenant General Richard H. Anderson's Confederate corps. About one and one half miles from their camp, the Twentieth Indiana and One Hundred and Twenty-fourth New York were thrown out as skirmishers, as the brigade neared the Hart House on the north bank of the Po River.[64] As the two regiments of skirmishers started to cross a small field, preparatory to wading the Po, Rebel sharpshooters concealed in a mill along the river opened a sharp fire on the unsuspecting men. Corporal James Torrence was struck in the head by a musket ball and killed instantly. Privates John Reynolds and David Fuller went down, both hit by the same bullet.[65]

The Ninety-ninth Pennsylvania was called forward, and the three regiments charged across a small swamp and a field, driving the Rebel gunmen out of their lair. They moved on across the Po River, scooping up a few prisoners along the way. Their advance continued for another three miles, where they awaited the remainder of Ward's brigade.[66] The brigade arrived at 8:00 P.M., a camp was made, and the bulk of the skirmishers were called in for the evening.[67]

The next morning Lieutenant Colonel George Meikel was informed that he was in temporary command of the Twentieth Indiana. Colonel Taylor had reached the limits of his physical capabilities and had become debilitated by the constant marching, fighting and lack of sleep.[68] At 10:00 A.M. Lieutenant Colonel Meikel was ordered directly by Major General David Birney to move out with the Ninety-ninth Pennsylvania and an artillery battery in support of skirmishers from Barlow's division who were making their way back across the Ny River, with the Rebels hot on their heels.[69]

The small expeditionary force marched to the furthest extreme of the right flank of the Union army resting on the Ny River. After ushering Barlow's men back to the north side of the Ny, the Hoosiers and Pennsylvanians, along with their artillery mates, trudged back to their camp. Their return was greeted with shouted commands to turn about and head back to the Ny. Major General William Mahone's division had pushed forward to the banks of the Ny in an effort to knock down any plans the Union force had for a flanking movement. The Twentieth Indiana was greeted at the approach to the Ny by a terrific artillery barrage. Shells flew thick, ripping through tree tops and plowing dirt and rocks up around the Indiana men.[70]

The men of the Twentieth moved into a protective hollow behind a hill which sheltered them from the exploding shells. After enduring the bombardment for several dangerous minutes, the Hoosiers were ordered to fall back along with the rest of Ward's brigade. While temporarily safe from the shells in the hollow, the Indiana boys were now subjected to the direct fire of the Rebel artillery as they hightailed it back to the Po River. The Confederates followed up their bombardment with an infantry attack which tried to take advantage of Union forces astride a river like a bull across a fence. Soon, determined Rebels charged headlong after Hancock's troops. The Indiana men formed a line to receive the attack and fire a volley which blunted the force of the Rebel advance. The Twentieth was nearly flanked and captured.[71]

Sergeant Thomas Stephens, Lieutenant John Price, Privates James McPheeters, and Amos Burch were lying in a woods to the rear of the Twentieth in an area thought safe before the Rebel attack. Enjoying their convalescence in the shade, they were rudely awakened and shaken by stray bullets zinging through their haven. They quickly two-stepped it out of the reach of the charging Confederates.[72]

Ward's men were driven back to the north side of the Po into the safe arms of their division. Fatigued from scurrying here and there, the Indiana men were ready to collapse and call it a day, but it wasn't to be. The main Confederate battle line on their left flank had been definitely located, and Hancock intended to launch an assault on it.

At sundown Ward's brigade moved into position and massed in column of regiments preparatory to an assault on the enemy's works. The brigade was stacked regiment upon regiment with the Eighty-sixth New York in the front line followed in order by the Third Maine, One Hundred and Twenty-fourth New York, Ninety-ninth Pennsylvania, One Hundred and Forty-first Pennsylvania, Twentieth Indiana, One Hundred and Tenth Pennsylvania, and the Fortieth New York.[73]

The Confederates held a steep hill about one hundred fifty feet high called Laurel Hill. Covered with pines and cedars, the crest was crowned with breastworks and well-developed defensive positions. The attack on Laurel Hill would consist of two divisions from Hancock's corps and two from Warren's corps.[74] Brigadier General Samuel Crawford passed in front of the Twentieth Indiana on the way back to his division after meeting with Hancock and the other division commanders. He was agitated and thoroughly disgusted that an assault was to be made. Fully within earshot of the Hoosiers, Crawford could be heard predicting a disaster for the attack, which he deemed suicidal.[75] This wasn't heartening to the Indiana men, but when Hobart Ward ordered bayonets to be fixed and the charge to be made, the men of the Twentieth complied.[76]

Ward's men advanced unopposed at first, but as they started to wind their way through the cedars and pines, Rebel pickets opened up on them. This alerted the main line of Confederate defenses, and soon the picket fire was joined by artillery fire and heavy volleys from the top of Laurel Hill. Private James Hoover's leg was nearly ripped off by an exploding shell as he charged up the hill.[77] Brigadier General Ward, keeping pace with his men, was struck in the side of the head by a shell fragment which dazed and shocked him, but spared his life.[78]

The Eighty-sixth New York and the Third Maine lost heavily on their advance up the hill, but were able to plant their colors on the works of the enemy. Rebels quickly counterattacked, driving Ward's men back down to the hill's base. With the attack, as Crawford had foretold, a suicidal failure, the fighting dissolved into scattered picket firing for the next twenty-four hours.[79]

An event of monumental proportion occurred on May 10, which would directly affect the Twentieth Indiana. Emory Upton, an energetic young colonel, commanding a brigade in Wright's division, came up with a simple, intriguing idea. He would mass a large number of soldiers, densely packed and many ranks deep, and bludgeon the defensive works of the Rebels with a swift, smashing attack. Upon opening a gap in the Rebel lines, the breach would be exploited by support troops following the shock troops. Upton was given permission to try his novel concept with five thousand men in the shock force and the support troops to be provided by Gershom Mott's division.[80]

Upton's attack was successful in opening a breach in the Confederate line, but Mott failed to exploit the opening, and a counterattack drove Upton's men back to their original position. Ulysses S. Grant, recognizing an innovation in military science when he saw one, was overheard talking to his staff, revealing what he thought of the attack: "A brigade today, a corps tomorrow."[81] Grant sat down that evening and penned a brief note to President Abraham Lincoln. In the note, Grant sent Lincoln a message that he had waited three years to see, "I propose to fight it out along this line if it takes all summer."[82] The note was penned in ink, but it would be underlined in blood.

Grant may have felt he was going to have to fight all year in front of Laurel Hill and Spotsylvania, with no apparent easy way around the Confederate flanks. He was faced with an interesting tactical situation in confronting Lee's Rebels. Lee had distributed his men along a steep ridge line that ran roughly in a northeasterly direction. In an effort to keep Major General Ambrose Burnside's Ninth Corps from getting around his right flank, he was forced to bend his line in a sharp southeasterly direction, giving Lee's line the appearance of an inverted V. It was a strong defensive position, with breastworks, trenches, and abatis, the sharp, spear-like limbs aimed forward to slow down any advancing attacker. The point of the V was heavily manned and, on May 10, thirty artillery pieces were mounted there. The point did stick out, however, and created an inviting target. In fact, it stuck out so much that Union forces referred to it as the "Mule Shoe."

Colonel Emory Upton's stormtrooper attack strategy struck a responsive chord with Grant because it gave him a tool to strike at the Mule Shoe. An attack by a full corps would take some time to put together and could not be carried out on May 11. This failure by the Union commander to renew his attacks on that day was misinterpreted by Lee as an indication that Grant was going to make another sidling move in an attempt to slip around his flank. Lee did not intend to allow Grant to get between his army and Richmond, so he alerted his men to be prepared to move at a moment's notice. Preparatory to the anticipated move, Lee ordered Richard Ewell to have twenty-two of his corps' artillery pieces limbered up and moved one mile and a half to the rear. This set the stage for the titanic events of the next day.

Tactics were not all that had changed on May 11. The weather, which had been unseasonably hot and blistering dry since the beginning of the month, now turned unseasonably cold and rainy. The feet of one hundred thousand men, mules, and wagon wheels quickly churned up the crude paths and roads into a muddy morass.[83]

At 9:00 P.M., May 11, the Twentieth Indiana methodically built extensive campfires at the base of Laurel Hill and in the woods and countryside around them and then set out on the long and fatiguing night march to the left of the existing Union line. The regiment trudged to the vicinity of the Landrum House to launch the coming attack. The Indiana men were now assembled twelve hundred yards from the Rebel lines at the Mule Shoe. Barlow's division formed on the left of the corps and Birney's division took its place on the right in the front of the densely massed battle formation. Gershom Mott's men backed up Barlow's division from the rear. Over fifteen thousand men gathered, awaiting the coming dawn and orders to attack.[84]

The cold night air gave rise to a dense blanket of fog which lay like a heavy shroud over the Union and Confederate lines, shielding movements and positions from the view of either army. The fog caused Winfield Hancock to delay his attack. He sent for all of the colonels from his corps for a strategy meeting, and they gathered behind the Twentieth Indiana, which was on the first line of the assembled masses. The men of the Twentieth eavesdropped while Hancock told his colonels that he wanted absolute silence as the corps advanced and that no man was to fire his rifle until the advancing troops had reached the first line of Confederate defenses. Hancock told the colonels that they were to use the Twentieth Indiana, which was in line on the left of the Ninety-ninth Pennsylvania, as the guide regiment. At 4:35 A.M. Hancock quietly asked his colonels, "Gentlemen, are you all ready now?" They replied in unison, "Yes."

"Then join your regiments and move forward," Hancock gently directed his officers.[85]

Brigadier General Hobart Ward had fussed and fretted all day about the movement to the left and was in an agitated and excitable state as the time to advance approached. Ward had taken the opportunity during the night to take some comfort, as many of his brother officers had done before him, from a bottle of whiskey. But rather than slipping into a stupor, Ward was on edge and full of fight, ready to rush headlong with his men toward the Rebel lines. Now, with the colonels returned to their regiments, Hancock's men quietly withdrew their bayonets from their scabbards and fastened them to the barrels of their guns with a gentle rattling which told each of the men that this new moment of destiny had come. Hobart Ward calmly ordered his men to move forward.[86]

The Hoosiers advanced in silence over a marsh and through a dense stand of low pines. From here the ground ascended sharply to the Rebel lines, which could not be seen by the men in the vanguard. The slope of the hill was heavily wooded, and the once-neat battle lines became ragged and mob-like as units became separated. Rebel pickets could hear men coming toward them and opened up with scattered shots, but still the Union troops held their fire and advanced. As Confederate picket fire rose in intensity, Colonel Thomas Biles of the Ninety-ninth Pennsylvania thought he had reached the main Rebel line and let out a yell which "woke people in Washington." Biles' earsplitting yell startled both the Union attackers and Confederates who were only now awakening to the reality that they were shortly to be under attack.[87]

The entire Union corps sent up a cheer and dashed up the slope toward the Confederate rifle pits. Four hundred yards from the Rebel line, trees disappeared, and the men exposed themselves to a killing zone in front of the breastworks and abatis. The Confederates were taken by complete surprise as the blue wave of screaming Union men washed over their works. Firing now opened from both sides and was brief and intense as the men of Colonel William Monaghan's Louisiana Brigade and Brigadier General James Walker's Stonewall Brigade were overwhelmed by the irresistible advance.[88]

Monaghan's men would throw down their guns in surrender and as the Union men ran past them, assuming that someone in the rear would scoop up the prisoners, the Louisianans would pick up their rifles and shoot the Northerners in the back. The Hoosiers witnessed this treachery and dealt with it severely and summarily, putting many of the Louisiana men to the bayonet in a brutal visitation of justice.[89]

The swift advance quickly evolved into a fierce melee of horrific dimensions. Lieutenant Colonel Charles Weygant, One Hundred and Twenty-fourth New York, described the fighting:

> *Then ensued one of those hand-to-hand encounters with clubbed rifles, bayonets, swords and pistols, which defies description. Officers of the opposing sides cut and slashed with their swords, and fired with their revolvers into the very faces of each other.*[90]

As it became obvious to Confederate Major General Edward Johnson that his lines were being attacked in force, he urgently called for the return of the artillery which had earlier been limbered up and withdrawn under orders from General Lee. The artillery returned on the fly; they quickly unlimbered and fired their first shots. However, the overpowering attack of Hancock's men swamped Johnson's division and rushed on toward the second line of Confederate defenses. Before the Rebel batteries could loose another round, the artillerymen were surrounded by blue-clad troops and were forced to surrender themselves and their guns. Private Jimmie Stephens was a member of a squad of soldiers from the Twentieth Indiana who captured two batteries of guns, turned the field pieces on the retreating Rebels and opened fire. The former Rebel guns ripped great holes in the backs of the panicked Confederates, accelerating the rout and piling up the dead.[91]

Johnson's division was totally shattered and thousands of men captured, along with most of Ewell's corps artillery. Major General Johnson was himself captured along with Brigadier General George "Maryland" Steuart. With the Rebels swept from the Mule Shoe and a gaping half-mile-wide breach in the Confederate line, the Union forces continued their rush to the third line of the Southern defenses.

The men of the Twentieth had fared well during the attack. The element of surprise, the lack of Confederate artillery and the ground cover had enabled the majority of the Hoosiers to escape serious injury. The apparent success emboldened the Indiana men, and their forward movement lost any semblance of order and discipline. Officers became separated from their men, and the once densely packed Second Corps was now strung out over a wide area.[92] It was a dangerous situation for the heretofore victorious Union forces and all but invited a Confederate counterattack.

Brigadier General John B. Gordon, commanding Early's division, quickly realized the potentially disastrous predicament for the Confederate army. He ordered his three brigades to throw up a hastily organized defense across the base of the Mule Shoe in an effort to stem the Federal tide. Gordon's men were joined by two brigades from Rodes' Division and together they moved forward at 5:30 A.M., directly toward the disorganized rabble which was once a powerful coordinated attack force.[93]

The Twentieth Indiana had just reached the third and final line of Confederate works when Gordon's men launched their counterstroke. Private William Archer had drawn near this line of breastworks and, placing his hands on the walls of the works, prepared to vault over them when he was shot in the head.[94] Quickly, all around the lifeless Archer, men began to drop like leaves in autumn. Privates Lawrence Frantz, Dan Briner, and John Coppeck were killed, ripped to pieces by the destructive volleys fired by Colonel John Hoffman's Virginians and Colonel Clement Evans' Georgians.[95] The force of Gordon's counterattack drove Hancock's men back toward the toe of the Mule Shoe, forcing them over the breastworks to their outer edge.

Jimmie Stephens was struck below the knee by a musket ball which splintered the bone and rendered him incapable of moving. Stephens' brother, Thomas, and Private George Lackham grabbed Jimmie's arms and dragged him to the rear.[96] Captain Daniel Corey was severely wounded and lay oozing blood on the Rebel breastworks.[97]

The Rebels pressed the Union men closely as they fell back to the first line of works. The intensity of the musket and artillery fire was "one deafening roar."[98] The Virginians, Georgians and North Carolinians of Early's division, commanded by Gordon, repeatedly smashed into the ranks of Hancock's men. They finally made it into the works, leaving Rebels in and Yankees out. In this position, the fight would rage on, unabated for the next eighteen hours. The Confederate "Stars and Bars" was implanted in the soft earth inside the parapet, and the proud flag of the Twentieth Indiana was firmly placed in the mud on the outside of the works.[99]

Red-faced Hobart Ward wildly waved his sword to rally his men outside the Confederate works and yelled for a counterattack—oblivious to the impossibility of a counterattack because he was drunk. Ward headed down the slope of the hill, heading for the original launching point of the predawn attack, incoherently mumbling about needing to find his horse and needing to attack. He passed Major General Birney who immediately smelled alcohol. Birney then ordered the brigadier general to the rear—under arrest.[100]

The fighting at the apex of the Mule Shoe marked a nadir in the ferocity and inhumanity of the Civil War. Prior to this moment of battle, there had been ample examples of chivalry, honor, compassion, and respect, even in the midst of the war's bloodiest battles. Men had often behaved as men and not as mindless, bloodlusting animals. Here, along the trenches of the Mule Shoe, no shred of honor remained. Soldiers of both armies, who had been subjected to every imaginable deprivation, inconvenience and suffering, finally snapped and reverted to their primal instincts.

Opponents stood toe-to-toe, bayoneting each other and swinging clubbed muskets, smashing heads and firing point blank into the faces of their opponents. No mercy was requested and none offered—only the mutual desire for annihilation. "Cheer and fire was all anyone did. Men tore off pieces of their clothing to wipe out their guns and then went to work firing again," Major Gilbreath reported.[101]

A Union artillery battery was run up close to the breastworks, where it fired round after round of canister at the Confederates. The battery's horses were all killed and its crews so thinned out by the heavy counter fire that the survivors were forced to drag the field pieces from the field by hand. Trees on both sides of the breastworks were cut in half by the buzz saw of lead fired by Confederates and Union men alike.[102]

The men of the Twentieth died by the score in the bloodbath, many falling face down in the ever-rising mud which had thickened from the driving, cold rain now falling. Officers and men died hideous deaths that morning in the Spotsylvania trenches. Captain John Thomas was felled by a bullet and his lifeless body was virtually dissected by the barrage of both Rebel and friendly bullets. Captain Lafayette Gordon nearly had his shoulder blown off by a musket shot fired from close range, a wound that soon after proved fatal. Lieutenant Michael Sheehan was struck down for the second battle in a row. Lieutenant John Bartholomew was severely wounded in the thick of the fight, and Captain Thomas Logan escaped with another slight wound, his second in one week.[103]

The Rebels relentlessly continued their efforts to recapture their works and repetitively sent wave after human wave of fresh men. Men stacked up in deep piles, and the dead, dying and wounded lay in inch-deep blood which flowed like a river inside the entrenchment. Hour after long hour the slaughter continued, allowing men neither rest nor sustenance, only the exhaustion of the melee. Finally, late in the evening of May 12, the Confederates still holding their ground, but barely, received word that a new line of works had been prepared eight hundred yards to the rear. The firing stopped and the Rebels slipped off to their new defensive position.

Their hands bloodied and mud-caked, lips black from the crusted gunpowder of their cartridges, the Indiana boys collapsed where they stood in the mud. Now, after midnight, a forlorn playing of Handel's "The Dead March" came wafting over the battlefield, played by a Confederate band. It was responded to by a Union rendition of "Nearer My God to Thee." Ending their woeful concert, the Union band played a version of the sentimental "Home Sweet Home." For a few brief hours, the killing stopped and the thoroughly worn out and broken young warriors of both sides cried themselves to sleep.[104] The nation itself could have well done the same had it been present for only a fraction of an hour at Spotsylvania.

When dawn came on May 13, the light of day revealed a surrealistic landscape of carnage. On the Rebel side of the works, the trench was filled with dead Confederates piled on top of Confederate wounded like so much cordwood. The Twentieth sorted through the piles of bodies, locating the wounded and helping them off the field to Union field hospitals. The Indiana men ventured out past the trench line looking for their regimental comrades who had been wounded during the early phases of the battle. Captain Corey's body was never found. Perhaps he was mutilated like the thick oak trees which were felled by the intense fire, as were the battery horses which were whittled down to a width of only ten inches by the incessant rifle fire. Captain Thomas' body was found, pierced by twelve bullets fired by both friend and foe.[105]

As the roll was called by the surviving officers of the Twentieth Indiana, fewer than one hundred and fifty men answered. Eighty-five Hoosiers who climbed the hill at the Mule Shoe were either dead, wounded, or missing.[106]

Private Samuel List sat down in the mud on the evening of May 13 and stretched a piece of paper over his knee and, with great difficulty, scribbled a note to his parents. List wrote:

For the first time since leaving Culpeper I have time and a chance to write. We have passed through the most severe battles that were ever fought. I will not attempt to give you an account of all our sufferings. This is the tenth day of the fight and there has not been a day that our regiment has not been under fire. Our loss is terrible. Our company has lost thirty men killed, wounded and missing. I tell you it was hard to see my comrades falling round me. We went into the field with fifty guns in the company and now we have about seventeen. The fight is still going on. Loss in our company occurred the first and second days' fight. Boys are very much worn out. Scarcely able to get along. Enemy strongly entrenched wherever we find them.[107]

Sadly, the new flag, presented to the regiment upon their departure from Indianapolis by the ladies of that town, was now torn by forty-seven bullet holes.[108] The men who carried the flag fared only slightly better; two color bearers were struck down in the fighting.[109]

On May 14 the regiment—or what was left of it—spent a relatively quiet day in a pelting rain in roughly the same location where they stood and fought on May 12. They did move a short distance to their right to shore up the Union defensive line. While lying in the mud trying to get some rest, Private Ira Allen had recklessly exposed himself to the view of the Confederate lines. In short order, a Rebel sniper drew a bead on the luckless private and killed him with one shot.[110]

Even though three days had passed since the terror of the Mule Shoe, Rebel wounded still dotted the landscape. In an act of compassion and humanity, several Hoosiers volunteered to venture out between the lines to bring in whatever gray-clad wounded they could find. The detail headed out under the command of the humanitarian Lieutenant Ed Sutherland, himself wounded in the battles of May 6 and 12. Several Confederate wounded were located and carried to Union medical facilities. In the process of removing one of the wounded, Lieutenant Sutherland offered himself as a target which an unidentified rebel marksman could not resist. Sutherland fell with a severe leg wound which would become infected, require amputation and result in an agonizingly painful death.[111]

That evening, the regiment moved two or three miles to their left to a position with their right flank resting on the Ta River with the breastworks now fronting west.[112] The men found some boards, placed them in the thick mud in their trenches and slept on them, finding comfort in small things.[113]

All day on May 16 and 17, the Twentieth spent their time working in the pouring rain on improving their defensive works. Out in front of the works there was continual skirmishing and frequent cannonading between the two armies. After dark on the seventeenth, Rebel forces ventured a weak attack on the Hoosiers' front and were beaten back. The Twentieth Indiana and the Ninety-ninth Pennsylvania were ordered to advance and enter the entrenchments they had captured on May 12.

On May 19 the brigade moved to the vicinity of the Anderson House and massed there with their division. Earlier that day, General Lee suspected that Grant had withdrawn Winfield Scott Hancock's and Horatio Wright's corps from their positions in the line. He determined to have Ewell's corps make a reconnaissance in force against what he perceived as a weakened Union line. His objective was to smash through the line and capture the Federal wagon train in the rear. In fact, the right of the Union line was not weak and had been significantly strengthened by the addition of seventy-five hundred fresh men, six thousand culled from heavy artillery units which had been defending Washington, D.C.[114]

At six that evening, the alarm was sounded in Hancock's corps and his troops rushed on the double quick to support the heavy artillerymen. Ewell's men were forced backward after a severe fight. The following morning, at first light, Egan's brigade formed a battle line and advanced in attack against the surprised Rebels. Colonel Egan's men scooped up five hundred prisoners at little loss to the brigade. However, Private James Smallwood had his arm shattered by a musket ball, requiring amputation.[115] At 11:00 A.M., the regiment returned to the Anderson House and, effectively, the Spotsylvania campaign came to an end.[116]

From May 5 through May 20, the Twentieth Indiana lost 223 men, including seven difficult-to-replace officers. The regiment found itself with only 192 men answering roll call.[117] The numbers were very similar throughout the Union army. Grant had suffered massive casualties at the hands of Lee, casualties that would not be replaced for some time. Grant suffered more than 36,000 casualties since May 5, compared to only 17,000 for the Confederate army. In addition, 14,000 men had either deserted, returned home at the expiration of their enlistment or were recovering in Washington hospitals from a variety of non-battle maladies. The Union army was now reduced to approximately 56,000 combat troops, roughly equal to the size of Lee's army. For the first time in the war, the next campaign would be waged on somewhat equal terms.[118]

Christopher Fraunberg, Company E, was promoted from the ranks and became first lieutenant of Company B. (Carlile collection)

Private John M. Smith, Company I, was promoted to sergeant, but he deserted on July 8, 1864, at Petersburg. (U.S. Army Military History Institute)

Second Lieutenant James P. Stallard, Company D, was promoted from the ranks in January 1864. (Dunn collection)

First Lieutenant William W. Stevens, Company I. (Dunn collection)

First Lieutenant Harry Geisendorff, Company H. (Dunn collection)

Second Lieutenant Warren J. Hauk, Company A. (Carlile collection)

Captain Charles A. Bell, Company B, was killed by an artillery shell on July 9, 1864, in front of Petersburg. (Carlile collection)

Captain John F. Thomas, Company A, was wounded at Chancellorsville and killed at Spotsylvania. (Carlile collection)

Lieutenant Colonel George W. Meikel rose from first lieutenant, Company H, to command of the regiment from Spotsylvania until his death in September at Petersburg. (Carlile collection)

Second Lieutenant Joseph A. Clark, Company B. (Carlile collection)

Colonel William C. L. Taylor was a former city attorney who rose from lieutenant of Company G to head the regiment at the Battle of the Wilderness. (Carlile collection)

Corporal Nicholas Thayer,
Company G, and his wife. (U.S.
Army Military History Institute)

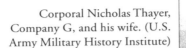

First Lieutenant Edward
C. Sutherland, Company
F, died of wounds on June
26, 1864. (Dunn
collection)

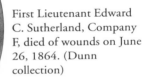

Private William H. Staley,
Company A, was wounded at
Spotsylvania. (Dunn
collection)

Captain Albert S.
Andrews,
Company E,
transferred to the
regiment from the
Fourteenth
Indiana. (Dunn
collection)

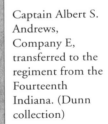

Private Thomas Johnson,
Company F, served for the entire
war. (Dunn collection)

First Lieutenant Hiram Crawford, Company E. (Carlile collection)

First Lieutenant Marquis Kinneard, Company D, resigned on July 2, 1864. (Dunn collection)

First Lieutenant William O. Sherwood, Company H, resigned on April 3, 1863. (Carlile collection)

Captain William D. Vatchett, Company D, was wounded at Oak Grove. (Dunn collection)

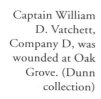

An unidentified private of the Twentieth Indiana. (Dunn collection)

Three unidentified lieutenants of the Twentieth Indiana (*top and center*), and two unidentified privates (*below*). (Carlile collection)

CHAPTER TWELVE

THE END OF A WILD ROMANCE

Ulysses S. Grant had his fill of the inconclusive and costly slugfest waged near Spotsylvania.

Headlong assaults had cost the Army of the Potomac huge numbers of manpower which would take months to replace. Grant resolved to revert to his earlier strategy of attempting to slip around the right flank of Lee's army. Grant's plan was simple and showed both a lack of knowledge of the terrain he was to encounter and a naiveté about his opponent's skill and determination. Winfield Scott Hancock's Second Corps would be sent east and south around the right flank of the Confederate army in the direction of Milford Station. If Hancock could reach Milford Station before Lee, then the Confederate army would either be forced to attack the Second Corps or withdraw on inferior roads toward Richmond. If Lee attacked Hancock, Grant would follow with three corps and smash into the Rebel forces.

The Twentieth Indiana and Egan's brigade quietly slipped out of their breastworks at 11:00 P.M. on May 20 and started on the long march to Guiney's Station via Massaponax Church. The regiment arrived at Guiney's Station at 8:00 A.M. and from there proceeded through Bowling Green. The march continued to Milford Station, and the regiment finally came to rest for the evening about two miles beyond the Mattapony River. The long, winding trek had moved east, then south and finally southwest before stopping—a distance of thirty miles.[1]

When they arrived at Coleman's House, Lieutenant Colonel George Meikel ordered the men to the spade. If Lee was to attack, Meikel wanted the full protection of entrenchments. The Hoosiers quickly threw up "a splendid line of works" and then just as quickly fell asleep.[2] Early the next morning, the Twentieth was dispatched on picket duty, moving out two miles in advance of the Second Corps, perilously close to Lieutenant General Richard Ewell's corps.[3] The proximity of the Rebels did not deter the Hoosiers from liberating several enslaved chickens, pigs, and ducks from the farms of their oppressive masters. The regiment had quite a feast that evening, dining on mush, chicken, and fresh pork. Bellies full, they were lulled asleep by the distant booming of an artillery duel on their right.[4]

At 5:30 A.M. on May 23 the Twentieth was on the move with its brigade, marching in the direction of Chesterfield Station. The cavalry led the movement, with Birney's division following on the Telegraph Road leading to the bridge across the North Anna River. When the line of marchers drew close to the North Anna, they could see Colonel John Henagan's South Carolinians boldly maintaining breastworks on the north bank of the river.[5] With defenders on both sides of the river, the forcing of the North Anna would require a two-part assault.

The first assault required the Union attackers to move five hundred yards over an open expanse with the ground ascending sharply at the Rebels' position. Speed was the order of the day as the Twentieth Indiana and the Third Maine were placed in the first line of attackers to be followed by the balance of the brigade. The attackers charged furiously across the open space, not halting to fire and reload. With bayonets fixed, Egan's brigade ran screaming toward the earthworks and were in among the startled Confederates before the enemy could fire much more than a volley or two.[6]

The losses in the brigade amounted to fewer than a hundred and fifty men, and the Twentieth fared well, except for Private Robert Duncan, Company H, who was killed by the first Rebel volley.[7] Major General Hancock witnessed the brave assault and declared it "brilliant and spirited."[8]

The second assault in the attempt to cross the North Anna would be much tougher. The river crossing presented a tactical problem of real difficulty. The assault would need to be made across a rickety, hastily constructed wagon-wide bridge which stood high across the water. The bridge was five hundred feet long and had been erected the year before to replace one which had been destroyed. This bridge itself was to have been burned, but the quick arrival and capture of the north bank of the river and the resulting fire kept up on the south end of the bridge all evening precluded the Rebels from setting it ablaze.[9]

Early in the morning on May 24, Lieutenant Colonel Meikel took part of the Twentieth Indiana down the steep northern bank of the North Anna, while the remainder of the brigade kept up a steady rifle fire on the Rebel pickets on the south side. The Hoosiers quickly chopped down several trees on the north bank which fell across the river toward the south bank. Two brave Indiana men swiftly ran on the trunks of the trees as far as they could and then leapt into the river and waded to the south side. With axes in hand, they chopped down two fairly good-sized trees, dropping them toward the north bank. The two Hoosiers were followed by several additional men who formed a small skirmish line. The scene was now set for the climactic assault.[10]

The bridge was so narrow that it did not allow for a large storming force to cross. This perilous crossing would need to be initially made by a small squad of "brave hearts." Once again, Hancock had chosen the Twentieth for the Devil's duty. With Meikel and his small force down in the deep ravine of the North Anna, volunteers were called for to storm the bridge. Captain John C. Brown of Monticello volunteered with twenty of his men for the crossing. Companies A and B also offered their services.[11]

The detachment waited impatiently for the trees to be felled across the river and the skirmish line to be established. When all was ready, Captain Brown gave the order for his small band of men to charge, and they dashed for the south end of the bridge, running into the swarm of Rebel bullets and artillery shells thrown at them. Sergeant Thomas Stephens was on a full run, leaping from rail to rail on the bridge when he heard an artillery shell whistling toward him. He froze in his tracks as the shell ripped into his knapsack, nearly knocking him down. No worse for wear, save for a severely dented frying pan, Stephens continued sprinting across the bridge, not taking the time to question the wisdom of bringing a skillet into an attack.[12]

When Captain Brown reached the south end of the bridge, he stopped to direct the men following him to fan out on both sides of the bridge to assault its defenders. At that instant, a .58-caliber musket ball slammed into Brown, entering below his left eye and exiting just below his right ear, taking the earlobe with it. Brown slumped to the deck of the bridge. His men rushed to his side but were admonished by their fallen captain to stick to their duty. Convinced that they had heard their captain's last words, the men of Company K rushed on to obey his command.[13]

Safely across the bridge, the Hoosiers now opened up their own fire on the Rebel pickets. The pickets, seemingly stunned by the audacity and the alacrity of the attack, quickly were put to flight. Sergeant Jonathan C. Kirk, one of the volunteers who had crossed the North Anna on a tree trunk, stormed up the slope on the south side of the river. He surprised a group of thirteen Confederate pickets and ordered them to throw down their guns. Supposing he had a large force behind him, the Rebels complied and surrendered to the sergeant. Kirk proudly marched the chagrined and embarrassed Confederates back down the slope and into captivity. His achievement would earn him the Medal of Honor.[14]

With the Confederate defenders driven off by the audacious Hoosiers, the remainder of Egan's brigade were able to cross the North Anna; by 1:00 P.M. the brigade was massed behind the Fox House. At 3:00 P.M. the brigade moved out in front of the Fox House and began constructing strong fortifications, all the while under a heavy Confederate artillery bombardment. By the time the line of entrenchments were finished, it was discovered that Ewell's corps had formed in extremely strong works opposite the Union troops. Their furious trenching now being to no avail, the Indiana men filed out of the earthworks and recrossed to the north bank of the river, destroying the bridge after their crossing.[15] All in all, an exhilaratingly successful assault was relegated to the scrap heap of wasted opportunities and lost dreams.

The Second Corps moved on May 27 from the north bank of the North Anna and marched in the direction of Hanover Town, arriving three miles north of the Pamunkey River, a distance of twenty miles.

The next day the Twentieth renewed their march, moving southeast and south, reaching the Pamunkey at 3:00 P.M.. There they halted, filled their canteens, and immersed themselves—uniforms and all—in the river. After that short stop, they crossed the river on a pontoon bridge and fanned out on the left flank, erecting breastworks. After two long years, and hundreds of casualties and many battles later, the Twentieth Indiana had returned to the Peninsula.[16]

On May 29 the regiment moved five miles to the southwest, the line of their march littered with dead Confederates who were lying, bloated and blackened from the sun. The Hoosiers halted late that evening in the immediate presence of the Rebels. Egan's brigade formed a battle line facing southwest and west. At 11:00 the following morning, the regiment moved out on the skirmish lines to build breastworks, enduring shelling by the Confederates the entire time. Private Azariah Leath was seriously wounded by the bombardment, and Private Alred was killed by a shell fragment.[17]

May 31 opened with a lively exchange of fire by pickets from both sides. At 11:00 A.M. Egan's brigade formed in battle line and advanced toward the Confederate rifle pits to the southwest. The thin Rebel line fired a few volleys and then retired from the field. Several Rebels intentionally loitered in the works and allowed themselves to become prisoners. It was a relatively inexpensive and insignificant victory but not one without cost. Privates Charles Sentman, Jeremiah Pherson, and Augustus Fritz were struck by enemy bullets and wounded.[18]

The Hoosiers were allowed to remain in their works all day on June 1, receiving a much-needed rest. However, the rest was merely a brief respite, which would come to an end at 1:00 A.M. later that evening. Birney's division marched, following Barlow's and Gibbon's divisions on a suffocating, hot and dusty ten-mile trek from the extreme right flank of the Union army to its extreme left flank at Cold Harbor.[19] Grant had reached a moment of fatal decision as he found the territory to conduct a flanking movement reduced. The general decided to launch a massive attack on the Confederate right flank; he wanted his best corps at the critical point. Moving along unfamiliar roads, the Second Corps soon lost its direction and marched six miles out of their way. They finally arrived on the left flank in an utterly fatigued state and were completely incapable of attacking that morning. Grant allowed a one-day reprieve and set the attack for the next day.

After arriving at Cold Harbor, the regiment was allowed to rest, while Lieutenant Colonel Meikel and Major Gilbreath were sent out to reconnoiter the ground in front of Second Corps. It was this ground over which an attack would be made. Meikel moved out on the right, and Gilbreath crept through the brush three hundred yards to his left. The men passed over a small stream and a marsh, determined to find the best place to pass troops. Intent on their work, the two officers failed to notice that they had moved perilously close to Rebel lines. From out of the brush to Gilbreath's front, the major heard a twangy Southern voice call out, "Yank, if you don't get into your lines pretty quick, you will go to Richmond." Gilbreath didn't need to be told twice. Meikel heard the commotion and he also began running for the rear. Less congenial Confederate pickets opened fire on the fleeing officers, and the zip, pop and zing of their bullets added to the urgency of Gilbreath's and Meikel's escape.[20]

The Confederacy had had ample time over the two years since the Peninsula campaign to strengthen and improve the defensive works around Richmond. Wide killing zones had been created, elaborate breastworks constructed and artillery positions laid out in such a way as to enable enfilading fire at almost any point along the lines. In addition, trees had been felled, and sharpened obstructions placed in front of the Rebel trenches to slow down the attackers. It was the strongest Confederate defensive position yet, and into the teeth of this defensive line Grant proposed to attack.

At 4:45 A.M. on June 3, Grant launched his attack at Cold Harbor. Rebel artillery and musketry fire was devastatingly accurate, ripping huge gaps in the advancing Federals ranks. Birney's division was assigned the role of the Second Corps reserve. Gibbon's and Barlow's divisions smashed into the Confederate wall, briefly gained a toehold on the Rebel line and then were repulsed by the powerful defensive fire. The Second Corps and the remainder of the Union attack force were driven back. The losses were formidable: nearly seven thousand Federal troops in Hancock's, Wright's, and Smith's corps were shot down in the hour-long attack and retreat.[21]

The Second Corps suffered early in the advance from an apparent lack of communication and intelligence. Gibbon and Barlow had failed to coordinate their attack, becoming separated by two hundred yards near the swamp where Lieutenant Colonel Meikel and Major Gilbreath had been warned by the friendly Rebel.[22] This was a mistake that cost hundreds of lives and was just another example of the wastefulness that Lieutenant General Grant seemed willing to tolerate in achieving his singular purpose of fighting it out until the end. His strategy, or lack thereof, had now cost the Union army nearly fifty thousand men since May 5.

For the next week the Twentieth Indiana occupied itself with the tiring and tedious task of building breastworks, digging trenches, marching, countermarching and standing picket duty. Temperatures were in the nineties daily, and adding to the discomfort was the dangerous presence of Rebel pickets and snipers, who never missed an opportunity to take pot shots at anything in blue that moved.[23] It was a tense, nerve-wracking experience, preparing for and awaiting an enemy to attack. General Lee had fully intended to attack his blue-coated nemesis if the opportunity presented itself. He had no desire to continually drop back on Richmond, knowing full well that the Confederacy could not withstand a siege. But before he could take aggressive action against Grant's army, he needed to beef up his own depleted forces.

Privates Robert Duncan, Company K, and Nathaniel Black, Company A, both learned of the dangers lurking in the underbrush of the Cold Harbor terrain when Rebel pickets rushed the men of the Twentieth while they were out on picket duty. Black was seriously wounded and Duncan killed as the Hoosier pickets rapidly fell back before the howling Confederate pickets.[24]

This feigned attack on June 5 directly contributed to the death of Private John Fisher. Fisher was a rough-and-tumble, vulgar country boy, who had thoroughly irritated and, at times, enraged the more religious men of the Twentieth Indiana. Many of the pious Hoosiers took offense at his drinking, gambling and profanity. Unfortunately for Private Fisher, the nerves of his brother soldiers on picket duty were ragged and on edge. Guns were loaded and hammers cocked as each picket anticipated a Rebel behind every rock, hill, and tree. It only took the slightest unidentified noise in the brush or trees for the men to open up on an unseen enemy, deer or rabbit. A nervous soldier from his own ranks recklessly discharged his rifle and blew out the back of Fisher's head.[25]

When it became obvious to the common soldiers of each army that severe combat was not imminent, the pickets gradually relaxed their tense demeanor and started communicating with each other across the lines. Yelling at each other from a distance at first, the distance between pickets grew closer until the men in blue and gray sat down with each other and again swapped tobacco, coffee, and newspapers. Most of the Confederate pickets participated in this discourse, with the exception of the Virginians on the right of the Hoosiers, who seemed bitter and unwilling to participate in barter and banter.[26]

The Twentieth Indiana received a vital boost of manpower during this lull in the fighting. The Fourteenth Indiana Volunteers, which had originally been mustered in June 1861, were due to be mustered out upon expiration of their three-year enlistment. The exit of the majority of the surviving members of this proud regiment left fewer than sixty men fit for duty. Because that was not a sufficient number to maintain the charade of even a skeleton regiment, the soldiers whose enlistment were not up were transferred to the Twentieth Indiana. They were formed into two companies, and the balance of the Twentieth was consolidated into six companies for organizational purposes. The reconstituted Twentieth Indiana could now muster 258 men for duty.[27]

The truth of the matter was that every regiment in the Union army was below strength, resulting in brigades the size of pre-1862 regiments and divisions the size of pre-1862 brigades. It was with this organizational tangle that Grant would be forced to bring the war to a conclusion. Fortunately for the Union cause, Robert E. Lee labored under the same disadvantage—magnified several times.

Lieutenant General Grant had decided on June 5 to make a bold, strategic move in an effort to break the bloody stalemate on the road to Richmond. He had suffered his fill of the seemingly fruitless slaughter which characterized the Wilderness, Spotsylvania, North Anna, and Cold Harbor. The reason the ugly disaster at Cold Harbor had occurred at all was that Grant felt that he had run out of room to continue his technique of sidling around the right flank of his opponent. The risks of moving a hundred thousand men through the marshes and morass of the Chickahominy River to the James River seemed too dangerous to chance. After Grant saw what the alternative to a further flanking movement would be, the dangers of moving his force through the same territory where McClellan's army was lost in 1862 shrank in comparison.

The move Grant proposed carried great risks. It was a daunting task, to slip away from an enemy along a ten-mile front, march nearly fifty miles across swampy, ravine-laden ground, and cross a tidal river at a point where it was nearly a half mile wide, all the while risking engagement by an aggressive foe and Confederate naval gunboats. If successful, the Union army would be transferred south of the James River and be in excellent position to capture the vital communication and rail center of Petersburg, and the fall of Petersburg would necessitate the evacuation of Richmond.

The plan was put in motion late in the evening of June 12. With Union cavalry in the advance, the Fifth Corps and Second Corps moved out in the dark of night. The Hoosiers of the Twentieth quietly slipped out of their entrenchments, trying to muffle the rattling of canteens, swords, bayonets and rifles so as to move unnoticed by the opposing Rebel lines. Each man carried four days' rations and fifty rounds of ammunition. That would be enough food, but each Indiana man wondered whether the ammunition would be sufficient for the task ahead. The march began in earnest at 11:00 P.M. and continued in shuffling silence as the Second Corps plodded along in stifling heat on dusty, twisted roads. The Twentieth crossed the Chickahominy River at 9:30 the following morning, and the men were allowed to make a brief stop and cook breakfast.[28]

After this short stop, the regiment restarted the hike for the James River, finally arriving there at 5:30 P.M. The Hoosiers had quickly and quietly covered thirty-five miles since the previous evening, an admirable accomplishment. Upon arriving at the James, the regiment formed in line of battle, each man nearly ready to drop in his tracks from fatigue. To their relief, the Rebels were still in their trenches at Cold Harbor, under the illusion that Grant's men were still there.[29]

At eleven the next morning the Indiana men filed on board the steamer *Eliza Hancock* and were ferried across the James River, landing at Wind Hill Point. Upon landing, the regiment moved up the river a short distance, stacked arms and lounged around until early evening, when they continued further up river and formed in line of battle.[30] The treat for the evening was a fat heifer which the boys of Company A killed, butchered and served up as a feast.[31]

The entire Second Corps finally completed the crossing of the James at 5:00 A.M. on June 15. At 10:30, after waiting in vain for rations to arrive, the corps moved off in the direction of Petersburg. The Twentieth marched briskly to the cadence of booming artillery fire coming from the Rebel-held town.[32] Major General William. F "Baldy" Smith was to move at daylight, with a force of sixteen thousand men, on what he assumed was to be a lightly defended Rebel citadel. Smith became bogged down on the periphery of the town before the chain of strongly constructed, artillery-laden fortifications. His attack degenerated into a brutal artillery duel supporting fruitless Union attacks. Hancock's men now marched toward Petersburg to add their weight to the struggle.

The Hoosiers covered eighteen grueling miles and arrived at Petersburg after sunset to find that Smith's men had captured a portion of the Confederate line and, with it, seventeen pieces of artillery.[33] The Indiana men also got their first good look at a new breed of comrade in the Northern army, the Negro soldier. Early in the war, the men of the Twentieth had derided every Negro they encountered, slave, freedman or soldier. The

Hoosiers had now come to respect the Negro soldier, who had earned that respect with blood shed in the name of the Union and freedom. In fact, the Negro regiments had captured two forts and several artillery pieces during the fighting. Too late to join in the attack, Hancock's corps was allowed to bed down for the night, serenaded to sleep by continuous cannon fire.[34]

Major Gilbreath was denied the opportunity to rest. Once again, Major General Birney pressed the major into service as a scout. Birney ordered Gilbreath to ride down a nearby road for several miles to see what turned up, a dangerous assignment at best. Gilbreath rode off into the pitch-black night with no escort and proceeded for two miles before he encountered obstructions in the road and was forced to ride through the trees. A mile later, Sammy, the major's bay horse, heard some strange noise and pricked up his ears. Gilbreath drew his revolver, halted the horse, and called out to his unseen threat to surrender. The major heard a plaintive, "For God sake, boss, don't shoot!" From out of the shadows came an old Negro slave. Gilbreath queried the old man as to where the road went and was informed, "Down here to de Cote House and up dar to Petersburg." Major Gilbreath returned to General Birney with his captive, who delighted in telling the division commander every bit of intelligence he could summon up.[35]

Tired eyelids had barely opened on June 16 when Confederate artillery began bombarding the Second Corps lines. The intense fire instantly wounded and killed several men and sent everyone ducking for cover. Lieutenant Colonel Meikel called his men to form a line of assault, ordering them, along with the Seventeenth Maine, to charge the Rebel works opposite them. As the attackers ran across several hundred yards of cleared fields, they were subjected to the severest of cannon fire. Man after man was struck by shell fragments and sent tumbling in a lifeless mass of blood and gore.[36]

The Hoosiers did not pause in the face of these staggering losses and the resultant screams and cries of the wounded and the dying. The attack was finally slowed when the regiments reached the intricate outer defenses of the Confederate line and ran into the sharpened abatis constructed by the Rebels. The Indiana men and their Maine brethren picked their way through the obstacles as quickly as possible, but the delay allowed reinforcements to be rushed to the defense of the Confederate line. The strengthened Rebel line opened a withering fire on the attackers, taking advantage of their exposed position to drop man after man with well-aimed fire. The Indiana men could neither advance nor withdraw. They were forced to the ground like so many vermin, burying their faces and burrowing into the Virginia soil.[37]

The Hoosiers and the men from Maine lay, pinned by rifle fire, until 3:00 P.M., when the remainder of the brigade formed and attacked the Confederate line. When the brigade reached the Twentieth, the Indiana boys jumped to their feet and joined the attack. Once again, the attack was repelled and driven back to its original starting point. At 6:00, one final attempt was made to capture the Rebel works, this time with Birney's entire division. The Hoosiers rushed headlong into this attack but not with the illusions that they had entertained during their first attempt.[38] This last try at smashing the Confederate lines was just as futile as the first two and as darkness fell, the Civil War moved one step closer to a conflict of siege warfare.

Twenty-six men from the regiment had been killed or wounded in the attacks of the day. Sergeant Thomas Stephens' messmate, Cenas Hartleroad, was shot in the head and died with the setting sun. Stephens implored his diary, "Who will fall next? Oh God, prepare us for death and eternity."[39]

Stephens' question was answered two days later when another abortive attack was made on the strengthened Confederate line. Late in the evening on June 17, Union officers turned to the old strategy to induce men to rush blindly into the face of death. A healthy whiskey ration was issued to each man in preparation for an attack to be made by the brigade before dawn the following day by nine regiments in column. When the charging Hoosiers, who were acting as skirmishers, reached the Rebel lines, they found only a few remnant soldiers. The main body of Confederate defenders had fallen back to a fortified line some three hundred yards to the rear. After flushing the Rebel pickets from the first line, Egan's brigade advanced on, and ran into, a wall of flame and fire. Driven back, the Hoosiers hunkered down and expended fifty rounds per man, blasting away at their not-so-distant enemy.[40]

The Indiana men found themselves seeking shelter in the stables of the lush horse farm of loyal Confederate O. P. Hare. A beautiful mansion graced the grounds, and the former farmhands from Indiana admired and envied the wealth of this fortunate landowner. However, Mr. Hare's fortunes changed permanently later that evening when the firing between the two forces grew so intense that the mansion and all of its stables were totally obliterated.[41]

Several men in the Twentieth were killed and wounded. Sergeant Stephens finally collapsed in exhaustion in the small hours of the following morning, his shoulder swollen and bruised from the repetitive loading and firing of the day. He did bed down with a full belly, his whiskey ration traded for extra grub.[42] The Federal attacks all along the Confederate perimeter on June 18 marked the end of any pretense of tactical maneuver. Plainly and simply, the struggle for Petersburg, and the Civil War itself, was now to be fought and settled in trenches and redoubts, a situation reminiscent of Cornwallis' predicament at Yorktown in the Revolutionary War.

When morning broke on June 19, Egan's brigade began the dangerous and laborious task of constructing a fort on the grounds of the former Hare estate. The men threw up huge piles of dirt and filled baskets woven from sticks—called gabions—with dirt. All the while, huge Confederate mortar shells, their fuses burning brightly, could be seen lofting their way into the Union lines. When the fort was finished, built under the noses of the men it was constructed to repel, it bristled with eight artillery guns. The men named it Fort Stedman.[43]

The Hoosiers were not allowed to enjoy the protection of Fort Stedman for long. On June 21 the Twentieth and Egan's brigade were ordered to a new position on the left of the Jerusalem Plank Road. The trek to their new position was scorchingly hot and made on roads which were so dusty that uniforms were gray and throats choked by the time the march ended.[44]

The following morning, Colonel Egan, in an act of generalship deemed "most foolhardy" by all involved, formed his brigade in line and, with flags flying and bands playing, marched them out to their new breastworks as if on parade. All of this was conducted under the watchful and shocked gaze of the Confederates manning their lines. Fortunately for the Indiana boys, who were placed out in front of the brigade, the Rebels appeared to be too surprised by the fanfare to fire a volley. By the time their surprise had faded, the Indiana men were safe in their new works.[45]

The new line of works consisted of a large fort on the Hoosiers' left flank, an ominous earthen structure, mounting eleven cannon, dubbed "Fort Hell" by the men defending it. The Ninety-ninth Pennsylvania was detailed to man the fort, and the Indiana men felt more secure knowing their trusted Pennsylvania comrades held the key position.[46]

Other elements of Birney's division were not as safe from the incursions of their enemy. The Second Brigade worked in advance of the main Union line, constructing defensive works near the Weldon Railroad. Lieutenant General A. P. Hill's corps moved beyond the flank of the Second Brigade and swooped down on them, killing many and capturing seventeen hundred prisoners. The attack also drove the survivors back to the Jerusalem Plank Road. Thus, Grant's attempt to have Birney turn the Confederate right flank ended in abject failure.[47]

The Twentieth Indiana, leading its brigade forward in an effort to regain the ground lost the previous day, came upon the battlefield to find it deserted, except for the bloated bodies of the dead, stripped of their clothing by scavenging Rebels desperate for their own resupply of pants, jackets, and shoes. After burying their dead, the brigade moved back to the protective shelter of Fort Hell.[48]

The Hoosiers were sandwiched between Fort Hell and a deep ravine on their right. In front of them, running between picket lines, lay another deep ravine, at the bottom of which bubbled a fine, cool spring. The weather had been insufferably hot for weeks on end, and potable water was in short supply. The spring's value increased exponentially daily as the heat also increased. Owing to the close proximity of the opposing picket lines and the stalemated inaction, men on both sides struck up conversations and agreed to make the spring a "no-fire" zone. Guns were prohibited in the area, and a lively trade sprang up as enemies traded boots, shoes, tobacco, and coffee. The system worked well for the common soldier but, as usual, rankled the senior officers. Major General Birney ordered Major Gilbreath to put an end to the fraternization.[49]

Fort Hell became the focal point of a visit by several curious dignitaries from England. The English were keenly interested in examining the American conflict and had observers attached to both armies. The English guests were intrigued by the huge guns at the fort and asked Colonel Thomas Biles if he might be able to arrange a demonstration of their firing. Biles, an Irishman and no Anglophile, was more than happy to comply. He knew any firing of his guns would stir the Confederates to respond in kind, giving the Englishmen more show than they had bargained for. Colonel Biles ordered one gun to fire; when more than fifty Rebel guns responded, Biles ran for cover, laughing all the way to his bombproof shelter as he watched his panicked guests.[50]

At this time the command structure was altered. Major General Birney was elevated to temporary command of the corps. Brigadier General Gershom Mott was promoted to command of Birney's division. Colonel Philippe De Trobriand was promoted to the command of the brigade encompassing the Twentieth Indiana. Major Erasmus Gilbreath was temporarily placed in command of the Seventeenth Maine, an unusual move in those politically sensitive times.[51]

For the next month, the survivors of the Twentieth Indiana moved into a tense, dangerous and exhaustive time of digging, building and waiting. Grant had undertaken a full-scaled siege operation which required the extensive construction of trenches edging ever closer to the Confederate lines. This work was done in almost unbearable heat and under continuous artillery and small arms fire. Men who stood too tall or failed to take safe paths during their movements soon fell to the keen-eyed Rebel sharpshooters. Construction parties were subject to shelling without warning. All the while, the working and the living were done under the pervasive stench of partially buried bodies rotting in the hot Virginia sun.

On July 9 Captain Charles Bell, Company D, the last of the regimental captains still commanding, was leading a work party at the site of a new fort under construction when a Confederate spherical case shell exploded in the air above the men. A small shell fragment ripped into Captain Bell's groin, severing an artery, and he died in a geyser of blood. As the blood spurted from his wound, though, Bell called to his friend John Luther. He gave Luther his personal effects and an address to which Luther could send them.[52]

In a solemn letter sent home to the *Plymouth Republican*, Lieutenant John Williams informed the readers of the death of Captain Bell and concluded his missive with these words:

> *There are now only thirteen of Company C, left. There were forty-four when they started on the present campaign. Some four or five have been captured; eight or ten died; the rest are sick and wounded. The thinned ranks of the Twentieth attests that it has been in the thickest of the fight.*[53]

On July 22 another sad day arrived in the saga of the Twentieth Indiana. Colonel William C. L. Taylor led eighty battle-hardened veterans home to Indiana upon the expiration of their three-year term of service. It was a sad parting, but one borne with pride in the many battles and hardships that each man in the Twentieth had shared. Major General Birney lauded the brave heroes in official orders and wished them well on their journey.[54]

There was little time for the remaining men of the Twentieth to become melancholy. A new plan of action had been hatched in an attempt to break the stalemate, and the services of Second Corps were in demand. The plan called for Pennsylvania coal miners to tunnel beneath the Confederate lines and explode a huge charge of gunpowder. Two divisions of black troops were then to rush through the opening in the Rebel line while other units followed up to exploit the breach. The role to be played by Second Corps was to advance on the extreme right of the Confederate line and prevent any support from that quarter moving to Rebel center. The task necessitated the movement of Second Corps from the extreme left flank of the Union lines to the extreme right flank.

At 4:30 P.M. on July 26 the Twentieth Indiana slipped away from its lines and began the long and winding march to the nether reaches of the Union right flank. It was not the first time that these men had made such a movement, and it came as no surprise to the fatigued boys. They marched wearily and steadily throughout the night and into the next morning before crossing the James River at 6:30 A.M., marching across on a pontoon bridge. The bridge had been covered with hay to muffle the sound of tramping feet and pounding hooves. Second Corps' three divisions immediately took their places in battle line, Mott's division on the right, Barlow's in the center and Gibbon's on the left.[55]

Fifteen minutes after the last regiment crossed the James River, the Twentieth Indiana, acting as skirmishers, moved forward, leading the Second

Corps on a rushing attack up a slope toward the Rebel line of works. By 7:00 A.M., the Confederates had been completely flushed out of their works and sent flying. Four twenty-pounder Parrott guns fell to the attackers as the powerful Second Corps pressed forward to Bailey's Creek, the Potteries, and New Market. The advancing Federal forces were supported in their advance by the huge mortars mounted on gunboats anchored in the James River, which pounded any organized Rebel resistance.[56]

The following day, Second Corps extended its line to the right toward Malvern Hill. However, at 8:00 P.M., Mott's division was ordered to return to their former position on the grounds of the former Hare Estate at Fort Stedman. It was from this location that the Twentieth Indiana would witness the great events of July 30.[57]

The explosion beneath the Confederate lines was to be detonated early on the morning of July 30. It had not been a closely guarded secret on the Federal side, and men rose at an early hour in anticipation of the long-awaited event. Major Gilbreath was up early to bathe and shave before the explosion. He was attended by his black servant, who was in the process of pouring water into Gilbreath's hands when a sniper's bullet came whistling by the major's head, crashing into the corner of his bombproof shelter. The startled camp servant, major, and wash basin all went tumbling in one big pile to the bottom of the shelter.[58] Ablutions were aborted, but not the day's plan.

At 5:00 A.M. the mine was finally exploded, raising earth in a massive tumult into the air. The tunnel immediately came crashing down into a deep crater, devoid of its former Confederate defenders who had been blown to bits. Into the crater ran the excited men of Ledlie's and Ferrero's divisions, their commanders safe in a bombproof shelter, drinking. The leaderless divisions paused too long to examine the effects of the explosion, and Major General William Mahone's Confederate division was given time to launch a vicious counterattack. Mahone's men slaughtered the black soldiers in the base of the crater and ended any hope for a successful end to the siege on this day.[59]

On August 13 the Twentieth Indiana moved north of the James River to make a demonstration on the Union right to draw Confederate artillery fire so the location of their batteries might be ascertained. As the Hoosiers moved from their base at Deep Bottom, Rebel skirmishers fell back before them. The men advanced further without coming under the expected artillery bombardment. Perplexed at how they could flush out the enemy batteries, Major Gilbreath hatched an idea which he thought might get a Confederate response. Noting the sensitivity of Rebel sharpshooters and artillery to the actions of Union signal stations, Gilbreath tied a red bandana on the end of a stick and waved it in the air. Immediately, the area around the Hoosiers was awash in artillery shells as the Confederate cannoneers wasted no time in trying to silence the supposed signal station.[60]

The Twentieth Indiana returned to its old camp at Fort Hell on August 18. Here they would remain for several weeks. Their duties amounted to maintaining the defense of this critical position on the Union left flank and keeping their heads down. There was time for the Hoosiers to debate the issues of the day, including the upcoming presidential election between Abraham Lincoln and George B. McClellan. Emotions ran high as the boys argued the relative merits of a president they respected and the general they had loved. Lieutenant Colonel Meikel sat in his dimly lit bombproof shelter and wrote to his friend, the publisher of the *Logansport Journal,* giving him his thoughts on the great domestic political conflict:

My Dear Friend:

Well, things here are little changed. We still hold the Weldon Road and shall continue to hold it as long as we want it, in spite of all the Rebels may do to drive us off. And while holding the road we are also employing our time well in other directions, which will be seen at the proper time, though not proper to be spoken of at present.

The pickets still continue to be on good terms and become more sociable every day. I never go along the line but I think what a strange picture it is; both parties embracing every opportunity to drop their rifles and be friends. As one of their men said to one of my men the other day: "If we private soldiers had the settling of this War, we would soon settle it. Jeff Davis need not tell Lincoln that the South will accept peace only upon a recognition of their independence, for he knows he lies." This was said in a group of Confederate soldiers who all endorsed what the man said. For the last few days the leading topic between the pickets has been the Chicago Convention. The Johnnies take an immense interest in the results of that convention. The Richmond and Petersburg papers have been full of it for the last three days, writing long articles about the nomination and at the same time trying to prove how little the nomination will affect the Southern cause, and that they don't care three straws who is nominated. But the very fact that they write so much about and that their pickets are so anxious in regard to it proves that it is the all absorbing topic among them.

Well, McClellan is their man, it seems. How have the mighty fallen! The man at one time the Commander-in-Chief of our armies in this same war steps upon the public stage in a new character. Instead of fighting against Rebels he is now going to fight for them. Instead of fighting for the Union he is going to fight the Administration, now straining every nerve to save it from destruction. Oh, the once idolized leader of this great army, how utterly has thou crushed the last spark of love and affection that remained in our hearts by this last act of thine.

We have today the news of the fall of Atlanta. This will be a great blow to the enemy. A Richmond paper a day or two ago admitted that the fall of either Richmond or Atlanta would be a very serious blow, and it has come sooner than they expected. Sherman's army is so large. If he once gets them started, I am sure he will keep them going. Grant's plans here depend somewhat on Sherman.

The weather the last few days has been cool and pleasant and the nights so cold as to make sleeping without blankets just the least uncomfortable, so the boys say who have tried it.[61]

Although the nights may have been uncomfortable, Lieutenant Colonel George Meikel was more uncomfortable with the position of his men. Fort Hell was within thirty yards of Confederate skirmishers, affording the enemy marksmen the opportunity to take pot shots at will at any unwitting or careless Federal who might show his head. Plenty of unthinking or unlucky Union troops lost their lives to these marksmen, and Meikel had suffered his share of the casualties. He proposed a bold attack to capture the Confederate skirmishers and their protected lair.[62]

On September 10 Lieutenant Colonel Meikel suggested to Brigadier General De Trobriand that he be allowed to lead an attack from Fort Hell on the Confederates in its front. De Trobriand ordered Meikel to take the Twentieth Indiana and the Second U.S. Sharpshooters on the dangerous mission. At 1:00 A.M. Meikel personally led his men from the ramparts of Fort Hell, down the steep ravine and into the teeth of the Confederate skirmishers. The attack was made with fixed bayonets and no shot was to be fired until the Union men were in among the Rebels. When the brief but brutal attack was over, the Union force controlled the former Confederate position, and had captured four officers and taken more than one hundred and eighty prisoners.[63] The cost to the attacking force was thirty-seven men killed and wounded.[64]

The Rebels exacted their revenge on Meikel shortly after daylight, when the lieutenant colonel advanced his men to an exposed position, inviting a Rebels counterstroke. Hundreds of Confederates moved outside the left flank of the advanced position and came rushing in on the Hoosiers and the sharpshooters. Meikel tried to rally his men to turn and meet the attackers, but he was struck and mortally wounded by a Rebel musket ball, thus going from live hero to just another dead martyr in the hell that was Petersburg.[65]

The fighting raged through the next week, with a constant whistling of bullets. The regiment fired more than thirteen thousand bullets during the week. The Hoosiers called the bullets "little kittens" and poured them freely into the Confederate lines while they were out on picket. The expenditure of the "little kittens" was not without cost—the Twentieth Indiana had at least one man killed each day during the week.[66]

Ulysses S. Grant determined in October of 1864 that the Army of the Potomac required serious reorganization in order to make it a more effective fighting force, in anticipation of the coming climactic campaigns of the Civil War. He recognized that virtually all existing regiments were woefully undermanned and mere shams of effective organizations. The Twentieth Indiana had declined to less than two hundred men, and the regiment was now used as a skirmishing force, a task that early in the war was assigned to a full company. Grant ordered the consolidation of understrength regiments into reconstituted fighting forces. The Nineteenth Indiana, into which the Seventh Indiana had been folded after the Wilderness Campaign, was to be combined with the Twentieth Indiana into a reorganized Twentieth Indiana Veteran Volunteer Infantry.[67]

Before the consolidation could occur, on October 7, 1864, Lieutenant William P. Thompson, Medal of Honor winner and rising Union star, was shot and killed by another of the ubiquitous Confederate sharpshooters. Having successfully eluded Rebel musketry and artillery fire for three years, Thompson was the victim of one Confederate sharpshooter. He became the last man to die in the Twentieth before consolidation.[68]

On October 18 the old Twentieth Indiana, or what was left of it, assembled for one final time to sign muster-out rolls. The few men who would help constitute the newly reorganized Twentieth were required to sign muster-in rolls. The remaining fortunate souls who found themselves as supernumeraries began the long trip back home again to Indiana. From its humble beginning on the windswept shores of Cape Hatteras, the Twentieth Indiana had proudly written its history in blood on the battlefields of the Peninsula, Second Manassas, Fredericksburg, Chancellorsville, Gettysburg, the Wilderness, Spotsylvania, North Anna, and in the trenches at Petersburg. The few survivors who safely returned to the Hoosier state bore laurels which had indeed been fairly won.

EPILOGUE

To the Green Fields Beyond

The history of the Twentieth Indiana Volunteer Infantry ceased on October 18, 1864, when the regiment joined with the Nineteenth Indiana to form the Reorganized Twentieth Indiana. However, a few of the original volunteers continued in the service of the Twentieth in its remaining battles and campaigns.

The regiment fought at the Boydton Plank Road and Hatcher's Run on October 27 and 28, 1864; and they participated in the raid on the Weldon Railroad on December 7 through 12, 1864. The following year the Indiana men fought at Dabney's Mills and Hatcher's Run, February 5 through 7; Watkins' House, March 25; Vaughn Road, March 29; Crow's House, March 31; Saylor's Creek, April 6; and at Farmville on April 7. Finally, they were present at Lee's surrender at Appomattox Court House on April 9.

In early June 1865, the remaining seventy-four men of the Twentieth Indiana returned to Indianapolis after participating in the Grand Review staged in Washington, D.C. A large reception was planned for the boys, but the homesick Hoosiers wanted only two things, to be paid and to go home. The festivities were canceled, and the war-weary farm boys returned home.[1]

The Civil War did not end for several of the officers of the regiment after they left its service. The four principal conspirators in the anti-Colonel Brown campaign in 1861 all moved on to greater achievements. Major George F. Dick eventually became colonel of the Eighty-sixth Indiana Volunteers and was rewarded at the war's conclusion with brevet promotion to brigadier general.[2] Adjutant Israel N. Stiles also rose to the rank of colonel in the Sixty-third Indiana Volunteers and was breveted to brigadier general.[3]

266

Lieutenant Colonel Charles D. Murray became colonel of the Eighty-ninth Indiana Volunteers and Assistant Surgeon Anson Hurd moved to the Fourteenth Indiana Volunteers, where he became surgeon.[4] Captain Thomas Logan left the Twentieth Indiana after suffering two wounds in combat; he eventually become colonel of the Twenty-eighth United States Colored Troops.[5] He was joined in that regiment by Will Emery Brown, who left the Twentieth as a private and was promoted to lieutenant.[6] Abraham Haines and John Guffin were promoted from assistant surgeons to surgeons in the One Hundred and Forty-sixth Indiana and the One Hundred and Fifty-sixth Indiana regiments, respectively.[7] Captain Oliver Bailey was advanced to lieutenant colonel of the Seventy-third Indiana Volunteers.[8]

It will be remembered that in 1861, Quartermaster Isaac Hart and several of his comrades were captured on board the steamer *Fanny* and subsequently escorted to Libby Prison. Years later, and in an odd turn of fate, it was quite a shock to the survivors of the Twentieth Indiana living in or near LaPorte County, Indiana, when they learned that the infamous Confederate prison had ended up in their own back yard: it had been disassembled and moved to Chicago, where it was reconstructed for the 1893 World's Fair. Afterwards, it was once again torn down and moved to LaPorte County, where it was reconstructed as a barn, thereby completing its strange journey.[9]

Many of the men from the Twentieth Indiana who were captured during the Wilderness and Spotsylvania campaigns were not as lucky as Quartermaster Hart, who had survived and returned from prison. Eleven men from the Twentieth died in the cramped, disease-ridden, and starvation-plagued Andersonville Prison during 1864. Simpson Brasier, Duane Ellis, William Galliger, Giles Goodwin, Noah Helvie, Jacob Hicks, John McBeth, Samuel Pangburn, James St. Clair, Charles Stone, and Eli Stuck all perished from malnutrition or disease between May and November of that year.[10]

The prison pen at Salisbury, North Carolina, was almost as deadly as the one at Andersonville. Henry Marshall, Eli Gregory, Newton Land, Harvey Artis, Christopher Marsh, John Foster, Alva Hordly, and John Horn starved to death there.[11]

Many of the officers and enlisted men of the Twentieth Indiana went on to distinguished postwar careers. Major Erasmus C. Gilbreath discovered that he had both an affinity and a knack for military command. He decided to continue his military career, becoming a lieutenant in the Eleventh Infantry Regiment, United States army. He fought throughout the Indian Wars and eventually rose to the rank of major.[12] Likewise, Captain Thomas Logan felt the boundaries of his world in Logansport too confining, and he also joined the United States army. He served in the Thirty-ninth, Fortieth, and Fifth United States Infantry Regiments. While serving in the Fifth Regiment, he participated in the hard fighting between the Cheyenne and the Kiowa. He retired with the rank of major and lived out his days as a building contractor in El Paso, Texas.[13]

Dennis Tuttle, the only Yale graduate in the Twentieth Indiana, returned to New Haven, Connecticut, after the war and spent his time growing cranberries and serving as the chairman of the city's board of education.[14] Reverend William C. Porter, chaplain of the regiment, moved to Naperville, Illinois, and then to Coldwater, Michigan, after the fighting ceased. He later became chairman of the board of missions at Fort Scott, Kansas. His biography notes that he missed only one appointment in his life and that was when he fell off a train.[15]

Captain Alfred F. Reed returned to White County to serve as an Indiana state senator and common pleas judge.[16] Private Phillip Dobbins, who enlisted in the regiment at the age of sixteen, lived to the ripe old age of ninety-one and achieved the distinction of surviving longer than any other Civil War veteran in Monon Township, White County.[17] Private John Boulson, the boy who was too young to enlist in the regiment, hung around the camps of the Twentieth Indiana until he reached age sixteen. He then served with the regiment through the remainder of the war and, at its conclusion, studied medicine and became a physician in Jackson, Michigan.[18]

Private William W. McColloch, an unfortunate soldier who lost his leg during combat, the amputation performed by Rebel surgeons, returned to Monticello, Indiana, to be elected county recorder. He held that post for eight years and then served as postmaster until his death.[19] Seymour T. Montgomery, the loquacious columnist for the *Howard Tribune* who so ably chronicled the history of the Twentieth Indiana in his letters home, traded in his knapsack and rifle for journalist's hat and became the co-publisher of the *Howard Tribune*.[20]

Colonel William Taylor returned to Lafayette, thoroughly exhausted from his service with the Twentieth. He practiced law successfully until 1874, when he moved to Bloomington, Indiana. He was active in Republican Party politics for all of his postwar years.[21]

Captain John C. Brown, who was given up for dead after his brave charge across the North Anna Bridge, showed similar bravery for the rest of his long life. The bullet that had entered under his eye and exited under his ear left a both a disfiguring wound and chronic, excruciating pain thereafter. He bore both with courage and became a leading citizen in Monticello, Indiana. He spent much of his time as an active, prominent member of the Masonic and Odd Fellows orders. He died in 1898 on his eightieth birthday.[22]

Some of the worst wounds of the Civil War scarred the soul while leaving the body whole. Colonel John Van Valkenburg returned in shame to his hometown of Peru after his abrupt and brutal dismissal from the service. He moved to Huntsville, Alabama, in 1866, unable or unwilling to tolerate the oppressive Republican politics of the North. He was active in Democratic politics in northern Alabama and in 1871 became the focus of a Congressional investigation looking into the activities of the Ku Klux Klan. While apparently not a Klan member himself, he found it impossible to be active in Democatic politics in the South without some contact with the group. He was called upon to give testimony to a visiting Congressional committee about several questionable persons.[23] Colonel Van Valkenburg received a measure of vindication on April 27, 1866—long after it was due—when the War Department revoked his dismissal and awarded him an honorable discharge.[24]

Brigadier General Hobart Ward, removed from his command for drunkenness, never faced either a day in court or received vindication. Although many prominent military men lauded Ward's heroism and valor, Secretary of War Stanton refused to reinstate him to command so that he could be court-martialed and have an opportunity to restore his good name. Almost recklessly brave throughout his Civil War career, Ward was tortured by the stain of his dismissal for years after the war. Finally, in 1903, Ward was struck and killed by a freight train when he stepped in front of it.[25] Suspicions of suicide abounded and hound his memory to this day, much as the accusations of his drunkenness had hounded him during his life.

The Twentieth Indiana Volunteers and the State of Indiana made every effort in postwar years to keep the memory of the gallant regiment alive. The veterans maintained an active regimental association, which held annual reunions well into the 1900s. Colonel Taylor served as the association's president for many years, and Will Emery Brown served as the secretary for most of its organizational life.[26] In 1913 the fiftieth anniversary of the Battle of Gettysburg was held on the battlefield there. Only three of the elderly veterans from the Twentieth could attend and join in patriotic brotherhood with their comrades from the North and South.[27]

In the late 1800s and early 1900s, the state of Indiana erected a huge Soldiers and Sailors Monument in the center of Indianapolis. When it came time to place a cornerstone, it was decided to enclose a flag from one of the great regiments which had served in the Civil War. The regimental flag selected was the bullet-ridden flag of the Twentieth Indiana Volunteers.[28] No higher tribute could have been paid to its brave defenders.

It is heartening to know that the valor and heroics of those brave soldiers who have defended our liberties and fought for freedom throughout our nation's history have not been forgotten. Lieutenant William Thompson was awarded the Medal of Honor for capturing the flag of the Fifty-fifth Virginia at the Battle of the Wilderness. He was killed on October 7, 1864, before he actually received the medal. Through the efforts of modern-day patriots living in Thompson's hometown, the Medal of Honor was presented posthumously at a ceremony held at Greenbush Cemetery in Lafayette, Indiana, on July 4, 1991.[29] The brave lieutenant received his just reward with full military honors.

On June 10, 1864, Private Charles W. Moores, a Union soldier serving in the Western theatre of the war, was killed in battle near Stevenson, Alabama. Before his death, he penned these words, which speak to this day:

> *When I was a boy, the books I read at different periods kindled a flame, an enthusiasm, an ambition to be a great general, orator, poet or scholar. The increasing cares and happiness of life dissipated or modified these ambitions till place and honor came to be esteemed wonderfully lower than desert and no man's success disturbed me. Now there is but one man I envy. I meet him on the street, his armless sleeve hanging by his side, or a wooden leg replacing the one he left at Vicksburg or Antietam. I esteem that mutilation a more honorable badge than all the stars, garters and crosses of the old world's nobility. It is the badge of Nature's nobleman. It tells, and will always tell that he loved his country and gave so much of his happiness to preserve her existence. I envy that man.*[30]

One may say the same of the veteran of Normandy Beach, Heartbreak Ridge, or Khe Sahn. It is well we remember them and their sacrifices in detail, the least tribute we can pay.

TWENTIETH (THREE YEARS) REGIMENT INDIANA VOLUNTEERS.

Company	NAMES AND RANK.	Residence.	Date of Commission.	Date of Muster.	REMARKS.
	Colonel.				
	WILLIAM L. BROWN	Logansport	July 23, 1861	July 22, 1861	Killed at battle Manassas Plains, August 24, 1862.
	JOHN VAN VALKENBURG	Peru	Aug. 30, 1862	Dec. 7, 1862	Dishonorably discharged, Feb. 10, 1863.
	JOHN WHEELER	Crown Point	Feb. 11, 1863	Mar. 16, 1863	Killed at Gettysburg, July 2, 1863.
	WILLIAM C. L. TAYLOR	Lafayette	July 3, 1863	July 3, 1863	Mustered out Oct. 5, 1864.
	Lieutenant Colonel.				
	CHARLES D. MURRAY	Kokomo	July 23, 1861	July 22, 1861	Resigned; re-entered service as Colonel 89th Regiment.
	BENJAMIN H. SMITH	Logansport	Dec. 28, 1861	Dec. 28, 1861	Resigned January 31, 1862.
	JOHN VAN VALKENBURG	Peru	Feb. 16, 1862	Feb. 16, 1862	Promoted Colonel.
	JAMES H. SHANNON	La Porte	Aug. 30, 1862	Aug. 30, 1862	Promoted Colonel.
			Feb. 11, 1863	April 9, 1863	Resigned June 5th, 1863; re-entered service as Colonel 138th Regiment.
	WILLIAM C. L. TAYLOR	Lafayette	June 6, 1863	June 6, 1863	Promoted Colonel.
	GEORGE W. MEIKEL	Indianapolis	July 3, 1863	July 3, 1863	Killed front Petersburgh, Va. September 10, 1864.
	Major.				
	BENJAMIN H. SMITH	Logansport	July 23, 1861	July 22, 1861	Promoted Lieutenant Colonel.
	JOHN VAN VALKENBURG	Peru	Dec. 28, 1861	Dec. 28, 1861	Promoted Lieutenant Colonel.
	JOHN WHEELER	Crown Point	Feb. 16, 1862	Feb. 16, 1862	Promoted Lieutenant Colonel.
	GEORGE F. DICK	Attica	Aug. 30, 1862	Oct. 13, 1862	Promoted Lieutenant Colonel 86th Regiment.
	JAMES H. SHANNON	La Porte	Oct. 21, 1862	Dec. 7, 1862	Promoted Lieutenant Colonel.
	WILLIAM C. L. TAYLOR	Lafayette	Fer. 12, 1863	April 9, 1863	Promoted Lieutenant Colonel.
	GEORGE W. MEIKEL	Indianapolis	June 6, 1863		Revoked; Com. Lieutenant Colonel.
	ERASMUS C. GALBREATH	Valparaiso	June 6, 1863	July 3, 1863	Mustered out on consolidation October 19. 1864.

Adjutant.

Name	Residence			Remarks
ISRAEL N. STILES	Lafayette	July 22, 1861	July 22, 1861	Promoted Major 63d Reg't, Aug. 28, 1862.
JOHN F. THOMAS	Peru	Aug. 30, 1862	Dec. 7, 1862	Promoted Captain Co. "A."
JOHN E. LUTHER	Indianapolis	May 27, 1863	June 10, 1863	Mustered out Oct. 13, 1864; term expired.

Quartermaster.

ISAAC W. HART	Attica	July 22, 1861	July 22, 1861	Promoted.
DENNIS TUTTLE	Hudson, Wis.,	Aug. 11, 1863	Aug. 20, 1863	Transferred to 20th Regiment, re-organization.

Chaplain.

WILLIAM C. PORTER	Plymouth	July 22, 1861	July 22, 1861	Transferred to 20th regiment, re-organization.

Surgeon.

ORPHEUS EVERTS	La Porte	July 23, 1861	July 22, 1861	Transferred to 20th regiment, re-organization.

Assistant Surgeon.

ANSON HURD	Oxford	July 23, 1861	July 22, 1861	Resigned Jan. 9, 1862; re-entered ser. as Surg. 14th Reg.
HENRY C. GROVER		Jan. 13, 1862	Dec. 7, 1862	Mustered out.
DANIEL H. PRUNK	Indianapolis	June 28, 1862	July 2, 1862	Dismissed March 13, 1863, to date Nov. 15, 1862.
THOMAS H. EVERTS	Valparaiso	Mar. 20, 1863		Declined.
JOHN GUFFIN	Huntington	April 25, 1863	May 13, 1863	Transferred to 20th regiment, re-organization.

Captain.

JOHN VAN VALKENBURG	Peru	July 22, 1861	July 22, 1861	Promoted Major.
WILLIAM B. REYBURN	Peru	Dec. 28, 1861	Dec. 28, 1861	Resigned Jan. 15, 1863.
JONAS HOOVER	Peru	Jan. 16, 1863	April 11, 1863	Resigned Aug. 20, 1863
JOHN F. THOMAS	Peru	May 21, 1863	June 6, 1863	Killed, May 12, 1864, in action.
JAMES DE LONG	Peru	Aug. 1, 1864		Not mustered; resigned as 1st Lieut., Sept. 3, 1864.

First Lieutenant.

WILLIAM B. REYBURN	Peru	July 22, 1861	July 22, 1861	Promoted 1st Lieutenant.
JONAS HOOVER	Peru	Dec. 28, 1861	Dec. 28, 1861	Promoted 1st Lieutenant.
CHARLES R. PEW	Peru	Jan. 16, 1863	Jan. 16, 1863	Discharged April 17, 1863, as 2d Lieut.
JAMES DE LONG	Peru	April 13, 1863	April 18, 1863	Promoted Captain; resigned Sept. 3, 1864.
WILLIAM TRIPPEER	Peru	Aug. 1, 1863	Sept. 4, 1864	Promoted Capt. Co. "H," 20th reg't, re-organization.

TWENTIETH (THREE YEARS) REGIMENT INDIANA VOLUNTEERS.—Continued.

Company.	NAMES AND RANK.	Residence.	Date of Commission.	Date of Muster.	REMARKS.
	Second Lieutenant.				
	JONAS HOOVER	Peru	July 22, 1861	July 22, 1861	Promoted 1st Lieutenant.
	JOHN F. THOMAS	Peru	Dec. 28, 1861	Dec. 28, 1861	Promoted Captain.
	CHARLES R. PEW	Peru	Aug. 30, 1862	Sept. 1, 1862	Promoted 1st Lieutenant.
	JAMES DELONG	Peru	Jan. 16, 1863	Jan. 16, 1863	Promoted 1st Lieutenant.
	WARREN J. HAWK	Peru	April 18, 1863	May 26, 1863	Honorably discharged July 7, 1864.
	WALLACE RICHARDSON	Peru	Aug. 1, 1864		Mustered out as Sergeant on consolidation, Oct. 29, '64.
B	*Captain.*				
	JOHN WHEELER	Crown Point	July 22, 1861	July 22, 1861	Promoted Major.
	CHARLES A. BELL	Corydon	Feb. 16, 1862	Feb. 16, 1862	Killed July 9, 1864, in front of Petersburg.
	First Lieutenant.				
	CHARLES A. BELL	Corydon	July 22, 1861	July 22, 1861	Promoted Captain.
	MICHAEL SHEEHAN	Crown Point	Feb. 16, 1862	Feb. 16, 1862	Resigned Sept. 6, 1864.
	CHRISTOPH FRAUNBERG		Aug. 1, 1864		Mustered out Oct. 10, '64, as 2d Lieutenant Co. "E."
	Second Lieutenant.				
	MICHAEL SHEEHAN	Crown Point	July 22, 1861	July 22, 1861	Promoted 1st Lieutenant.
	WILLIAM S. BABBIT		Feb. 16, 1862	March 1, 1862	Promoted Captain Co. "C."
	JOSEPH A. CLARK		Sept. 16, 1862	Sept. 16, 1862	Resigned Oct. 25, 1864.
	AMORY K. ALLEN	Loogootee	Aug. 1, 1864	Dec. 15, 1864	Transferred to Co. "B," 20th Regiment, re-organization.

Captain.

OLIVER H. P. BAILEY	Plymouth	July 22, 1861	July 22, 1861	Resigned Dec. 31, 1861.
WILLIAM BABBINGTON	Plymouth	Jan. 1, 1862	July 1, 1862	Resigned Sept. 15, 1862.
WILLIAM S. BABBITT	Plymouth	Sept. 16, 1863	Nov. 1, 1862	Honorably discharged July 22, 1863.
LaFAYETTE GORDON	Plymouth	July 23, 1863	Oct. 25, 1863	Died of wounds June 9, 1864.
JOHN W. WILLIAMS	Plymouth	Aug. 1, 1864	Sept. 2, 1864	Transferred to Co. "D," 20th Regiment, re-organization.

First Lieutenant.

WILLIAM C. CASSELMAN	Plymouth	July 22, 1861	July 22, 1861	Resigned.
WILLIAM BABBINGTON	Plymouth	Dec. 16, 1861	Dec. 16, 1861	Promoted Captain.
JOHN W. DAVIS	Plymouth	Jan. 1, 1862	Jan. 1, 1862	Resigned, 1863.
EZRA B. ROBBINS	Plymouth	May 21, 1863	May 21, 1863	Killed, 1863.
JOHN W. WILLIAMS	Plymouth	July 23, 1863	Oct. 25, 1863	Promoted Captain.
FRANK M. DAWSON	Plymouth	Aug. 1, 1864	Oct. 21, 1864	Transferred to Co. "D," 20th Regiment, re-organization.

Second Lieutenant.

JOSEPH LYNCH	Plymouth	July 22, 1861	July 22, 1861	Resigned.
WILLIAM BABBINGTON	Plymouth	Dec. 4, 1861	Dec. 4, 1861	Promoted 1st Lieutenant.
JOHN W. DAVIS	Plymouth	Dec. 16, 1861	Dec. 16, 1861	Promoted 1st Lieutenant.
EDWIN S. WARCUP	Plymouth	Jan. 1, 1862	Jan. 1, 1862	Resigned Nov. 11, 1862.
JOHN W. HEWITT	Plymouth	Nov. 12, 1862	Nov. 12, 1862	Resigned April 3, 1863.
EZRA B. ROBBINS	Plymouth	April 1, 1863	April 25, 1863	Promoted 1st Lieutenant.
LaFAYETTE GORDON	Plymouth	May 21, 1863	June 10, 1863	Promoted Captain.
JAMES R. BENNETT	Plymouth	Aug. 1, 1864		Mustered out as sup'y Sergt on consolidation, Oct. 29, '64.

Captain.

GEORGE F. DICK	Attica	July 22, 1861	July 22, 1861	Promoted Major.
CHARLES REESE	Attica	Aug. 30, 1862	Dec. 7, 1862	Honorably discharged Oct. 22, 1863.
WILLIAM D. VATCHETT	Indianapolis	Oct. 23, 1863	Dec. 4, 1863	Mustered out Oct. 6, 1864; term expired.

First Lieutenant.

CHARLES REESE	Attica	July 22, 1861	July 22, 1861	Promoted Captain.
WILLIAM D. VATCHETT	Indianapolis	Aug. 30, 1862	Sept. 1, 1862	Promoted Captain.
MARQUIS L. KINNEARD	Attica	Oct. 23, 1863	March 1, 1864	Resigned July 2, 1864.

A

TWENTIETH (THREE YEARS) REGIMENT INDIANA VOLUNTEERS—Continued.

Company.	NAMES AND RANK.	Residence.	Date of Commission.	Date of Muster.	REMARKS.
H	*Second Lieutenant.*				
	James A. Wilson	Attica	July 22, 1861	July 22, 1861	Resigned Oct. 14, 1861.
	William D. Vatchett	Indianapolis	Jan. 9, 1862	Jan. 9, 1862	Promoted 1st Lieutenant.
	Albert R. Norris	Attica	Aug. 30, 1862		Discharged Jan. 23, 1864.
	James P. Stallard	Attica	Jan. 24, 1864	Dec. 7, 1862	Mustered out as supernumerary Sergeant on consolidation, Oct. 29, 1864.
	Captain.				
	James H. Shanson	Laporte	July 22, 1861	July 22, 1861	Promoted Major.
	John E. Sweet	Laporte	Oct. 21, 1862	Nov. 21, 1862	Mustered out Oct. 8, 1864; term expired.
	Albert S. Andrews	Terre Haute	Aug. 1, 1864	Sept. 2, 1864	Transferred to Co. "B," 20th Regiment, re-organization.
	First Lieutenant.				
	John W. Andrew	Laporte	July 22, 1861	July 22, 1861	Killed in action before Richmond, June 30, 1862.
	John E. Sweet	Laporte	July 1, 1862	July 1, 1862	Promoted Captain.
	Hiram Crawford	Laporte	Oct. 21, 1862	Nov. 21, 1862	Mustered out Oct. 8, 1864; term expired.
	William H. Cole	Bloomfield	Aug. 1, 1864	Sept. 2, 1864	Transferred to Co. "B," 20th Regiment, re-organization.
	Second Lieutenant.				
	John E. Sweet	Laporte	July 22, 1861	July 22, 1861	Promoted 1st Lieutenant.
	Hiram Crawford	Laporte	July 1, 1862	July 1, 1862	Promoted 1st Lieutenant.
	William R. Muir	Laporte	Oct. 21, 1862	Nov. 21, 1862	Resigned Jan. 17, 1863.
	Christoph Fraunberg	Laporte	Jan. 18, 1863	Jan. 18, 1863	Promoted 1st Lieut. Co. "B;" mustered out Oct. 10, '64.
	William Brown	Laporte	Aug. 1, 1864		Mustered out as sup'y Ser't on consolidation, Oct. 29, 64.

F

Captain.

Name	Residence	Enrolled	Mustered	Remarks
John Kistler	Danville	July 22, 1861	July 22, 1861	Discharged Nov. 14, 1862.
Thomas H. Logan	Logansport	Nov. 15, 1862	Nov. 16, 1862	Promoted Sept. 19, 1864.

First Lieutenant.

Name	Residence	Enrolled	Mustered	Remarks
Thomas H. Logan	Logansport	July 22, 1861	July 22, 1861	Promoted Captain.
Ed. C. Sutherland	Logansport	Nov. 15, 1862	Nov. 15, 1862	Died May 26, 1864.
William A. Anderson	Indianapolis	Aug. 1, 1864	Sept. 2, 1864	Promoted Adjutant 20th Regiment, re-organization.

Second Lieutenant.

Name	Residence	Enrolled	Mustered	Remarks
Ed. C. Sutherland	Logansport	July 22, 1861	July 22, 1861	Promoted 1st Lieutenant.
Harvey H. Miller	Logansport	Nov. 15, 1862	Nov. 15, 1862	Discharged July 8, 1864.
Jonathian C. Kirk	Wilmington	Aug. 1, 1864		Promoted 1st Lt. Co. "F," 20th Reg't, re-organization.

G

Captain.

Name	Residence	Enrolled	Mustered	Remarks
Nathaniel Herron	Delphi	July 22, 1861	July 22, 1861	Promoted.
William C. L. Taylor	Lafayette	Nov. 20, 1861	Nov. 20, 1861	Promoted Major.
Henry Quigley	Lafayette	Feb. 12, 1863	May 13, 1863	Killed May 12, 1864.
Robert H. Taylor	Cordova, Ills.	Aug. 1, 1864	Sept. 2, 1864	Transferred to Co. "F," 20th Regiment, re-organization.

First Lieutenant.

Name	Residence	Enrolled	Mustered	Remarks
William C. L. Taylor	Lafayette	July 22, 1861	July 22, 1861	Promoted Captain.
Henry Quigley	Lafayette	Nov. 20, 1861	Nov. 20, 1861	Promoted Captain.
Robert H. Taylor	Cordova, Ills.	Feb. 12, 1863	May 13, 1863	Promoted Captain.
William P. Thompson	Lafayette	Aug. 1, 1864	Sept. 2, 1864	Mustered out; term expired.

Second Lieutenant.

Name	Residence	Enrolled	Mustered	Remarks
William B. Brittingham	Lafayette	July 22, 1861	July 22, 1861	Resigned.
Stephen E. Bartholomew	Lafayette	Jan. 15, 1862	Jan. 15, 1862	Resigned Oct. 31, 1862.
Robert H. Taylor	Cordova, Ills.	Nov. 1, 1862	Nov. 1, 1862	Promoted 1st Lieutenant.
Isaac V. C. Ensey	Lafayette	Feb. 12, 1863	May 13, 1863	Cashiered July 16, 1864.
William Zimmerman	Lafayette	Aug. 1, 1861		Mustered out as sup'y Serg't on consolidation, Oct. 19, '64.

TWENTIETH (THREE YEARS) REGIMENT INDIANA VOLUNTEERS.

Company.	NAMES AND RANK.	Residence.	Date of Commission.	Date of Muster.	REMARKS.
H	*Captain.*				
	GEORGE W. GEISENDORFF	Indianapolis	July 22, 1861	July 22, 1861	Resigned.
	GEORGE W. MEIKEL	Indianapolis	Dec. 4, 1861	Dec. 4, 1861	Promoted Lieut. Col.
	CHARLES LINER	Indianapolis	June 6, 1863	Aug. 26, 1863	Mustered out Oct. 10, 1864; term expired.
	First Lieutenant.				
	GEORGE W. MEIKEL	Indianapolis	July 22, 1861	July 22, 1861	Promoted Captain.
	WILLIAM O. SHERWOOD	Indianapolis	Dec. 4, 1861	Dec. 4, 1861	Resigned April 3, 1863.
	CHARLES LINER	Indianapolis	April 4, 1863	April 24, 1863	Promoted Captain.
	HARRY GEISENDORFF	Indianapolis	June 6, 1863	Sept. 3, 1863	Mustered out Oct. 10, 1864; term expired.
	Second Lieutenant.				
	WILLIAM O. SHERWOOD	Indianapolis	July 22, 1861	July 22, 1861	Promoted 1st Lieutenant.
	FRED. W. GEISENDORFF	Indianapolis	Dec. 4, 1861	Dec. 4, 1861	Resigned July 29, 1862.
	CHARLES LINER	Indianapolis	July 30, 1862	July 30, 1862	Promoted 1st Lieutenant.
	HARRY GEISENDORFF	Indianapolis	April 4, 1863	April 25, 1863	Promoted 1st Lieutenant.
	WILLIAM DICKASON	Indianapolis	Aug. 1, 1864		Mustered out as sup'y Serg't on consolidation, Oct. 29, '64.
I	*Captain.*				
	JAMES M. LYTLE	Valparaiso	July 22, 1861	July 22, 1861	Died Aug. 19, 1862, of wounds.
	ERASMUS C. GALBREATH	Valparaiso	Aug. 20, 1862	Dec. 7, 1862	Promoted Major.
	LORENZO D. COREY	Valparaiso	June 6, 1863	Nov. 1, 1863	Mustered out; term expired.

First Lieutenant.

Name	Residence			Remarks
ERASMUS C. GALBREATH	Valparaiso	July 22, 1861	July 22, 1861	Promoted Captain.
WILLIAM T. CARR	Valparaiso	Aug. 20, 1862	Aug. 20, 1862	Dismissed March 20, 1863.
LORENZO D. COREY	Valparaiso	Mar. 21, 1863	April 24, 1863	Promoted Captain.
WILLIAM W. STEVENS	Valparaiso	June 6, 1863	Nov. 1, 1863	Mustered out Oct. 10, 1864; term expired.

Second Lieutenant.

Name	Residence			Remarks
WILLIAM T. CARR	Valparaiso	July 22, 1861	July 22, 1861	Promoted 1st Lieutenant.
LORENZO D. COREY	Valparaiso	Aug. 20, 1862	Dec. 7, 1862	Promoted 1st Lieutenant.
WILLIAM W. STEVENS	Valparaiso	Mar. 21, 1863	April 25, 1863	Promoted 1st Lieutenant.
JOHN W. VANDERBANK	Kokomo	June 6, 1863	July 3, 1864	Promoted Capt. Co. "K," 20th reg't, re-organization.

Captain.

Name	Residence			Remarks
ALFRED REED	Monticello	July 22, 1861	July 22, 1861	Resigned Dec. 19, '62; re-ent. ser. as Lt. Col. 12th Cav.
JOHN C. BROWN	Monticello	Dec. 20, 1862	Dec. 20, 1862	Honorably discharged, Oct. 25, 1864.

First Lieutenant.

Name	Residence			Remarks
JOHN T. RICHARDSON	Monticello	July 22, 1861	July 22, 1861	Resigned July 16, 1862.
JOHN C. BROWN	Monticello	July 18, 1862	Dec. 7, 1862	Promoted Captain.
JOHN PRICE	Monticello	Dec. 20, 1862	Dec. 20, 1862	Mustered out Oct. 10, 1864; term expired.

Second Lieutenant.

Name	Residence			Remarks
DANIEL D. DALE	Monticello	July 22, 1861	July 22, 1861	Resigned July 17, 1862.
JONATHAN B. HARBOLT	Monticello	July 18, 1862		
JOHN PRICE	Monticello	Aug. 30, 1862	Dec. 7, 1862	Promoted 1st Lieutenant.
JOHN C. BARTHOLOMEW	Monticello	Dec. 20, 1862	Dec. 20, 1862	Died May 28, 1864, of wounds.
SAMUEL E. BALL	Monticello	Aug. 1, 1864		Promoted 1st Lt. Co. "K," 20th reg't, re-organization

TWENTIETH REGIMENT—THREE YEAR'S SERVICE.

REGIMENTAL NON-COMMISSIONED STAFF AND BAND.

Name and Rank.	Residence.	Date of Muster. 1861.	Remarks.
Sergeant Major			
Comly, Charles H.........	....	July 22........	
Quartermaster Sergeant.			
Heath, William............	....	July 22........	
Commissary Sergeant.			
Evans, John..................	....	July 22........	
Hospital Steward.			
Fawcett, Joseph...........	....	July 22........	
Principal Musicians.			
Pierson, Joseph............	....	Aug. 28......	
Salisbury, Alfred B.......	....	Aug. 28......	
Band.			
Benney, Octavius W.....	....	Aug. 28......	
Bumstead, John A........	....	Aug. 28......	
Dennison, George S.......	....	Aug. 28......	
Manahan, Calvin..........	....	Aug. 28......	
Salisbury, Francis M.....	....	Aug. 28......	
Whitehead, Samuel F...	....	Aug. 28......	
Foster, Almon..............	....	Aug. 28......	
Whitehead, John...........	....	Aug. 28......	
Pierson, George H........	....	Aug. 28......	
Wells, Theodore H........	....	Aug. 28......	
Montgomery, John H....	....	Aug. 28......	
Krimbill, William........	....	Aug. 28......	
Campbell, Henry H......	....	Aug. 28......	
Christy, William..........	....	Aug. 28......	
Fessenden, Charles H....	....	Aug. 28......	
Ireland, Amos P...........	....	Aug. 28......	
Jewell, William............	....	Aug. 28......	
Lans, Henry.................	....	Aug. 28......	
Loomis, Seth................	....	Aug. 28......	
Main, John H...............	....	Aug. 28......	
Richards, Clark R.........	....	Aug. 28......	
Salisbury, Francis L......	....	Aug. 28......	
Stoddard, Henry...........	....	Aug. 28......	

ENLISTED MEN OF COMPANY "A."

Name and Rank.	Residence.	Date of Muster. 1861.	Remarks.
First Sergeant.			
Thomas, John F	Peru.	July 22........	Promoted 2d Lieutenant.
Sergeants.			
Bright, John T.............	Miami co..........	July 22........	
Strive, George A...........	Miami co..........	July 22........	
Deibert, Henry W.........	Miami co..........	July 22........	
Pew, Charles R.............	Peru.	July 22........	Promoted 2d Lieutenant.
Corporals.			
Deibert, Charles F	Miami co..........	July 22........	Mustered out July 29, '64.
Weisner, Hezekiah........	Miami co..........	July 22........	" " "
Trippeer, William.........	Peru.	July 22........	Veteran; promoted 1st Lieutenant.
Dangerfield, William H	Miami co..........	July 22........	
Reeder, William C. H...	Miami co..........	July 22........	Mustered out July 29, '64.
Hawk, Warren J...........	Peru.	July 22........	Promoted 2d Lieutenant.

TWENTIETH REGIMENT INFANTRY.

NAME AND RANK.	Residence.	Date of Muster. 1861.	REMARKS.
Smith, Nichoias I.........	Miami co.........	July 22......	[organized.
Dunlap, John T.............	Miami co.........	July 22......	Vetn; w'ded, Wild'ns; transf'd, 20th Regt. re-
Musicians.			
Mabie, John P.............	Miami co.........	July 22,.....	
Miller, William B.........	Miami co.........	July 22......	Mustered out July 29, '64.
Wagoner.			
Thorn, Hopthni B........	Miami co.........	July 22......	
Privates.			
Ash, Amos D................	Miami co.........	July 22......	Killed at Gettysburg.
Barbour, Marion F......	Miami co.........	July 22	Mustered out July 29, '64.
Blood, Nathan W.........	Miami co.........	July 22......	Vet'n; transf'd 20th Regt. re-organized.
Blackburn, Nathaniel...	Miami co.........	July 22......	Vet'd; w'ded June 6, '64, transf'd 20th Regt.
Bennell, Nerthew S......	Miami co.........	July 22......	[re-organized.
Busey, Samuel G.........	Miami co.........	July 22......	Vet'n; transf'd to 20th Regt. re-organized.
Cockley, George...........	Miami co.........	July 22......	
Conner, Newton...........	Miami co.........	July 22......	Vet'n; transf'd to 20th Regt. re-organized.
Courter, William J.......	Miami co.........	July 22......	Vet'n; capt'd Spottsylvania; must'd out June
Dauily, Jonathan W.....	Miami co.........	July 22......	[27, '65
Darr, George W...........	Miami co.........	July 22......	
DeLong, James...........	Miami co.........	July 22......	Promoted 2d Lieutenant.
Edmond, William J......	Miami co.........	July 22......	Mustered out July 29, '64.
Edson, Ira B................	Miami co.........	July 22......	" " "
Fairman, John B.........	Miami co.........	July 22......	" " "
Fisher, Wilson.............	Miami co.........	July 22......	
Flook, Isaac...............	Miami co.........	July 22......	
Fulwiler, Louis B.........	Miami co.........	July 22......	
Goff, Delford C...........	Miami co.........	July 22......	
Goodwin, John H.........	Miami co.........	July 22......	Mustered out July 29, '64.
Hann, John B.............	Miami co.........	July 22......	
Harvey, Elias.............	Miami co.........	July 22......	Vet'n; transf'd to 20th Regt. re-organized.
Hoffman, William T.....	Miami co.........	July 22......	
Holman, Solomon.........	Miami co.........	July 22......	
Irvin, Henry..............	Miami co.........	July 22......	Died at City Point, Va.
Johnson, Dickoson......	Miami co.........	July 22......	
Kelley, Morris.............	Miami co.........	July 22......	Mustered out July 29, '64.
King, Lucian A...........	Miami co.........	July 22......	Mustered out Aug. 1, '64.
LaRue, Philip H..........	Miami co.........	July 22......	
Lee, Thomas...............	Miami co.........	July 22......	Vet'n; transf'd to 20th Regt. re-organized·
Muryrsip, Isaac N........	Miami co.........	July 22......	
Marsh, Simeon S..........	Miami co.........	July 22......	Mustered out July 29, '64.
McGrew, Henry I.........	Miami co.........	July 22......	
McMellen, Joseph.........	Miami co.........	July 22......	Vet'n; transf'd to 20th Regt. re-organized.
McCulloch, William M...	Miami co.........	July 22......	Mustered out July 29, '64.
Morris, William A.......	Miami co.........	July 22......	Vet'n; transf'd to 20th Regt. re-organized.
Montgomery, Geo. S.....	Miami co.........	July 22......	Vet; w'ded, Spotts'ia; tr'fd 20th Regt. re-org.
Mowbray, William G...	Miami co.........	July 22......	[one year in Navy; must'd out May 8,'65.
Murray, Jeremiah........	Miami co.........	July 22......	Deserted; N. Y. City, Oct. '63; enlisted, served
Murphy, George V.......	Miami co.........	July 22......	Vet'n; w'ded Wild'ns, tr'fd 20th Regt. re-org.
Newbern, William........	Miami co.........	July 22......	Mustered out July 29, '64.
Owens, William B.........	Miami co.........	July 22......	
Passage, William B......	Miami co.........	July 22......	
Patterson, William H....	Miami co.........	July 22......	Mustered out July 29, '64.
Parrish. Meredith G.....	Miami co.........	July 22......	Vet; w'ded Petersburg; tr'fd 20th Regt. re-org.
Pelky, Robert.............	Miami co.........	July 22......	Mustered out July 29, '64.
Peir, John W..............	Miami co.........	July 22......	
Pierson, Eli H............	Miami co.........	July 22......	Vet'n ; transf'd to 20th Regt. re-organized.
Plotner, Conrad...........	Miami co.........	July 22......	
Proctor, William..........	Miami co.........	July 22......	Vet'n; transf'd to 20th Regt. re-organized.
Preble, John W...........	Miami co.........	July 22......	" " " "
Richardson, Reuben.....	Miami co.........	July 22......	" " " "
Richardson, Wallace.....	Miami co.........	July 22......	Vet; promoted 2d Lieut.
Rogers, Rickard R........	Miami co.........	July 22......	
Roe, Elijah	Miami co.........	July 22......	Mustered out July 29. '64.
Rock, Theodore, F.......	Miami co.........	July 22......	Vet; w'ded Spotts'ia; tr'fd 20th Regt. re-org.
Robinson, George W.....	Miami co.........	July 22......	Died at Alexandria, Mar. 25, '64.
Sager, Levi A.............	Miami co.........	July 22......	Mustered out July 29, '64.
Sager, John M.............	Miami co.........	July 22......	Killed at Gettysburg.
Scholl, Charles A.........	Miami co.........	July 22......	Vet; w'ded Petersburg, tr'fd 20th Regt. re-org.
Schaeffer, Henry F.......	Miami co.........	July 22......	Vet'n; transf'd to 20th Regt. re-organized.
Sharp, Jacob...............	Miami co.........	July 22......	
Shue, Jacob I.............	Miami co.........	July 22......	Vet; w'ded Wild'ns, tr'fd 20th Regt. re-org·
Sigarfoos, Andrew........	Miami co.........	July 22......	
Smallwood, James H....	Miami co.........	July 22......	Vet; w'ded May 19,'64; tr'fd 20th Regt. re-org
Smith, Charles A.........	Miami co.........	July 22......	
Smith, Charles W.........	Miami co.........	July 22......	Killed at Gettysburg.
Southard, Henry A......	Miami co.........	July 22......	
Stanford Sylvester........	Miami co.........	July 22......	
Staley, William H........	Miami co.........	July 22......	Vet; w'ded Spotts'ia, tr'fd 20th Regt. re-org.

NAME AND RANK.	Residence.	Date of Muster, 1861.	REMARKS.
Stuber, Jacob...............	Miami co.........	July 22......	
Swaggart, Samuel O......	Miami co..........	July 22......	Mustered out July 29, '64.
Tinkham, Benjamin F...	Miami co.........	July 22......	
Tice, John M...............	Miami co.........	July 22......	Killed at Gettysburg. [burg.
Tumblin, Reuben R......	Miami co.........	July 22......	Dischg'd July 11, '64; wounds rec'd at Gettys-
Tumblin, Henry S........	Miami co.........	July 22......	Veteran; wounded Wilderness; transferred to
Tucker, John M............	Miami co.........	July 22......	[20th Regiment, re-organized.
Weist, Edwin B............	Miami co.........	July 22......	Veteran; transf'd 20th Reg't, re-organized.
Wentling, Emanuel......	Miami co.........	July 22......	
Williams, Jesse B..........	Miami co.........	July 22......	
Wisel, Jacob...............	Miami co.........	July 22......	Veteran; transf'd 20th Reg't, re-organized.
Wright, Daniel G..........	Miami co.........	July 22......	
Recruits.			
Brownlee, David P......			
Conner, Napoleon B......	Miami co..........	Sept. 21, '62	Transferred to 20th Regiment, re-organized.
Counts, William............	Miami co.........	Mar. 20, '64	Transferred to 20th Regiment, re-organized.
Cook, Benjamin F........	Miami co.........	Sept. 19, '64	Died, Washington, July 4, '64. [organized.
Flook, John W............	Miami co.........	Mar. 20, '64	Wounded, Petersburg; transf'd 20th Regt., re-
Fenton, Richard............	Miami co.........	Mar. 20, '64	Wou'd, Wilderness; trans. 20th Regt., re-org.
Hurley, Levin...............	Tippecanoe co..	Sept. 21, '62	Transferred to 20th Regt., re-organized.
Herrell, Noah...............	Miami co.........	Mar. 28, '64	Transferred to 20th Regt., re-organized.
McMillen, David............	Miami co.........	Mar. 28, '64	Wou'd, Spottsylvania; trans. 20th Regt.re-org.
Martin, James J............	Miami co.........	Mar. 28, '64	Transferred to 20th Regt., reorganized.
McDonald, John............	Miami co.........	Mar. 28, '64	" " " "
McMillen, Peter............	Miami co.........	Sept. 19, '62	
Olinger, James M........	Miami co.........	Sept. 19, '62	Transferred to 20th Regt., re-organized.
O'Brien, Martin............	Miami co.........	Sept. 13, '62	" " " "
Richardson, John.........	Miami co.........		Veteran; transf'd to 20th Regt., reorganized.
Stowe, George A...........			Killed at Chickhominy, —, '62.

ENLISTED MEN OF COMPANY "B."

NAME AND RANK.	Residence.	Date of Muster. 1861.	REMARKS.
First Sergeant.			
Babbitt, William S........	Valparaiso	July 22........	Promoted 2d Lieutenant.
Sergeants.			
Clark, Joseph A.............	Lake co............	July 22........	Promoted 2d Lieutenant.
Zouvers, Charles............	Lake co............	July 22........	Discharged Nov. 22, '61; disability.
Curtice, George G........	Lake co............	July 22........	Vet.; wou'd Wilderness,trans.20th Regt re-org.
Sprague, Edwin R........	Lake co............	July 22........	Died at Harrison's Landing, Aug. 10, '62.
Corporals.			
Jones, Jarias...............	Lake co............	July 22........	Vet.; wd'd Wilderness; trans. 20th Regt,re-org.
Root, Charles...............	Lake co............	July 22........	Discharged Feb. 25, '63.
Dutton, Oscar...............	Lake co............	July 22........	Wou'd, Spottsylvania; must'd out July 29, '64.
Dwyer, John M..	Lake co............	July 22........	Wou'd, Wilderness; must'd out July 29, '64.
Pangburn, Samuel..........	Lake co............	July 22........	Captured, Spottsylvania; died, Andersonville
Sherats, Frank P............	Lake co............	July 22........	Discharged April 27, '63. [Nov. 6, '64.
Luther, Amos O............	Lake co............	July 22........	App'd principal musician; discharged.
Foster, George D...........	Lake co............	July 22........	Discharged July 22,'63; disability.
Musicians.			
Luther, Albert W........	Lake co............	July 22........	App'd prin'l musician; must'd out July 29,'64.
Frazier, Benjamin F.....	Lake co............	July 22........	Deserted, Fort Schuyler, N. Y., Sept. 2, '63.
Wagoner.			
Williams, Ralph P........	Lake co............	July 22........	Mustered out July 29, '64.
Privates.			
Abrams, George............	Lake co............	July 22........	Wou'd, North Anna; disch'd Aug. 20, '64.
Benjamin, David............	Lake co............	July 22........	Veteran; transf'd 20th Reg't, reorganized.
Burch, Timothy C........	Lake co............	July 22........	Mustered out July 29, '64.
Bloomfield, Lott............	Lake co............	July 22........	Disch'd for promotion Aug. '62.
Carl, Goliah...............	Lake co............	July 22........	Discharged Nov. 15, '61; disability.
Castle, George L............	Lake co............	July 22........	Mustered out July 29, '64, as Corporal.
Chapman, Asher V......	Lake co............	July 22........	Discharged Sept. 18, '63; disability.
Clark, Milo W............	Lake co............	July 22........	Discharged Oct. 6, '62; disability.
Clark, William............	Lake co............	July 22........	Wou'd, Petersburg; must'd out July 29, '64.
Colby, Ezekiel............	Lake co............	July 22........	Veteran; transf'd 20th Reg't, re-organized.
Corvine, James............	Lake co............	July 22........	Captured, Wilderness, May 6, '64.
Darst, Abraham F........	Lake co............	July 22........	Vet.; w'd, Wilderness; trans. 20th Regt, re-org.
Davis, Frederick M.......	Lake co............	July 22........	Dest'd, Fredericksburg on eve battle,Dec.11'62.
Dean, Charles............	Lake co............	July 22........	Vet.; transf'd 20th Reg't' reorganized.

TWENTIETH REGIMENT INFANTRY

Name and Rank.	Residence.	Date of Muster. 1861.	Remarks.
Degroff, Charles	Lake co	July 22	Vet.; wo'd, Wilderness; transf. 20th Reg't, re-
Deyo, James A	Lake co	July 22	Veteran; died, Aug. 9, '64; wounds. [or'g'd.
Dittloff, John	Lake co	July 22	Transferred Co. "G," March 1, '62.
Dodd, Horace W	Lake co	July 22	Mustered out July 29, '64.
Doehlier, George	Lake co	July 22	Discharged, Feb. 18, '63; disability.
Drake, Jeremiah W	Lake co	July 22	Died of wounds, received Petersburg.
Dolin, Hiram	Lake co	July 22	Discharged, Dec. 9. '61; disability.
Edgerton, George W	Lake co	July 22	Killed, Gettysburg, July 2, '63.
Elison, John	Lake co	July 22	Veteran; transf. 20th Regiment, re-organized.
Fairman, Charles A	Lake co	July 22	Discharged, March 16, '62; disability.
Foster, George W	Lake co	July 22	Veteran; transf. 20th Reg't, re-organized.
Frazier, Alexander	Lake co	July 22	Vet; w'd Wild'n's; transf. 20th R'g't, re-org.
Fry, Charles	Lake co	July 22	Missing in action, Charles City Cross Roads,
Fuller, Albert L	Lake co	July 22	Disch'gd, Jan. 17,'62; disability. [Je. 30,'62.
Gilger, Christopher R	Lake co	July 22	Discharged, Oct. 8, '62; disability.
Glazier, Joel	Lake co	July 22	Discharged, disability.
Griesell, John D	Lake co	July 22	Died, David Isl'd, N. Y., Aug. 16,'62; w'ds rec.
Hafey, Michael	Lake co	July 22	Vet'n; died, Petersburg, Va. [Chickahominy.
Haley, John	Lake co	July 22	Vet'n; transf. 20th Regiment, re-organized.
Hill, William	Lake co	July 22	Must'd out July 29, '64, as musician.
Hoffman, Jacob	Lake co	July 22	Veteran; transf. 20th Regiment, re-org.
Hazworth, Christian	Lake co	July 22	Died, Wash'n, May 26,'63; w'ds rec. Man. Pl'n.
Jaques, Thomas	Lake co	July 22	Vet; w'd Je. 16,'64; transf. 20th R'g't, reorg.
Jewett, Oris W	Lake co	July 22	Veteran; transf. 20th Regiment, re-organized.
Johnson, William M	Lake co	July 22	Veteran; killed, Petersburg, June 18, '64.
Jones, Christopher	Lake co	July 22	W'd Wilderness; mustered out July 29, '64.
Kale, Albert	Lake co	July 22	Died, Camp Hampton, Va., Dec. 17, '61.
Kronkright, Eugene	Lake co	July 22	Mustered out July 29, '64.
Luther, John E	Lake co	July 22	Discharged for promotion, June 9, '63.
Meshum, Thomas G	Lake co	July 22	Veteran; transf. 20th Regiment, re-org.
Metcalf, George W	Lake co	July 22	Discharged, Aug. 8, '62; disability.
Mulliken, George W	Lake co	July 22	Mustered out July 29, '64, as Sergeant.
Mushrush, Thomas	Lake co	July 22	Mustered out July 29, '64.
Mutchler, William	Lake co	July 22	Died, Camp Smith, Va., April 25, '62.
Mutchler, Peter	Lake co	July 22	Died, Washington, July 15, '62; wounds rec'd
Myers, John H	Lake co	July 22	Mustered out July 29, '64. [Chickahominy.
Norton, Oliver	Lake co	July 22	Mustered out July 29, '64.
Patter, Constantine C	Lake co	July 22	Discharged, Dec. 22, '62; disability.
Patter, Casimer	Lake co	July 22	Captured, Gettysburg, July 2, '63.
Phillips, Peter	Lake co	July 22	Mustered out July 29, '64.
Pinckerton, David	Lake co	July 22	Died of wounds received Wilderness.
Reed, Elias	Lake co	July 22	Veteran; transf. 20th Regiment, re-org.
Richmond, David	Lake co	July 24	Mustered out July 29, '64.
Rollings, George	Lake co	July 22	W'd, Fredericksburg; must'd out July 29, '64.
Rollings, Samuel	Lake co	July 22	Discharged, Aug. 22, '62; disability.
Rollings, Charles	Lake co	July 22	Veteran; transf. 20th Regiment, re-org.
Root, William	Lake co	July 22	Mustered out July 29, '64, as musician.
Runnebaugh, John	Lake co	July 22	Transf. Co. "G," 20th Regiment, March 1,'62.
Sake, Conrad	Lake co	July 22	Veteran; transf. 20th Regiment, re-org.
Sanders, John	Lake co	July 22	Discharged, Dec. 25, '62.
Schritchfield, Jacks'n H	Lake co	July 22	W'd, Spottsylvania; must'd out July 29, '64.
Shamhorst, Henry C	Lake co	July 22	Discharged, Dec. 29, '64; disability.
Sheehan, John	Lake co	July 22	W'd, Petersburg; must'd out July 29, '64.
Sheehan, Maurice	Lake co	July 22	Discharged, Oct. 27, '62; disability.
Sisson, Harvey B	Lake co	July 22	Died, Brandy Station, Va., Feb. 21, '64.
Snyder, Charles	Lake co	July 22	W'd Wildn's; sent Hosp'l; not since heard from.
Stewart, Chas. [Jer. W.]	Lake co	July 22	Deserted, Fredericksburg, Dec. 11, '62.
Tarr, John F	Lake co	July 22	Died, Washington, Nov. 24, '62.
Thompson, Amos P	Lake co	July 22	Vet'n; w'd Wild'n's; transf. 20th R'gt, re-org.
Topham, John	Lake co	July 22	Capt'd, Chickahominy; must'd out.
Tripp, David E	Lake co	July 22	Veteran; transf. 20th Regiment, re-org.
Wabb, Samuel	Lake co	July 22	Deserted while on furlough.
Warren, George W	Lake co	July 22	Discharged, Aug. 21, '62.
Wilcox, Stephen H	Lake co	July 22	Mustered out July 29, '64.
Williams, Isaac	Lake co	July 22	Died, July 5, '63; wounds rec'd Gettysburg.
Winters, Charles	Lake co	July 22	Vet'n; died, City P't, Va., Je. 19,'64; w'ds rec.
Wright, William	Lake co	July 22	Disch'gd, Dec. 28,'61; disability. [Petersb'g.
Zimmer, Peter	Lake co	July 22	Vet'n; transf. 20th Regiment, re-organized.
Recruits.			
Archer, James			Vet'n; transf. 20th Regiment, re-organized.
Curtis, George G		July 31, '63	
Crawford, Samuel		Feb. 28, '62	Discharged, Nov. 3, '62; disability.
Frazier, James B		Feb. 4, '62	Discharged, Dec. 27, '62.
Fuller, Horace		Aug. 15, '62	Killed, Wilderness, May 5, '64.
Farmer, Thompson	Lake co	July 22, '61	Mustered out July 29, '64.
Frantz, Lawrence	Lake co	Feb. 28, '62	Vet'n; killed, Spottsylvania, May 12, '64.
Fields, George W		Dec. 23, '63	Transferred 20th Regiment, re-organized.
Flockhart, L			" " " "
Glazier, Melvin		Feb. 28, '62	Discharged, disability.
Gerbing, Frederick	Jefferson co	Sept. 1, '62	Transferred 20th Regiment, re-organized.

INDIANA VOLUNTEERS.

Name and Rank.	Residence.	Date of Muster.	Remarks.
			[Reg't, re-organized.
Hackett, Horace H.	Lake co	Feb. 4, '62	Vet'n; wounded, Spottsylvania; transf'd 20th
Hale, John		Mar. 4, '64	Transferred to 20th Regiment, re-organized.
Kinney, Oscar	Porter co	Feb. 17, '62	Discharged Dec. 22, '62; disability.
Kelmer, Joseph	Jefferson co	Sept. 15, '62	Transferred to 20th Regiment, re-organized.
Kimball, Richard	Lake co	Sept. 15, '62	" " "
Kirsch, Frantz	Jefferson co	Sept. 15, '62	" " "
Love, William H		Aug. 19, '62	" " "
Merrill, James D	Lake co	Feb. 28, '62	Veteran; killed at Wilderness May 5, '64.
Montgomery, John			Veteran; transf'd to 20th Reg't, re-organized.
Pattie, James		Aug. 20, '62	Captured at Gettysburg July 2, '63.
Pierce, John	Vigo co	Sept. 19, '62	Transferred to 20th Regiment, re-organized.
Rotger, Henry	Jefferson co	Aug. 25, '62	Woun'd May 30, '64; transf'd 20th Reg't, re-
Richmond, Joshua		Aug. 2, '62	Killed, Gettysburg July 2, '63. [organized.
Rottgen, Henry		Aug. 18, '62	Wounded May 24, '64. [out Sept. 5, '65.
Richard, John W		Mar. 29, '64	Woun'd Spottsylv'a; transf'd V. R. C.; must.
Smith, John			Veteran; transf'd to 20th Reg't, re-organized.
Thomas, James C	Lake co	Sept. 21, '62	Transferred to 20th Regiment, re-organized.
Taylor, William C			Veteran; transf'd to 20th Reg't, re-organized.
Van Ness, Israel	Porter co	Feb. 4, '62	Transferred to 20th Regiment, re-organized.
Van Slyke, Alfred		Aug. 25, '62	Discharged Jan. 9, '63.
Wilson, Robert R	Lake co	Feb. 14, '64	Veteran; deserted while on veteran furlough.
Welch, Michael	Porter co	Dec. 16, '62	Transferred to 20th Regiment, re-organized.
Wood, Lewis	Porter co	Mar. 26, '62	" " "
Worsler, Hiram	Porter co	Mar. 26, '62	" " "
Weyper, Richard J		Aug. 20, '62	

ENLISTED MEN OF COMPANY "C."

Name and Rank.	Residence.	Date of Muster. 1861.	Remarks.
First Sergeant.			
Babbington, William	Plymouth	July 22	Promoted 2d Lieutenant.
Sergeants.			
Mattingley, Moses B	Marshall co	July 22	
Hewitt, John W	Plymouth	July 22	Promoted 2d Lieutenant.
Wright, Forrest	Marshall co	July 22	
O'Blenis, Abel	Marshall co	July 22	
Corporals.			
Turner, John	Marshall co	July 22	Killed at Gettysburg.
Robbins, Ezra B	Plymouth	July 22	Promoted 2d Lieutenant.
Davis, John W	Plymouth	July 22	" " "
Williams, Paul	Marshall co	July 22	
Botset, Henry	Marshall co	July 22	Mustered out July 29, '64, as private.
Pensinger, John	Marshall co	July 22	
Shrighley, Samuel	Marshall co	July 22	
Warcup, Edwin S	Plymouth	July 22	Promoted 2d Lieutenant.
Musicians.			
Reynolds, George	Marshall co	July 22	
Koontz, Frederick J	Marshall co	July 22	Captured; mustered out June 28, '65.
Wagoner.			
McDonough, Harmes	Marshall co	July 22	Veteran; transf'd to 20th Reg't, re-organized.
Privates.			
Baxter, John	Marshall co	July 22	
Bennet, James R	Marshall co	July 22	Veteran; woun'd, Spottsylv'a; prom'd 2d Lt.
Black, John B	Marshall co	July 22	Mustered out July 29, '64.
Bowles, John G	Marshall co	July 22	
Burkett, Wilson W	Marshall co	July 22	Mustered out July 29, '64.
Clark, Abraham E	Marshall co	July 22	[May 22, '62.
Clark, George W	Marshall co	July 22	Captured on gunboat "Fanny"; discharged
Clepper, Henry	Marshall co	July 22	Mustered out July 29, '64.
Coon, Stephen V	Marshall co	July 22	
Copley, David	Marshall co	July 22	
Creviston, William W	Marshall co	July 22	Captured; mustered out July 29, '64.
Darnell, Walter J. A	Marshall co	July 22	Veteran; died at Petersburg, Va.
Dawson, William H	Marshall co	July 22	
Dawson, Francis M	Marshall co	July 22	Vet'n; wounded, Petersburg; promoted 2d Lt.
Elder, Benjamin F	Marshall co	July 22	
Erwin, William H. H.	Marshall co	July 22	Veteran.
Erwin, Uriah B	Marshall co	July 22	
Fergerson, John W	Marshall co	July 22	
Glass, Seymour	Marshall co	July 22	

NAME AND RANK.	Residence.	Date of Muster. 1861	REMARKS.
Gordon, Lafayette	Marshall co	July 22	Promoted 2d Lieutenant.
Griffiths, Elias	Marshall co	July 22	Wounded; mustered out July 29, '64.
Grimes, Albert A	Marshall co	July 22	
Grimes, William J	Marshall co	July 22	
Hall, William	Marshall co	July 22	Captured; mustered out June 27, '65.
Head, Benjamin F	Marshall co	July 22	Veteran.
Head, Francis M	Marshall co	July 22	Vet.; transferred to 20th Reg't, re-organized.
Hedglen, Alexander N.	Marshall co	July 22	[22, '62.
Helsel, John	Marshall co	July 22	Capt'd on gunboat "Fanny;" must'd out May
Howard, Rupert	Marshall co	July 22	[22, '62.
Ingles, Robert A	Marshall co	July 22	Capt'd on gunboat "Fanny," must'd out May
Inks, Joseph	Marshall co	July 22	
Inks, Jonah	Marshall co	July 22	
Jones, John O	Marshall co	July 22	Vet.; transf'd to 20th Regiment, re-organized.
Kehr, Henry	Marshall co	July 22	
Kesselring, Jacob	Marshall co	July 22	Mustered out July 29, '64.
Kilgore, General W	Marshall co	July 22	" " " [Reg't, re-org.
Kuntz, Adam P	Marshall co	July 22	Vet.; captured June 1, '64; transf'd to 20th
Kreighbaum, Cyrus	Marshall co	July 22	[re-organized.
Kreighbaum, Uriah	Marshall co	July 22	Vet.; wounded, Wilderness, transf'd 20th Reg.
Lacy, Nathaniel M	Marshall co	Jnly 22	[Reg't, re-organized.
Lewis, William J	Marshall co	July 22	Vet.; wounded, Wilderness; transf'd to 20th
Logston, Perry	Marshall co	July 22	
Morris, Elihu	Marshall co	July 22	Mustered out July 29, '64.
Neidig, Jacob	Marshall co	July 22	
Neidig, David	Marshall co	July 22	[July 29, '64.
O'Blenis, Henry F	Marshall co	July 22	Captured on gunboat "Fanny," must'd out
Osplister, John	Marshall co	July 22	[re-organized.
Owens, Francis M	Marshall co	July 22	Vet.; wounded, Petersb'g; transf'd 20th Reg.,
Owens, Elijah E	Marshall co	July 22	Vet.; w'd May 29,'64; tr'f'd 20th Reg., re-org.
Parker, Francis L	Marshall co	July 22	Vet.; transf'd to 20th Reg't, re-organized.
Penrod, John	Marshall co	July 22	Vet.; w'd Spottsylv'a; tr'f' 20th Reg't, re-org.
Pickerl, James	Marshall co	July 22	Mustered out July 29, '64.
Poff, Peter	Marshall co	July 22	Transferred to 13th Regiment, re-organized.
Pohlmann, Bernhard	Marshall co	July 22	
Rash, James	Marshall co	July 22	
Reed, David	Marshall co	July 22	Vet.; transf'd to 20th Reg't, re-organized.
Richhart. William H	Marshall co	July 22	Vet.; wounded at Petersburg; transferred to
Robbins, David	Marshall co	July 22	[20th Reg'nt, re-org.
Rowell, George J	Marshall co	July 22	
Sapp, William R	Marshall co	July 22	Vet.; killed, Wilderness, May 5, '64.
Shade, William	Marshall co	July 22	
Simmons, Goodman	Marshall co	July 22	Vet.; transf'd to 20th Reg't, re-organized.
Sippey, John M	Marshall co	July 22	[out May 22,'62.
Stickley, William	Marshall co	July 22	Captured at Chicomicomico 'Island; mustered
Stickley, Simon	Marshall co	July 22	
Stickley, Samuel	Marshall co	July 22	Mustered out July 29, '64.
Stuck, Eli	Marshall co	July 22	Died at Andersonville prison, May 5, '64.
Stuck, George	Marshall co	July 22	Mustered out July 29, '64.
Swapka, Frederick	Marshall co	July 22	Vet.; transf'd to 20th Reg't, re-organized.
Taylor, James	Marshall co	July 22	Vet.; wounded at Petersburg; transf'd to 20th
Teaker, William	Marshall co	July 22	[Reg't, re-org.
Thompson, David	Marshall co	July 22	Vet.; died at Washington, June 1, '64.
Tribbey, James	Marshall co	July 22	[May 22,'62.
Unruh, Henry A	Marshall co	July 22	Captured at Chicomicomico Island; must'd out
Weldon, Franklin	Marshall co	July 22	Vet.; transf'd to 20th Reg't, re-org.
Welte, Isidon	Marshall co	July 22	[re-organized.
Wentzler, Christian	Marshall co	July 22	Wounded, Wilderness; transf'd to 20th Reg't,
Williams, John W	Marshall co	July 22	Promoted 1st Lieutenant.
Wise, Abraham N	Marshall co	July 22	[Reg't, re-organized.
Wolf, Peter	Marshall co	July 22	Vet.; wounded, Petersburg; transf'd to 20th
Woodruff, Jesse V	Marshall co	July 22	
Young, Adam	Marshall co	July 22	
Recruits.			
Black, William T	Marshall co		Veteran.
Baxter, Joseph	Marshall co	Oct. 20, '62.	Wounded, Wild'ness; tr'f'd to 20th Reg., re-or.
Baxter, Wyman	Marshall co	Sept. 16, '62	" " " " "
Buster, Joseph F	Marshall co	Oct. 18, '62.	
Cross, Jacob W	Marshall co	Oct. 18, '62.	
Gordon, John	Marshall co	Mar. 12, '62	[re-org.
Head, Jacob B	Marshall co	Mar. 12,'62.	Wounded, Aug. 4, '64; transf'd to 20th Reg't,
Hutchison, Joseph	Marshall co	Sept. 10, '62	Transferred to 20th Regiment, re-organized.
Hussey, Jonathan	Marshall co	Mar. 12,'62.	
Kerr, Alexander	Marshall co	Sept. 10, '62	Transferred V. R. C., must'd out June 28,'65.
Lewis, Albert T		Oct. 20, '62.	W'ded, Wild'ness; tr'f'd to 20th Reg't, re-org.
Lewis, George W		Nov. 1,'62.	Transferred to 20th Reg't, re-organized.
Morgan, Jonathan W.	Marshall co	Mar. 12,'62	Vet.; transferred to 20th Reg't, re-organized.
Murphy, Oliver P	Marshall co	Oct. 10, '62	Transf'd to 20th Reg't, re-organized.
Marks, Thomas P	Marshall co	Oct. 18, '62.	
Nichols, Edward	Marshall co	Sept. 10, '62	Transf'd to 20th Regiment, re-organized.

NAME AND RANK.	Residence.	Date of Muster.	REMARKS.
Pickerd, Aaron H.........	Marshall co......	Mar. 12, '62	
Radabaugh, William......	Marshall co......	Oct. 21, '62..	Transferred to 20th Regiment, re-organized.
Robinson, Christopher..	Marshall co......	Oct. 18, '62..	[re-organized.
Swihart, Joshua...........	Marshall co......	Sept. 20, '62	Wounded Oct. 14, '64; transf'd to 20th Reg't
Simons, Wiliam D.........	....	April 15, '64	Transferred to 20th Regiment, re-organized.
Sutton, George.............	....	....	Killed Fredericksburg Dec. 15, '62.
Williams, Richard........	Marshall co......	April 13, '64	Wounded Spottsylvania; transf'd to 20th Reg.
Young, Fletcher...........	Marshall co......	Sept, 10, '62	Killed Gettysburg. [re-organized.

ENLISTED MEN OF COMPANY "D."

NAME AND RANK.	Residence.	Date of Muster. 1861.	REMARKS.
First Sergeant.			
Kinneard, Marquis L...	Attica...............	July 22........	Promoted 1st Lieutenant.
Sergeants.			
Campbell, Henry E. W.	Fountain co......	July 22........	
Engel, Ferdinand.........	Fountain co......	July 22........	Cap'd, Chicomicomico Island; discharged June
Longsdorf, Edgar.........	Fountain co......	July 22........	Veteran. [28, '62.
Stallard, James P.........	Attica...............	July 22........	Vet.; woun'd Wilderness; promoted 2d Lieut.
Corporals.			
Vatchett, William D.....	Indianapolis ...	July 22........	Promoted 2d Lieutenant.
Shafer, Otho J.............	Fountain co......	July 22........	Mustered out July 29, '64, as private.
Norris, Albert R...........	Fountain co......	July 22........	Promoted 2d Lieutenant.
Bernhard, Jacob..........	Fountain co......	July 22........	Mustered out July 29, '64, as Serg't.
Martin, David B...........	Fountain co......	July 22........	Mustered out July 29, '64; as 1st Serg't.
Magruder, Jonas E........	Fountain co......	July 22........	
Hughes, John W...........	Fountain co......	July 22........	
Painter, George W........	Fountain co......	July 22........	Veteran; transf'd to 20th Reg't, re-organized.
Musicians.			
Chesley. Edwin............	Fountain co......	July 22........	Veteran.
Liggett, James K.........	Fountain co......	July 22........	
Wagoner.			
Dukes, Samuel H.........	Fountain co......	July 22........	Veteran.
Privates.			
Adams, William J........	Fountain co......	July 22........	Died, Washington, July 28, '62.
Barwick, Henry...........	Fountain co......	July 22........	
Barfell, Othias.............	Fountain co......	July 22........	
Beever, Edwin D..........	Fountain co......	July 22........	
Beedle, William A........	Fountain co......	July 22........	Mustered out July 29, '64. [Reg't, re-org'd.
Berry, Edwin A...........	Fountain co......	July 22........	Veteran; woun'd Spottsylvania; transf'd 20th
Blake, James L.............	Fountain co......	July 22........	Veteran; transf'd to 20th Reg't, re-organized.
Bowers, Joseph............	Fountain co......	July 22........	
Brown, George.............	Fountain co......	July 22........	Veteran; transf'd to 20th Reg't, re-organized.
Bunce, Thomas C.........	Fountain co......	July 22........	" " " "
Bunch, America...........	Fountain co......	July 22........	
Campbell, Mark T........	Fountain co......	July 22........	
Cox, Albert J...............	Fountain co......	July 22........	Mustered out July 29, '64.
Crabb, Andrew J	Fountain co......	July 22........	
Crabb, Joseph..............	Fountain co......	July 22........	
Crawford, Robert A......	Fountain co......	July 22........	
Davidson, John T.........	Fountain co......	July 23.. ...	
Davidson, Marsh F......	Fountain co......	July 22........	
Day, William W...........	Fountain co......	July 22........	
Day, Theodore.............	Fountain co......	July 22........	Killed Gettysburg.
Deford, James..............	Fountain co......	July 22........	
Deshler, Roman...........	Fountain co......	July 22........	
Dickenson, Michael......	Fountain co......	July 22........	
Doll, James A..............	Fountain co......	July 22........	Mustered out July 29, '64.
Doubleday, John M......	Fountain co......	July 22........	" " "
Doubleday, Harry A......	Fountain co......	July 22........	
Donaldson, Madison.....	Fountain co......	July 22........	
Duke, Thomas S...........	Fountain co......	July 22........	Veteran.
Farmer, James..............	Fountain co......	July 22........	Veteran.
Fitzpatrick, John..........	Fountain co......	July 22........	Mustered out July 29, '64.
Fix, John R..................	Fountain co......	July 22........	Veteran; transf'd to 20th Reg't, re-organized.
Fleshman, Lorence........	Fountain co......	July 22........	Mustered out July 29, '64.
Froreich, Hermann......	Fountain co......	July 22........	" " "
France, George.............	Fountain co......	July 22........	
Gallaher, Fielding.........	Fountain co......	July 22........	
Gillaspy, George T........	Fountain co......	July 22........	Veteran; transf'd to 20th Reg't, re-organized

Name and Rank.	Residence.	Date of Muster. 1861.	Remarks.
Glover, Francis M	Fountain co	July 22	Capt'd Chicomicomico Isl'd; must'd out May [22, '62.
Greennuk, Harry	Fountain co	July 22	Vet; tr'fd 20th Regt. re-organized.
Haler, Michael	Fountain co	July 22	" " "
Hawkins, Daniel	Fountain co	July 22	" " "
Hawkins, Isaac W	Fountain co	July 22	" " "
Helderbraut, James K	Fountain co	July 22	
Himmebright, Thos. J	Fountain co	July 22	
Hollett, John S	Fountain co	July 22	Veteran; transf'd to 20th Regt re-organized.
Idle, George	Fountain co	July 22	
Jackson, Isaac H	Fountain co	July 22	
Jansen, Jacob	Fountain co	July 22	
Johnson, John	Fountain co	July 22	Mustered out July 29, '64.
Kadle, John	Fountain co	July 22	" " "
Kane, Jonathan	Fountain co	July 22	Veteran; transf'd to 20th Regt. re-organized.
Kane, Agrifa	Fountain co	July 22	
Koffman, Jacob	Fountain co	July 22	Veteran; transf'd to 20th Regt. re-organized.
Ketcham, William P	Fountain co	July 22	Mustered out July 29, '64.
Kiser, William F	Fountain co	July 22	
Leath, Azariah T	Fountain co	July 22	Vet; w'ded May 30,'64; tr'fd 20th Regt. re-org.
Liggett, Andrew J W	Fountain co	July 22	Veteran.
Neal, Samuel W	Fountain co	July 22	Veteran; transf'd to 20th Regt. re-organized.
Orwig, Lemuel J	Fountain co	July 22	Leg amputated Gettysburg.
Parker, William.,	Fountain co	July 22	
Peltz, John A	Fountain co	July 22	
Pierce, George	Fountain co	July 22	
Pierce, Thomas	Fountain co	July 22	Mustered out July 29, '64.
Probus, Washington	Fountain co	July 22	Capt'd Chicomicomico Isl'd; must'd out May
Ridgeway, Wesley J	Fountain co	July 22	Mustered out July 29, '64. [22, '62.
Savage, John E	Fountain co	July 22	
Seaman, Thomas J	Fountain co	July 22	
Sentman, Charles W	Fountain co	July 22	Vet; w'ded June 1, '64; tr'fd 20th Regt. re-org.
Sible, Thomas H. B	Fountain co	July 22	Veteran; transf'd 20th to Regt. re-organized.
Simpson, James	Fountain co	July 22	Mustered out July 29, '64.
Slaughter, John	Fountain co	July 22	" " "
Slusser, William D	Fountain co	July 22	" " "
Smith, Abraham	Fountain co	July 22	
Thomas, James N	Fountain co	July 22	Mustered out July 29, '64.
Tollivar, Archibald	Fountain co	July 22	Died at Alexandria, Oct. 28, '62.
Tollivar, Reuben	Fountain co	July 22	Veteran; transf'd to 20th Regt. re-organized.
Walker, John	Fountain co	July 22	Mustered out July 29, '64.
Warner, William	Fountain co	July 22	Veteran; transf'd to 20th Regt. re-organized.
Wolf, George J	Fountain co	July 22	Veteran.
Woolverton, George W.	Fountain co	July 22	Veteran; died at Washington, May 19, '64.
Wood, William	Fountain co	July 22	
Wood, Ira C	Fountain co	July 22	
Yates, Nathaniel	Fountain co	July 22	Veteran; transf'd to 20th Regt. re-organized.
Recruits.			
Barnick, Franklin	Franklin co		Vet; w'ded Spotts'ia tr'fd 20th Regt. re-org.
Bruner, Nicholas	Tippecanoe co	Jan. 4, '62	Transferred to 20th Regt. re-organized.
Crawford, John A	Fountain co	Oct. 12, '62	" " "
Cole, William H			Killed at Fredericksburg, Dec 15, '62.
Clifton, Perry	Fountain co	Aug. 22, '62	
Davis, Lewis	Fountain co	Jan. 4, '64	Transferred to 20th Regt. re-organized.
Dunkin, J	White co	April 9, '62	Discharged Oct. 1. '62.
Engle, Ferdinand	Fountain co	Aug. 30, '62	Transf'd to 20th Regt. re-organized
Glover, Frances	Fountain co	Jan. 7, '64	" " "
Griffith, Nathaniel	Fountain co	Jan. 7, '64	" " "
Hawkins, Joseph J	Fountain co	Jan. 7, '64	W'ded Petersburg; tr'fd to 20th Regt. re-org.
Harrell J. M			Killed at Fredericksburg Dec. 15,'62.
Harper, Columbus	Fountain co	Aug. 22, '62	
Hart, Charles W	Fountain co	Aug. 22, '62	
Houts, David	Fountain co	Aug. 22, '62	
Harper, Columbus	Fountain co	Jan. 7, '64.	
Johnson, William C	Fountain co	Aug. 7, '62.	W'ded at Wild'nss; transf'd 20th Regt. re-org.
Johnston, Grandy			Killed Fredricksburg, Dec. 15, '62. [22,'62.
Kinneard, Marcus L	Fountain co	Aug. 22, '62	Capt'd Chicomicomico Isl'd; must'd out May
Morgan, Francis M	Fountain co	Aug. 10, '62	Transferred to 20th Regt. re-organized.
Manlove, Charles	Fountain co	Jan. 7, '64.	W'ded, Wild'nss; tr'fd 20th Regt. re-org.
Mentzer, Samuel C	Fountain co	Aug. 22, '62	Transferred to 20th Regt. re-organized.
Odom, John	Fountain co	Jan. 7, '64.	W'ded, Wild'nss; tr'fd 20th Regt. re-org.
Pearson, John C	Fountain co	Sept. 8, '62.	Transferred to 20th Regt. re-crganized.
Probus, Washington	Fountain co	Aug. 22, '62	
Reegan, P. E			Killed at Fredericksburg Dec. 15, '62.
Thomas, George	Fountain co	Aug. 22, '62	
Wood, Ira C	Fountain co	Jan. 7, '64.	W'ded Spotts'ia, tr'fd 20th Regt. re-org.
Williams, George W			Killed at Fredericksburg, Dec. 15, '62.

ENLISTED MEN OF COMPANY "E."

Name and Rank.	Residence.	Date of Muster. 1861.	Remarks.
First Sergeant.			
Abbey, Edward S	Laporte co	July 22	
Sergeants.			
Crawford, Hiram	Laporte co	July 22	Promoted 2d Lieutenant.
Thompson, John C	Laporte co	July 22	
Muir, William R	Laporte co	July 22	Promoted 2d Lieutenant.
Woodworth, Leonard	Laporte co	July 22	
Corporals.			
Lamb, Alonzo H	Laporte co	July 22	Mortally wounded, Gettysburg.
Bingaman, David N	Laporte co	July 22	
Fonstel, Charles	Laporte co	July 22	
Hinstis, George F	Laporte co	July 22	
Martin, William H	Laporte co	July 22	
Behan, Samuel E	Laporte co	July 22	
Cissna, Isaac N	Laporte co	July 22	Mustered out July 29, '64, as private.
Easton, Nathan B	Laporte co	July 22	Capt'd, Spottsylvania; must'd out May 3, '65.
Musicians.			
Smith, Thomas J	Laporte co	July 22	Veteran.
Bixby, Warren D	Laporte co	July 22	Veteran; transferred 20th Regiment, re-org.
Wagoner.			
Powers, John	Laporte co	July 22	
Privates.			
Aldrich, Charles	Laporte co	July 22	
Barkhurst, Amos	Laporte co	July 22	Mustered out July 29, '64.
Bartow, John D	Laporte co	July 22	Capt'd Fredericksburg; must'd out July 29,'64.
Bingaman, John M	Laporte co	July 22	
Biser, Daniel	Laporte co	July 22	
Briley, Elias F	Laporte co	July 22	
Bruch, Philip	Laporte co	July 22	Veteran; transf. 20th Reg't, re-organized.
Burke, Michael	Laporte co	July 22	
Burns, Royal S	Laporte co	July 22	
Carney, Matthew	Laporte co	July 22	
Carr, Frazee	Laporte co	July 22	
Drake, George	Laporte co	July 22	Vet'n; transf. 20th Regiment, re-organized.
Eberly, Jacob	Laporte co	July 22	Mustered out July 29, '64.
Egan, Michael	Laporte co	July 22	" " "
Farnsworth, Edward M	Laporte co	July 22	
Fraunberg, Christopher	Laporte co	July 22	Promoted 2d Lieutenant.
Fuller, Warren	Laporte co	July 22	
Gallegan, Michael	Laporte co	July 22	Veteran; transf. 20th Reg't, re-organized.
Griffin, Patrick	Laporte co	July 22	Killed, Gettysburg.
Goodenough, Francis H.	Laporte co	July 22	
Goodsell, Henry M	Laporte co	July 22	
Hackett, David	Laporte co	July 22	
Hatfield, William C	Laporte co	July 22	Veteran; w'd North Anna; transf. 20th Reg't, [re-organized.
Helmouth, Henry	Laporte co	July 22	
Hendricks, John H	Laporte co	July 22	Killed, Gettysburg.
Hickman, Benjamin F.	Laporte co	July 22	Vet'n; transf. 20th Reg't, re-organized,
Hollingsworth, Reuben	Laporte co	July 22	Capt'd Mine Run; must'd out March 18, '65.
Johnson, George W	Laporte co	July 23	
Jones, Charles E	Laporte co	July 22	Capt'd Chicomicomico Island; must'd out May [22, '62.
Kannard, David	Laporte co	July 22	
Kistler, John J	Laporte co	July 22	Mustered out July 29, '64.
Legyard, William B	Laporte co	July 22	
Lewalter, John	Laporte co	July 22	
Logan, William	Laporte co	July 22	
Louder, William H	Laporte co	July 22	Vet'n; transf. 20th Regiment, re-organized.
Lytle, John T	Laporte co	July 22	
Magnesun, Israel	Laporte co	July 22	
March, John	Laporte co	July 22	
McAnany, Peter	Laporte co	July 22	Vet'n; transf. 20th Regiment, re-organized.
McFey, Bernard	Laporte co	July 22	
Morrow, James	Laporte co	July 22	Mustered out July 29, '64.
Murphy, Edward	Laporte co	July 22	
Orb, Fernando C	Laporte co	July 22	
Paddock, Harvey S	Laporte co	July 22	Veteran.
Parker, George M	Laporte co	July 22	Capt'd Chicomicomico Island; mustered out [May 22, '62.
Pealer, David	Laporte co	July 22	Veteran.
Phillips, Oscar	Laporte co	July 22	
Price, Salathiel C	Laporte co	July 22	Killed, Gettysburg.
Raber, Samuel	Laporte co	July 22	Mustered out July 29, '64.
Reynolds, Christopher	Laporte co	July 22	" " "
Richards, Benjamin F.	Laporte co	July 22	

Name and Rank.	Residence.	Date of Muster. 1861.	Remarks.
Richardson, Arthur	Laporte co	July 22	[May 22, '62.
Riley, Leonard	Laporte co	July 22	Capt'd at Chicomlcomico Island; mustered out
Ruff, Lawrence	Laporte co	July 22	Capt'd at Chicomicomico Island; mustered out
Sabin, Orlando W	Laporte co	July 22	[May 22, '62.
Scanlen, Dennis	Leporte co	July 22	
Shay, Cornelius	Laporte co	July 22	Veteran; transf'd 20th Regt, re-organized.
Smith, Andrew J	Laporte co	July 22	
Smith, Frederick	Laporte co	July 22	
Smith, Stephen R	Laporte co	July 22	
Smith, William	Laporte co	July 22	May 22, '92.
Snyder, Eli	Laporte co	July 22	Capt'd at Chicomicomico Island; mustered out
St. Clair, Nathan	Laporte co	July 22	
Swingle, John W	Laporte co	July 22	Killed at Gettysburg.
Tappan, Noah M	Laporte co	July 22	Mustered out July 29, '64.
Taylor, John D	Laporte co	July 22	
Travis, Curtis	Laporte co	July 22	Veteran; transf'd 20th Regt, re-organized.
Vandusen, Cornelius	Laporte co	July 22	Veteran.
Vandusen, Dennis F. F.	Laporte co	July 22	Mustered out July 29, '64.
Vandusen, Henry H	Laporte co	July 22	
Verrel, Stephen	Laporte co	July 22	
Washburn, George W	Laporte co	July 22	Mustered out July 29, '64.
Watson, Frank	Laporte co	July 22	
Weed, Charles F	Laporte co	July 22	
Whiteraft, Thomas	Laporte co	July 22	
Whitney, Henry M	Laporte co	July 22	
Williams, Frank	Laporte co	July 22	
Wilson, Ellicott,	Laporte co	July 22	Wou'd, Wilderness; mustered out July 29, '64.
Winch, Marquis R	Laporte co	July 22	Mustered out July 29, '64.
Young, William	Laporte co	July 22	
Zimmerman, Thomas	Laporte co	July 22	
Zimmerman, William	Laporte co	July 22	Veteran; promoted 2d Lieut., Co. "G."
Recruits			
Andrews, Abram C	Laporte co	Jan. 27, '62	
Berry, Franklin		Jan. 24, '64	Transf'd to 20th Regt, re-organized.
Fields, Daniel H			Vet.; traneferred to 20th Regt, re-organized.
Fields, Thomas S			" " " "
Gilkenson, Archibald		Aug. 30, '62	Transferred to 20th Regt, re-organized.
Hannah, Andrew J	Laporte co	Dec. 2, '63	
Johnson, Isaac E		Sept. 1, '62	Transferred to 20th Regt, re-organized.
Layton John	Laporte co	Jan. 27, '62	
Overman, James T			Vet.; transferred to 20th Regt, re-organized.
Poachiner, A. A			Transferred to 20th Regt, re-organized.
Pearman, Adam	Clay co	Dec. 26, '63	" " " "
Phillips, Norman	Parke co	Jan. 26, '64	Wou'd; trans'fd to 20th Regt, re-organized.
Roberts, Edwiu A	Parke co	Dec. 18, '63	Transferred to 20th Regt, re-organized.
Robinson, Charles			" " " "
Reed, J. C			" " " "
Raburn, William J		Dec. 11, '61	Killed at Gettysburg.
Sturgis, L. J			Wou'd, Wilderness; transf'd 20th Regt, re-org.
Simons, Price	Montgomery co	Jan. 7, '64	Transferred to 20th Regt, re-organized.
Vail, Oliver G	Vigo co	Feb. 27, '64	" " " "
Welterman, T. J			" " " "

ENLISTED MEN OF COMPANY "F."

Name and Rank.	Residence.	Date of Muster. 1861.	Remarks.
First Sergeant.			
Miller, Harvey H	Logansport	July 22	Promoted 2d Lieutenant.
Sergeants.			
Hock, Jacob B	Cass co	July 22	
Haslett, John W	Cass co	July 22	
Cavanaugh, George E	Cass co	July 22	
Cornwell, Jesse L	Cass co	July 22	Mustered out July 29, '64, as private.
Corporals.			
McAnally, Thomas J	Cass co	July 22	Vet.; transferred 20th Regt, re-organized.
Yund, Isaac V	Cass co	July 22	
Reddick, George H	Cass co	July 22	Leg amputated at Gettysburg.
Swadener, Abraham	Cass co	July 22	Vet.; transferred to 20th Regt, re-organized.
Anderson, William A	Indianapolis	July 22	Promoted Adjutant.
Moore, Nathan M	Cass co	July 22	
Winsch, Frederick	Cass co	July 22	Mustered out July 29, '64, as private.
Stipe, Henry T	Cass co	July 22	Veteran.

Name and Rank.	Residence.	Date of Muster. 1861.	Remarks.
Musicians.			
Bray, John	Cass co	July 22	
McBride, Joseph	Cass co	July 22	
Wagoner.			
Doyle, William	Cass co	July 22	
Privates.			
Allen, Ira T	Cass co	July 22	Killed.
Arnold, Gilbert	Cass co	July 22	Veteran; transf'd to 20th Reg't, reorganized.
Benefield, Enoch	Cass co	July 22	[re-organized.
Bliss, Henry H	Cass co	July 22	Vet.; woun'd Wilderness; transf'd 20th Reg't,
Booth, George	Cass co	July 22	
Brophy, John	Cass co	July 22	
Brennan, Michael	Cass co	July 22	
Burr, Amadeus B	Cass co	July 22	Mustered out July 29, '64.
Carey, James	Cass co	July 22	
Clapp, Michael D	Cass co	July 22	Capt'd Gettysburg; mus'd out July 29, '64.
Cook, Isaac W	Cass co	July 22	[22, '62.
Comingore, John A.	Cass co	July 22	Capt'd Chicomicomico Island; must'd out May
Cuppy, Perry C	Cass co	July 22	Mustered out July 29, '64.
Cummins, John W	Cass co	July 22	Veteran; transf'd to 20th Reg't, re-organized.
Cunningham, Jesse H	Cass co	July 22	
Cullen, Joseph W	Cass co	July 22	Mustered out July 29, '64.
Davis, Joshua	Cass co	July 22	
Davidson, James I	Cass co	July 22	
Douglas, James	Cass co	July 22	Transferred to 20th Regiment, re-organized.
Dasch, George W	Cass co	July 22	Killed at Chancellorsville.
Duncan Richard	Cass co	July 22	
Emmons, William	Cass co	July 22	Mustered out July 29, '64.
Everman, William H	Cass co	July 22	
Fenters, James	Cass co	July 22	Veteran.
Finke, John A	Cass co	July 22	
Floyd, John	Cass co	July 22	Veteran; transf'd to 20th Reg't, re-organized.
Foxworthy, Samuel F	Cass co	July 22	
Gates, William H C	Cass co	July 22	
Goodare, Charles	Cass co	July 22	
Goodwin, Giles N	Cass co	July 22	Captured May 16, '64.
Gross, John A	Cass co	July 22	
Henry, Charles	Cass co	July 22	Veteran; transf'd to 20th Reg't, re-organized.
Howland, Marcus J	Cass co	July 22	
Jennings, Curtis	Cass co	July 22	Mustered out July 29, '64.
Jennings, Edward W	Cass co	July 22	" " "
Jenkins William I	Cass co	July 22	" " "
Johnson, Thomas	Cass co	July 22	Veteran; transf'd to 20th Reg't, re-organized.
Kelley, William	Cass co	July 22	
Knoud, Frank	Coss co	July 22	Veteran.
Landus, James	Cass co	July 22	
Laprell, Joseph	Cass co	July 22	
Loman, Samuel	Cass co	July 22	Veteran; transf'd to 20th Reg't, re-organized.
Maddox, James	Cass co	July 22	Capt'd Chicom'mico Isl.; mus. out May 22,'62.
May, James	Cass co	July 22	Veteran; transf'd to 20th Reg't, re-organized.
Miller, Robert	Cass co	July 22	Veteran.
Moore, Charles	Cass co	July 22	
Moore, David F	Cass co	July 22	
McCauley, James Q	Cass co	July 22	
McDonald, David	Cass co	July 22	
Morgan, John W	Cass co	July 22	Veteran; transf'd to 20th Reg't, re-organized.
Morgan, Murrell	Cass co	July 22	Woun'd Wilderness; must'd out July 29, '64.
Morrisey, Patrick	Cass co	July 22	Killed Gettysburg.
Murphy, Harrison	Cass co	July 22	
Murphy, Peter	Cass co	July 22	Mustered out July 29, '64.
Newell, Jeremiah	Cass co	July 22	
Papena, Romeo	Cass co	July 22	Mustered out July 29, '64.
Pherson, Jeremiah	Cass co	July 22	Woun'd June 1, '64; must'd out July 29, '64.
Rariden, Henry C	Cass co	July 22	
Radpearn, Richard	Cass co	July 22	
Redpearn, James W	Cass co	July 22	Mustered out July 29, '64.
Replogle, Solomon	Cass co	July 22	
Replogle, Harrison	Cass co	July 22	Wounded Petersburg.
Ross, Robert H	Cass co	July 22	Mustered out July 29, '64. [re-organized.
Shields, Frederick C	Cass co	July 22	Vet.; woun'd Wilderness; transf'd 20th Reg't,
Shell, Jacob H	Cass co	July 22	Mustered out July 29, '64.
Scott, Richard R	Cass co	July 22	
Smiley, Archibald	Cass co	July 22	
Smiley, John A	Cass co	July 22	Wounded Chancellorsville.
Staff, Henry	Cass co	July 22	
Terrill, Joseph	Cass co	July 22	
Torrence, James H	Cass co	July 22	Veteran.
Thomas, John	Cass co	July 22	
Truax, Simon P	Cass co	July 22	Veteran.

NAME AND RANK.	Residence.	Date of Muster. 1861.	REMARKS.
Walters, Joseph	Cass co	July 22	Veteran; transf'd to 20th Reg't, re-organized.
Walters, John Isaac	Cass co	July 22	" " "
Wall, Leander	Cass co	July 22	" " "
Weaver, George W	Cass co	July 22	
West, James O	Cass co	July 22	Mustered out July 29, '64. [May 22, '62.
Wilkinson, Henry	Cass co	July 22	Captured on gunboat "Fanny"; must'd out
Wayrick, John A	Cass co	July 22	Mustered out July 29, '64.
Wayrick, James W	Cass co	July 22	" " " [Reg't, re-org.
Yount, Lewis	Cass co	July 22	Vet'n; wounded at Wilderness; transf'd 20th
Recruits.			
Bliss, William C	Cass co	Mar. 25, '64	Woun'd, Wilderness; transf'd 20th Reg't, re-
Bliss, Henry H	Cass co	Feb. 20, '64	[organized.
Grant, William	Cass co		Veteran.
Hoffman, Mathias	Jefferson co	Sept. 15, '62	Killed at Gettysburg.
Jones, Thomas	Cass co	Mar. 30, '64	Transferred to 20th Regiment, re-organized.
Lambkin, Christian	Cass co	Mar. 20, '64	" " "
Mason, John S	Cass co		Veteran.
Morway, Lewis	Cass co	Aug. 25, '62	Transferred to 20th Regiment, re-organized.
Morarity, Eugene	Cass co	Mar. 23, '64	Woun'd, Wilderness; transf'd 20th Reg't, re-
Murphy, Patrick	Cass co	Dec. 25, '63	[organized.
Noland, Israel	Cass co	Nov. 23, '63	
Skinner, Ira H	Cass co	Sept. 15, '62	
Wilkinson, Henry C	Cass co	Oct. 20, '62	Transferred to 20th Regiment, re-organized.
Washburn, Eli P	Cass co	Nov. 23, '63	" " "
Weyand, George W	Cass co	Nov. 23, '63	" " "
Welsh, Clay			Killed at Fredericksburg Dec. 15, '62.
Walters, Eli	Cass co	Sept. 15, '62	

ENLISTED MEN OF COMPANY "G."

NAME AND RANK.	Residence.	Date of Muster. 1861.	REMARKS.
First Sergeant.			
Taylor, Robert H	Cordova, Ill	July 22	Promoted 2d Lieutenant.
Sergeants.			
McCurdy, Archibald	Tippecanoe co	July 22	
Castater, Andrew J	Tippecanoe co	July 22	
Bartholomew, Steph. E.	Lafayette	July 22	Promoted 2d Lieutenant.
Pruitt, William H. H.	Tippecanoe co	July 22	Veteran; transf'd to 20th Reg't. re-organized.
Corporals.			
Quigley, Henry	Lafayette	July 22	Promoted 1st Lieutenant.
McCarty, Reuben	Tippecanoe co	July 22	Mustered out July 29, '64, as private.
Ensey, Isaac V. C	Lafayette	July 22	Promoted 2d Lieutenant.
Railing, Joseph R	Tippecanoe co	July 22	
Hungerford, Courtl'd L	Tippecanoe co	July 22	
Castater, John H	Tippecanoe co	July 22	
Burdett, Leander	Tippecanoe co	July 22	Veteran.
Mulford, William S	Tippecanoe co	July 22	
Musicians.			
Glick, Monroe B	Tippecanoe co	July 22	
Newton, Norman	Tippecanoe co	July 22	
Wagoner.			
Neville, Isaac H	Tippecanoe co	July 22	
Privates.			
Alexander, George B	Tippecanoe co	July 22	
Bailey, John W	Tippecanoe co	July 22	['64, as Corporal.
Baker, Marion	Tippecanoe co	July 22	Wounded at Laurel Hill; must'd out July 29,
Beker, Henry	Tippecanoe co	July 22	Mustered out July 29, '64.
Boen, Perry	Tippecanoe co	July 22	Veteran; transf'd to 20th Reg't, re-organized.
Bodwell, Edwin C	Tippecanoe co	July 22	
Bonebrake, George	Tippecanoe co	July 22	
Branham, Vernon	Tippecanoe co	July 22	Veteran; transf'd to 20th Reg't, re-organized.
Brashares, Hiram C	Tippecanoe co	July 22	
Brown, Solomon	Tippecanoe co	July 22	[20th Reg't, re-organized.
Brown, Thomas	Tippecanoe co	July 22	Veteran; wounded at Petersburg; transf'd to
Bryan, James M	Tippecanoe co	July 22	
Buck, Robert	Tippecanoe co	July 22	
Bulla, Levi D	Tippecanoe co	July 22	Wounded, Spottsylv'a; must'd out July 29, '64.
Burdsall, William H	Tippecanoe co	July 22	Des'd; charge of desert'n removed Mar. 25, '64.

INDIANA VOLUNTEERS.

Name and Rank.	Residence.	Date of Muster. 1861.	Remarks.
Campbell, Thomas N....	Tippecanoe co...	July 22.....	Veteran; transferred to 29th Reg't, re-org.
Chapman, William A...	Tippecanoe co...	July 22.....	" " " " "
Chestnut, Venilar M.....	Tippecanoe co...	July 22.....	
Cox, Edward................	Tippecanoe co...	July 22.....	[prison, July 1, '62.
Creek, Albert................	Tippecanoe co...	July 22.....	Captured at Chickahominy; died, Richmond
Cunningham, George B	Tippecanoe co...	July 22.....	
Cuppy, George W.........	Tippecanoe co...	July 22.....	Mustered out July 29, '64.
Curtis, Andrew G.........	Tippecanoe co...	July 22.....	" " "
Davison, David............	Tippecanoe co...	July 22.....	
Dazey, John................	Tippecanoe co...	July 22.....	Veteran; transferred to 20th Reg't, re·org.
Dey, Richard D............	Tippecanoe co...	July 22.....	
Dill, William H............	Tippecanoe co...	July 22.....	Veteran; transferred to 20th Reg't, re-org.
Dwinney, Cyrennus......	Tippecanoe co...	July 22.....	
Dixon, James................	Tippecanoe co...	July 22.....	Absent since June 29, '62; supposed deserter.
Downing, Francis A.....	Tippecanoe co...	July 22.....	
Driskill, Dennis...........	Tippecanoe co...	July 22.....	
Dugan, John D.............	Tippecanoe co...	July 22.....	Captured; mustered out July 29, '64.
Eldridge, Henry J........	Tippecanoe co...	July 22.....	Died.
Emory, William W......	Tippecanoe co...	July 22.....	Vet'n; transf'd to 29th Reg't, re-organized.
Fitzpatrick, Walter.....	Tippecanoe co...	July 22.....	Wounded, Gettysburg; must'd out July 29,'64.
Flanagan, Martin.........	Tippecanoe co...	July 22.....	
Foster, Richard T........	Tippecanoe co...	July 22.....	
Fast, Thomas B............	Tippecanoe co...	July 22.....	
French, Edward C.......	Tippecanoe co...	July 22.....	[out May 22, '65.
Gross, Charles M..........	Tippecanoe co...	July 22.....	Captured at Chicomicomico Island; mustered
Hall, Peter..................	Tippecanoe co...	July 22.....	
Hampton, James M.....	Tippecanoe c0...	July 22.....	
Harnden, John.............	Tippeзanoe co...	July 22.....	Mustered out July 29, '64.
Haun, Isaac................	Tippecanoe co...	July 22.....	Mustered out July 29, '64, as Sergeant.
Himiller, Daniel...........	Tippecanoe co...	July 22.....	
Huey, William H.........	Tippecanoe co...	July 22.....	
Hughes, George W.......	Tippecanoe co...	July 22.....	
Hunter, Joseph O.........	Tippecanoe co...	July 22.....	Vet'n; transf'd to 20th Reg't, re-organized.
Hutton, Seymour.........	Tippecanoe co...	July 22.....	Mustered out July 29, '64.
Jett, Henry..................	Tippecanoe co...	July 22.....	
Johnson, William.........	Tippecanoe co...	July 22.....	Wounded at Mine Run; must'd out July 29,'64.
Kennedy, James H......	Tippecanoe co...	July 22.....	
Kidney, George W........	Tippecanoe co...	July 22.....	
Largent, William.........	Tippecanoe co...	July 22.....	Vet'n; transf'd to 20th Reg't, re-organized.
McCowen, Cory E........	Tippecanoe co...	July 22.....	
McKee, Robert C.........	Tippecanoe co...	July 22.....	
McPherson, Alexander	Tippecanoe co...	July 22.....	
Moffatt, Joab..............	Tippecanoe co...	July 22.....	
Nierbury, Nicholas	Tippecanoe co...	July 22.....	
Parker, Francis M......	Tippecanoe co...	July 22.....	
Park, James................	Tippecanoe co...	July 22.....	Vet'n; transf'd to 20th Reg't, re-organized.
Pauley, John W...........	Tippecanoe co...	July 22.....	" " " " "
Penrod, Allen..............	Tippecanoe co...	July 22.....	
Peterson, Andrew J......	Tippeconoe co...	July 22.....	Capt'd; must'd out July 29, '64.
Peterson, George W.....	Tippecanoe co...	July 22.....	Vet'n; transf'd to 20th Reg't, re-organized.
Printy, Thomas............	Tippecanoe co...	July 22.....	
Rooker, William M......	Tippecanoe co...	July 22.....	
Rion, John N...............	Tippecanoe co...	July 22.....	
St. Clair, James M........	Tippecanoe co...	July 22.....	
Simeon, John J............	Tippecanoe co...	July 22.....	
Smith, Nathaniel C......	Tippecanoe co...	July 22.....	
Stringer, George W......	Tippecanoe co...	July 22.....	
Sweeney, William........	Tippecanoe co...	July 22.....	Vet'n; transf'd to 20th Reg't, re-organized.
Taylor, David..............	Tippecanoe co...	July 22.....	Veteran.
Thacker, William R......	Tippecanoe co...	July 22.....	
Thayer, Nicholas.........	Tippecanoe co...	July 22.....	
Thompson, William D...	Tippecanoe co...	July 22.....	Veteran; promoted 1st Lieutenant.
Webb, James A............	Tippecanoe co...	July 22.....	
Wiles, William P.........	Tippecanoe co...	July 22.....	Wounded, Wilderness.
Woodham, Herbert C...	Tippecanoe co...	July 22.....	
Young, Andrew S........	Tippecanoe co...	July 22.....	Wounded, Mine Run; must'd out July 29, '64.
Zuercher, Conrad.........	Tippecanoe co...	July 22.....	
Recruits.			
Alexander, Emory B....	Tippecanoe co...	....	Veteran.
Arnett, William...........	Tippecanoe co...	Aug. 12, '62	Transferred to 20th Regiment, re-organized.
Arnold, John H............	Tippecanoe co...	Dec. 26, '63..	" " " "
Ashby, Daniel..............	Tippecanoe co...	Aug. 22, '62	" " " "
Alred, Garrison............	Tippecanoe co...	Aug. 22, '62	
Armstrong, William H	Tippecanoe co...	Nov. 17, '63	
Bennett, John..............	Tippecanoe co...	Aug. 22, '62	
Bury, James C..............	Tippecanoe co...	Aug. 22, '62	
Beeher, John................	Tippecanoe co...	Aug. 22, '62	
Barnes, Horatio W.......	Tippecanoe co...	Aug. 22, '62	
Bunch, James M..........	Tippecanoe co...	Aug. 22, '62	[Regiment, re-organized.
Bonebrake, John C.......	Tippecanoe co...	Mar. 14, '64	Wounded at Petersburg; transferred to 20th

Name and Rank.	Residence.	Date of Muster. 1861.	Remarks
Bryant, Orin P	Tippecanoe co...	Mar. 14, '64	W'ded at Spotts'ia, tr'fd 20th Regt. re-org.
Bowen, William H		Aug. 11, '62	W'ded at N. Anna, tr'fd 20th Regt. re-org.
Creese, James	Tippecanoe co...	Sept. 5, '62..	
Campbell, Patrick	Cass co	Sept. 15, '62	Transf'd to 20th Regt. re-org.
Cullen, Peter H		Dec. 16, '62.	" " "
Campbell, Morris	Cass co	Aug. 25, '62	" " "
Clute, James P	Tippecanoe co...	Aug. 11, '62	" " "
Cavanaugh, James	Tippecanoe co...	Dec. 22, '63.	" " "
Crock, Thomas	Tippecanoe co...	Nov. 13, '63	
Davidson, Samuel W...	Tippecanoe co...	Sept. 5, '62..	
Fultz, John W		Oct. 31, '62..	Transferred to 20th Regt. re-organized.
Fultz, Cyrus	Cass co	Dec. 25, '63.	W'ded Spotts'ia ; tr'fd 20th Regt. re-org.
Fritz, Augustus		Oct. 21, '62..	Miss'g in act'n June 1,'64; t'fd 20th Reg. re-org
Ferguson, Howell	Tippecanoe co...	Aug. 22, '62	W'ded wild'nss, tr'fd 20th Regt. re-org.
Faulkner, Joseph	Tippecanoe co...	Aug. 22, '62	
Grant, Lewis			Vet'n tr'fd to 20th Regt. re-organized.
Gunning, Barney	Tippecanoe co...	Dec. 29, '63.	Transferred to 20th Regt. re-organized.
Hammel, Jeremiah	Tippecanoe co...	Aug. 11, '62	W'ded Petersburg ; transf'd 20th Regt. re-org.
Homan, Charles W...	Tippecanoe co...	Jan. 5, '64...	Transferred to 20th Regt. re-organized.
Hicks, Jacob	Tippecanoe co...	Dec. 7, '63...	W'ded Wilderness transf'd 20th Regt. re-org.
Hickman, Lewis	Tippecanoe co...	Aug. 22, '62	" " " "
Hartman, Samuel	Tippecanoe co...	Aug. 22, '62	
Jett, John	Tippecanoe co...	Nov. 11, '63	Transf'd to 20th Regt. re-organized.
Julian, Evan	Tippecanoe co...	Aug. 22, '62	
Jones, Chauncey	Tippecanoe co...	Aug. 22, '62	
Jones, George A	Tippecanoe co...	Aug. 22, '62	
Kirk, Jonathan C	Marshall co	Oct. 21, '62..	W'ded Petersburg, tr'fd to 20th Regt. re-org.
Kauffman, Jacob C	Marshall co	Sept. 24, '62	Transferred to 20th Regt. re-organized.
Kieker, Frederick C	Jefferson co	Sept. 15, '62	" " "
Keiker, August	Jefferson co	Sept. 15, '62	Transferred to 20th Regt. re-org.
Lynch, Michael			Killed at Gettysburg.
Olds, William W	Tippecanoe co...	Dec. 22, '63.	Transferred to 20th Regt. re-org.
Pauley, Lenias	Tippecanoe co...	April 16; '64	" " "
Peurad, Levi	Tippecanoe co...	Aug. 22, '62	
Quigley, William	Tippecanoe co...	Aug. 27, '62	Transferred to 20th Regt. re-org.
Rolley, William	Boone co	Dec. 11, '63.	" " "
Sexton, Joseph C	Tippecanoe co...	Aug. 15, '62	" " "
Shaw, Isaiah J	Tippecanoe co...	Aug. 12, '62	" " "
Sweeny, Charles	Tippecanoe co...	April 2, '64.	" " "
Stanley, Charles I	Tippecanoe co...	Dec. 21, '63.	W'ded Wilderness; tr'fd 20th Regt re-org.
Staff, Henry		July 22, '61.	Transferred to 20th Regt. re-organized.
Shaut, John	Tippecanoe co...	Aug. 22, '62	
Stephenson, Perry	Tippecanoe co...	Aug. 22, '62	
Songer, Andrew	Tippecanoe co...	Sept. 24, '62	
Stone, Charles	Tippecanoe co...	Dec. 22, '63.	
Thompson, George	Tippecanoe co...	Dec. 22, '63.	W'ded Spotts'ia, tr'fd 20th Regt. re-organized.
Thompson, Charles E		Sept. 14, '63	Transferred to 20th Regt re-organized.
Toomar, Richard	Tippecanoe co...	Aug. 22, '62	
Vaughn, James J	Tippecanoe co...	Aug. 22, '62	
Van Alst, William	Tippecanoe co...	Aug. 22, '62	
Wolf, Philip	Tippecanoe co...	Aug. 11, '62	Transferred to 20th Regt. re-organized.

ENLISTED MEN OF COMPANY "H."

Names and Rank.	Residence.	Date of Muster. 1861.	Remarks.
First Sergeant.			
Geisendorff, Fred. W	Marion co	July 22	Promoted 2d Lieutenant.
Sergeants.			
Kemper, John W	Marion co	July 22	App'd 1st Sergt; disch'd Dec. —,'62; disability.
Davis, Moses	Marion co	July 22	Discharged Aug. —, '62.
Liner, Charles	Marion co	July 22	Promoted 2d Lieutenant.
Geisendorff, Harry	Indianapolis	July 22	Promoted 2d Lieutenant.
Corporals.			
Crunkleton, Joseph	Marion co	July 22	Discharged Dec. —, '61; disability.
Meek, James C	Marion co	July 22	Capt'd on gun boat Fanny; discn'd May 22,'62.
Dickenson, William	Indianapolis	July 22	Vet; prom'd 2d Lieut. died in pris'n, Wil'gton
Ellsworth, Andrew	Marion co	July 22	Dis; w'ds rec'd, Orchards. [N. C. July —,'64.
Springer, David	Marion co	July 22	Transf'd to Invalid Corps. —, '62; disch'd July
Archer, William	Marion co	July 22	Vet; killed at Spotsylvania. [22, '64.
Hiner, William	Marion co	July 22	Wounded at Mine Run.
Kelley, John	Marion co	July 22	Mustered out July —, '65.

Name and Rank.	Residence.	Date of Muster. 1861.	Remarks.
Musicians.			
Sackett, Frederick P.	Marion co	July 22	Capt'd, Gunb't "Fanny;" disch'gd May 22,'62.
Andrews, John	Marion co	July 22	" " "
Wagoner.			
Tull, Newton	Marion co	July 22	Died, Alexandria, Va., Aug., '62.
Privates.			
Allen, Henry C	Marion co	July 22	Discharged, disability.
Allen, John	Marion co	July 22	Discharged, Dec., '61; disability.
Allen, William	Marion co	July 22	Discharged, Aug., '62; disability.
Anderson, John	Marion co	July 22	Mustered out July 29, '64.
Bassett, Harvey	Marion co	July 22	W'd, Chickah'ny, Je. 25,'62; died, Rich'd pr'n,
Baylor, James	Marion co	July 22	Deserted, Aug. 29,'62. [July 3,'63.
Beaver, Isaac	Marion co	July 22	Capt'd, Mine Run; must'd out Feb. 9, '65.
Bennett, Lucias L	Marion co	July 22	Captured, Oct., '61.
Black, Edward A	Marion co	July 22	Killed, Gettysburg, July 4, '63.
Briner, Daniel L	Marion co	July 22	Killed, Spottsylvania, Va.
Bushnell, Franklin	Marion co	July 22	Discharged, on account of wounds.
Cassell, George W	Marion co	July 22	Discharged, Dec., '61; disability.
Caywood, Samuel	Marion co	July 22	Transferred Invalid Corps.
Chriswell, Thomas	Marion co	July 22	Killed Gettysburg.
Clayton, James	Marion co	July 22	Capt'd, Chicomicomico Is.; disch'd May 22,'62.
Clow, David	Marion co	July 22	Vet'n; des'td, April, '64; ret'd, Oct.,'64; must'd
Cooper, Ephraim	Marion co	July 22	Discharged, '62. [out July, '65.
Cottrell, David	Marion co	July 22	Veteran; transf. 20th Reg't, re-organized.
Craner, Eli	Marion co	July 22	" " "
Custer, James	Marion co	July 22	Died, Newport News, April, '62. [re-org.
Dennis, Irvin	Marion co	July 22	Veteran; w'd, Sept. 10, '64; trans,. 20th Reg't,
Dickey, John	Marion co	July 22	Veteran; transf. 20th Regiment, re-org.
Fagen, Lambert	Marion co	July 22	Killed, Battle Orchards, June 25, '62.
Finley, James	Marion co	July 22	Veteran; transf. 20th Regiment, re-org.
Ford, James A	Marion co	July 22	Veteran; mustered out July, '65.
Frizell, Allen	Marion co	July 22	App'd Drum Maj.; must'd out Oct., '64.
Gamble, Henry	Marion co	July 22	Died, Cockeysville, Md., Aug., '61.
Gardner, James	Marion co	July 22	Mustered out July 22, '64.
Geek, Michael	Marion co	July 22	Mustered out July 29, '64.
Hagen, Samuel	Marion co	July 22	Killed, Gettysburg, July 2, '63.
Harris, Charles	Marion co	July 22	Disch'gd, on acc't wounds rec'd Gettysburg.
Hays, Abram	Marion co	July 22	Discharged, Dec., '61.
Hill, Samuel	Marion co	July 22	Mustered out July 29, '64.
Hulburt, George	Marion co	July 22	Veteran; transf. 20th Regiment, re-org.
Hufman, John	Marion co	July 22	Killed, Battle Orchards, June 25, '62.
Irick, Daniel	Marion co	July 22	Discharged, Dec., '61; disability.
Irick, Morris	Marion co	July 22	Discharged, on acc't w'ds rec'd Fredericksb'g.
Iholtz, Christopher	Marion co	July 22	Mustered out July 29, '64.
James, Jacob	Marion co	July 22	Veteran; died Petersburg.
Jenkins, William	Marion co	July 22	Veteran; transf. 20th Regiment, re-org.
King, James	Marion co	July 22	Deserted, Falmouth, Va., Nov., '62.
Kurtz, Frederick	Marion co	July 2?	Mustered out July 29, '64.
Lang, Fredrick	Marion co	July 22	Discharged, Sept., '62; disability.
Lawrence, Frank	Marion co	July 22	Killed, Wilderness.
Leffel, George	Marion co	July 22	Discharged, on account of wounds.
Lewis, Joshua	Marion co	July 22	Discharged, Aug., '62; disability.
Long, Noah	Marion co	July 22	Discharged.
Miller, Nelson	Marion co	July 22	Veteran; transf. 20th Regiment, re-org.
Mourer, Michael	Marion co	July 22	" " "
Monter, Lewis	Marion co	July 22	W'd, Oct. 29, '63; must'd out July 29, '64.
Ohaver, Warren	Marion co	July 22	Disch'gd, Dec., '61; disability. [May 19,'62.
Oxford, Elias	Marion co	July 22	Capt'd on Gunb't "Fanny;" died, Wash'gt'n,
Piersons, Frank B	Marion co	July 22	Capt'd on gunb't "Fanny;" disch'gd May 22,
Powers, Michael	Marion co	July 22	Mustered out July 29, '64. ['62.
Rance, Albert	Marion co	July 22	Wounded, Spottsylvania.
Robinson, Solomon B	Marion co	July 22	Deserted, Aug., '61.
Ruh, William	Marion co	July 22	Discharged, disability.
Rule, James M	Marion co	July 22	Veteran; transf. 20th Regiment, re-org.
Russell, William P	Marion co	July 22	Killed, in front of Richmond, Va., Je. 29, '62.
Serach, Christian	Marion co	July 22	C'pd, Chicomicomico Is.; disch'd May 22, '62.
Shallenberger, Benton	Marion co	July 22	Disch'gd, on acc't w'ds rec'd Battle Orchards.
Sharp, Colonel P	Marion co	July 22	Veteran; transf. 20th Regiment, re-org.
Shoaf, Jacob	Marion co	July 22	Capt'd, Chicomicomico Isl'd; discharged May
Shur, Christian	Marion co	July 22	Mustered out July 29, '64. [22,'62.
Simpson, Richard	Marion co	July 22	Deserted, Aug., '61.
Simpson, William	Marion co	July 22	Deserted, Sept., '61.
Smith, Samuel S	Mrrion co	July 22	Deserted, July, '61.
Smith, Edward C	Marion co	July 22	Died, Alexandria, Va., '63.
Steavens, David	Marion co	July 22	Capt'd, Fredericksb'g; not since heard from
Stockwell, Robert	Marion co	July 22	Died, Harrison's Landing, Aug. 9, '62.
Sweet, Nelson	Marion co	July 22	Killed, Battle Orchards, June 25, '62.
Talbertt, Overton	Marion co	July 22	Discharged, Dec., '61; disability.
Templin, George W	Marion co	July 22	Wounded, Greendale, Va.

NAME AND RANK.	Residence.	Date of Muster. 1861.	REMARKS.
Ten Eyck, John............	Marion co........	July 22.......	Mustered out July 29, '64.
Thompson, William......	Marion co.........	July 22.......	Discharged ——, '62; disability.
Tilbason, John.............	Marion co.........	July 22.......	Died June 25, '62; wounds.
Tristy, Miles...............	Marion co.........	July 22.......	Captured at Gettysburg.
Vanhorn, Abraham.......	Marion co.........	July 22.......	
Whealan, Timothy.......	Marion co.........	July 22.......	Deserted at Cockeysville, Md., Sept. —, '61.
White, Charles H........	Marion co.........	July 22.......	Drowned Oct. —, '61, attempting to escape
Wilson, Robert............	Marion co.........	July 22.......	Transf'd to Co. "A." [from Hatteras Island.
Windle, William..........	Marion co.........	July 22.......	Captured on gunboat "Fanny"; disch'd May [22, '62.
Recruits.			
Ambrose, Harrison......	Sommersett	Sept. 26, '61	Died Sept. —,'63, wounds rec'd at Gettysburg.
Angevine, Edward G....	Marion co.........	Sept. 26, '61	Deserted at Washington, D. C., March 5, '64.
Atkins, William A.......	Marion co.........	Oct. 21, '62..	Transferred to 20th Regiment, re-organized.
Broderick, John...........	Marion co.........	April 1, '64..	" " "
Barbour, Calvin S........	Marion co.........	Oct. 22, '62..	" " "
Brewer, John...............			Discharged; disability.
Beach, Henry...............	Marion co.........	Aug. 28, '62	
Breneshaltz, Sylvester..	Marion co.........	Oct. 27, '62..	
Clouse, Joseph H........	Marion co.........	Oct. 21, '62..	Transferred to 20th Regiment, re.organized.
Cloidt, Joseph.............	Marion co.........	Oct. 21, '62..	Wounded Wild'ss; transf'd 20th Regt, re-org.
Cain, Hyatt.................	Marion co.........	April 12, '64	Transferred to 20th Regiment, re-organized.
Chainey, William B......		Sept. 26, '61	Died at Falmouth, Va., March —, '63.
Coppeck, John.............		April —, '64	Killed at Spottsylvania.
Duncan, Robert............	Bradford..........	Feb. —, '62..	Killed at Cold Harbor, Va., May 22, '64.
Davis, Jeremiah...........		Sept. 26, '64	Killed at Gettysburg.
Eaton, John N.............	Marion co.........	April 12, '64	Transferred to 20th Regiment, re-organized.
Fuller, Morris..............	Marion co.........	Aug. 28, '62	
Frazier, James.............	Vermillion co...	Feb. —, '62..	Transferred to Co. "B."
Furgison, John.............	Marion co.........	Oct. 21, '62..	Transferred to 20th Regiment, re-organized.
Gordonier, Edwin J......	Marion co.........	Oct. 21, '62..	" " "
Gardner, Mathew.........	Marion co.........	Mar. 12, '64	Wounded, Battle Orchards; disch'd; disability.
Gardner, Jerome..........	Marion co.........	Oct. 21, '62..	
Hurlburt, George W.....	Marion co.........		Veteran.
Hutchens, Thomas E....	Marion co.........	Oct. 28, '62..	Transferred to 20th Regiment, re-organized.
Haushorn, James..........		Oct. 11, '61..	Discharged; wounds.
Harris, Simon..............		Nov. 6, '62..	Killed at Gettysburg.
Heckler, Frederick.......		Sept. 26, '61	Deserted at Poolsville, Md., Oct. —, '62.
Hunt, William.............		April —, '64	Mustered out July —, '65.
Hooker, E. M. B..........	Marion co.........	Sept. 26, '61	Appointed Sergeant Major.
Homer, Bazil...............	Marion co.........	Aug. 28, '62	
Johnson, Hiram...........		Sept. 26, '61	Killed at Orange Grove, Va., Nov. 30, '63.
King, William A..........	Marion co.........	Oct. 21, '62..	
Karad, Joseph..............	Marion co.........	Oct. 21, '62..	
Lee, John C.................	Marion co.........	Oct. 17, '63..	Died at Richmond, Va.
Lewis, B. L.................	Bradford..........	Oct. 24, '62..	Discharged; wounds.
Lowder, Martin............			Discharged Feb. 25, '62.
Lang, Fritz..................	Marion co.........	Oct. 21, '62..	Transferred to 20th Regiment, re-organized.
Lacox, William............	Marion co.........	Oct. 16, '62..	Wounded Oct. 1, '64; transf'd 20th Reg't, re-
Meek, Irvin D..............	Marion co.........	April 12, '64	Disch'd June 13, '65; disability. [organized.
Miller, Frederick..........	South Bend......	Feb. 24, '62..	Veteran; wounded, Spottsylvania; must'd out.
Miller, Jacob S............	Marion co.........	Feb. 24, '62..	Wounded, Petersburg; transf'd to 20th Reg't
McKown, William........		Sept. 26, '61	Discharged; disability. [re-organized.
Morse, James H...........	Lafayette	Feb. 24, '62..	Wounded, Spottsylv'a; must'd out July —,'65.
Moore, Harrison..........	Marion co.........	Nov. 5, '62..	
McCollough, Jefferson..		Feb. 24, '62..	Died at Portsmouth, Va., Aug. —,'62.
Noland, James H..........	Marion co.........	Oct. 21, '62..	Transferred to 20th Regiment, re-organized.
Orr, James P...............	Monticello	Feb. 24, '62..	Wounded at Po River, Va.; transf'd V. R. C.;
Olinger, Henry E.........	Marion co.........	Aug. 28, '62	[must'd out July 15, '65.
Pritchard, Ephraim.......		Oct. 4, '61...	Discharged; disability.
Piper, Levi.................	Marion co.........	Mar. 12, '62	[Reg't, re-organized.
Potts, Peter H..............	Marion co.........	Dec. 23, '63..	Wounded at Spottsylvania; transf'd to 20th
Piper, Lewis...............	Marion co.........	Mar. 12, '62	Transf'd 20th Reg't, re-organized. [re-org.
Rantz, Robert..............	Marion co.........		Vet'n; woun'd, Wild'ness; transf'd 20th Reg't,
Rantz, Charles E..........	Marion co.........	April 12, '64	Transferred to 20th Regiment, re-organized.
Rantz, Calvin J............	Marion co.........	April 12, '64	" " "
Rugg, Noah.................	Sommersett	Oct. 4, '61...	Captured at Glen Dale, Va.; not since heard
Richmond, Robert J.....	Marion co.........	Aug. 28, '62	[from.
Sparks, John...............	Marion co.........	Aug. 26, '62	Transf'd to 20th Reg't, re-organized. [org.
Sparks, Lyman E..........	Marion co.........	Oct. 21, '62..	Woun'd, Wilderness; transf'd 20th Reg't, re-
Sharpe, Henry.............	Marion co.........	Feb. 12, '62..	Discharged; disability.
Sharpe, William...........	Marion co.........	Feb. 28, '62..	" " "
Souther, Jacob............		Aug. —, '62	" " "
Simes, William............		Oct. 4, '61...	" " "
Sharpe, George...........	Marion co.........	Feb. 28, '62..	
Strode, George W........	Marion co.........	Oct. 21, '62..	
Shelton, Jonathan.........	Marion co.........	Nov. 5, '62..	
Winch, Frederick.........	Marion co.........	July 22, '61..	Transferred to Co. "F."
Walters, Solomon.........	Marion co.........	Aug. 28, '62	
Wilson, Moses............	Marion co.........	Aug. 28, '62	
Wilkey, Benjamin F.....	Marion co.........	Aug. 28, '62	

NAME AND RANK.	Residence.	Date of Muster. 1861.	REMARKS.
Weiper, Richard J..	Marion co.........	Aug. 28, '62	
Walters, Levi...............	Marion co.........	Oct. 4. '61...	Vet.; killed, Wilderness, May 5, '64.
Walters, John...............	Marion co.........	Oct. 4, '61...	Vet.; mustered out July —, '65.
Wilmot, Horace...........	Marion co.........	Feb. 18, '63..	Transferred 20th Regt, re-organized.
White, William H.......	Marion co.........	Oct. 2, '62...	W'd Nov. 2, '63; trans. 20th Regt. re-org.
Wyatt, William E.......	Marion co.........	Oct. 13, '62..	Transferred 20th Regt, re-organized.
Wooley Charles............	Marion co.........	Oct. 21, '62..	Vet.; transferred 20th Regt, re-organized.
Younkin, Michael.........	Marion co.........		" " " "
Younkin, Christopher...	Marion co.........		

ENLISTED MEN OF COMPANY "I."

NAME AND RANK.	Residence.	Date of Muster. 1861.	REMARKS.
First Sergeant.			
Corey, Lorenzo D...........	Valparaiso	July 22........	Promoted 2d Lieutenant.
Sergeants.			
Fluhart, Edwin W........	Porter co.........	July 22......	
Johnston, Hiram B.......	Porter co.........	July 22......	
Bartlett, Theodore M....	Porter co.........	July 22......	
De Motte, Charles W.....	Porter co.........	July 22......	Cap'd, Chicomicomico Isl'd; disch'd May 22,'62
Corporals.			
Baker, Isaac.................	Porter co.........	July 22......	
Kitchell, David.............	Porter co.........	July 22......	Vet.; transf'd 20th Reg't, re-organized.
Robinson, William H....	Porter co.........	July 22......	
Brown, Charles C.........	Porter co.........	July 22......	Vet.; transf'd 20th Reg't, re-organized.
Ball, Charles C. H.........	Porter co.........	July 22......	" " " "
Brown, Elmer H...........	Porter co.........	July 22......	
Reeves, William H........	Porter co.........	July 22......	Vet.; transf'd 20th Reg't, re-organized.
Cannover, Vorhees........	Porter co.........	July 22......	
Musicians.			
Johnston, Edwin B.......	Porter co.........	July 22......	Mustered out July 29, '64.
Shores, Eugene..............	Porter co.........	July 22......	Vet., transf'd 20th Reg't, re-organized.
Wagoner.			
Hart, William D...........	Porter co.........	July 22......	Vet.; transf'd 20th Reg't, re-organized.
Privates.			
Babbit, William H........	Porter co.........	July 22......	
Baum, Napoleon...........	Porter co.........	July 22......	Capt'd on gun boat "Fanny;" dis. May 22,'62.
Benhart, George..	Porter co.........	July 22......	
Bernhart, Paul..............	Porter co.........	July 22......	Cap'd, Chicomicomico Isl'd; disch'd May 22,'62.
Beringer, John..............	Porter co.........	July 22......	" " " " " "
Bays, John...................	Porter co.........	July 22......	Mustered out July 29, '64, as absent sick.
Bowen, Jonathan...........	Porter co.........	July 22......	[mustered out May 10, '65.
Bowen, John D.............	Porter co.........	July 22......	Deserted, Rappahannock Station, Jan. 26, '63;
Budd, William...............	Porter co.........	July 22......	Veteran.
Carlin, Elza..................	Porter co.........	July 22......	Vet.; transf'd 20th Reg't, re-organized.
Conner, James T...........	Porter co.........	July 22......	
Corbin, Martin.............	Porter co.........	July 22......	
Cooley John W.............	Porter co.........	July 22......	
Cox, Reuben H..............	Porter co.........	July 22......	
Cox, Joseph.................	Porter co.........	July 22......	Mustered out July 29, '64, as Corp.
Cromer, James R..........	Porter co.........	July 22......	Wounded at Fredericksburg.
Drury, John.................	Porter co.........	July 22......	Cap'd, Chicomicomico Isl'd; disch'd May22,'62.
Dumphrey, Nicholas.....	Porter co.........	July 22......	Wounded June 25, '62.
Dunham, Luther S........	Porter co.........	July 22......	Mustered out July 29, '64.
Dunham, Henry............	Porter co.........	July 22......	
Ferguson, Sylvester E...	Porter co.........	July 22......	
Fielman, Frederick......	Porter co.........	July 22......	
French, Alpheus C........	Porter co.........	July 22......	Veteran.
Freeman, John W.........	Porter co.........	July 22......	Vet.; transf'd 20th Reg't, re-organized.
Gouldsbury, Jonathan..	Porter co.........	July 22......	
Gouldsbury, William....	Porter co.........	July 22......	
Gray, James J..............	Porter co.........	July 22......	
Hankins, Albert...........	Porter co.........	July 22......	Vet.; transf'd 20th Reg't, re-organized.
Haun, John.................	Porter co.........	July 22......	
Harrold, William.........	Porter co.........	July 22......	
Hettmansperger F. R...	Porter co.........	July 22,......	
Hughs, Joseph..............	Porter co.........	July 22......	
Hyde, Hiram................	Porter co.........	July 22......	Capt'd on gunboat"Fanny;"disch'd May22,'62.
Kitchen, Mathews........	Porcer co.........	July 22......	
Kopp, Louis.................	Porter co.........	July 22......	Wounded at Petersburg; transf'd 20th Reg't.

NAME AND RANK.	Residence.	Date of Muster. 1861.	REMARKS.
Lewis, James	Porter co	July 22	
Lynch, James	Porter co	July 22	
Mangon, James	Porter co	July 22	
Mathews, James G. D	Porter co	July 22	
McCarty Charles	Porter co	July 22	
Millard, Varnham W	Porter co	July 22	Veteran; transferred to 20th Regiment.
Montgomery, SeymourT	Porter co	July 22	Appointed Hospital Steward; veteran.
Moore, William H	Porter co	July 22	Mustered out July 29, '64.
Morehouse, Homer	Porter co	July 22	
Morris, Edwin D	Porter co	July 22	['62.
Muster, John	Porter co	July 22	Capt'd on gunboat " Fanny;" disch'd May 22,
Myers, Daniel H	Porter co	July 22	
Osborn, Francis A	Porter co	July 22	Discharged Aug. 13, '62.
Pullins, William	Porter co	July 22	
Pursall, Henry	Porter co	July 22	Capt'd Chicomocomico Isl.; disch'd May 22,'62.
Quinn, James L	Porter co	July 22	Mustered out July 29, '64.
Ragan, Joseph H	Porter co	July 22	
Rice, Jacob	Porter co	July 22	Veteran; transferred to 20th Reg't, re-org'd.
Rowland, Isaac D	Porter co	July 22	
Ruchong, James	Porter co	July 22	
Rust, John E	Porter co	July 22	Veteran; transferred to 20th Reg't, re-org'd.
Rustling, Richard	Porter co	July 22	
Shaffer, John	Porter co	July 22	Died, Washington, Dec. 7, '62.
Shanning, John	Porter co	July 22	
Sillman, Stephen	Porter co	July 22	Veteran.
Sleight, Charles H	Porter co	July 22	
Smith, John	Porter co	July 22	
Stevens, William W	Porter co	July 22	Promoted 2d Lieutenant.
Stoddard, Robert	Porter co	July 22	Veteran. ['62.
Sparks, John	Porter co	July 22	Capt'd on gunboat " Fanny;" disch'd May 22,
Sutton, John M	Porter co	July 22	
Sutton, Addison P	Porter co	July 22	Veteran; transferred to 20th Reg't, re-org'd.
Swisher, Jackson	Porter co	July 22	
Thompson, Peter	Porter co	July 22	
Torpy, John	Porter co	July 22	Killed Gettysburg.
Turner, James	Porter co	July 22	
Vanderbark, John	Porter co	July 22	Veteran; promoted 2d Lieutenant.
Vanater, Thomas	Porter co	July 22	Veteran; died, Washington, June 6, '64.
Vore, Thomas	Porter co	July 22	Veteran; transferred to 20th Reg't, re-org'd.
Vistal, Lafayette	Porter co	July 22	
Wallace, John	Porter co	July 22	Veteran.
Weaver, Samuel	Porter co	July 22	Veteran; transferred to 20th Reg't, re-org'd.
Wick, Jacob	Porter co	July 22	
Wilson, Stephen C	Porter co	July 22	Veteran; wounded Wilderness; transf'd 20th
Wood, Milton	Porter co	July 22	[Regiment, re-organized.
Wood, Lyman T	Porter co	July 22	Mustered out July 29, '64.
Yates, Jonathan	Porter co	July 22	
Recruits.			
Artist, Harvey	Porter co	Feb. 28, '62	Veteran; transferred to 20th Reg't, re-org'd.
Antrim, Thomas C	Pulaski co	Feb. 28, '62	
Archer, David	Porter co	Mar. 12, '62	
Bousher, Anthony	Porter co	Feb. 28, '62	Veteran; transferred to 20th Reg't, re-org'd.
Beadle, Norris	Porter co	Sept. 25, '62	Transferred to 20th Regiment; re-organized.
Ballard, Henry W	Pulaski co	Mar. 12, '62	
Beebe, William J	Porter co	Mar. 12, '62	
Bauman, John	Porter co	Oct. 21, '62	
Conover, John	Porter co		Veteran. [org'd.
Carman, Charles G	Porter co	Oct. 2, 62	Woun'd Wilderness; transf'd 20th Reg't, re-
Conner, John	Pulaski co	Feb. 10, '64	Transf'd to 20th Regiment, re-organized.
Cook, John H	Porter co	Feb. 28, '62	Killed Gettysburg.
Cloidt, Anton	Porter co	Oct. 21, '62	
Fuller, ——			Killed Chickahominy.
Fuller, William H	Porter co	Mar. 12, '62	
Green, Francis	Porter co	Nov. 25, '63	Transferred to 20th Regiment, re-organized.
Hamilton, Alexander		Aug. 15, '62	" " " "
Huttendoff, Conrad	Jefferson co	Sept. 1, '62	" " " "
Hoffman, John	Jefferson co	Sept. 1, '62	Wou'd Petersb'g; transf'd 20th Reg't, re-org.
Hepp, Antony	Jefferson co	Sept. 1,'61	Wou'd Wild'ness; transf'd 20th Reg't, re-org.
Jones, John		Sept. 1, '62	Capt'd on gunboat " Fanny;" must'd out May.
Johnson, Hiram B		Sept. 1, '62	Transf'd 20th Reg't, re-org'd. [22, '62.
Kruse, Henry	Jefferson co	Sept. 1, '62	Wou'd Wild'ness; transf'd 20th Reg't, re-org'd.
Kitchum, Jerome B	Porter co	Mar. 12, '62	
Locke, Otho	Porter co	Nov. 25, '63	Wou'd Wild'ness; transf'd 20th Reg't, re-org.
Lewis, Lewis B	Porter co	Feb. 28, '62	Veteran; transferred to 20th Reg't, reorg'd.
Livingston, Moses	Porter co	Mar. 12, '62	
Livingston Robert	Porter co	Mar. 12, '62	
Markins, Benjamin F	Pulaski co	Feb. 15, '62	Transferred to 20th Regiment, reorganized.
Moorhouse, John		Aug. 1, '62	
McCay, Fielding		Sept. 1, '62	Won'd Wild'ness; transf'd 20th Reg't, re-org.
McCumsey, John	Porter co	Sept. 1, '62	Veteran; transferred to 20th Reg't, re-org'd.

Name and Rank.	Residence.	Date of Muster. 1861.	Remarks.
Metcalf, Jacob	Pulaski co	Sept. 1, '62.	
Moore, Reuben S	Porter co	Mar. 12, '62.	
McCumsey, Isaac W	Porter co	Sept. 15, '62	Transf'd to V. R. C.; must'd out July 11, '65.
Mount, Nicholas D	Porter co	Sept. 25, '62	
Neron, William	Porter co	Sept. 1, '62	Transf'd to 20th Regiment, re-organized.
Osborn, Charles T	Porter co	Sept. 25,'62	[Reg't, re-organized.
Rogers, Joseph H	Porter co		Vet'n; wounded, Wilderness; transf'd to 20th
Robinson, Michael	Pulaski co	Feb. 18, '62	Wounded, Wilderness; transf'd to 20th Reg't,
Rhu, William	Porter co	Feb. 28, '62.	[re-organized·
Robinson, Edward L	Porter co	Mar. 12, '62	
Robinson, Jacob G	Porter co	Mar. 12, '62	
Smith, Anthony W	Porter co	Feb. 24, '62	Veteran; transf'd to 20th Reg't, re-organized.
Swisher, Levi	Pulaski co	Feb. 12, '61.	Transf'd to 20th Reg't, re-organized.
Shafer, John	Porter co	Feb. 1, '62	" " "
Sullivan, Matthew	Porter co	Feb. 28, '62	Transf'd to V. R. C.; must'd out Feb. 18,'65.
Waugh, William		Aug. 15, '62	Wo'd, Spottsylv'a; tr'f'd 20th Reg't, re-org'd.
Wheeler William E	Porter co	Feb. 28,'62	Transf'd to 20th Reg't, re-organized.
Wheeler, Charles W	Porter co	Feb. 28,'62	
Yorgenson, Hans	Porter co	Oct.18, '62	

ENLISTED MEN OF COMPANY "K."

Name and Rank.	Residence.	Date of Muster. 1861.	Remarks.
First Sergeant.			
Brown, John C	White co	July 22	Promoted 1st Lieutenant.
Sergeants.			
Price, John	White co	July 22	Promoted 2d Lieutenant.
Bartholomew, John C	White co	July 22	Promoted 2d Lieutenant.
Harvey, Rufus L	White co	July 22	
Thompson, George W	White co	July 22	
Corporals.			[as absent sick.
Stevenson, John S	White co	July 22	Wounded, Gettysburg; must'd out July 29,'64.
Smith, Mahlon F	White co	July 22	Mustered out July 29, '64.
Harbolt, Jonathan B	White co	July 22	Promoted 2d Lieutenant.
Ball, Samuel E	White co	July 22	Veteran; promoted 2d Lieutenant.
Dobbins, John W	White co	July 22	Died at Philadelphia, Aug. 18, '62.
Uhl, George	White co	July 22	Veteran; transf'd to 20th Reg't, re-organized.
Bowen, Elias	White co	July 22	
Berkey, James S	White co	July 22	
Musicians.			
Snyder, Peter	White co	July 22	
Baker, George W	White co	July 22	
Wagoner			
McBeth, John S	White co	July 22	Veteran.
Privates.			
Albright, Jacob	White co	July 22	
Bacon, Sylvester	White co	July 22	
Baum, John C	White co	July 22	
Bliss, John W	White co	July 22	Vet'n; transf'd to 20th Reg't, re-organized.
Brannan, John W	White co	July 22	Wounded, Wilderness; must'd out July 29,'64.
Brown, Joseph A	White co	July 22	
Brunnell, Horatio	White co	July 22	
Brunnell, Nathaniel W	White co	July 22	Died of wounds received at Gettysburg.
Burch, Amos	White co	July 22	Vet'n; transf'd to 20th Reg't, re-organized.
Burch, John	White co	July 22	Veteran.
Bussard, Philip A	White co	July 22	
Cooper, Michael	White co	July 22	
Chapman, Wyman	White co	July 22	
Cole, Benjamin F	White co	July 22	
Corbin, Calvin J	White co	July 22	Mustered out July 29, '64.
Cragun, Joshua W	White co	July 22	
Cry, Hugh	White co	July 22	
Crose, William C	White co	July 22	
Davis, William H	White co	July 22	Mustered out July 29, '64.
Dawson, Abram	White co	July 22	Died at Philadelphia, Sept 20, '62.
Demint, William R	White co	July 22	Mustered out July 29, '64.
Dibra, Samuel	White co	July 22	" " "
Dickey, Elias	White co	July 22	

Name and Rank.	Residence.	Date of Muster. 1861.	Remarks.
Dyer, James W	White co	July 22	Killed at Gettysburg.
Dillon, Burgess H	White co	July 22	Vet'n; transf'd to 20th Reg't, re-organized.
Dobbins, Abraham	White co	July 22	Mustered out July 29, '64.
Dobbins, Martin	White co	July 22	
Dobbins, Samuel P	White co	July 22	Wounded, Wilderness; must'd out July 29,'64.
Duncan, Abram S	White co	July 22	
Duncan, Isaac	White co	July 22	
Faire, John	White co	July 22	Wounded, Wilderness; must'd out July 29,'64.
Fisher, John C	White co	July 22	Veteran.
Fuller, David	White co	July 22	Vet.; w'd Wild'ness; transf. 20th R'gt; re-org.
Furguson, Edgar	White co	July 22	Vet; transf. 20th Regiment re-org.
Hartelrhode, Cenas	White co	July 22	Veteran.
Hart, George W	White co	July 22	Veteran; transf. 20th Regiment re-org.
Hendrixon, Enoch	White co	July 22	Veteran; transf. 20th Regiment, re-org.
Herrick, William	White co	July 22	
Hinds, Van	White co	July 22	Capt'd, gunb't "Fanny;" disch'gd May 22,'62.
Horine, William T	White co	July 22	W'd Gettysb'g; must'd out July 29, '64; Sergt.
Hufty, Thomas C	White co	July 22	[re-organized.
Imes, Richard	White co	July 22	Veteran; w'd June 30, '64; transf. 20th Reg't,
Keefer, Calvin W	White co	July 22	Capt'd, gunb't "Fanny;" disch'gd May 22,'62.
Kelley, Noah	White co	July 22	Capt'd, gunb't "Fanny;" disch'gd May 22,'62.
Lackum, George	White co	July 22	Missing since battle of Cold Harbor.
Mason, John S	White co	July 22	
McBeth, Joseph	White co	July 22	Mustered out July 29, '64.
McClintick, Robert J	White co	July 22	
McCollock, William W	White co	July 22	
McEntire, Henry H	White co	July 22	
McPheeters, James A. M	White co	July 22	Veteran; w'd June 20, '64; transf. 20th Reg't,
Miller, Jacob	White co	July 22	[re-organized.
Nordyke, Parris	White co	July 22	Veteran; w'd, Wilderness; transf. 20th Reg't,
Parker, Martin B	White co	July 22	Must'd out July 29, '64. [re-org.
Reams, Samuel L	White co	July 22	
Reams, Tavner W	White co	July 22	Veteran.
Reynolds, John G	White co	July 22	W'd, Spottsylvania; must'd out July 29, '64.
Rhodes, David S	White co	July 22	Veteran; transf. 20th Regiment, re-org.
Rhody, William	White co	July 22	
Rinker, John D	White co	July 22	
Robbins, Canada	White co	July 22	
Rogers, Luke	White co	July 22	W'd Gettysburg; must'd out July 29,'64; S'gt.
Sibbett, Oliver P	White co	July 22	
Silince, Stephen L	White co	July 22	
Skevington, John	White co	July 22	
Smith, Edward D	White co	July 22	
Smith, James B	White co	July 22	Capt'd on gunboat "Fanny;" must'd out May
Smith, Joseph	White co	July 22	[22, '62.
Snyder, John	White co	July 22	
Staton, Thomas	White co	July 22	
Stevens, James C	White co	July 22	W'd Spottsylvania; must'd out July 29,'64, as
Stephens, Thomas W	White co	July 22	Must'd out July 29, '64; Sergt. [Corp'l.
Styers, Theodore	White co	July 22	Mustered out July 29, '64.
Stone, David F	White co	July 22	" " "
Stone, William	White co	July 22	
Thrasher, Notley H	White co	July 22	
Turner, Samuel	White co	July 22	Veteran; transf. 20th Regiment, re-org.
Vinson, James V	White co	July 22	Wounded, Wilderness.
Williams, Joseph M	White co	July 22	Mustered out July 29, '64.
White, George D	White co	July 22	
White, Nathan	White co	July 22	Mustered out July 29, '64.
White, Samuel J	White co	July 22	" " "
Recruits.			
Baum, Adam P	White co	Feb. 28, '62	
Croce, William C	White co	April 12,'64	Transferred 20th Regiment, re-organized.
Duncan, Robert	White co	Feb. 28, '62	Veteran; killed, Cold Harbor, June 5, '64.
Dobbins, Amos M	White co	Dec. 11, '61	
Duncan, Isaac	White co	April 9, '62	
Furguson, Edwin M	White co	Feb. 28, '62	
Grover, George W	Clinton co		Veteran; transf. 20th Regiment, re-org.
Haver, Samuel B	Tippecanoe co		" " " "
Hughes, Milton	White co	Dec. 11, '61	
Hogeland, William S	White co	Dec. 18, '61	
Hoover, James	White co	Feb. 28, '62	
Hoover, Emanuel B	White co	April 9, '62	
Judah, Samuel	White co	Feb. 28, '62	
Jessup, Clark W	White co	Feb. 28, '62	
Lear, George W	Carroll co		Transferred 20th Regiment, re-org.
Little, George		Apr. 28,'64	" " "
Rodgers, Joseph	White co	Dec. 9, '61	Veteran; transferred 20th Regiment, re-org.
Ream, David K	White co	Jan. 21,'64	Transferred 20th Regiment, re-organized.
Reed, William	White co	Dec. 11, '61	
Ryan, Richard	White co	Dec. 14, '61	

INDIANA VOLUNTEERS.

NAME AND RANK.	Residence.	Date of Muster. 1861.	REMARKS.
Sweet, Frank		Feb. 28, '62.	Vet'n; transf'd to 20th Reg't, re-organized.
Smith, Jacob J	White co	Feb. 28, '62.	
Stowe, Samuel M	White co	Apr. 9, '62..	
Taylor, Ross J	White co	Apr. 9, '62..	
Wilm, Augustus		Oct. 20, '62.	Vet'n; transf'd to 20th Reg't, re-organized.
Wright, James M	White co	Feb. 28, '62.	
White, George D	White co	Feb. 28, '62.	
Weirick, John E	White co	Feb. 28, '62.	

UNASSIGNED RECRUITS.

NAME AND RANK.	Residence.	Date of Muster.	REMARKS.
Baker, James A	Marshall co	April 12, '64	
Brunes, Francis M	Vermillion co..	April 15, '64	
Cappock, Seth	Cass co	April 1, '64..	
Crose, William C	White co	April 12, '64	
Current, Samuel	Vermillion co...	April 15, '64	
Dixon, James A	Lake co	Mar. 29, '64	
Ellis, Duane, M	Porter co	Jan, 4, '64...	
Gable, Jacob W	Pulaski co	April 12, '64	
Gaskins, William D	Marion co	April 14, '64	
Green, Robert	Jefferson co	Sept. 15, '62	
Harting, Carl	Jefferson co	Sept. 15, '62	
Hannan, John	Tippecanoe co...	Dec. 29, '63.	
Helvie, Noah C	Cass co	Feb. 20, '64.	
Hichlay, Thomas W	Grant co	Mar. 22, '64	
Kimball, Monroe D	Porter co	Jan. 4, '64...	
McClure, Henry	Tippecanoe co...	June 2, '64..	
Naggal, William N		June 23, '62	
Ochsumr, Frederick		Sept. 15, '62	[re-organized.
Richards, John			W'ded at Spottsylvania transf'd to 20th Regt.
Rupe, Andrew	Tippecanoe co..	Dec. 29, '63.	
Rice, Jacob	Tippecanoe co..	Dec. 29, '63.	
Rose, Joseph	Fountain co	Jan. 7, '64...	
Ream, David K	White co	Jan. 23, '64.	
Richards, John W	Lake co	May 29, '64.	
Stainbury, Jeremiah	Cass co	April 6, '64..	
Spleen, Robert	Gibson co	April 9, '64..	
Souther, Martin	Jefferson co	Sept. 15, '62	
Tumblin, George	Miami co	Mar. 31, '64	
Thorp, Love	Tippecanoe co..	Jan. 7, '64..	Transferred to 20th Regt. re-organized.
Tulley, James	Tippecanoe co..	Dec. 29, '63.	
Watson, Henry B	Hancock co	Feb. 2, '64..	
Young, James E	Marion co	Jan. 18, '64.	

ENDNOTES

CHAPTER 1 – THEY MAKE LITTLE
FUSS

1. *Marshall County Republican*, June 20,
   1861, p. 2.
2. Brown letter to O. P. Bailey, *Marshall
   County Republican*, June 20, 1861,
   p. 2.
3. Gilbreath manuscript, p. 2.
4. Ibid.
5. Stephens diary, p. 8.
6. Hamelle, *History of White County*,
   p. 180.
7. Wheeler letter to his Uncle J. C.
   Hudson, March 18, 1863.
8. Ibid.
9. Family history as told by Nancy Van
   Valkenburgh.
10. Gilbreath manuscript, p. 2.
11. Ibid.
12. Lester, *One of the Fighting Three
    Hundred*, p. 1.
13. Gilbreath manuscript, p. 2.
14. *Biographical Record and Portrait
    Album of Tippecanoe County
    Indiana*, p. 452.
15. *Ball Encyclopedia of Genealogy and
    Biography of Lake County*, Indiana,
    p. 54.
16. Ibid., p. 60.
17. *Monticello Herald*, December 1,
    1898, p. 3.
18. *History of North and West Texas*,
    p. 502.
19. Research of Benedict R. Maryniak.
20. Archer letter to Zack Scott,
    February 17, 1862, Robertson's *Out
    of the Spirit and the Soil*, p. 17.
21. Gilbreath manuscript, p. 4.
22. *Lafayette Journal*, July 22, 1861,
    p. 3.
23. Gilbreath manuscript, p. 4.
24. Ibid., p. 4.
25. J. Finley letter to Governor Morton,
    July 21, 1861.
26. H. H. Miller letter to his wife
    Emmie, July 7, 1861.
27. *Lafayette Journal*, July 17, 1861,
    p. 3.
28. *Soldier of Indiana*, p. 484.
29. *Logansport Journal*, July 9, 1861,
    p. 2.
30. Lewis manuscript, p. 5.
31. Stephens diary, p. 8.
32. Gilbreath manuscript, p. 4.
33. Ibid, p. 4.
34. Lewis manuscript, p. 6.
35. Bowen letter to wife, July 24, 1861.
36. *Report of the Adjutant General of the
    State of Indiana* (hereafter referred
    to as IAG), Vol. 2, pp. 178–185.
37. Gilbreath manuscript, p. 6.
38. Lester, *One of the Fighting Three
    Hundred*, p. 1.
39. *Marshall County Republican*, July
    31, 1861, p. 1.
40. *Valparaiso Republic*, August 15,
    1861, p. 2.
41. Gilbreath manuscript, p. 7.
42. Lewis manuscript, p. 6.
43. Gilbreath manuscript, p. 7.
44. Reed letter to wife, *Monticello
    Spectator*, August 16, 1862, p. 2.
45. Ibid., p. 7.
46. Ibid., p. 8.
47. Ibid., p. 8.
48. *Soldier of Indiana*, p. 483.
49. Ibid., p. 484.

CHAPTER 2 – STRANGERS IN A
STRANGE LAND

1. Stoddard letter to the *Valparaiso
   Republic*, August 22, 1861, p. 2.
2. Ibid.
3. Stiles letter to the *Lafayette Journal*,
   August 10, 1861, p. 3.
4. *Soldier of Indiana*, p. 484.
5. Lytle letter to the *Valparaiso Republic*,
   August 15, 1861, p. 2.
6. *Soldier of Indiana*, pp. 484–485.
7. Stiles letter to the *Lafayette Journal*,
   August 13, 1861, p. 3.

8. Ibid., p. 3.
9. Stoddard letter to the *Valparaiso Republic*, September 5, 1861, p. 2.
10. Lytle letter to the *Valparaiso Republic*, September 5, 1861, p. 1.
11. *Howard Tribune*, August 27, 1861, p. 2.
12. Luther letter to father, August 18, 1861.
13. Lytle letter to the *Valparaiso Republic*, September 5, 1861, p. 1.
14. *Indianapolis Daily Journal*, September 17, 1861, p. 1.
15. Lytle letter to the *Valparaiso Republic*, September 19, 1861, p. 1.
16. Luther letter to father, August 18, 1861.
17. Mattingly letter to the *Marshall County Republican*, September 19, 1861, p. 1.
18. Stiles letter to the *Lafayette Journal*, August 13, 1861, p. 2.
19. Lytle letter to the *Valparaiso Republic*, September 26, 1861, p. 2.
20. *Indianapolis Journal*, September 17, 1861, p. 3.
21. Lewis manuscript, p. 9.
22. Ibid., p. 7.
23. Pealer letter to his brother, December 8, 1861.
24. Hooker letter to the *Marshall County Republican*, October 3, 1861, p. 2.
25. Ibid., p. 2.
26. *Soldier of Indiana*, p. 485.
27. Gilbreath manuscript, p. 9.
28. Porter, *Naval History of the Civil War*, p. 44.
29. Ibid., p. 46.
30. Hooker letter to the *Marshall County Republican*, October 3, 1861, p. 2.
31. Ibid, October 10, 1861, p. 2.
32. Ibid., p. 2.
33. Kistler letter to Emily, Luce and Saby Hill, November 17, 1861.
34. Bartlett letter to the *Valparaiso Republic*, October 24, 1861, p. 2.
35. Montgomery letter to the *Howard Tribune*, October 21, 1861, p. 1.
36. Ibid., p. 1.
37. Hooker letter to the *Marshall County Republican*, October 10, 1861, p. 2.
38. *Soldier of Indiana*, p. 487.
39. Ibid., p. 487.
40. Montgomery letter to the *Howard Tribune*, October 21, 1861, p. 2.
41. Ibid., October 21, 1861, p. 2.
42. Gragg, *Civil War Quiz and Fact Book*, p. 129.
43. O.R., Report of Brigadier General Joseph K. Mansfield, USA, October 5, 1861, Series I, Vol. 4, p. 597.
44. *Lafayette Journal*, January 11, 1862, p. 2.
45. O.R., Report of Brigadier General Benjamin Huger, CSA, October 5, 1861, Series I, Vol. 4, p. 597.
46. O.R., Report of Colonel A. R. Wright, CSA, October 2,1861, Series I, Vol. 4, p. 597.
47. *One of the Fighting Three Hundred*, p. 2.
48. O.R., Report of Brigadier General Joseph K. Mansfield, USA, October 5, 1861, Series I, Vol. 4, p. 597.
49. *Soldier of Indiana*, p. 488.
50. Kistler letter to Emily Sally Luce and Saby Hill, November 17, 1861.
51. *One of the Fighting Three Hundred*, p. 2.
52. Ibid.
53. Ibid.
54. *Marshall County Republican*, October 17, 1861, p. 2.
55. *Soldier of Indiana*, p. 488.
56. *Logansport Journal*, October 19, 1861, p. 2.
57. Ibid.
58. Ibid.
59. Montgomery letter to the *Howard Tribune*, October 21, 1861, p. 2.
60. Comly letter to his mother, *Marshall County Republican*, November 7, 1861, p. 1.
61. *Marshall County Republican*, October 17, 1861, p. 2.
62. *Logansport Journal*, October 19, 1861, p. 2.

63. *Soldier of Indiana*, p. 489.
64. Brown letter to George Winter, November 4, 1861.
65. *One of the Fighting Three Hundred*, p. 3.
66. *Marshall County Republican*, October 17, 1861, p. 2.
67. *Soldier of Indiana*, p. 490.
68. Ibid., p. 491.
69. Wheeler diary, October 11, 1861.
70. *Howard Tribune*, October 21, 1861, p. 1.
71. *O.R.*, Series I, Vol. 4, p. 627.
72. Andrew letter to his sister, October 20, 1861.
73. *Logansport Journal*, October 19, 1861, p. 2.
74. Lewis manuscript, p. 11.
75. Petition of officers of the Twentieth to Governor Oliver P. Morton, October 21, 1861.
76. Lewis manuscript, p. 12.
77. Wheeler diary, October 12, 1861.
78. *O.R.*, Series I, Vol. 4, p. 626.
79. Montgomery letter to the *Howard Tribune*, October 29, 1861, p. 2.
80. Ibid., p. 2.
81. Reese letter to brother, September 30, 1861.
82. Andrew letter to his sister, October 20, 1861.
83. *Soldier of Indiana*, p. 493.
84. Ibid., p. 493.
85. Lewis manuscript, p. 12.
86. Gilbreath manuscript, p. 12.
87. Lewis manuscript, p. 13.
88. Andrew letter to his sister, November 6, 1861.
89. *Lake County in the Civil War*, p. 7.
90. Murray letter to his wife, *Howard Tribune*, November 12, 1861, p. 2.
91. Andrew letter to his sister, November 6, 1861.
92. Murray letter to his wife, *Howard Tribune*, November 12, 1861, p. 2.
93. *Soldier of Indiana*, p. 494.
94. Murray letter to his wife, *Howard Tribune*, November 12, 1861, p. 2.
95. Montgomery letter to *Howard Tribune*, November 19, 1861.

96. *Valparaiso Republic*, November 21, 1861, p. 2.
97. Stephens diary, page 18.
98. *Valparaiso Republic*, November 21, 1861, p. 2.
99. Ibid., November 28, 1861, p. 1.

CHAPTER 3 – IRON SHIPS AND LEAD BULLETS

1. Stephens diary, p. 18.
2. Lytle letter to the *Valparaiso Republic*, August 15, 1861, p.2.
3. *Valparaiso Republic*, February 6, 1862, p. 2.
4. Montgomery letter to the *Howard Tribune*, October 29, 1861, p. 2.
5. *Marshall County Republican*, December 26, 1861, p. 1.
6. *Lake County in the Civil War*, p. 19.
7. Wheeler letter to his wife, November 13, 1861.
8. Ibid., November 11, 1861.
9. Montgomery letter to the *Howard Tribune*, November 25, 1861, p. 2.
10. Murray letter to Morton, December 5, 1861.
11. Brown letter to Morton, December 26, 1861.
12. Comly letter to Muggie, November 16, 1861. as printed in *Logansport Pharos*, December 11, 1861, p. 3.
13. *Soldier of Indiana*, p. 496.
14. Ibid., p. 498.
15. Ibid.
16. *Indianapolis Daily Journal*, January 13, 1862, p. 3.
17. *Soldier of Indiana*, p. 500.
18. *Indianapolis Daily Journal*, April 1, 1862, p. 3.
19. Murray letter to the *Howard Tribune*, November 18, 1861, p. 3.
20. *Lake County in the Civil War*, p. 18.
21. Lytle letter to the *Valparaiso Republic*, January 2, 1862, p. 1.
22. Stephens diary, p. 20.
23. Montgomery letter to the *Howard Tribune*, November 20, 1861, p. 1.
24. Lytle letter to the *Valparaiso Republic*, January 2, 1862, p. 1.
25. Montgomery letter to the *Howard*

Tribune, January 4, 1862, p. 2.

26. Ibid., p. 2.

27. Lytle letter to the *Valparaiso Republic*, January 30, 1862, p. 1.

28. Montgomery letter to the *Howard Tribune*, November 20, 1861, p. 1.

29. Ibid., p. 1.

30. *Indianapolis Daily Journal*, January 22, 1862, p. 2.

31. Stone letter to John Nolison, December 24, 1862.

32. Hendricks letter to mother, December 8, 1861.

33. *Indianapolis Daily Journal*, January 3, 1862, p. 2.

34. *Soldier of Indiana*, Vol. 1, p. 501.

35. Ireland diary, March 10, 1862.

36. *Valparaiso Republic*, February 6, 1862, p. 1.

37. Montgomery letter to the *Howard Tribune*, January 5, 1862, p. 2.

38. Hooker letter to the *Indianapolis Daily Journal*, January 21, 1862, p. 2.

39. Montgomery letter to the *Howard Tribune*, January 28, 1862, p. 2.

40. *Indiana Adjutant General Report*, Vol. 2, p. 178.

41. *Hudson Star Observer*, April 13, 1995, p. 3A.

42. Wheeler letter to J. C. Hudson, March 18, 1863.

43. Ibid.

44. Porter, *Naval History of the Civil War*, p. 119.

45. Gibreath manuscript, p. 17.

46. Ibid., p. 18.

47. Stiles, *Mollus War Papers: Illinois*, Vol. 1, p. 125.

48. Wheeler letter to J. C. Hudson, March 18, 1863.

49. Ibid.

50. Lewis manuscript, p. 18.

51. Lytle letter to A. M. Higgins, *Valparaiso Republic*, March 26, 1862, p. 3.

52. Stiles, *Mollus War Papers: Illinois*, Vol. 1, p. 128.

53. Sibel letter to his father, March 11, 1862.

54. Montgomery letter to the *Howard Tribune*, March 12, 1862, p. 1.

55. Wheeler letter to his wife, March 8, 1862.

56. Meikel letter to *Indianapolis Daily Journal*, March 15, 1862., p. 2.

57. Lytle letter to the *Valparaiso Republic*, March 26, 1862, p. 2.

58. Lytle letter to the *Valparaiso Republic*, March 29, 1862, p. 2.

59. Gilbreath manuscript, p. 19.

60. *Soldier of Indiana*, Vol. 1, p. 503.

61. Montgomery letter to the *Howard Tribune*, March 9, 1862.

62. French letter to cousins, March 30, 1862.

63. Lewis manuscript, p. 18.

64. Bassett letter as printed in *Soldier of Indiana*, Vol. 1, p. 503.

65. Porter, *The Naval History of the Civil War*, p. 126.

66. Gilbreath manuscript, p. 20.

67. Ibid.

68. Stiles, *Mollus War Papers: Illinois*, Vol. 1, p. 131.

69. *Soldier of Indiana*, Vol. 1, p. 504.

70. Porter, *The Naval History of the Civil War*, p. 129.

71. Tuttle letter to wife, March 16, 1862.

72. Montgomery letter to the *Howard Tribune*, March 12, 1862, p. 1.

CHAPTER 4 – "I CAN DIE WITH A CLEAR CONSCIENCE"

1. Brown letter to the *Logansport Pharos*, April 30, 1862, p. 2.

2. Dunn, *Iron Men, Iron Will: The Nineteenth Indiana Regiment of the Iron Brigade*, p. 19.

3. Montgomery letter to the *Howard Tribune*, March 23, 1862, p. 3.

4. Meikel letter to the *Indianapolis Daily Journal*, April 8, 1862, p. 2.

5. Warner, *Generals in Blue*, p. 290–291.

6. Miller, *The Peninsula Campaign of 1862*, p. 178–181.

7. Ibid.

8. Wheeler letter to J. C. Judson,

March 18, 1863.

9. Montgomery letter to the *Howard Tribune*, April 29, 1862, p. 2.

10. Lytle letter to the *Valparaiso Republic*, May 1, 1862, p. 1.

11. Montgomery letter to the *Howard Tribune*, April 13, 1862, p. 2.

12. Ibid., May 12, 1862, p. 1.

13. Meikel letter to the *Indiana Daily Journal*, May 19, 1862, p. 2.

14. Montgomery letter to the *Howard Tribune*, April 12, 1862, p. 1.

15. Ibid.

16. Montgomery letter to the *Howard Tribune*, May 26, 1862, p. 1.

17. Meikel letter to the *Indiana Daily Journal*, May 19, 1862, p. 2.

18. Montgomery letter to the *Howard Tribune*, May 12, 1862, p. 1.

19. Ibid.

20. *Soldier of Indiana*, Vol. 1, p. 505–506.

21. Montgomery letter to the *Howard Tribune*, May 12, 1862, p. 1.

22. Wheeler letter to J. C. Judson, March 18, 1863.

23. Winch War Reminiscences, Part 1, unnumbered.

24. Lytle letter to the *Valparaiso Republic*, May 29, 1862, p. 2.

25. Ibid.

26. Montgomery letter to the *Howard Tribune*, May 12, 1862, p. 1.

27. Ibid., May 26, 1862, p. 1.

28. Meikel letter to the *Indianapolis Daily Journal*, May 29, 1862, p. 2.

29. *Soldier of Indiana*, Vol. 1, p. 507.

30. *Indianapolis Daily Journal*, June 1, 1862, p. 3.

31. Montgomery letter to the *Howard Tribune*, May 26, 1862, p. 1.

32. Archer letter to Zack Scott, June 2, 1862, Robertson's *Out of the Spirit and the Soil*, p. 22.

33. Meikel letter to the *Indianapolis Daily Journal*, May 29, 1862, p. 2.

34. Wheeler letter to his wife, May 31, 1862.

35. *Soldier of Indiana*, Vol. 1, p. 506.

36. Montgomery letter to the *Howard Tribune*, May 26, 1862, p. 1.

37. Warner, *Generals In Blue*, p. 407.

38. Ibid., p. 407–408.

39. Lytle letter to the *Valparaiso Republic*, May 29, 1862, p. 2.

40. Ibid.

41. Meikel letter to the *Indianapolis Daily Journal*, June 18, 1862, p. 2.

42. Ibid.

43. Reeder letter to Daniel Reeder, June 10, 1862.

44. Meikel letter to the *Valparaiso Republic*, June 18, 1862, p. 2.

45. Robbins letter to his brother, *Northern Indianan*, July 3, 1862, p. 2.

46. Archer letter to Zack Scott, May 20, 1862.

47. Boatner, *The Civil War Dictionary*, p. 272–273.

48. Gilbreath manuscript, p. 24.

49. Warner, *Generals in Blue*, p. 258–259.

50. *Soldier of Indiana*, p. 521.

51. Lewis manuscript, p. 22.

52. Andrew letter to his sister, June 1, 1862.

53. Ibid.

54. Reeder letter to Daniel Reeder, June 10, 1862.

55. Ibid.

56. Ibid.

57. Archer letter to Zack Scott, June 23, 1862, Robertson's *Out of the Spirit and the Soil*, p. 24.

58. Reeder letter to Daniel Reeder, June 10, 1862.

59. Reeder letter to parents, June 21, 1862.

60. Brown Report, June 19, 1862, *O.R.*, Vol. 11, p. 1068.

61. Meikel letter to the *Indianapolis Daily Journal*, July 7, 1862, p. 2.

62. Ibid.

63. Brown Report, June 19, 1862, *O.R.*, Vol. 11, p. 1068.

64. Ibid.

65. Hogeland letter to the *Lafayette Daily Courier*, June 27, 1862, p. 2.

66. Archer letter to Zack Scott, June 23, 1862, Robertson's *Out of the Spirit and the Soil*, p. 23.

CHAPTER 5 – SEVEN DAYS OF HELL

1. *Soldier of Indiana*, Vol. 1, p. 523.
2. Sears, *To the Gates of Richmond*, p. 183.
3. Reeder letter to parents, June 21, 1862.
4. Hooker letter to *Indianapolis Daily Journal*, July 28, 1862, p. 2.
5. Sears, *To the Gates of Richmond*, p. 183.
6. Andrew letter to his sister, June 15, 1862.
7. Meikel letter to the *Indianapolis Daily Journal*, July 7, 1862, p. 2.
8. Reeder letter to parents, June 21, 1862.
9. Lewis manuscript, p. 22.
10. Ibid., p. 22.
11. Robinson report to Kearny, *O.R.*, Series I, Vol. 11, p. 174.
12. Reeder letter to parents, July 1, 1862.
13. *One of the Fighting Three Hundred* (no page number given).
14. Lewis manuscript, p. 22.
15. Robinson report to Kearny, *O.R.*, Series I, Vol. 11, p. 175.
16. Ibid., p. 175.
17. Lewis manuscript, p. 22.
18. Reeder letter to parents, July 1, 1862.
19. Robinson report to Kearny, *O.R.*, Series I, Vol. 11, p. 175.
20. Ibid., p. 175.
21. Sears, *To the Gates of Richmond*, p. 185.
22. *Indianapolis Daily Journal*, July 4, 1862, p. 2.
23. Sears, *To the Gates of Richmond*, p. 185.
24. Heintzelman report to Williams, *O.R.*, Series I, Vol. 11, p. 96.
25. Smith report to Mahone, *O.R.*, Series I, Vol. 11, p. 804.
26. Robinson report to Kearny, *O.R.*, Series I, Vol. 11, p. 174.
27. Lewis manuscript, p. 23.
28. Robinson report to Kearny, *O.R.*, Series I, Vol. 11, p. 174.
29. Lewis manuscript, p. 23.
30. Reeder letter to parents, July 1, 1862.
31. Robinson report to Kearny, *O.R.*, Series I, Vol. 11, p. 174.
32. Hart letter to the editor, *Lafayette Daily Courier*, July 26, 1862, p. 2.
33. Ibid.
34. *Indianapolis Daily Journal*, July 28, 1862, p. 3.
35. Hooker letter to the *Indianapolis Daily Journal*, August 13, 1862, p. 2.
36. Ibid.
37. Stephens diary, p. 23.
38. Hooker letter to the *Indianapolis Daily Journal*, August 13, 1862, p. 2.
39. Ibid.
40. Lewis manuscript, p. 23.
41. Ibid.
42. Ibid.
43. Robinson report to Kearny, *O.R.*, Series I, Vol. 11, p. 174.
44. Lewis manuscript, p. 23.
45. Fox, *Regimental Losses in the American Civil War*, p. 429.
46. Ibid.
47. Wheeler letter to J. C. Judson, March 18, 1863.
48. Gilbreath manuscript, p. 27.
49. Ibid.
50. *Valparaiso Republic*, July 17, 1862, p. 1.
51. Gilbreath manuscript, p. 27.
52. Wright report to Lt. Colonel S. S. Anderson, July 8, 1862, *O.R.*, Series I., Vol. 11, p. 811.
53. Reeder letter to parents, July 1, 1862.
54. *Soldier of Indiana*, p. 528.
55. Sears, *To the Gates of Richmond*, pp. 189–191.
56. Ibid., pp. 189–203.
57. Ibid., p. 208.
58. Ibid., pp. 223–235.
59. Ibid., pp. 235–248.

60. Ibid., p. 250.
61. *Soldier of Indiana*, Vol. 1, p. 535.
62. Kearny report to McKeever, July 6, 1862, *O.R.*, Vol. 11, p.162.
63. Sears, *To the Gates of Richmond*, p. 267.
64. Ibid., p. 274.
65. Gilbreath manuscript, p. 29.
66. Ibid.
67. Lewis manuscript, p. 24.
68. Kearny report to McKeever, July 6, 1862, *O.R.*, Vol. 11, p. 162.
69. Lewis manuscript, p. 25.
70. Ibid.
71. Gilbreath manuscript, p. 29.
72. Lewis manuscript, p. 25.
73. Ibid., p. 25.
74. Ibid.
75. Sears, *To the Gates of Richmond*, p. 297.
76. Heintzelman report to Williams, July 21, 1862, *O.R.*, Vol. 11, Part 2, p. 100.
77. Tuttle letter to his wife, July 5, 1862.
78. Lewis manuscript, p. 25.
79. Heintzelman report to Williams, July 21, 1862, *O.R.*, Vol. 11, Part 2, p. 100.
80. Pryor report to Sorrel, July 29, 1862, *O.R.*, Vol. 11, Part 2, p. 779.
81. Brown report to Robinson, June 30, 1862, *O.R.*, Vol. 11, Part 2, p. 177.
82. Featherston report to Sorrel, July 12, 1862, *O.R.*, Vol. 11, Part 2, p. 786.
83. Thompson report to Moore, July 11, 1862, *O.R.*, Vol. 11, Part 2, p. 172.
84. Gilbreath manuscript, p. 30.
85. McCowan report to Gregg, July 12, 1862, *O.R.*, Vol. 11, Part 2, p. 871.
86. Humphrey report to Wilson, July 5, 1862, *O.R.*, Vol. 11, Part 2, p. 189.
87. Brown report to Robinson, June 30, 1862, *O.R.*, Vol. 11, Part 2, p. 177.
88. Thompson report to Moore, July 11, 1862, *O.R.*, Vol. 11, Part 2, p. 172.
89. Lewis manuscript, p. 26.
90. Brown report to Robinson, June 30, 1862, *O.R.*, Vol. 11, Part 2, p. 177.
91. Lewis manuscript, p. 26.
92. Stiles, *Mollus War Papers: Illinois*, Vol. 3, p. 54.
93. McCowan report to Gregg, July 12, 1862, *O.R.*, Vol. 11, Part 2, p. 871.
94. Kearny report to McKeever, July 6, 1862, *O.R.*, Vol. 11, Part 2, p. 162.
95. Robinson report to Kearny, July 4, 1862, *O.R.*, Vol. 11, Part 2, p. 176.
96. *Logansport Journal*, August 2, 1862, p. 1.
97. *Soldier of Indiana*, Vol. 1, p. 538.
98. Ibid.
99. *Logansport Journal*, August 2, 1862, p. 1.
100. Tuttle letter to wife, July 5, 1862.
101. *Soldier of Indiana*, Vol. 1, P. 539.
102. Gilbreath manuscript, p. 30.
103. Lewis manuscript, p. 26.
104. Hooker letter to the *Indianapolis Daily Journal*, July 11, 1862, p. 2.
105. Tuttle letter to wife, July 5, 1862.
106. Hooker letter to the *Indianapolis Daily Journal*, July 11, 1862, p. 2.
107. Gilbreath manuscript, p. 32.
108. Hendricks letter to mother, July 6, 1862.

CHAPTER 6 – WE HAVE ROUSED THE REAL CRITTER

1. Wheeler letter to J. C. Judson, March 18, 1863.
2. Hooker letter to the *Indianapolis Daily Journal*, August 13, 1862, p. 2.
3. *Indianapolis Daily Journal*, July 20, 1862, p. 3.
4. *Indianapolis Daily Journal*, August 5, 1862, p. 3.
5. Reeder letter to his parents, July 1, 1862.
6. *Valparaiso Republic*, July 17, 1862, p. 1.
7. *History of Porter County*, p. 88.
8. *Indianapolis Daily Journal*, August 5, 1862, p. 3.
9. Stiles, *Mollus War Papers: Illinois*, Vol. 3, p. 54.

10. Ibid., p. 45.
11. Ibid.
12. Ibid., p. 54–55.
13. Ibid., p. 56–57.
14. Ibid., p. 58.
15. Ibid.
16. Montgomery letter to the *Howard Tribune*, August 10, 1862., p. 2.
17. Tuttle letter to wife, July 19, 1862.
18. Hooker letter to the *Indianapolis Daily Journal*, July 26, 1862, p. 2.
19. Ibid., July, 13, 1862, p. 2.
20. Tuttle letter to wife, July 13, 1862.
21. Ibid., July 19, 1862.
22. Hooker letter to the *Indianapolis Daily Journal*, July 13, 1862, p. 2.
23. Montgomery letter to the *Howard Tribune*, August 10, 1862, p. 2.
24. *Indianapolis Daily Journal*, August 5, 1862, p. 2.
25. Reese letter to his brother, July 27, 1862.
26. Gilbreath manuscript, p. 35.
27. Wheeler letter to his wife, July 12, 1862.
28. Ibid.
29. Wheeler letter to James Luther, August 10, 1862.
30. *Howard Tribune*, August 10, 1862, p. 2.
31. Clark letter to his sisters, July 5, 1862.
32. Reese letter to his brother, July 27, 1862.
33. Ibid.
34. Hart letter to the *Lafayette Daily Courier*, July 26, 1862, p. 2.
35. Hooker letter to the *Marshall County Republican*, September 11, 1862, p. 1.
36. Ibid.
37. Montgomery letter to the *Howard Tribune*, September 4, 1862, p. 1.
38. Hooker letter to the *Marshall County Republican*, September 11, 1862, p. 1.
39. Montgomery letter to the *Howard Tribune*, September 4, 1862, p. 1.
40. Ibid.
41. Ibid.
42. Ibid.
43. Hooker letter to the *Marshall County Republican*, September 11, 1862, p. 1.
44. Ibid.
45. Montgomery letter to the *Howard Tribune*, September 4, 1862, p. 1.
46. Hooker letter to the *Marshall County Republican*, September 11, 1862, p. 1.
47. Ibid.
48. Gilbreath manuscript, p. 35.
49. Kelly, *The Battle and Campaign, Second Manassas*, pp. 15–16.
50. Gilbreath manuscript, p. 35.
51. Hooker letter to the *Indianapolis Daily Journal*, September 16, 1862, p. 2.
52. Ibid.
53. Heintzelman report to Ruggles, October 21, 1862, *O.R.*, Series I, Vol. 16, p. 413.
54. Hooker letter to the *Indianapolis Daily Journal*, September 16, 1862, p. 2.
55. Hennessy, *Return to Bull Run*, pp. 245–257.
56. Ibid.
57. Robinson report to Mindil, August 31, 1862, *O.R.*, Series I, Vol. 16, p. 421.
58. Hennessy, *Return to Bull Run*, pp. 245–257.
59. Gilbreath manuscript, p. 37.
60. Ibid.
61. Hooker letter to the *Logansport Journal*, September 13, 1862, p. 2.
62. Ibid.
63. McCrady report to brigade, September, 1862, *O.R.*, Series I, Vol. 16, p. 687.
64. Hooker letter to the *Indianapolis Daily Journal*, September 16, 1862, p. 2.
65. McCrady report to brigade, September, 1862, *O.R.*, Series I, Vol. 16, p. 687.
66. Hooker letter to the *Indianapolis Daily Journal*, September 16, 1862, p. 2.

67. *Valparaiso Republic*, September 18, 1862, p. 1.
68. *Lake County in the Civil War*, p. 28.
69. McCrady report to brigade, September, 1862, *O.R.*, Series I, Vol. 16, p. 687.
70. Hooker letter to the *Indianapolis Daily Journal*, September 16, 1862, p. 2.
71. Gilbreath manuscript, p. 38.
72. Hooker letter to the *Indianapolis Daily Journal*, September 16, 1862, p. 2.
73. Hooker letter to the *Logansport Journal*, September 13, 1862, p. 2.
74. Hooker letter to the *Indianapolis Daily Journal*, September 16, 1862, p. 2.
75. Gilbreath manuscript, p. 39.
76. Ibid.
77. Ibid.
78. Ibid.
79. Taylor letter to his father, the *Lafayette Weekly Journal*, September 18, 1862, p. 2.
80. *Voices of the Civil War, Second Manassas*, p. 150.
81. Winch War Reminiscences, Part 2, p. 3.

CHAPTER 7 – THE LEAST POSSIBLE GOOD

1. *The Condition of Affairs in the Late Insurrectionary States*, Alabama, Vol. 2, p. 799.
2. Gilbreath manuscript, p. 42.
3. Miller letter to his grandmother, September 6, 1862.
4. Reese letter to his brother, August 14, 1862.
5. Montgomery letter to the *Howard Tribune*, October 30, 1862, p. 2.
6. Wheeler diary, September 25, 1862.
7. *Indiana Adjutant General Report*, Vol. 2, pp. 178–185.
8. Gilbreath manuscript, p. 42.
9. Montgomery letter to the *Howard Tribune*, October 9, 1862, p. 2.
10. Ibid.
11. Montgomery letter to the *Howard Tribune*, October 30, 1862, p. 2.
12. Ibid.
13. Tuttle letter to his wife, October 5, 1862.
14. Wheeler letter to his wife, October 14, 1862.
15. Winch War Reminiscences, Part 3, p. 5.
16. Montgomery letter to the *Howard Tribune*, November 13, 1862, p. 1.
17. Ibid.
18. Montgomery letter to the *Howard Tribune*, November 20, 1862, p. 2.
19. Meikel letter to the *Marshall County Republican*, November 22, 1862, p. 2.
20. Montgomery letter to the *Howard Tribune*, November 20, 1862, p. 2.
21. Ibid.
22. Meikel letter to the *Marshall County Republican*, November 22, 1862, p. 2.
23. Montgomery letter to the *Howard Tribune*, November 20, 1862, p. 2.
24. Ibid.
25. Ibid.
26. Ibid.
27. Winch War Reminiscences, Part 3, p. 6.
28. Montgomery letter to the *Howard Tribune*, November 27, 1862, p. 2.
29. Ibid., November 20, 1862, p. 2.
30. Ibid.
31. Ibid.
32. Time-Life Books, The Civil War Series, *Rebels Resurgent: Fredericksburg to Chancellorsville*, p. 24.
33. Ibid., p. 30.
34. Meikel letter to the *Marshall County Republican*, November 22, 1862, p. 2.
35. Reese letter to his sister, November 15, 1862.
36. *Indiana Adjutant General Report*, Vol. 2, pp. 178–185.
37. Wheeler diary, September 9, 1862.
38. Reese letter to his sister, November 15, 1862.
39. Ibid.
40. Ibid.

41. Time-Life Books, The Civil War Series, *Rebels Resurgent: Fredericksburg to Chancellorsville*, p. 30.
42. Ibid., p. 31.
43. Ibid., p. 32.
44. Ibid., p. 33.
45. Ibid., p. 35.
46. Reese letter to his brother, December 6, 1862.
47. Wheeler letter to Morton, December 4, 1862.
48. Time-Life Books, *The Civil War, Rebels Resurgent: Fredericksburg to Chancellorsville*, pp. 40–41.
49. *The Soldier of Indiana*, Vol. 3, pp. 58–62.
50. Robinson report to F. Birney, December 15, 1862, *O.R.*, Vol. 1, Series 31, p. 366.
51. Gilbreath manuscript, p. 52.
52. James Longstreet, "The Battle of Fredericksburg," *Battles and Leaders of the Civil War*, Vol. 3, pp. 73–75.
53. Ibid., p. 75.
54. William F. Smith, "Franklin's Left Grand Division," *Battles and Leaders of the Civil War*, Vol. 3, p. 135.
55. Ibid.
56. Logan letter to the *Logansport Pharos*, December 29, 1862, p. 3.
57. Robinson report to F. Birney, *O.R.*, Vol. 1, Series 31, p. 366.
58. Gilbreath manuscript, p. 52.
59. Luther letter to his father, December 19, 1862.
60. Montgomery letter to the *Howard Tribune*, December 25, 1862, p. 2.
61. Montgomery letter to the *Howard Tribune*, January 8, 1863, p. 1.
62. Logan letter to the *Logansport Pharos*, December 29, 1862, p. 3.
63. Ibid.
64. Ibid.
65. Order of battle: "The Opposing Forces at Fredericksburg," *Battles and Leaders of the Civil War*, Vol. 3, pp. 143–47.
66. Gilbreath manuscript, p. 52.
67. Montgomery letter to the *Howard Tribune*, December 25, 1862, p. 2.
68. Montgomery letter to the *Howard Tribune*, January 8, 1863, p. 1.
69. Gilbreath manuscript, p. 53.
70. Ibid.
71. Winch War Reminiscences, Part 4, p. 2.
72. Wheeler letter to his wife, December 16, 1862.
73. Gilbreath manuscript, p. 54.
74. Luther letter to his father, December 19, 1862.
75. Tuttle letter to his wife, December 21, 1862.
76. Ibid.
77. Logan letter to the *Logansport Pharos*, December 29, 1862, p. 3.
78. Tuttle letter to his wife, December 25, 1862.
79. Ibid.
80. Weaver letter to Kate, October 27, 1862.
81. Montgomery letter to the *Howard Tribune*, January 8, 1863, p. 1.

CHAPTER 8 – MUD, BLOOD, AND CHEERS

1. Hendricks letter to his mother, January 1, 1863.
2. Montgomery letter to the *Howard Tribune*, January 15, 1863, p. 2.
3. Ibid.
4. Ibid.
5. Gilbreath manuscript, p. 56.
6. Gilbreath manuscript, p. 55.
7. Tuttle letter to his wife, January 5, 1863.
8. Tuttle letter to his wife, January 10, 1863.
9. Tuttle letter to his wife, January 8, 1863.
10. Stephens diary, p. 45.
11. Montgomery letter to the *Howard Tribune*, February 5, 1863, p. 2.
12. Ibid.
13. Ibid.
14. Ibid.
15. Tuttle letter to his wife, January 23, 1863.

16. Montgomery letter to the *Howard Tribune*, February 5, 1863, p. 2.

17. Luther letter to his father, January 30, 1863.

18. Montgomery letter to the *Howard Tribune*, February 5, 1863, p. 2.

19. Montgomery letter to the *Howard Tribune*, February 12, 1863, p. 2.

20. Tuttle letter to his wife, February 20, 1863.

21. Ibid.

22. General Orders No. 39, February 10, 1863, signed by General Lorenzo Thomas.

23. Tuttle letter to his wife, February 20, 1863.

24. Ibid.

25. *The Condition of Affairs in the Late Insurrectionary States: Alabama*, Vol. 2, p. 799.

26. Ibid.

27. Ibid.

28. Ibid., p. 802.

29. Ibid.

30. Ibid.

31. Vincent letter to Morton, March 21, 1863, .

32. *The Condition of Affairs in the Late Insurrectionary States*, Alabama, Vol. 2, pp. 803–807.

33. Wheeler diary, March 1, 1863.

34. Wheeler diary, April 25, 1863.

35. Wheeler letter to Morton, February 24, 1863.

36. *Indiana Adjutant General Report*, Vol. 2, p. 178.

37. Ibid., pp. 179–185.

38. General Orders number 119, March 13, 1863, Lorenzo Thomas.

39. Winch War Reminiscences, Part 4, unnumbered page.

40. Montgomery letter to the *Howard Tribune*, February 26, 1863, p. 2.

41. Montgomery letter to the *Howard Tribune*, March 26, 1863, p. 2.

42. Ibid.

43. Gilbreath manuscript, p. 55.

44. Tuttle letter to his wife, March 6, 1863.

45. Montgomery letter to the *Howard Tribune*, April 23, 1863, p. 1.

46. Tuttle letter to his wife, April 3, 1863.

47. Tuttle letter to his wife, March 6, 1863.

48. Ibid.

49. Tuttle letter to his wife, February 25, 1863.

50. Tuttle letter to his wife, March 6, 1863.

51. Warner, *Generals in Blue*, p. 537.

52. Meikel letter to the *Marshall County Republican*, April 16, 1863, p. 1.

53. Montgomery letter to the *Howard Tribune*, April 2, 1863, p. 2.

54. Stephens diary, p. 55.

55. Montgomery letter to the *Howard Tribune*, April 16, 1863, p. 1.

56. Montgomery letter to the *Howard Tribune*, April 23, 1863, p. 1.

57. Ibid.

58. Stephens diary, p. 59.

59. Montgomery letter to the *Howard Tribune*, April 23, 1863, p. 1.

60. Stephens diary, p. 59.

61. Time-Life Books, The Civil War Series, *Rebels Resurgent: Fredericksburg to Chancellorsville*, p. 120.

62. Stephens diary, p. 60.

63. Gilbreath manuscript, p. 61.

64. Stephens diary, p. 61.

65. Wheeler letter to Governor Morton, April 24, 1863.

66. Everts letter to the *LaPorte Union* as printed in the *Valparaiso Republic*, May 7, 1863, p. 1.

67. Stephens diary, p. 62.

68. Ibid.

69. Ibid.

70. Ibid.

71. Ward report to Brevoort, May 9, 1863, *O.R.*, Series I, Vol. 25/1, S#39, p. 429.

72. Ibid.

73. Ibid, p. 63.

74. Ibid.

75. Ibid, p. 64.

76. Ibid., p. 429.

77. Bell letter to the editor, *Marshall County Republican*, May 21, 1863, p. 2.
78. Ibid.
79. Birney report to Hart, May 9, 1863, *O.R.*, Series I, Vol. 25/1, S#39, p. 408.
80. Bell letter to the editor, the *Marshall County Republican*, May 21, 1863, p. 2.
81. Sickles report to Williams, May 20, 1863, *O.R.*, Series I, Vol. 25/1, S#39, p. 386.
82. Wheeler report to Henry, May 7, 1863, *O.R.*, Series I, Vol. 25/1, S#39, p. 432.
83. Best report to Von Borke, May 8, 1863, *O.R.*, Series I, Vol. 25/1, S#39, p. 980.
84. Ibid.
85. Ibid.
86. Ibid.
87. Gilbreath manuscript, p. 59.
88. Ibid.
89. Winch War Reminiscences, unnumbered page.
90. Gilbreath manuscript, p. 59–60.
91. Ibid., p. 60.
92. Winch War Reminiscences, unnumbered page.
93. Bell letter to the editor, *Marshall County Repulican*, May 21, 1863, p. 2.
94. Stephens diary, p. 64.
95. Winch War Reminiscences, unnumbered page.
96. Gilbreath manuscript, p. 60.
97. Ibid.
98. Hendricks letter to his mother, May 25, 1863.
99. Winch War Reminiscences, unnumbered page.
100. *Indianapolis Daily Journal*, May 11, 1863, p. 3.
101. Gilbreath manuscript, p. 61.
102. Stephens diary, p. 65.
103. Montgomery letter to the *Howard Tribune*, May 14, 1863, p. 2.
104. Bell letter to the *Marshall County Republican*, May 21, 1863, p. 2.
105. Stephens diary, p. 65.
106. Ibid., p. 66.
107. Ibid.
108. Gilbreath manuscript, p. 61.
109. Stephens diary, p. 66.
110. Bell letter to the *Marshall County Republican*, May 21, 1863, p. 2.

CHAPTER 9 – A GLORIOUS FIELD OF GRIEF

1. Stephens diary, p. 68.
2. Ibid.
3. Tuttle letter to his wife, May 10, 1863.
4. Stephens diary, p. 70.
5. Ibid.
6. *Lake County in the Civil War*, p. 32.
7. Stephens diary, p. 70.
8. Hendricks letter to his mother, May 21, 1863.
9. *Lake County in the Civil War*, p. 33.
10. Stephens diary, p. 69.
11. Ibid., p. 73.
12. Ibid., p. 72.
13. Tuttle letter to his wife, May 21, 1863.
14. Wheeler letter to his wife, May 28, 1863.
15. Stephens diary, p. 73.
16. Tuttle letter to his wife, June 2, 1863.
17. Ibid., June 4, 1863.
18. *Lake County in the Civil War*, p. 32.
19. Gilbreath manuscript, p. 73.
20. Stephens diary, p. 75.
21. Ibid., p. 76.
22. Lash, "The March of the 124th New York to Gettysburg," *Gettysburg* magazine, No. 9, p. 8.
23. Stephens diary, p. 77.
24. Lash, "The March of the 124th New York to Gettysburg," *Gettysburg* magazine, No. 9, p. 8.
25. Stephens diary, p. 77.
26. Ibid.
27. Tuttle letter to his wife, June 17, 1863.

28. Reeder letter to his parents, June 18, 1863.
29. Stephens diary, p. 77.
30. Tuttle letter to his wife, June 17, 1863.
31. Stephens diary, p. 78.
32. Lash, "The March of the 124th New York to Gettysburg," *Gettysburg* magazine, No. 9, p. 10.
33. Stephens diary, p. 78.
34. Ibid., p. 79.
35. Tuttle letter to his wife, June 23, 1863.
36. Stephens diary, p. 79.
37. Ibid., p. 80.
38. Ibid.
39. Ibid., p. 81.
40. Time-Life Books, The Civil War Series, *Gettysburg: Confederate High Tide*, p. 34.
41. Stephens diary, p. 81.
42. Reese letter to his brother, June 29, 1863.
43. Stephens diary, p. 82.
44. Ibid.
45. Ibid., p. 83.
46. Lash, "The March of the 124th New York to Gettysburg," *Gettysburg* magazine, No. 9, p. 13.
47. Ibid.
48. Birney report to Williams, August 7, 1863, *O.R.*, Series I, Vol. 27, Part 2, p. 482.
49. Stephens diary, p. 83.
50. Lash, "The March of the 124th New York to Gettysburg," *Gettysburg* magazine, No. 9, p. 15.
51. Birney report to Williams, August 7, 1863, *O.R.*, Series I, Vol. 27, Part 2, p. 482.
52. Stephens diary, p. 83.
53. Gilbreath manuscript, p. 71.
54. Birney report to Williams, August 7, 1863, *O.R.*, Series I, Vol. 27, Part 2, p. 482.
55. Wheeler letter to his wife and children, July 2, 1863.
56. Birney report to Williams, August 7, 1863, O.R., Series I, Vol. 27, Part 2, p. 482.

57. Gilbreath manuscript, p. 71.
58. Ibid.
59. Birney report to Williams, August 7, 1863, *O.R.*, Series I, Vol. 27, Part 2, p. 482.
60. Collier, *They'll Do To Tie To, The Story of the Third Arkansas Infantry, C.S.A.*, pp. 135–136.
61. Ibid., p. 137.
62. Ibid., p. 138.
63. Ibid.
64. Ibid., p. 139.
65. Ibid.
66. Ibid.
67. Gilbreath manuscript, p. 72.
68. Ward report to Torbert, August 4, 1863, *O.R.*, Series I, Vol. 27, Part 2, p. 493.
69. A. W. Luther letter to his father, July 13, 1863; *Lake County in the Civil War*, p. 30.
70. Gilbreath manuscript, p. 72.
71. *Lake County in the Civil War*, p. 28.
72. *Logansport Pharos*, July 15, 1863, p. 3.
73. List of deaths at the Battle of Gettysburg, p. 27.
74. Ibid., pp. 27–28.
75. Jorgensen, "Anderson Attacks the Wheatfield," *Gettysburg* magazine, No. 14, p. 69.
76. Gilbreath manuscript, p. 72.
77. Taylor report to AAG, Second Brigade, Undated, *O.R.*, Series I, Vol. 27, Part 2, p. 506.
78. Ibid.
79. Pearson letter to Reese's father, July 10, 1863.
80. Sibel letter to his father, July 6, 1863.
81. Stephens diary, p. 83.
82. Ward report to Torbert, August 4, 1863, *O.R.*, Series I, Vol. 27, Part 2, pp. 493–494.
83. Woodall, "The Fifty-ninth Georgia Infantry at Gettysburg," *The Atlanta Historical Journal*, Vol. 23, No. 1, p. 56.
84. Gilbreath manuscript, p. 72.
85. Ibid.

86. List of deaths at the Battle of Gettysburg, pp. 27–29.
87. A. W. Luther letter to his father, July 13, 1863.
88. Ibid.
89. Collier, *They'll Do To Tie To: The Story of the Third Regiment Arkansas Infantry, C.S.A.*, p. 140.
90. Woodall, "The Fifty-ninth Georgia Infantry at Gettysburg," *The Atlanta Historical Journal*, Vol. 23, No. 1, p. 57.
91. Gilbreath manuscript, p. 73.
92. Ibid.
93. *Soldier of Indiana*, Vol. 2, p. 110.
94. List of Deaths at the Battle of Gettysburg, pp. 27–29.
95. Gilbreath manuscript, p. 74.
96. Ibid.
97. Ibid.
98. Henry J. Hunt, "The Third Day At Gettysburg," *Battles and Leaders of the Civil War*, Vol. 3, p. 371.
99. Ibid., p. 374.
100. E. Porter Alexander, "Artillery Fighting At Gettysburg," *Battles and Leaders of the Civil War*, Vol. 3, pp. 362–365.
101. Gilbreath manuscript, pp. 74–75.
102. Ibid., p. 75.
103. Ibid.
104. Brown letter to Bachelder, July 1, 1887.
105. Gilbreath manuscript, p. 75.
106. Quigley letter to his father, the *Lafayette Daily Courier*, July 13, 1863, p. 1.
107. Gilbreath manuscript, p. 75.
108. Quigley letter to his father, the *Lafayette Daily Courier*, July 13, 1863, p. 1.
109. Tuttle letter to his wife, July 5, 1863.
110. A. W. Luther letter to his father, July 13, 1863.
111. Welch, "Gettysburg Finale," *America's Civil War*, July 1993, p. 52.
112. Time-Life Books, The Civil War Series, *Gettysburg: Confederate High Tide*, pp. 146–151.
113. Zimmerman letter to his father, the *LaPorte Herald*, August 17, 1863. P. 1.
114. Time-Life Books, The Civil War Series, *Gettysburg: Confederate High Tide*, p. 156.
115. Ibid.
116. Reeder letter to his parents, July 22, 1863.
117. Montgomery letter to the *Howard Tribune*, July 30, 1863, p. 1.
118. Tuttle letter to his wife, July 17, 1863.

CHAPTER 10 – BULLETS ON BROADWAY

1. Halleck order to Meade, July 30, 1863, *O.R.*, Series I, Vol. 43, Part 2, p. 108.
2. Tuttle letter to his wife, July 17, 1863.
3. Ibid., July 30, 1863.
4. Ibid., August 2, 1863.
5. Gilbreath manuscript, p. 79.
6. Driscoll, Holiday in New York, *Civil War Times Illustrated*, November 1992, p. 49.
7. Gilbreath manuscript, p. 79.
8. Meikel letter to the *Marshall County Republican*, August 20, 1863, p. 2.
9. Gilbreath manuscript, p. 79.
10. Ibid.
11. Ibid.
12. Stephens diary, September 14, 1863.
13. List of deaths at the Battle of Gettysburg, p. 27.
14. Head letter to his father, the *Marshall County Republican*, September 24, 1863.
15. Stephens diary, July 3, 1863.
16. Ibid., August 13, 1863.
17. Ibid., August 25, 1863.
18. Ibid., September 29, 1863.
19. Ibid.
20. Gilbreath manuscript, p. 80.
21. Stephens diary, October 15, 1863.
22. Ibid.
23. Tuttle letter to his wife, October 30,

1863.

24. Ibid.

25. Montgomery letter to the *Howard Tribune*, November 26, 1863.

26. Stephens diary, October 19, 1863.

27. Tuttle letter to his wife, November, 1, 1863.

28. Ibid.

29. Stephens diary, October 21, 1863.

30. Ibid., October 22–26, 1863.

31. Ibid., October 30, 1863.

32. Jimmie Stephens diary, November 6, 1863.

33. Tuttle letter to his wife, November 2, 1863.

34. Ibid, November 11, 1863.

35. Gilbreath manuscript, p. 81.

36. Jimmie Stephens diary, November 7, 1863.

37. Gilbreath manuscript, p. 81.

38. Ibid.

39. Jimmie Stephens diary, November 7, 1863.

40. Gilbreath manuscript, p. 82.

41. Tuttle letter to his wife, November 11, 1863.

42. Gilbreath manuscript, p. 82.

43. Tuttle letter to his wife, November 16, 1863.

44. Ibid., November 22, 1863.

45. Ibid., November 24, 1863.

46. Gilbreath manuscript, p. 82.

47. Ibid., p. 83.

48. Montgomery letter to the *Howard Tribune*, December 24, 1863, p. 1.

49. Ibid.

50. Ibid.

51. Stephens diary, November 28, 1863.

52. Gilbreath manuscript, p. 83.

53. *Soldier of Indiana*, Vol. 3, p. 600.

54. Ibid.

55. Gilbreath manuscript, p. 83.

56. *Soldier of Indiana*, Vol. 3, p. 600.

57. Gilbreath manuscript, p. 83.

58. Ibid.

59. Jimmie Stephens diary, November 30, 1863.

60. Montgomery letter to the *Howard*

Tribune, December 24, 1863, p. 1.

61. Tuttle letter to his wife, December 3, 1863.

62. Gilbreath manuscript, p. 83.

63. Alotta, *Civil War Justice, Union Army Executions Under Lincoln*, p. 89.

64. Stephens diary, December 4, 1863.

65. Jimmie Stephens diary, December 4 and December 18, 1863.

66. Tuttle letter to his wife, December 18, 1863.

67. Ibid., December 22, 1863.

68. Ibid., December 26, 1863.

69. *Lake County In the Civil War*, p. 38.

70. *Indianapolis Journal*, March 9, 1864, p. 1.

71. *History of Tippecanoe County*, p. 454.

72. *Indianapolis Journal*, April 15, 1864, p. 1.

73. Letter to Morton from men of Company I, April 14, 1864.

CHAPTER 11 – DESCENT INTO THE INFERNO

1. Tuttle letter to his wife, April 25, 1864.

2. Tucker, *Hancock the Superb*, p. 177.

3. *Soldier of Indiana*, Vol. 3, p. 617.

4. Tuttle letter to his wife, April 25, 1864.

5. Ibid., April 28, 1864.

6. Stephens diary, May 4, 1864.

7. Tucker, *Hancock the Superb*, p. 181.

8. *Lake County in the Civil War*, p. 38.

9. Montgomery letter to the *Howard Tribune*, July 28, 1864, p. 1.

10. IAG, Vol. 2, pp. 178–185.

11. Tucker, *Hancock the Superb*, p. 181.

12. Priest, *Nowhere to Run*, p. 136.

13. Cannan, *The Wilderness Campaign*, p. 106.

14. DeTrobriand Report, October 20, 1864, *O.R.*, Series I, Vol. 36, p. 469.

15. Priest, *Nowhere to Run*, p. 139.

16. Ibid.

17. Rhea, *The Battle of the Wilderness*,

May 5–6, 1864, p. 197.

18. Priest, *Nowhere to Run*, p. 187.

19. Stephens diary, May 5, 1864.

20. Priest, *Nowhere to Run*, p. 192.

21. Priest, *Victory Without Triumph*, p. 254.

22. Jimmie Stephens diary, May 5, 1864.

23. DeTrobriand Report, October 20, 1864, *O.R.*, Series I, Vol. 36, p. 469.

24. Priest, *Victory Without Triumph*, p. 14.

25. Jimmie Stephens diary, May 6, 1864.

26. Ibid.

27. Stephens diary, May 6, 1864.

28. Version: Scriptures.com, University of Virginia.

29. *Logansport Journal*, June 4, 1864, p. 2.

30. Tuttle letter to his wife, May 8, 1864.

31. Jimmie Stephens diary, May 6, 1864.

32. Priest, *Victory Without Triumph*, p. 61.

33. Ibid.

34. Ibid., p. 62.

35. Ibid., p. 87.

36. Ibid., p. 111.

37. Gilbreath manuscript, p. 90.

38. DeTrobriand Report, October 20, 1864, *O.R.*, Series I, Vol. 36, p. 469.

39. Jimmie Stephens diary, May 6, 1864.

40. Jace B. Head letter to the editor, the *Marshall County Republican*, May 15, 1864, p. 2.

41. Priest, *Victory Without Triumph*, p. 154.

42. Ibid., p. 155.

43. Ibid.

44. Jimmie Stephens diary, May 6, 1864.

45. Priest, *Victory Without Triumph*, p. 156.

46. Gilbreath manuscript, p. 90.

47. Priest, *Victory Without Triumph*, p. 158.

48. Gilbreath manuscript, p. 90.

49. Priest, *Victory Without Triumph*, p. 160.

50. Gilbreath manuscript, p. 90.

51. Priest, *Victory Without Triumph*, p. 163.

52. Gilbreath manuscript, p. 90.

53. Time-Life Books, The Civil War Series, *The Killing Ground: Wilderness to Cold Harbor*, p. 81.

54. Gilbreath manuscript, p. 91.

55. Ibid.

56. Ibid.

57. Time-Life Books, The Civil War Series, *The Killing Ground: Wilderness to Cold Harbor*, p. 81.

58. Gilbreath manuscript, p. 91.

59. Ibid.

60. Ibid.

61. Ibid.

62. Ibid.

63. Stephens diary, May 8, 1864.

64. Gilbreath manuscript, p. 92.

65. Jimmie Stephens diary, May 9, 1864.

66. Stephens diary, May 9, 1864.

67. Gilbreath manuscript, p. 92.

68. *Crown Point Register*, May 26, 1864, p. 2.

69. DeTrobriand Report, October 20, 1864, *O.R.*, Series I, Vol. 36, p. 470.

70. Jimmie Stephens diary, May 10, 1864.

71. Ibid.

72. Stephens diary, May 10, 1864.

73. Gilbreath manuscript, p. 93.

74. Ibid.

75. Matter, *If It Takes All Summer: The Battle of Spotsylvania*, p. 154.

76. Gilbreath manuscript, p. 93.

77. Jimmie Stephens diary, May 10, 1864.

78. DeTrobriand Report, October 20, 1864, *O.R.*, Series I, Vol. 36, p. 470.

79. Gilbreath manuscript, p. 93.

80. Time-Life Books, The Civil War Series, *The Killing Ground:*

Wilderness to Cold Harbor, p. 90.

81. Ibid., p. 92.

82. Ibid.

83. Gilbreath manuscript, p. 93.

84. Ibid.

85. Ibid.

86. DeTrobriand Report, October 20, 1864, Series I, Vol. 36, p. 470.

87. Gilbreath manuscript, p. 94.

88. Ibid.

89. Montgomery letter to the *Howard Tribune*, May 29, 1864, p. 1.

90. Time-Life Books, The Civil War Series, *The Killing Ground: Wilderness to Cold Harbor*, p. 98.

91. Jimmie Stephens diary, May 12, 1864.

92. Gilbreath manuscript, p. 94.

93. Time-Life Books, The Civil War Series, *The Killing Ground: Wilderness to Cold Harbor*, p. 100.

94. Montgomery letter to the *Howard Tribune*, June 9, 1864.

95. IAG, Vol. 4., p. 411

96. Jimmie Stephens diary, May 12, 1864.

97. Tuttle letter to his wife, May 16, 1864.

98. Ibid., May 13, 1864.

99. Gilbreath manuscript, p. 94.

100. DeTrobriand report, October 20, 1864, *O.R.*, Vol. 36, p. 471.

101. Gilbreath manuscript, p. 94.

102. Ibid.

103. Tuttle letter to his wife, May 13, 1864.

104. Time-Life Books, The Civil War Series, *The Killing Ground: Wilderness to Cold Harbor*, p. 105.

105. Gilbreath manuscript, p. 95.

106. Tuttle letter to his wife, May 13, 1864.

107. *Soldier of Indiana*, Vol. 3, p. 630.

108. Montgomery letter to the *Howard Tribune*, May 26, 1864, p. 1.

109. *Indianapolis Daily Journal*, May 19, 1864, p. 3.

110. Stephens diary, May 14, 1864.

111. Ibid, May 15, 1864.

112. Gilbreath manuscript, p. 95.

113. Stephens diary, May 15, 1864.

114. Time-Life Books, The Civil War Series, *The Killing Ground: Wilderness to Cold Harbor*, p. 125.

115. Montgomery letter to the *Howard Tribune*, June 9, 1864, p. 2.

116. Gilbreath manuscript, p. 95.

117. Montgomery letter to the *Howard Tribune*, June 9, 1864, p. 2.

118. Time-Life Books, The Civil War Series, *The Killing Ground: Wilderness to Cold Harbor*, p. 130.

CHAPTER 12 – THE END OF A WILD ROMANCE

1. Gilbreath manuscript, p. 97.

2. Ibid.

3. Stephens diary, May 22, 1864.

4. Ibid.

5. Gilbreath manuscript, p. 97.

6. Ibid.

7. Stephens diary, May 23, 1864.

8. Gilbreath manuscript, p. 97.

9. Ibid.

10. Ibid., p. 98.

11. Ibid.

12. Stephens diary, May 24, 1864.

13. *The Monticello Herald*, December 1, 1898, p. 2.

14. Gilbreath manuscript, p. 98.

15. Ibid.

16. Stephens diary, May 28, 1864.

17. Ibid., May 29–30, 1864.

18. Ibid., May 31, 1964.

19. Gilbreath manuscript, p. 99.

20. Ibid., p. 102.

21. Time-Life Books, The Civil War Series, *The Killing Ground: Wilderness to Cold Harbor*, p. 165.

22. Gilbreath manuscript, p. 99.

23. Stephens diary, June 4–12, 1864.

24. Ibid., June 5–6, 1864.

25. Ibid., June 7, 1864.

26. Ibid., June 9, 1864.

27. Montgomery letter to the *Howard Tribune*, June 4, 1864, p. 1.

28. Gilbreath manuscript, p. 104.

29. Ibid.

30. Ibid.

31. Stephens diary, June 14, 1864.
32. Gilbreath manuscript, p. 104.
33. Ibid.
34. Stephens diary, June 15, 1864.
35. Gilbreath manuscript, p. 105.
36. Ibid.
37. Ibid.
38. Ibid.
39. Stephens diary, June 16, 1864.
40. Ibid., June 18, 1864
41. Gilbreath manuscript, p. 107.
42. Stephens diary, June 18–19, 1864.
43. Gilbreath manuscript, p. 108.
44. Ibid., p. 109.
45. Gilbreath manuscript, p. 110.
46. Ibid.
47. Stephens diary, June 22, 1864.
48. Ibid., June 23, 1864.
49. Gilbreath manuscript, p. 111.
50. Ibid.
51. Ibid., p. 112.
52. Luther letter to his father, July 9, 1864
53. Williams letter to the *Plymouth Republican*, July 21, 1864, p. 2.
54. Gilbreath manuscript, p. 114.
55. Ibid.
56. Ibid., p. 115.
57. Ibid.
58. Ibid.
59. Ibid.
60. Ibid, p. 117.
61. Meikel letter to the *Logansport Journal*, September 3, 1864.
62. Gilbreath manuscript, p. 118.
63. Luther letter to his father, September 10, 1864.
64. Gilbreath manuscript, p. 118.
65. Ibid.
66. Tuttle letter to his wife, September 19, 1864.
67. Gilbreath manuscript, p. 119.
68. Ibid., p. 121.

EPILOGUE

1. *Indianapolis Journal*, June 9, 1865, p. 2.
2. *Official Army Register of the Volunteer Force*, Part 6, p. 61.
3. Ibid.
4. Ibid., p. 147. and p. 50.
5. Ibid., p. 61.
6. Ibid., Part 8, p. 85.
7. Ibid., Part 6, p. 61.
8. Ibid., p. 459.
9. *LaPorte Herald Argus*, January 5, 1854, p. 3.
10. Monument Commission, *Dedication of the Indiana Monument*: Andersonville Prison 864–1865, pp. 76–77.
11. Regimental descriptive list, National Archives.
12. Gilbreath manuscript, cover page.
13. *History of North and West Texas*, p. 502.
14. National Archives, The papers of Dennis Tuttle.
15. Details provided by Benedict R. Maryniak.
16. Charles L. Foster, article at the White County Historical Society, August 3, 1861.
17. Details provided by Charles Ervin.
18. Gilbreath manuscript, p. 5.
19. *History of White County*, p. 476.
20. Montgomery letter to the *Howard Tribune*, September 15, 1864, p. 1.
21. *History of Tippecanoe County*, p. 454.
22. *History of White County*, p. 440.
23. Joint Select Committee, *The Condition of Affairs in the Late Insurrectionary States*, Alabama, Vol. 2, pp. 790–813.
24. Brundage, *Men of 1861–1865 Miami County and Their Families*, Indiana, Vol. 1, p. 1072.
25. Warner, *Generals in Blue*, p. 538.
26. *Sixth Annual Reunion Program*, Twentieth Indiana Regiment, 1891.
27. *Lake County in the Civil War*, p. 98.
28. Gilbreath manuscript, p. 122.
29. *Lafayette Journal and Courier*, July 6, 1991, p. SC 20.
30. *Soldier of Indiana*, Vol. 3, p. 804.

BIBLIOGRAPHY

MANUSCRIPTS
    David Canright Collection, Chesterton, Indiana
        Marquis Winch War Reminiscences
        Twentieth Indiana Collection
    Crown Point Community Library, Crown Point, Indiana
        Lake County in the Civil War
    Indiana Historical Society, Indianapolis, Indiana
        James C. Stephens Collection
    Indiana State Archives
        Governor's Correspondence (Oliver Perry Morton)
        Regimental Files
        Governor's Telegram Log Book (Oliver Perry Morton)
        Soldier Records
    Indiana State Library, Manuscript Division, Indianapolis, Indiana
        Joshua Lewis Collection S861
        Erasmus C. Gilbreath Manuscript
        Francis A. Osbourn Manuscript
    Gettysburg National Military Park Library
        List of Dead
    Library of Congress
        Dennis Tuttle Collection
    National Archives
        Descriptive Lists
        Regimental Book
        Regimental Files
        Order Book
    United States Army Military History Institute
        Thomas White Stephens Collection
        William C. H. Reeder Collection
        Soldier Images

GOVERNMENT PUBLICATIONS
    Annual Reports to the Secretary of War, 1893–1901. Washington: Gettysburg National Military Park Commission, Government Printing Office, 1902.
    Guide to Indiana Civil War Manuscripts. Indianapolis: Civil War Centennial Commission, 1965.
    Indiana at Gettysburg. Indianapolis: Fiftieth Anniversary Commission, 1913.
    Indiana's Battle Flags. Indianapolis: McCormick, Indiana Battle Flag Commission, 1929.
    Indiana in the Civil War: 1861–1865. Indianapolis: Civil War Centennial Commission, 1865.
    Maine at Gettysburg. Portland: Maine Gettysburg Commissioners, 1898.

Official Army Register of the Volunteer Force of the United States Army. Nine Volumes. Washington: War Department, Congressional Printing Office, 1865.

Report of the Adjutant General of the State of Indiana. Eight Volumes. Indianapolis: Conner, 1869.

Report of Dedication Indiana Monument: Andersonville. Indianapolis: Andersonville Monument Commission, 1909.

The Condition of Affairs in the Late Insurrectionary States, Alabama, Voll. 2, AMS Press, New York, New York, 1872.

War of the Rebellion: Official Records of the Union and Confederate Armies. 128 Volumes. Washington: United States War Department, Government Printing Office, 1880–1901

DIARIES AND LETTERS

Andrew, John W. Letters to sisters. Transcripts from David Canright, Chesterton, Indiana.

Bowen, John. Letter to his wife. John Bowen Collection, White County Historical Society, Monticello, Indiana.

Brown, John C. Letter to John B. Bachelder. Gettysburg N. M. P. Library, Gettysburg, Pennsylvania.

Brown, William Lyon. Letters to Governor Morton. Oliver P. Morton Collection, Indiana State Archives, Indianapolis, Indiana.

Brown, William Lyon. Letter to George Winter. George Winter Collection, Indiana Historical Society, Indianapolis, Indiana.

Clark, William. Letter to sisters. Gilbert Young, Jr. Collection, Huntington, Indiana.

Finley, John. Letter to Governor Morton. Oliver P. Morton Collection, Indiana State Archives, Indianapolis, Indiana.

French, Alpheus C. Letter to his cousins. Alpheus C. French Collection, Indiana Historical Society, Indianapolis, Indiana.

Hendricks, John H. Letters to his mother. John H. Hendricks Collection, Indiana Historical Society, Indianapolis, Indiana.

Ireland, A. P. Diary. A. P. Ireland Collection, Indiana Historical Society, Indianapolis, Indiana.

Kistler, John. Letter to Emily, Sally, Luce, and Saby Hill. Craig Dunn Collection, Kokomo, Indiana.

Men of Company I. Letter to Governor Morton. Oliver P. Morton Collection, Indiana Archives, Indianapolis, Indiana.

Miller, H. H. Letters to his wife. H. H. Miller Collection, Indiana Historical Society, Indianapolis, Indiana.

Murray, Charles D. Letter to Governor Morton. Oliver P. Morton Collection, Indiana State Archives, Indianapolis, Indiana.

Officers of Regiment. Letters to Governor Morton. Oliver P. Morton Collection, Indiana State Archives, Indianapolis, Indiana.

Pealer, David. Letter to his brother. Transcript from David Canright, Chesterton, Indiana.

Pearson, John C. Letter to brother of Charles Reese. John C. Pearson Collection, Indiana Historical Society, Indianapolis, Indiana.

Reeder, William C. H. Letters to his parents. Reeder Folder: Personal Correspondence, 1862–1865, United States Military History Institute, Carlisle, Pennsylvania.

Reese, Charles. Letter to brother. Gilbert Young, Jr. Collection, Huntington, Indiana.

Reese, Charles. Letter to brother. Charles Reese Collection, Indiana Historical Society, Indianapolis, Indiana.

Reese, Charles. Letters to brother. David Stone Collection, Anderson, Indiana.

Reese, Charles. Letter to sister. David Stone Collection, Anderson, Indiana.

Sibel, Thomas. Letters to Hiram Sibel. Thomas Sibel Collection, Indiana State Library, Manuscript Division, Indianapolis, Indiana.

Stephens, James C. Diary. James C. Stephens Collection, Indiana Historical Society, Indianapolis, Indiana.

Stephens, Thomas W. Diary. Thomas White Stephens Collection, United States Military History Institute, Carlisle, Pennsylvania.

Stone, Charles. Letter to John Nolison, Craig L. Dunn Collection, Kokomo, Indiana.

Thomas, Lorenzo, Special Orders 39. Twentieth Indiana Collection, Indiana Archives, Indianapolis, Indiana.

Thomas, Lorenzo, Special Orders 119. Twentieth Indiana Collection, Indiana Archives, Indianapolis, Indiana.

Turpin, Henry. Diary. Henry Turpin Collection, Indiana Historical Society, Indianapolis, Indiana.

Tuttle, Dennis. Letters to his wife. Dennis Tuttle Collection, Library of Congress, Washington, D.C.

Vatchett, William D. Letters to Christopher Reese. Charles Reese Collection, Indiana Historical Society, Indianapolis, Indiana.

Vincent, Strong. Letters to Governor Morton. Oliver P. Morton Collection, Indiana Archives, Indianapolis, Indiana.

Weaver, George W. Letter to Kate. George W. Weaver Collection, Indiana Historical Society, Indianapolis, Indiana.

Wheeler, John. Diary. Boyd F. Cole Collection, Libertyville, Illinois.

Wheeler, John. Letters. Boyd F. Cole Collection, Libertyville, Illinois.

Wheeler, John. Letter to J. C. Hudson. Gilbert Young, Jr. Collection, Huntington, Indiana.

Wheeler, John. Letter to James H. Luther. Ball Collection, Indiana Historical Society, Indianapolis, Indiana.

Wheeler, John. Letters to Governor Morton. Oliver P. Morton Collection, Indiana Archives, Indianapolis, Indiana.

Wilkerson, John A. Excerpts of Gettysburg diary, Transcript from David Canright, Chesterton, Indiana.

NEWSPAPERS

Crown Point Register

Howard Tribune

Hudson Star Observer

Indianapolis Daily Journal

Lafayette Daily Courier

Lafayette Journal

Lafayette Daily Courier

Lafayette Weekly Journal

LaPorte Herald Argus

Logansport Journal

Logansport Pharos

Marshall County Republican

Monticello Herald
Monticello Spectator
National Tribune
Northern Indianian
Plymouth Republican
Valparaiso Republic

ARTICLES AND ESSAYS

Alexander, E. Porter. "Artillery Fighting at Gettysburg." *Battles and Leaders of the Civil War*, Vol. 3. New York: The Century Co., 1884.

Dorrel, Ruth. "Military Deaths from the *Indianapolis Daily Journal.*" July 1862. *The Hoosier Geneologist*, December 1993, pp. 228–236.

Driscoll, T. Jeff. "Holiday in New York." *Civil War Times Illustrated*, November/December, 1992, Vol. 31, Number 5, pp. 48–53.

Haas, Steve. "They Did Their Job: The 124th New York Volunteers at Houck's Ridge, Gettysburg, 1863." www.arthes.com:1030/haas.html, pp. 1–6.

Hunt, Henry J. "The Third Day at Gettysburg." *Battles and Leaders of the Civil War*, Vol. 3. New York: The Century Co., 1884.

Jorgenson, Jay. "Anderson Attacks The Wheatfield." *Gettysburg* magazine, January 1996, No. 14, pp. 64–100.

Kelly, Dennis. "The Battle and Campaign Second Manassas." Reprint of *Civil War Times Illustrated*, Eastern Acorn Press, 1983.

Lash, Gary. "The March of the 124th New York to Gettysburg." *Gettysburg* magazine, July 1993, Issue 9, pp. 5–16.

Longstreet, James. "The Battle of Fredericksburg." *Battles and Leaders of the Civil War*, Vol. 3. New York: The Century Co., 1884.

Miller, J. Michael. "Even To Hell Itself." *The North Anna Campaign, May 21–26, 1864.* Lynchburg: H. E. Howard, Inc., 1989.

Moss, Bennett R. "The Chicamacomico Races: A Prelude to Courage." chicamac.htm@www.clis.com, pp. 1–5.

National Park Service. "The Battles of Wilderness and Spotsylvania Court House." www.nps.gov/frsp/wshist.htm.

Smith, Robbie. "M. G. Washington Smith, Company D, 59th Regiment, Anderson's Brigade." Gettysburg N. M. P. Library, Gettysburg, Pennsylvania.

Smith, William F. "Franklin's Left Grand Division." *Battles and Leaders of the Civil War*, Vol. 3. New York: The Century Co., 1884.

Stiles, Israel N. "On To Richmond In 1862." *Mollus War Papers: Illinois*, Vol. 3, pp. 45–59.

Stiles, Israel N. "The Merrimac and the Monitor." *Mollus War Papers: Illinois*, Vol. 1, pp. 125–133.

Welch, "Gettysburg Finale." *America's Civil War*, July 1993, p. 52.

Woodall, Ann E. (Editor) "The 59th Georgia at Gettysburg." *The Atlanta Historical Journal*, Vol. 23, No. 1, Spring 1979, pp.53–59.

BOOKS

Alotta, Robert I. *Civil War Justice: Union Army Executions Under Lincoln.* Shippensburg: White Mane Publishing, 1989.

Ball Encyclopedia of Genealogy and Biography of Lake County (no publisher listed).

Biographical Record and Portrait Album of Tippecanoe County, Indiana. Chicago: Lewis Publishing, 1888.

Boatner, Mark M. III. *The Civil War Dictionary.* New York: David McKay Company, Inc., 1959.

Bowers, John. *Stonewall Jackson: Portrait of a Soldier.* New York: Avon Books, 1989.

Brant and Fuller. *History of Miami County, Indiana.* Chicago: Brant and Fuller Publishing, 1887.

Brown, William Emery. *Fifth Annual Reunion of the 20th Indiana Veteran Volunteer Association.* Valparaiso: Brown, 1890.

Brundage, Donald K. *Men of 1861–1865 Miami County, Indiana, and Their Families,* Vol. 1. Peru: Brundage, 1990.

Cannan, John. *The Wilderness Campaign: May 1864.* Conshohocken: Combined Books, Inc., 1993.

Coddington, Edwin B. *The Gettysburg Campaign: A Study in Command.* New York: Charles Scribner's Sons, 1968.

Collier, Captain Calvin L. *They'll Do To Tie To: The Story of the Third Regiment Arkansas Infantry, CSA.* Jacksonville: James D. Warren, USAF, 1959.

Cross, Andrew B. *The War: Battle of Gettysburg and the Christian Commission.* Gettysburg: Cross, 1865.

Dabney, R. L. *Life and Campaigns of Lieutenant General T. J. (Stonewall) Jackson.* Harrisonburg: Sprinkle Publications, 1983.

Davis, Burke. *The Long Surrender.* New York: Random House, 1985.

Death In the Trenches: Grant at Petersburg. The Civil War Series. Alexandria: Time-Life Books, 1986.

Dunn, Craig. *Iron Men, Iron Will: The Nineteenth Indiana Regiment of the Iron Brigade.* Carmel: Guild Press of Indiana, Inc., 1995.

Dyer, Frederick H. *A Compendium of the War of the Rebellion.* Des Moines: The Dyer Publishing Company, 1908.

Forward to Richmond: McClellan's Peninsular Campaign. The Civil War Series. Alexandria: Time-Life Books, 1983.

Fox, William F. *Regimental Losses in the American Civil War 1861–1865.* Albany: Albany Publishing Company, 1889.

Gettysburg: The Confederate High Tide. The Civil War Series. Alexandria: Time-Life Books, 1985.

Goodspeed, Weston A. *Counties of Porter and Lake Indiana.* Chicago: F. A. Battey & Co., 1882.

Gragg, Rod. *Civil War Quiz and Fact Book.* New York: Harper and Row, 1985.

Hamelle, W. H. *History of White County.* Chicago: The Lewis Publishing Company, 1915.

Head, Benjamin F. *Rally on Argos.* Argos: Head Publishing, 1891.

Hassler, Warren W., Jr. *Crisis at the Crossroads: The First Day at Gettysburg.* Gettysburg: Stan Clark Military Books, 1970.

Hebert, Walter H. *Fighting Joe Hooker.* Gaithersburg: Butternut Press, 1987.

Hennessy, John J. *Return to Bull Run: The Campaign and Battle of Second Manassas.* New York: Simon and Schuster, 1993.

History of Miami County. Chicago: Hall and O'Donald Publishing, 1887.

History of North and West Texas. (No author or publication information available: Internet source.)

Hood, Lt. Gen. J. B. *Advance and Retreat.* Secaucus: Blue and Grey Press, 1985.

Horn, John. *The Petersburg Campaign: June 1864–April 1865.* Conshohocken: Combined Books, 1993.

Hunt, Roger D. and Jack R. Brown. *Brevet Brigadier Generals in Blue.* Gaithersburg: Olde Soldier Books, Inc., 1990.

Killing Ground: Wilderness to Cold Harbor. The Civil War Series. Alexandria: Time-Life Books, 1986.

Ladd, David L. and Audrey J. Ladd. *John Bachelder's History of the Battle of Gettysburg.* Dayton: Morningside House, Inc., 1997.

Lee Takes Command: From Seven Days to Second Bull Run. The Civil War Series. Alexandria: Time-Life Books, 1984.

Lester, Robert E. *Civil War Unit Histories* (Part 4): *The Union Midwest and West: Regimental Histories and Personal Narratives: One of the Fighting Three Hundred.* Bethesda: University Publications of America, 1993.

Matter, William D. *If It Takes All Summer: The Battle of Spotsylvania.* Chapel Hill: The University of North Carolina Press, 1988.

Miller, William J. *The Peninsula Campaign of 1862.* Campbell: Savas Woodbury Publishers, 1995.

Nofi, Albert A. *The Gettysburg Campaign: June–July 1863.* Conshohocken: Combined Books, 1986.

O'Connor, Richard. *Hood: Cavalier General.* New York: Prentice-Hall, Inc., 1949.

Phillips, Stanley S. *Civil War Corps Badges and Other Related Awards: Badges, Medals of the Period.* New York: Phillips Company, 1982.

Poore, Ben. *Life of Burnside.* Providence: Reid Publishers, 1882.

Porter, Admiral David D. *Naval History of the Civil War.* Secaucus: Castle Publishing, 1984.

Pfanz, Harry W. *Gettysburg, The Second Day.* Chapel Hill: University of North Carolina Press, 1987.

Priest, John Michael. *Nowhere to Run: The Wilderness, May 4th and 5th, 1864.* Shippensburg: White Mane Publishing Co., 1995.

_____. *Victory Without Triumph, The Wilderness, May 6th and 7th, 1864.* Shippensburg: White Mane Publishing Co., 1996.

Pursuit to Appomattox: The Last Battles. The Civil War Series. Alexandria: Time-Life Books, 1987.

Rebels Resurgent: Fredericksburg to Chancellorsville. The Civil War Series. Alexandria: Time-Life Books, 1985.

Rhea, Gordon C. *The Battles for Spotsylvania Court House and the Road to Yellow Tavern: May 7–12, 1864.* Baton Rouge: Louisiana State University Press, 1997.

Robertson, D. Andrew. *Out of the Spirit and the Soil: A Complete History of Forest Township in Clinton County, Indiana.* Forest: Enniskillen Fruit Company, 1992.

Robertson, James I. *General A. P. Hill: The Story of a Confederate Warrior.* New York: Random House, 1987.

_____. *The Battle of the Wilderness May 5–6, 1864.* Baton Rouge: Louisiana State University Press, 1994.

Scott, Robert Garth. *Into the Wilderness with the Army of the Potomac.* Bloomington: Indiana University Press, 1988.

Sears, Stephen W. *George B. McClellan: The Young Napoleon.* New York: Ticknor and Fields, 1988.

_____. *To the Gates of Richmond: The Peninsula Campaign.* New York: Ticknor and Fields, 1992.

Smith, John. *1860 Federal Population Census for Miami County, Indiana.* Chicago: Smith Publishing, 1860.

Soldier Of Indiana in the War for the Union. Indianapolis: Bobbs-Merrill, 1869.

Stackpole, General Edward J. *They Met at Gettysburg.* Harrisburg: Stackpole Books, 1956.

Stafford, Frederick H. *Medal of Honor: Awarded for Distinguished Service During the War of the Rebellion.* Washington: Stafford, 1886.

Tucker, Glenn. *Hancock the Superb.* Indianapolis: Bobbs-Merrill, 1960.

Voices of the Civil War: Chancellorsville. Alexandria: Time-Life Books, 1996.

Voices of the Civil War: Second Manassas. Alexandria: Time-Life Books, 1995.

Warner, Ezra J. *Generals in Blue.* Baton Rouge: Louisiana State University Press, 1964.

Warner, Ezra J. *Generals In Gray.* Baton Rouge: Louisiana State University Press, 1959.

Wheeler, Richard. *Lee's Terrible Swift Sword.* New York: Harper Collins Publishers, 1992.

INDEX

Note: An asterisk (*) after a number
indicates that a photo appears on that page.